GREGORIAN CHANT AND THE CAROLINGIANS

GREGORIAN CHANT
AND THE CAROLINGIANS

Kenneth Levy

PRINCETON UNIVERSITY PRESS   PRINCETON, NEW JERSEY

Library of Congress Cataloging-in-Publication Data

Levy, Kenneth, 1927–
Gregorian chant and the Carolingians / Kenneth Levy.
p.   cm.
Includes bibliographical references and index.
ISBN 0-691-01733-6 (cl : alk. paper)
1. Chants (Plain, Gregorian, etc.)—History and criticism.
I. Title.
ML3082.L44   1998
782.32'22'009021—dc21   97-21957   CIP   MN

This book has been composed in Sabon

Princeton University Press books are printed
on acid-free paper and meet the guidelines
for permanence and durability of the Committee
on Production Guidelines for Book Longevity
of the Council on Library Resources

Printed in the United States of America

1 3 5 7 9 10 8 6 4 2

Contents

Acknowledgments

I HAVE RUN UP DEBTS to many friends for conversations that helped keep me on track while this project was taking shape; among them, Bob Snow, Peter Jeffery, and Susan Rankin. I am also much indebted to the Fellows of Emmanuel College, Cambridge, for ideal working conditions during the Easter Term of 1995, when this work reached final form. In the course of production, I have benefited greatly from the professionalism of Malcolm Litchfield and Jane Low at Princeton University Press, who went far beyond routine in giving polish to the result.

Abbreviations

AcM	*Acta musicologica*
AfMw	*Archiv für Musikwissenschaft*
AH	Guido Maria Dreves, Clemens Blume, and Henry Marriott Bannister, eds., *Analecta hymnica,* 55 vols. (Leipzig, 1886–1922).
AMS	René-Jean Hesbert, ed., *Antiphonale missarum sextuplex* (Brussels, 1935).
CAO	René-Jean Hesbert, ed., *Corpus antiphonalium officii,* Rerum ecclesiasticarum documenta, Series maior, Fontes, 7–12 (Rome, 1963–79).
CLA	Elias A. Lowe, *Codices latini antiquiores,* 11 vols. (Oxford, 1934–66).
CLLA	Klaus Gamber, *Codices liturgici latini antiquiores,* 2nd ed., part 1. (Freiburg, Switzerland, 1968).
CS	Edmond de Coussemaker, *Scriptorum de musica medii aevi novam seriem,* 4 vols. (Paris, 1864–76).
CSM	*Corpus scriptorum de musica* (Rome, 1950–present).
CT	Corpus troporum, Studia Latina Stockholmiensia (Stockholm, 1975–present).
EG	*Études grégoriennes*
EMH	*Early Music History*
GR	*Graduale Sacrosanctae Romanae Ecclesiae* (Paris, Tournai, Rome, 1952).
GS	Martin Gerbert, *Scriptores ecclesiastici de musica sacra potissimum,* 3 vols. (Sankt-Blasien, 1784).
GT	Marie-Claire Billecocq and Rupert Fischer eds., *Graduale triplex* (Solesmes, 1979).
JAMS	*Journal of the American Musicological Society*
JPMMS	*Journal of the Plainsong & Medieval Music Society*
LeGR	*Le Graduel Romain: Édition critique par les moines de Solesmes.* Vol. 2, *Les sources* (Solesmes, 1957).
Mf	*Die Musikforschung*
MGG	*Die Musik in Geschichte und Gegenwart,* 17 vols. (Kassel, 1949–86).
MGH	*Monumenta Germaniae historica*
MMMA	*Monumenta monodica medii aevi* (Kassel, 1956–present).
NGD	Stanley Sadie, ed., *The New Grove Dictionary of Music and Musicians,* 20 vols. (London, 1980).

PalMus   *Paléographie musicale: Les principaux manuscrits de chant grégorien, ambrosien, mozarabe, gallican* (Solesmes, 1889–present).

PL   J.-P. Migne, ed., *Patrologiae cursus completus, series latina* (Paris, 1844–64).

RG   *Revue grégorienne*

GREGORIAN CHANT AND THE CAROLINGIANS

CHAPTER 1

From Gregory to the Ottonians

THIS BOOK will consider Gregorian chant's passage from oral to written transmission. Much of what happened during this passage remains obscure, as ultimate origins reside in prehistoric states before musical notations were used, and even then the beginnings of noted transmission are still prehistoric in the sense that no written records survive. The first preserved documentary evidence using neumatic notations comes from ca. 900. Yet even in them, the written factor is only a minor one. The neumes are in a mutual dependency with verbatim memory, where memory still has the essential role, much as it did during the improvisational, notationless stages that went before. The neumes are secondary, supplying silhouettes of melodic substances that are fixed and quite accurately remembered, yet useless unless someone has the full melodic substances in memory. All the same, the neumes are what make possible the precise memory control that is the essence of the transmission. Their pitch descriptions are only approximate, but they are exact enough about rhythmic and other nuances of melodic contour to provide memory with the support it needs in order to effect verbatim recall.

Thus even with the neumes the Gregorian transmission has become written only in a limited sense. There is no oral dimension at all: the oral factor is memory, with no latitude for improvisational variability. What this suggests is that the terms oral and written need at least to be reconsidered. They appear constantly in discussions of Gregorian chant and other medieval monophonic and early polyphonic musical repertories, but their original association is with subject matters that are verbal,[1] and these terms are less well suited to musical matters. In what follows, I will experiment with the use of aural and notational as substitutes for oral and written. Something of the sort was suggested years ago in a remark of Bruno Nettl's, " . . . oral (or more correctly, aural transmission) . . . ,"[2] and it has since been picked up by Peter Jeffery.[3] The oral/written di-

---

[1] Recent uses of "orality" in applications closer to its origins are found in *Schriftlichkeit im frühen Mittelalter*, ed., Ursula Schaefer, ScriptOralia 53 (Tübingen, 1993).

[2] *The Study of Ethnomusicology: Twenty-Nine Issues and Concepts.* (Urbana, 1983) 200.

[3] *Re-Envisioning Past Musical Cultures*, Chicago Studies in Ethnomusicology) (Chicago, 1992) 48.

chotomy comes so readily to mind and tongue that it will be hard to root out; but some other terms may better serve the music.

For more than a thousand years, peoples' notions about Gregorian chant were summed up in a genial myth that linked the music's origins to the activity of Gregory the Great.[4] The Carolingians put this in pictures, showing the Holy Spirit, in the form of a dove, communicating musical (?) matter to Gregory's ear, and Gregory passing it on to a waiting scribe.[5] Gregory's role was also advertised in poems that appeared prominently at the beginnings of antiphoners.[6] It was not until the nineteenth century, with the movement to restore Gregorian chants to medieval states, that such pieties came into question. Further, it was not until the middle twentieth century that the notion took hold of Gregorian chant with its ultimate antecedents in transmissions that were aural rather than notational. Dom Cardine led the way at the International Congress of Sacred Music at Rome in 1950: "La notation musicale . . . ayant fait son apparition vers la fin du IXe siècle sous forme de neumes . . . nous n'aurons pas là le livre primitif sous sa forme matérielle, puisque la notation musicale était alors inconnue."[7] The nature and substance of the music during its aural transmission, and the circumstances of its writing down, have ever since been high on Gregorianists' agendas.

When most people think of Gregorian chant, they think of the melodies in square notations, as in the editions prepared for the Vatican by the Benedictines of Solesmes: the *Graduale* (1908) and *Antiphonale* (1912). Example 1.1 shows the alleluia verse for the mass of Christmas day in the Vatican *Graduale*.[8] In general terms, just a single, mainline tradition for the Gregorian melodies has come down from the Middle Ages. For most purposes, even for many scientific ones, the Solesmes-Vatican square note editions adequately represent the medieval melodies' pitch details and performance nuances. The Vatican readings trace back to square note versions of the twelfth century; behind them are accurately pitched versions in alphabetic notations of the early eleventh century; behind those are versions in staffless neumes, which reach back to ca. 900.

In recent decades, the general supposition has been that the Gregorian musical states, as represented in the Vatican editions, were firmed up as melodies in Carolingian times, that is, by ca. 800. Yet it has also been the

[4] David Hiley, *Western Plainchant* (Oxford, 1993) 503–513.

[5] Saint Gall, *Stiftsbibliothek* 390/391 (Antiphoner of Hartker), ca. 1000, reproduced in *PalMus* 2, (1891–92), Pl. 2.

[6] Bruno Stäblein, "'Gregorius Praesul', der Prolog zum römischen Antiphonale," in *Musik und Verlag: Festschrift Karl Vötterle* (Kassel, 1968), 537–61.

[7] "De l'édition critique du Graduel," in Higini Anglès, ed., *Atti del Congresso Internazionale di Musica Sacra* (1950; reprint, Tournai, 1952), 190.

[8] *Graduale Sacrosanctae Romanae Ecclesiae de Tempore et de Sanctis SS. D. N. Pii X Pontificis Maximi jussu restitutum et editum* (Roma, 1908), 34.

Example 1.1. Graduale, Vatican Edition, 1908

general supposition that those Gregorian melodies did not receive any neumings until a century later, ca. 900. One of the major departures from traditional thinking in this book is to see the melodies as being cast in an authoritative neumatic edition by ca. 800—at the same time and in the same process where they became musically fixed.

In 1979, the Benedictines of Solesmes brought out a valuable supplement to the Graduale. The *Graduale Triplex* parallels the square note versions of 1908 with two very detailed early neumings. Underneath the square notes are the neumes of tenth century Saint Gall; above them are the neumes of tenth century Laon. Example 1.2 shows the alleluia for Christmas day in this arrangement.[9] The two neumations represent almost the same melodic substances, down to fine details; and by and large the Vatican's square note readings conform with them. Those agreements in neumation and in musical substance show how specific the tenth-century melos had become: these were tunes with fixed details, chiseled melodic profiles that were accurately remembered. Yet with these melodic

---

[9] *Graduale Triplex seu Graduale Romanum Pauli PP. VI cura recognitum . . . ornatum neumis laudunensibus (cod. 239) et sangallensibus (codicum sangallensis 359 et einsidlensis 121 nunc auctum* (Solesmis, 1979), 49.

Example 1.2. Graduale Triplex, Solesmes, 1979

agreements, there are differences in the notational means used to represent the same musical details. The neumations of Laon and Saint Gall are distinct in calligraphic styles, and that raises questions. How did the same melos change to the different neumatic dress? Can the diverse neumations be outgrowths of a common neumed source, or were there independent written antecedents?

Between the sixth and tenth centuries, European plainchant went through three more or less simultaneous processes of change. In one of these, local chant repertories, with their distinctive musical dialects, were suppressed, and the single, authoritative Gregorian melodic repertory was substituted. In another, the melos went from something that might vary between one delivery and the next, to one that was fixed and should, in principle, always sound the same. In a third change, there was the turn from solely aural transmission to the one where verbatim memory had the support of memory-aid neumes. These three changes affected one another. They came about largely before neumes were introduced, or before there is record of their use. The changes were essentially complete by the time of the first extant Gregorian neumings, ca. 900.

The first change, suppression of regional musical dialects, was a priority of the Carolingian ecclesiastical reformers of the later eighth century. Their purpose was to have a single, nominally Roman, repertory sung throughout Europe. Charlemagne ascribes the initiative to his father:

> Ut cantum Romanum pleniter discant, et ordinabiliter per nocturnale vel gradale officium peragatur, secundum quod beatae memoriae genitor noster Pippinus rex decertavit ut fieret quando Gallicanum tulit ob unanimitatem apostolicae sedis et sanctae Dei aeclesiae pacificam concordiam.[10]

By about 800, an authoritative Carolingian-Gregorian repertory had supplanted the local chant dialects in most Carolingian domains. No neumings survive before the second quarter of the ninth century, so little is known of most earlier dialects, such as the German and Celtic. There are most abundant traces of an archaic Gallican repertory, while a full Old Hispanic repertory was spared Carolingian suppression by the Islamic presence on the Iberian peninsula, which began in the early eighth century. Italy also retained substantial earlier relics.[11] There is a full regional repertory at Milan, preserved in twelfth century sources, much of whose music is related to the Gregorian in fundamental ways.[12] There are other important regional survivals in central and southern Italy.[13]

---

[10] In the *Admonitio generalis* of March 789; Capitularia, vol. 1. *MGH, Legum Sectio 2,* ed., Alfred Boretius (Hanover, 1883) 61. The matter surfaces again in the Libri Carolini: ". . . in officiorum celebratione, venerandae memoriae genitoris nostri inlustrissimi atque excellentissimi viri Pippini regis cura et industria sive adventu in Gallias reverentissimi et sanctissimi viri Stephani Romanae urbis antestitis est ei etiam in psallendi ordine copulata, ut non esset dispar ordo psallendi, quibus erat conpar ordo credendi, et quae unitae erant unius sacrae legis sacra lectione, essent etiam unitae unius modulaminis veneranda traditione nec se iungeret officiorum varia celebratio quas coniunxerat unicae fidei pia devotio. Quod quidem et nos conlato nobis a Deo Italiae regno fecimus sanctae Romanae ecclesiae fastigium sublimare cupientes et reverentissimi papae Adriani salutaribus exhortationibus parere nitentes, scilicet ut plures illius partis ecclesiae, quae quondam apostolicae sedis traditionem in psallendo suscipere recusabant, nunc eam cum omni diligentia amplectantur, et cui adhaeserant fidei munere, adhaereant quoque psallendi ordine. Quod non solum omnium Galliarum provinciae et Germania sive Italia, sed etiam Saxones et quaedam aquilonalis plagae gentes per nos Deo annuente ad verae fidei rudimenta conversae facere noscuntur . . . ." *Libri carolini,* MGH, *Concilia 2,* Supplementum. ed. Hubertus Bastgen, (Hanover, Leipzig, 1924.) 21 (Bk. 1 ch. 6).

[11] David Hiley, *Western Plainchant,* 530–62; Kenneth Levy, "Latin Chant Outside The Roman Tradition," in *The New Oxford History of Music,* Vol. 2, *The Early Middle Ages, to 1300,* ed. Richard Crocker and David Hiley (Oxford, 1990), 69–110.

[11] Rembert G. Weakland, "The Office Antiphons of the Ambrosian Chant" (Ph.D. diss., Columbia University, forthcoming).

[13] Thomas F. Kelly, *The Beneventan Chant* (Cambridge, 1989); Kelly, *Les Témoins manuscrits du chant Bénéventains; Pal Mus* 21 (Solesmes, 1992).

The most significant of the archaic Italian repertories represents the musical use of Rome with full-year cycles of musical propers for the mass and office. Here the liturgical texts agree almost entirely with Carolingian-Gregorian usage.[14] However, the music has distinctive traits of an Old Roman dialect. This repertory was perhaps committed to notation before the later eleventh century, two centuries or more after the neumed Carolingian-Gregorian repertory was circulated. For many individual Old Roman chants, even for whole classes of chant, there is an underlying common melodic fund shared with liturgical-textual counterparts in the Gregorian and other musical dialects. There are also considerable differences between Carolingian-Gregorian repertory and the Old Roman in both style and detail, and how these are interpreted affects notions about the Carolingian musical reform.

The key question is, what shapes and styles did the musical repertory at Rome have during the later eighth century, at the time when the Carolingians, at their own word, were importing Gregorian musical substances from Rome?[15] There are many variables. One answer would see the Old Roman and Gregorian chants as having a common musical basis in a proto-Roman melodic repertory of the later eighth century. The material is taken up by the Carolingians who accurately consign it to memory, and at that time, or soon afterward, they add neumatic support. At Rome, meanwhile, the common source material would remain neumeless for a longer time, undergoing significant deteriorations, or at least changes, on the way to its eleventh century Old Roman noted forms. This would make the Carolingian-"Gregorian" music a better window on archaic Roman practice than what was eventually found at Rome itself.

Another answer would see the Old Roman and Gregorian repertories as again sharing a common musical fund in late eighth century Rome. But here the Carolingian-Gregorian repertory is more than an accurately recorded import. Instead, the Roman basis is deliberately edited; considerable stylistic changes suit it to northern musical tastes, and favorite Gallican music is worked in, sometimes accommodated to Roman liturgical texts. Meanwhile, at Rome, the initial repertory might undergo some change, yet remain much closer to its eighth century melodic state.

A rather different possibility has both the Old-Roman and Gregorian repertories descend from a common proto-Roman melodic fund, but both

[14] *MMMA* vol. 2, Band. *Die Gesänge des altrömischen Graduale, Vat. lat. 5319,* Introduction by Bruno Stäblein, Notes by Margareta Landwehr-Melnicki (Kassel, 1970); Max Lütolf, ed., *Das Graduale von Santa Cecilia in Trastevere,* 2 vols., (Cologny-Genève, 1987), (Bodmer C. 74 dated 1071, formerly Phillipps 16069); Helmut Hucke, "Gregorian and Old Roman Chant," *NGD* 7, 693–97; David Hiley, *Western Plainchant,* 530–40.

[15] Bonifazio Baroffio, "Il canto Gregoriano nel secolo VIII," *Lateinische Kultur im VIII. Jahrhundert. Traube-Gedenkschrift,* ed. Albert Lehner and Walter Berschin. (St. Ottilien, 1989) 9–23.

would already flourish as distinctive musical entities in late eighth century Rome. In one form of this hypothesis, the Old Roman music was the embellishment for ceremonies at basilicas and stational churches that enjoyed papal intervention, while the Gregorian music was used at other urban and extra-urban establishments. That external use destined it for export to the Franks, who then edited and supplemented it, though retaining much of what was received of Roman musical substance. A reverse twist on this two-Roman-repertories hypothesis sees the forerunner of the Carolingian-Gregorian music as the Roman music for basilical-stational use, while for the eleventh-century Old Roman it was the standard urban-suburban music.[16] These theories all labor under the difficulty that there is no documentation for the Roman music at Rome before the later eleventh century, and no large-scale documentation of the Gregorian musical repertory there before the thirteenth century.[17]

Behind both the Old Roman and Gregorian there was, in any case, a common musical fund, and somewhere along the way, whether during purely aural stages or after neumes were introduced, this underwent editorial tinkerings, borrowings, and supplementations. Some observations about this will appear in Chapters 2 and 3, but there is no attempt here at comprehensive treatment. The focus is instead on the other two changes, both taking place essentially within the Gregorian repertory: how the melos went from variable to fixed and how the transmission went from aural to notational.

Concerning the change from variable to fixed melos, it would seem that the musical substances of most Gregorian chants were settled as remembered melodies between the sixth and tenth centuries. Some of the crystallization may have come about during aural transmission; some may have had to wait until the availability of notation made practical the complex and refined referential (centonate) and accommodative niceties that mark the written versions. My view is that most of the Gregorian repertory had turned to remembered melody before there was any neuming, but the memories fell short of exact recall, and for so long as the trans-

---

[16] J. Smits van Waesberghe, "L'état actuel des recherches scientifiques dans la domaine du chant grégorien," *Troisième congrès internationale de musique sacrée* (Paris, 1957) 206; S. J. P. van Dijk, "The Urban and Papal Rites in Seventh- and Eighth-Century Rome," *Sacris erudiri* 12 (1961): 411–87; van Dijk "Recent Developments in the Study of the Old-Roman Rite," *Studia patristica* 8 (1966): 299; Bruno Stäblein, "Kann der gregorianische Choral im Frankenreich entstanden sein?" *AfMw* 24 (1967): 153; Stäblein "Nochmals zur angeblichen Entstehungs des gregorianischen Chorals im Frankenreich," *AfMw.* 27 (1970): 110.

[17] It makes a cameo appearance in the later eleventh century, with Gregorian tracts substituting for the Old Roman canticles on Holy Saturday: Stäblein, *Die Gesänge des altrömischen Graduale, Vat. lat. 5319,* 241–45, 647.

mission remained neumeless the music was only approximately replicated; verbatim reproduction was not even an aspiration until there was neuming.

Concerning the change from aural to notational transmission, for certain genres, such as tropes, sequences, and theorists' citations, there are extant neumations as far back as the 830s or 840s. But for the central repertory of Gregorian propers, the neumings reach back only to ca. 900. Most specialists have taken that relatively late date as a rough starting date for Gregorian neuming itself. That leaves a century or more of neumeless transmission between the fixing of melodic substances under Pippin and Charlemagne and the initial neuming. It raises questions about what happened to the music during the ninth century: could the melodies have remained unaltered through a century of unnotated transmission; could the neumed versions, with their networks of formulaic-centonate relationships and their wealths of accommodative detail, have been produced and then maintained in the memories of all the realm's choirmasters for a century without the support of music writing?

Most answers to these questions in recent decades have lined up with one or another of three scenarios, which can be described as the late independent, reimprovisation, and early archetype scenarios. The late independent scenario has been the favorite ever since the notion of aural antecedents took hold in the 1950s. It sees the Gregorian musical substances reaching fixed, definitive melodic states in the later eighth century, but the Carolingian musicians accomplish this without the use of neumes, which were invented a generation or so later. All operations, dictating, editing, teaching, memorizing, would be accomplished by aural means. Then, still without neumes, choirmasters everywhere maintained the fixed melodic forms without change for a full century or more, until neuming of the Gregorian repertory began ca. 900.[18] This traditional view of the repertory[19]

---

[18] Solange Corbin proposed in 1952 that neumes were applied late to Gregorian chant; "Les Notations neumatiques en France à l'époque carolingienne," *Revue d'histoire de l'église en France* 38 (1952): 226–27: "[les premiers témoins de la notation] sont tous des additions de quelques lignes de neumes ou de quelques neumes, faites á des livres déjà existants; aucune de ces additions ne peut être ramenée à une date antérieure à la fin du IXe siècle . . . . Il n'existe pas, jusqu'au Xe siècle, de livres spécialement écrits pour reçevoir une notation . . ." Jacques Froger endorsed this in 1954 when setting out the working methods of the Solesmes critical edition of the Gradual: ". . . l'invention des neumes s'est produite un bon siècle (sinon un siècle et demi) après le début de la diffusion des mélodies du Graduel dans les pays francs. Les mélodies se sont répandues d'abord par tradition purement orale et ont subi diverses modifications dans les diverses régions ou elles ont pénétré. Quand les neumes furent inventés, on fixa par écrit la musique auparavant retenue de mémoire"; in "L'Édition critique de l'*antiphonale missarum* romain par les moines de Solesmes," *EG* 1 (1954): 156.

[19] Recently reaffirmed by David G. Hughes, "Evidence for the Traditional View of the Transmission of Gregorian Chant," *JAMS* 40 (1987): 377–404.

sees the differences in neumatic ductus and technique between the Laon and Saint Gall species (Ex. 1.2 above), or the Breton, Aquitaine, Beneventan, and other species, as indications that Gregorian neumings got started more or less independently at different places. They seem too far apart to have a common source, and those independent initiatives would begin only ca. 900, at about the same time the first survivors appear.[20]

[20] "Or, dès les premiers témoins, nous nous trouvons en présence de plusieurs graphies bien différenciées, sans qu'il paraisse possible, actuellement, d'établir l'antériorité de l'une ou de l'autre d'entre elles, et j'insiste sur ce fait que tout se passe comme s'il y avait eu un prototype dont nous ignorons tout, sauf qu'il a été reproduit de façon différente suivant les régions, que ces différences se produisent dès la fin du IXe siècle, et qu'elles ont conservé leurs caractères jusqu'à la fin du XIIIe siècle . . . "; Corbin, "Les notations neumatiques" (1952): 228. That accurate assessment converted easily to the view that no privileged early written version existed; thus on variants among twelfth-thirteenth century French traditions: "The difference between one melodic tradition and another is easy to explain. For centuries plainsong had been handed down orally so that when it began to be written down, melodic variants, often between two neighboring churches, or even in one and the same cathedral were already established." Heinrich Husmann, "The Origin and Destination of the Magnus liber organi," *The Musical Quarterly* 49 (1963): 313. The Solesmes position has remained more flexible, supposing some sort of belated (ca. 900) authoritative neumation, even though differences among the early neumed relics do not allow full determination of its features. One of Froger's options in 1952 was: " . . . dans cette éventualitè, nos manuscrits neumés nous permettraient de restituer non pas l'archétype du VIIIe siècle, source de la diffusion orale, mais seulement l'archétype de la fin du IXe siècle, source de la diffusion écrite des neumes" J. Froger, *loc. cit.* Dom Cardine reframed this with characteristic good sense in 1977: "(L) es notations sont attestées par les documents seulement dans la seconde moitié du IXe s., d'abord dans les pays compris entre le Rhin et la Seine. Elles présentent de nombreux types d'écriture qui ont fait croire longtemps à leur indépendance; on les imaginait comme le fruit des 'dictées musicales' qui auraient fixé sur le parchemin la tradition orale de chaque école. La constation de quelques anomalies, au même endroit, dans l'ensemble de la tradition, porte aujourd'hui à penser qu'une 'copie visuelle' a été pratiquée, non seulement entre les manuscrits d'un même scriptorium, mais aussi entre les prototypes des diverses écoles. Si l'hypothèse est vrai, l'effort de restitution critique des mélodies grégoriennes serait limité à l'archétype d'écriture sans plus" "Vue d'ensemble sur le chant grégorien," *EG.* 16 (1977): 174. The view that the Gregorian melodies were precisely fixed in memory ca. 800 was reemphasized by David Hughes, "Evidence for the Traditional View of the Transmission of Gregorian Chant," *JAMS* 40 (1987): 400. "A body of chants fully fixed with respect to pitch was in use at the Carolingian court . . . as early as the time of Charlemagne, and was thence propagated to the rest of the Empire . . . . At the time of its radiation, it was transmitted orally, but the oral tradition was tightly controlled and hence highly uniform. The process of radiation was effected by court-trained singers going out into the provinces and teaching the singers there . . . . Notated manuscripts—at least the earlier ones—are faithful records of local practice at the time they were made." Hughes' position was more conservative than Cardines' concerning an eventual privileged neumatic archetype, and that conservatism continues to be widespread. David Hiley's magisterial survey has it: "As this book has tried to make clear, it is not at all certain that an 'original' form of this type ever existed"; *Western Plainchant. A Handbook* (Oxford, 1993), 628; this is also the position of David Hughes, who sets out "some of the indices that seem to me to argue against an early origin for musical notation, or, to put the matter more exactly, against the existence of an

Then there is the reimprovisation scenario, developed in the 1970s, chiefly the creation of Treitler, Hucke, and (independently) van der Werf. This agrees with the late independent scenario as to the independent, late (ca. 900) startup of Gregorian neuming.[21] It adds the notion that melodic stability, the replication of fixed melos, was not realized in the Carolingian liturgical-textual-musical operations of the later eighth century, or even at an eventual introduction of neumes ca. 900. Instead, improvisational strategies and freedoms as to pitch choice would continue long after Gregorian neuming began.[22]

---

authoritative notated exemplar as early as the time of Charlemagne." He concludes, "A much more satisfactory picture emerges if we assume that the dissemination of Gregorian chant under Charlemagne was oral, and that notation intervened only later." "The Implications of Variants for Chant Transmission," in *De Musica et Cantu. Studien zur Geschichte der Kirchenmusik und der Oper. Helmut Hucke zum 60. Geburtstag,* ed. Peter Cahn and Ann-Katrin Heimer (Hildesheim, 1993), 66, 72; so also the position taken in an admirable summary of Carolingian music by Susan Rankin: " . . . the varieties of notations made in the ninth century indicate that the invention of notation cannot be traced to a single, centrally determined enterprise (although such a step may have played a part), but to multiple initiatives." *Carolingian Culture: Emulation and Innovation,* ed. Rosamond McKitterick (Cambridge, 1994), 294.

[21] Leo Treitler: " . . . it is hard to see how a fully neumated Mass proper would have been in circulation as early as 800 . . . my supposition of the later date [i.e. ca. 900] is based on a whole series of indications that the performance of the Mass propers during the ninth century was based on an oral tradition, and that these indications are consistent with the fact that neumated Mass propers have not survived from that century"; "Communication," *JAMS* 41 (1988), 566. Similarly Helmut Hucke: " . . . the five complete chant books that survive from the ninth century, and three from the first half of the tenth century, contain only texts or incipits of texts, and whatever neumes they contain were added later. Even if one wishes, despite this evidence, to suppose that there were in certain localities chant books with neumes as early as the ninth century, chant books without neumes were written at least until the tenth century. We must be able to explain the beginning of chant transmission in the Frankish Empire without assuming the use of neumes . . . " "Toward a New Historical View of Gregorian Chant," *JAMS* 33 (1980): 447. Hucke in 1988 observed about the unneumed Carolingian Tonary in Metz 351: "Dass ein Kopist im zweiten Drittel des 9. Jahrhunderts im liturgisch-musikalischen Zentrum Metz einen Tonar schreibt und dabei von Neumen keinen Gebrauch macht, zeigt, dass die Neumenschrift im Zentrum Metz noch nicht zum Handwerkszeug des Kantors und zum Kommunikationsmittel unter Kantoren geworden war"; "Gregorianische Fragen," 309; and about the possibility of a neumatic model: "Wie soll nam dann erklären dass sie [Kopisten] die gregorianischen Melodien vom Anfang der Überlieferung an in unterschiedliche Neumenschriften notierten?"; *Mf* 41 (1988): 329–30.

[22] Treitler: " . . . the Gregorian Chant tradition was, in its early centuries, an oral performance practice . . . . The oral tradition was translated after the ninth century into writing. But the evolution from a performance practice represented in writing, to a tradition of composing, transmission, and reading, took place over a span of centuries . . . . The act of writing was thus a kind of performance analogous to singing out, and the written score served as an exemplification of the song, to be taken more as a model for performance than as a blueprint"; "The Early History of Music Writing in the West," *JAMS* 35 (1982): 237. Hucke: "The uniformity of melodic transmission of Gregorian chant books does not prove

Then there is the early archetype scenario developed in these pages.[23] This agrees with the late independent scenario in seeing the Gregorian repertory reach fixed melodic states during the later eighth century. But it goes on to see the neumes as essential agents in that stabilization. Neumes were needed for taking down aural deliveries, and then for the editorial revisions that produced the polished melodic states represented in the earliest extant neumings. Neumes continued to be needed as those same editorially-fixed melodies were handed on to choirmasters and soloists throughout the realm with a mandate for their accurate reproduction.

Six of the following chapters (Ch. 2 through 7) have appeared in periodicals and, with one exception, they reappear as first published: Chapter 7 has had some of its original background material shifted to the present chapter; Chapters 8 through 11 are new. From various points of view they address the turn from aural to notational.

---

uniformity of musical practice. A fundamental change of conception was needed before what had been written down at the beginning of the written tradition was understood, as it is in the current historical view of Gregorian chant, as a collection of melodies." "Toward a New Historical View of Gregorian Chant," *JAMS* 33 (1980): 466. Also Hendrik van der Werf: "The texts for the Proper and the Ordinary of the Franco-Roman Mass were precisely codified during the reign of Charlemagne. If the extant manuscripts are a reliable testimony, this codification took hold rather rapidly . . . . For the music, however, the situation must have been different. The practice of newly improvising a melody on the spot, or for a given liturgical service, must have begun to decline long before 800, but note for note recall from one year to the next was still unthought of. If the singers had wanted exact retention of their melodies, they could have made use of letter notation, as did the authors and copyists of treatises. The somewhat awkward term 'reimprovisation' seems to be best suited for the manner in which the melodies were recalled from year to year." *The Emergence of Gregorian Chant: A Comparative Study of Ambrosian, Roman, and Gregorian Chant.* Volume I of A Study of Modes and Melodies, Part One, Discourse. Rochester, New York: (Published by the author, 1983), 164. Hucke endorsed this notion of pitch variability as a factor in neumed Gregorian transmissions: " . . .aber über den 'pitch-content' . . . informieren sie uns schlecht. Und wir haben keinen Beweis, dass die Überlieferung hinsichtlich des 'pitch content' je einheitlich gewesen ist. Die Übersichtstafeln von Hendrik van der Werf in seinem Buch *The Emergence of Gregorian Chant* zeigen in eindrucksvoller Weise, dass die gregorianischen Melodien uns in der intervallisch lesbaren Tradition nicht als kanonisierte Intervallfolgen, sondern mit melodischen Varianten entgegen treten . . . . Die linienlosen Neumenschriften stellen kein einheitliches und geschlossenes Notationssystem dar. Eben darum lässt sich mit den Methoden der Editionskritik ein 'Urtext' nicht erschliessen." 'Gregorianische Frager," 326–27.

[23] Its main lines were set out in "Charlemagne's Archetype" and "On the Origin of Neumes," (both 1987, republished here as Chs. 4 and 5), and in a paper "Gregorian Chant and Oral Transmission," at a 1990 Harvard symposium, published in *Essays on Medieval Music in Honor of David G. Hughes*, ed. Graeme M. Boone. *Isham Library Papers* 4 (Harvard University Department of Music, 1955), 277–86.

Chapter 2 ("A Gregorian Processional Antiphon")[24] considers the earliest documented Gregorian chant. This is the processional antiphon *Deprecamur te,* which went with St. Augustine of Canterbury on his mission to England during the reign of Gregory the Great. Its musical states illumine the prehistory of the Gregorian propers and their relationship with archaic Italian musical dialects.

Chapter 3 ("Toledo, Rome, and the Legacy of Gaul")[25] is concerned with Gallo-Hispanic musical antecedents for certain Gregorian offertories. It identifies relics of an archaic offertory repertory, suggesting that substantial amounts of the eventual Gregorian offertories' musical substance represent Gallican rather than Roman chant style. The discussion turns on instances of "close multiples," where the neumed versions of a once aural plainchant, although written down at different times and places, turn out to have considerable melodic agreements. That points to the shared aural version behind the notational ones: a chant already having an essentially fixed melodic profile and the status of "remembered melody." Close multiples offer a unique avenue of access to archaic melodic states. In the case of these Old Hispanic, Gregorian, and Milanese multiples, the historical backgrounds suggest that their antecedents were already stable as remembered melodies before the Moorish invasion of the Iberian peninsula in 711.

Chapter 4 ("Charlemagne's Archetype of Gregorian Chant")[26] argues that an archetypal Carolingian-Gregorian model neumation of ca. 800 may have been the departure point for nearly all the later neumations.

Chapter 5 ("On the Origin of Neumes")[27] complements the projection in Chapter 4 with a fresh theory about early neuming. It sees an original stage of neuming (reflected only in Paleofrank notations), using a positional-graphic rationale; then a next stage (beginning near the end of the eighth century) which substitutes neumings based on a directional-gestural-chironomic rationale. The distinctive neume species of tenth-century Lorraine, Saint Gall, Brittany, Aquitaine, Burgundy, Benevento, etc., would all be outgrowths of a Carolingian model, or archetype, in existence ca. 800, whose own neumation was generated by the directional-gestural-chironomic rationale, with the differences among the eventual regional species resulting from local reimplementations of that rationale.

Chapter 6 ("On Gregorian Orality")[28] addresses an exceptionally fertile complex of close multiples. Among independently neumed regional recensions for the old-Gallican offertory *Elegerunt apostoli,* for St.

[24] *Schweizer Jahrbuch für Musikwissenschaft* NS 2 (1982): 91–102.
[25] *EMH* 4 (1984): 49–99.
[26] *JAMS* 40 (1987): 1–30.
[27] *EMH* 7 (1987): 59–90.
[28] *JAMS* 43 (1990): 185–227.

Stephen, there are melodic agreements, pointing to a stable melos, rooted in Gallican memories before the music was ever neumed. These local versions fall short of full melodic agreement, indicating that the melos during the neumeless transmission was not yet firm. Verbatim recall was not achieved, and may not have been a goal; it would become practical only with the addition of the memory-supportive staffless neumes.

Chapter 7 ("Abbot Helisachar's Antiphoner")[29] reviews the remarks of Helisachar, archchancellor to Louis the Pious, ca. 820, about singers, copyists, liturgical texts, and antiphoners in his day. In previous assessments, he has been seen as referring to a neumeless practice. Yet he may be describing not only melodies with musical details that were quite fixed, but also melodies that were, as a matter of course, accurately profiled in neumes.

Chapter 8 ("Aurelian's Use of Neumes") addresses the same issues of melodic fixity and use of neumes in the *Musica disciplina* of Aurelian of Réôme, likely composed ca. 850. Some plainchants were being neumed by then, and the treatise makes occasional use of neumes; some of the Gregorian musical details that Aurelian describes in words turn up with the same details in neumings ca. 900. There are arguments that the whole Gregorian repertory Aurelian knew was regularly supplied with neumes.

Chapter 9 ("Plainchant Before Neumes") turns to aural states before there was any neuming. Differences of musical behavior in the notational states suggest different behavior in the prior aural state. Four classes of Gregorian chant are distinguished, each with something of its own historical-procedural-stylistic features, and each perhaps with its own path from aural to notational. They are: remembered melodies (*idiomela,*) accommodated melodies (*automela/prosomoia,*) psalmic matrices, and centonate compilations.

Chapter 10 ("The Carolingian Visual Model") ties together proposals made in earlier chapters, concerning neume origins and the start of neumed Gregorian states. The repertory is seen as collected in an authoritative visual model—Charlemagne's Archetype—whose likely place of compilation is Metz,[30] or at least the region around Trier. The model's neumes supply choirmasters with the memory support they need to maintain the freshly edited Carolingian-Gregorian melodies throughout Europe. Eventual differences in neumatic ductus among the descendent species are an outcome of reapplying the model's own directional-gestural-chironomic rationale in later neumings of the universally familiar, memorized melodies.

Chapter 11 ("Memory, Neumes, and Square Notations") considers, finally, the nature and extent of melodic variance during the tenth through

[29] *JAMS* 48 (1995): 171–86.
[30] Claire Maître, *La Béforme cistercienne du plain-chant. Étude d'un traité théorique.* Cîteaux: Studi et Documenta, Vol. 6 (Brecht, 1995), 42–45,

eighteenth centuries. At the outset, by ca. 800, the Carolingian transmission couples professionals' memories, where the full melodic substances, fixed tunes, are stored, with the model neumings that provide silhouettes of the memorized melodies. Memory is essential, because the neumes are inadequate as to pitch; still, the neumatic memory aids enhance memory's sharpness; they make verbatim recall possible. That initial memory-neume relationship evolved during centuries to come. As the staffless neumes were turned into pitched signs heightened precisely on a lined staff, memory came to have a lesser role. Yet it remained a stabilizing force, usually supporting the mainline transmission, though at times it became a vehicle for perpetuating local variants; other variants arose from fresh stylistic initiatives.

In the end, none of the three main scenarios lays claim to solid proof. The late independent scenario relies on two chief points. One is that traces of about a dozen antiphoners survive from before ca. 900, and none of them has neumes; the reason is that neumed antiphoners were not produced before that time. That argues from silence, and countering arguments are proposed here in Chapters 4 and 10. The other support for the late independent scenario amounts to the difficulty of explaining how the range of rather different tenth and eleventh century regional neume-species can be the outcome of any single written model. My explanation for this, Chapters 5 and 10, identifies a directional-gestural-chironomic rationale as the generating force in all the eventual divergent neumings.

The reimprovisation scenario agrees with the late independent scenario about those two points, and adds two others of its own. One, that for some centuries after Gregorian neuming began, singers continued to exercise improvisational freedoms in their deliveries. Support is found in melodic variants of the twelfth and thirteenth centuries.[31] Yet those variants are slight as well as late, compared with the massive agreements of melodic-neumatic details in a great spread of early (tenth and eleventh century) neumings. These suggest that precisely fixed melodies were the rule by the first half of the ninth century.

The reimprovisation scenario's other point is a parallel with comparative literature. Dom Cardine's declaration about aural antecedents produced a general understanding that formulaic-centonate traits in Gregorian neumed states had antecedents in aural-improvisational deliveries. It left open the question of what the antecedents were like. The reimprovisation scenario approaches this through analogies with the practice of Homer and of modern Macedonian bards, as first analyzed by Parry

[31] Hendrik Van der Werf, *The Emergence of Gregorian Chant*, Volume 1, Part 2 (Rochester, NY, 1983).

and Lord.[32] However the verbal texts of the Homeric hexameters (which survive only in written traditions) and of the Balkan epic one-liners, are in substance and style at a considerable remove from the melodic matter of florid Gregorian chants. The melismatic music was also destined, in many cases, for choral performance, where license for improvisatory input was limited. One must also question how accurately the noted Gregorian states, on which the reimprovisational conjectures are based, represent the details of the aural melodic states. Any rearward see-through, from notational to prior aural, would vary from class to class within the Gregorian canon (see Ch. 9). The centonate-formulaic complexities seen in the tenth century neumed versions, may well be the result of editorial-compositional decisions taken in a notational medium rather than snapshots of aural deliveries.[33]

The three scenarios all address the same issues: means of access to unnoted melodic states, the nature of aural production, the capabilities of medieval musical memory, the origin of neumes, the partnership between memory and neumes in early notational transmissions, and the emergence of regional melodic and neumatic variants. In connection with these, there has been much recent discussion about the date of the first Gregorian neumings.[34] The late independent and reimprovisation scenarios both put this near 900; the early archetype scenario puts it roughly a century earlier. That difference of a century may in itself seem trivial, but where one sees the start of Gregorian neuming, and whether it is viewed as the outcome of a centrally organized process or of independent initiatives at different places, makes a difference in the way one deals with the repertory. That applies particularly to how one goes about preparing a Gregorian critical edition. Such an edition has been under way at Solesmes during the past half century. It has produced very valuable results, though more on the procedural and bibliographic sides than the musical side. So far, in music, there are the mass chants for the first Sunday in Advent.[35] This measured progress reflects an admirable, scientific caution. Yet at the same time it speaks for a difficulty with the assumptions on which the critical edition is based. The assumptions are those of the late independent scenario, which has the Gregorian chants attain melodic fixity under Pippin or Charlemagne. This provides a goal for melodic restoration and that

[32] Albert B. Lord, *The Singer of Tales* (Cambridge, MA: 1960); Dennis H. Green, "Orality and Reading: The State of Research in Medieval Studies," Speculum 65 (1990): 267–80.

[33] See the "Communications" by Peter Jeffery and Leo Treitler in *JAMS* 49 (1996): 175–79.

[34] "Communications" by Treitler, Levy, and Hughes in *JAMS* 41 (1988): 566–79.

[35] *LeGr*, Vol. 4. Le texte neumatique; 1: Le Groupement des manuscrits (1960); 2: Les relations généalogiques des manuscrits (1962): 69–89: "La messe *Ad te levavi*."

is where progress has been most substantial. Yet a critical edition might also aspire to the restoration of an authoritative, or at least early, neumatic state. The prevailing scenario has the fixed melodies established without the use of neumes in the later eighth century, with the neumes entering a century later, more or less independently at different places; in effect, there is no neumatic original to restore. Under the early archetype scenario, an authoritative Gregorian neumation is formulated in the same endeavors that establish the melodic forms; all of which takes place in the Carolingian heartland by ca. 800. It also sees the many different tenth and eleventh century neume species as descendents of that archetypal neumation, with their differences generated by reapplying the same directional gestural rationale that produced the original neumatic shapings. That puts the critical restoration of an authoritative Carolingian neumation well within reach.

CHAPTER 2

A Gregorian Processional Antiphon

No chant of the medieval liturgy comes better supplied with evidence of its origin, function, and change than the processional antiphon *Deprecamur te Domine*. No chant, in fact, has a better claim to be called «Gregorian,» for Deprecamur reaches us with a unique parcel of history attached. In 596, Pope Gregory the Great dispatched Augustine, the Italian-born prior of the monastery of Saint Andrew on the Caelian hill at Rome, to refound the Church of England, and before Augustine died in 604–5 he was ordained the first archbishop of Canterbury. In the 8th-century *History* of Bede and again in the *Vita* of Augustine it is recorded that as the Saint approached Canterbury in 597 there was sweetly sung the «litanialem antiphonam» *Deprecamur te Domine in omni misericordia tua.*[1] The full text of that antiphon is given by the two English histories, and it appears again in the 9th-century text-antiphonaries of Compiègne and Senlis among the provisions for the Great Litanies.[2] During the following centuries it reappears in neumed sources from all over Europe. Thus there is every reason to suppose that the verbal text was established in the Roman usage by the end of the 6th century. For the music, no fewer than three distinct chants circulate during the Middle Ages, and the present purpose is to examine them and see what they reveal.

The most widely diffused chant is a truly international one that appears in France (as early as the 10th century), Germany, Italy, and England. It is apparently the only melody in surviving English sources. A generation ago, one might have labelled a melody with such a pedigree as «Gregorian,» and with that have settled the question of what melody it was that Augustine heard in England. Today, however, it is clear that the question is knottier, and that there are arguments for assigning such a melody to a «Frankish»-fostered recension of the Roman chant, carried out north of the Alps some two centuries or more after Gregory's reign.[3] In the discussion that follows, I shall prefer to call that recension «Carolingian» rather than «Frankish,» on the one hand as describing the time-frame during which it took decisive shape, and on the other as describing what was in some respects a broad-based endeavor which, like its cultural progenitor, the «Carolingian Renaissance,» joined contributions of Visigoths and Lombards, Celts and Saxons, with those of Franks and Italians in shaping the musical tradition that for centuries thereafter was known as «Gregorian.»

1 *Bede's Ecclesiastical History of the English People,* ed. B. Colgrave, R. A. B. Mynors (Oxford, 1969), 74: ... *hanc laetaniam consona voce modularentur; Vita Sancti Augustini,* cap. 19; J.-P. Migne, *Patrologiae cursus completus ... Series Latina. . . ,* tomus 80 (Paris, 1863), col. 62: ... *tum hanc litanialem antiphonam dulcimode intonat, et ... consona modulatione ac devotione decantat.*
2 R.-J. Hesbert, *Antiphonale Missarum Sextuplex* (Brussels, 1935), No. 202a; p. cxxi.
3 H. Hucke, «Gregorianischer Gesang in altrömischer und fränkischer Überlieferung,» *Archiv für Musikwissenschaft,* 13 (1956), 74 ff.; idem, «Karolingische Renaissance und Gregorianischer Gesang,» *Die Musikforschung,* 28 (1975), 4 ff., especially 12–13; idem, *The New Grove Dictionary,* ed. Stanley Sadie (London, 1980), «Gregorian and Old Roman Chant,» 7, 696–7.

First published in *Schweizer Jahrbuch für Musikwissenschaft,* Neue Folge, 2 (1982), 91–102. Reprinted with permission.

Fig. 1 offers three early witnesses of Deprecamur te in the Carolingian tradition: one is from German Switzerland; another from central Italy; and a third from eastern Austria.

Fig. 1 *Deprecamur te* in Carolingian traditions: 1a. Saint Gall 339, 136 (plus Bamberg lit. 6, 90); 1b. Pistoia C. 119, 127; 1c. Graz 807, 116.

1 a

1 b (4) et i- ra tu- a

1 c

(Bamberg,   (St. Gall)
1 a lit. 6)

1 b (5) a ci- vi-ta- te i- sta

1 c

1 a

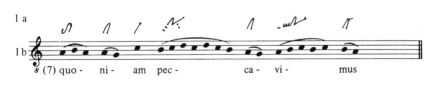

1 b (6) et de do- mo san-cta tu- a

1 c

1 a

1 b (7) quo- ni- am pec- ca- vi- mus

1 c

Fig. 1a is a staffless version in 11th-century St. Gall neumes.[4] Its neumation is essentially identical with that in some other prediastematic sources of the middle 10th through early 11th centuries, originating as far apart as Brittany, Picardy, and Aemilia.[5] Despite their spreads of time and place, the staffless versions are so united in details of graphic disposition that they all must represent the sort of single neumatic archetype that Dom Cardine and his associates have been adumbrating for many chants of the standard repertory, an archetype compiled at some scriptorium «between the Seine and the Rhine,» and presumably during the 9th century.[6]

Turning to Fig. 1b, we have a staffed reading descended from the neumatic archetype represented by Fig. 1a.[7] This 12th-century melodic version from Pistoia is quite close to Fig. 1a in its neumatic layout. In fact, it is remarkable how uniformly most of the early staffed versions have come through the process of transformation from neumatic outline to heighted melody. Essentially this same melodic version is found in England, though not to my knowledge in any source before the 13th century. The Worcester reading is descended from the same neumatic model as Fig. 1a, but with more considerable melodic decay than most, and its testimony seems to contribute little to the dossier of the chant's early history.

With Fig. 1b we have the substance of the melody, which was evidently thought of as representing a D-Authentic mode. There is the characteristic opening leap from D to A, though other modal earmarks are less indicative. The question of modality takes on further interest when we turn to Fig. 1c, which shows the 12th-century east Austrian version of Graz 807.[9] This version in its neumatic disposition reflects the same prediastematic model as the versions of Saint Gall (Fig. 1a) and Pistoia (Fig. 1b). But the modal premise is changed. Unlike the great majority of Carolingian-derived traditions, Graz is exceptional in presenting the familiar melodic substance at a different pitch-level. While still treating the chant as D-mode, it adjusts some modal-melodic details so that the resulting conception is D-Plagal rather than D-Authentic. This may have come about as a casual result of the process by which chants that originally circulated in staffless neumes became attached to different levels of the tonal system when decisions about staff and clefs were made. Yet like some other Germanic manuscripts, particularly Augustinian and Cistercian, the one at Graz systematically transposes chants like its Graduals of the *Justus ut palma* type, shifting them so as to avoid an upper B-flat. A similar logic may have prevailed in the choice of D-Plagal for Depre-

---

4 Saint Gall 339, 136 (*Paléographie musicale* [hereafter: *PM*], 1); variants after Bamberg lit. 6, 90.
5 *PM* 11, 126; *PM* 16, 44v; *PM* 18, 169.
6 E. Cardine, «A propos des formes possibles d'une figure neumatique,» in *Sacerdos et Cantus Gregoriani Magister: Festschrift F. X. Haberl* (Regensburg, 1977), 68: «On constate... que les manuscrits sont en accord entre eux pour noter les particularités les plus fines, d'autant mieux qu'ils sont plus anciens et qu'ils proviennent des pays situés entre la Seine et le Rhin, c'est-à-dire qu'ils sont plus rapprochés du lieu où fut établi l'archétype de la notation musicale.» The thrust of Cardine's argument is notably expanded by J. B. Göschl, *Semiologische Untersuchungen zum Phänomen der gregorianischen Liqueszenz,* 2 vols, (Wien, 1980).
7 Pistoia, Bibl. cap., C. 119, 127.
8 PM 12, 227; a 12th-century Winchester missal, Le Havre 330, was unavailable to me.
9 PM 19, 116; the manuscript's origin there assigned by Dom J. Froger to Klosterneuberg.

camur te. Yet whatever the motive behind the change in mode, the underlying neumation of Graz (Fig. 1 c) clearly reflects the «Carolingian» neumation of Fig. 1 a.

Turning to Fig. 2, we have a south-central Italian, «Beneventan» version of our antiphon after three sources of the 12th century: one from Troia in eastern Puglia, near Monte Gargano; another from Sora in the Abruzzi, near Subiaco to the southeast of Rome; and a third from Campanian Benevento itself.[10]

Fig. 2 *Deprecamur te* in Beneventan tradition:
Naples VI. G. 34, 6; Vat. reg. lat. 334, 68v; Benevento VI. 34, 157.

10 Napoli, Bibl. Naz., VI.G.34, 6; Vatican, Reg. lat. 334, 68v; Benevento, Bibl. cap., VI.34, 157 (PM 15).

No Beneventan version in staffless neumes has survived, but our three staffed readings are so close in details of neumation that there is likely to have been a single pre-diastematic model behind all of them, as there is for most of the rest of the Beneventan tradition. Like the east Austrian melody in Fig. 1c, our Beneventan melody is in D-Plagal, and it is in many respects so much like Fig. 1c that a first estimate might be that it represents the same kind of transmission: another derivative of the Carolingian neumatic archetype, again shifted from authentic to plagal. Still, the Beneventan reading departs somewhat more considerably from the Carolingian neumation than occurs elsewhere in the 11th–12th century readings, and the aggregate of the Beneventan variants of mode, neumatic disposition, and pitch-detail seems considerable enough to warrant a separate presentation of the Beneventan reading.[11] In a moment I shall return to consider some possibilities that are raised by the Beneventan variants.

There are still two melodies remaining. Fig. 3 shows the Urban-Roman, «Old-Roman» melody, an unicum in Vatican 5319, copied c. 1100.[12]

Fig. 3 *Deprecamur te* in Old Roman tradition:
Vat. lat. 5319, 141v.

(1) De - pre - ca - mur te Do - mi - ne

(2) in om - ni mi - se - ri - cor -

di - e tu - e

(3) ut au - fe - ra - tur fu - ror tu - us

(4) et i - ra tu - a

---

11 There are the following variants for the first five words: *De-pre-*, C[arolingian]: two puncta or punctum, virga; B[eneventan]: two ornamental(?) neumes (on this type see J. Boe, «The Beneventan Apostrophus in South Italian Notation,A.D. 1000–1100,» in *Early Music History,* 3, 1983, 43–66). *Do-*, C: torculus resupinus; B: torculus, punctum, clivis. *mi-*, C: virga; B: podatus. *ne-*. C: torculus; B: «pressus.» *in.* C: quilisma; B: torculus. *om-*. C: virga; B: torculus. Etc.
12 Vatican, Latin 5319, 141v; B. Stäblein, ed., *Monumenta monodica medii aevi,* II (Kassel, 1970), 565.

As at Benevento, the mode is D-Plagal; and these two «Italic» versions also show melodic relationships of a sort found elsewhere between the two neighboring traditions. This is not an occasion to review the problematic history of the Old-Roman repertory, but since the melodic evidence for Deprecamur te falls into an area so burdened with personal opinions, I should state that I favor the view that the Old-Roman chants, as they reach us in a small handful of 11th–13th century sources, represent a relatively late conversion to writing of a melodic tradition that persisted in circulating orally for somewhat longer than the Carolingian tradition.[13] Some years ago I pointed out the special channel that existed between the church of St. Cecilia in Trastevere, where in 1071 the earliest Urban-Roman Gradual was noted, and the abbey of Monte Cassino, whose abbott Desiderius, the most influential of Cassinese abbots after St. Benedict himself, was assigned St. Cecilia as his titular Urban church upon investing the functions of Cardinal-Priest in 1059. Desiderius continued in authority over church and monastery until his elevation to the papacy in 1087.[14] The considerable number of musical borrowings from Beneventan use found in the Old-Roman Gradual of 1071 may reflect that link. Moreover it would not be surprising if the impulse to convert an obsolescent Roman musical tradition from oral transmission to writing also came from Monte Cassino in the middle 11th century. In any case, the close neumatic agreement between the Gradual of 1071 and the slightly later Gradual, Vatican 5319 indicates that both are close to the same model, perhaps the archetype for the Roman noted tradition. As for the melodic substance of that tradition, however, what indications there are suggest that the Roman musicians clung to the stylistic integrity of their chant-dialect at least through the early 9th century. That is how one must interpret the conversion to a Roman melodic dia-

13 A view considered recently by P. Cutter, «The Old-Roman Chant Tradition: Oral or Written?,» *Journal of the American Musicological Society* [hereafter: *JAMS*], 20 (1967), 167–181; see also Cutter in *Acta Musicologica*, 39 (1967), 2–19, and *The Musical Quarterly*, 62 (1976), 182–194; compare T.H. Connolly, «The Gradual of S. Cecilia in Trastevere and the Old Roman Tradition,» *JAMS*, 28 (1975), 413–458.

14 K. Levy, «*Lux de luce:* The Origin of an Italian Sequence,» *The Musical Quarterly*, 57 (1971), 44 n. 11.

lect of the set of *Veterem hominem* antiphons for the Epiphany octave, which began their diffusion in the West during the early 9th century as a melodic translation from a Byzantine to a Carolingian melos, carried out by the order of Charlemagne.[15] Just when the *Veterem hominem* set was incorporated in Roman usage is not known, though this perhaps occurred no sooner than the exercise of Ottonian influence at Rome in the later 10th or early 11th century.[16] What is clear is that when those antiphons reached Rome, the Urban musicians still cared enough about their local dialect to effect the melodic conversion from the Carolingian dialect to the Old-Roman.

Finally, Fig. 4 shows us the melody for Deprecamur te in the Milanese tradition.[17]

Fig. 4 *Deprecamur te* in Milanese tradition:
Oxford, Bodl. lat. lit. a. 4, 87.

15 O. Strunk, «The Latin Antiphons for the Octave of the Epiphany,» *Recueil de travaux de l'institut d'Études byzantines, No. 8: Mélanges Georges Ostrogorsky,* 2 (Belgrade, 1964), 417–426; repr. in O. Strunk, *Essays on Music in the Byzantine World* (New York, 1977), 208–219.

16 Berno of Reichenau (d. 1048) (*De Quibusdam rebus ad missae officium spectantibus,* c. 2: Migne, *Patrologiae . . . lat.,* 142, col. 1060f.) recounts *(me coram assistente)* the astonishment of Henry II in 1014 on finding the Credo omitted from the Mass at Rome, which lead to its inclusion at public Masses by Benedict VIII (1012–24).

17 Oxford, Bodl., lat. liturg. a. 4 (30062), 87 (A. D. 1399).

(6) et de do - mo san - cta tu - a

(7) quo - ni - am pec - ca - vi - mus ti - bi

In light of the D-mode assignment for the antiphon in the Carolingian, Beneventan, and Old-Roman traditions, it is no surprise to discover again a chant in a
D-mode. Yet as usual at Milan, the distinction between plagal and authentic
forms is not clearly made, if made at all, and this chant is not indicative enough
in melodic idioms or focussed enough within its range to justify a characterization as either plagal or authentic. The text first appears at Milan in a series of
litanic services in an 11th century Ambrosian Manuale.[18] The musical version
in Fig. 4 is three centuries younger, though the melodic stability exhibited by
other Milanese chants as they progress through manuscripts of the early 12th
through late 14th centuries allows some possibility that the version of Deprecamur te sung at Milan in the 11th–12th century was not too different from the one
given here.
If we go on now to compare our three basic melodies – Carolingian-Beneventan
(Figs. 1–2), Old-Roman (Fig. 3), and Milanese (Fig. 4) – there is some ground for
supposing that they are fundamentally related. Thus there are parallels in the
rhetorical rise and fall of lines 1 and 2; in the melodic climaxes on *furor* (line 3)
and *ita* (line 4); in the recitations that open line 5. One of these three melodic
formulations may have served as the point of departure for another. But it is more
likely that behind all three there lies some ancestral modal-melodic formulation
whose stylistic details we can no longer ascertain.

*

Barring some unexpected circumstance, there will be no way of knowing what
melodic formulations lie behind our earliest noted sources. I am not about to propose that such an unexpected circumstance exists, yet there is something provocative about the melodic transmissions for Deprecamur te, and I do not want
to leave the question of this antiphon without sketching a scenario that may lift
something of the veil that shrouds the earlier, pre-notational centuries. It depends on the small differences that have already been observed between the Carolingian (Fig. 1) and Beneventan (Fig. 2) versions. What separates those two comes
to very little: the choice of authentic mode as opposed to plagal; and a handful
of neumatic-melodic details whose divergences reach a bit beyond those in other

18 M. Magistretti, *Monumenta veteris liturgiae ambrosianae: Manuale ambrosianum (saec XI), pars altera* (Milano, 1904–5), 265; *die tertio de litaniis,* Antiphona xvi.

early witnesses. This might be dismissed as representing no more than the same kind of decay attributed to the 13th-century English tradition: a reading farther removed in space from Cardine's archetype «between the Seine and the Rhine,» and a musical result correspondingly removed in neumatic-melodic detail. However there is an alternative explanation for the Beneventan variants. It supposes that Benevento's choice of the «Italic» D-Plagal mode (which it shares with Rome) and also the variants in melodic detail, amount to a Beneventan insistence on a well-entrenched local tradition, and one in fact that can claim some special authority: an attachment by the Italians to a musical version that they felt justified in maintaining in the face of the Carolingian rescension. There is some background for the idea of a Beneventan liturgical-musical practice having special authority. For one thing, the Benedictine mother abbey of Monte Cassino, established in 529, spread its usage from the Beneventan zone to the whole of Europe. In the later 6th century, Gregory the Great governed his monks by the Benedictine Rule, and when Augustine of Canterbury and his company reached England in 596–7 it was that Rule and presumably its accompanying music that they brought with them.[19] There is also the Lindisfarne Gospel, compiled in northeast Britain at the end of the 7th century. Its text model was not an Evangeliary of Roman provenance but one going back to a Campanian or Neapolitan exemplar – from the Beneventan zone.[20] As for music, Dom Hesbert has shown the extraordinary tenacity of the Beneventan scribes in preserving archaic details of the Carolingian neumatic recension more faithfully than elsewhere.[21] The other side of that Beneventan archaizing is the tenacity about the local musical liturgy: the scribes continued to copy the old-Beneventan proper chants for major feasts well into the 12th century, long after other regions had bowed to the liturgical unifications dictated by Charlemagne and abandoned the bulk of their local music for the Carolingian recension.[22]

Now if it can be supposed that the Beneventan variants for Deprecamur te represent a similar independence of mind, an archaic persuasion about how certain features of the antiphon must go, that may tell us something useful. At face value, the variants say only that the Italians were fussing over some very small details. Yet the insistence on apparent trifles betokens something more: in effect, an «endorsement» of the large amounts of melodic fabric that the Beneventan and

19 F. L. Cross, ed., *Oxford Dictionary of the Christian Church* (London, 1958), 155 («Benedictine Order»).

20 F. Cabrol and H. Leclercq, eds., *Dictionnaire d'archéologie chrétienne et de liturgie*, 12¹, 766 («Naples»); E. A. Lowe, *Codices latini antiquiores*, 2 (Oxford, 1935), No. 187.

21 *PM* 14 (1931 ff.), 143–196: «L'Archaïsme mélodique,» Hesbert's summary (p. 464): «Archaïque par son écriture, archaïque par maints traits de sa liturgie, archaïque par sa notation musicale, la tradition bénéventaine l'est encore au double point de vue mélodique et modal. Et, ici encore, nous entendons bien parler, non de la cantilène locale qui accompagnait les fonctions de l'ancien rite bénéventain, mais bien du chant romain [i.e. the recension here described as «Carolingian»] en tant qu'il est attesté par des témoins bénéventains.»

22 On the old-Beneventan chant repertory, see Dom B. Baroffio, «Liturgie im beneventanischen Raum,» *Geschichte der katholischen Kirchenmusik*, ed. K.-G. Fellerer, 1 (Kassel, 1972), 204; K. Schlager, «Beneventan rite, music of the,» in *The New Grove Dictionary*, 2, 482–4; K. Levy, «Latin Chant Outside the Roman Tradition,» in *New Oxford History of Music*, 2, rev. ed. (forthcoming), ed. R.L. Crocker. Editions are in preparation of the old-Beneventan proper chants by T.F. Kelly, and the sequences and tropes by A. Planchart and J. Boe.

Carolingian readings have in common. And clearly enough, any melodic fabric on which those two arguably «independent» recensions agree must have an extraordinary claim to antiquity. One can imagine it representing, down to the small details, a specific fund of melody that went north from Italy during the 8th–9th century to be enshrined in the neumes of the Carolingian recension.[23] To be sure, other scenarios are possible. There is the simple one already proposed, of Benevento representing a decaying Carolingian recension. There are more elaborate ones, supposing that Benevento preserves an archaic stage of a Carolingian neumatic formulation older than has survived elsewhere, and leaving open the question of whether the common melodic fabric in Figs. 1–2 was originally Italian or may represent a Gallican or Frankish formulation.

To pursue only the scenario of an Italian original transmitted independently by Benevento, before any claims can be made, there must be further testing of Carolingian-derived versions of Deprecamur te, and also tests of comparable processional antiphons. I have undertaken one such comparison with the antiphon *Peccavimus Domine et tu iratus es,* which offers a particularly close parallel to Deprecamur te. This is again an antiphon of the Great Litanies, transmitted in the same group as Deprecamur te by the Carolingian, Beneventan, and Old-Roman traditions. At Rome, Deprecamur and Peccavimus are in a sense musical twins: both are in D-Plagal, and they share more specific melodic substance with one another than either shares with any other Roman processional antiphon.[24] The point of the comparison, however, is in the Beneventan and Carolingian recensions. Unlike the case of Deprecamur, where the two recensions disagree about the mode, both now have Peccavimus in D-Plagal. Moreover the differences in melodic detail are much less considerable for Peccavimus than for Deprecamur.[25] Since the recensions agree about Peccavimus while disagreeing about Deprecamur, the likelihood seems increased that the Beneventans were adhering to an entrenched historical tradition in their variant reading of Deprecamur.

If such arguments can stand up to further testing, they may give us a unique grip, not only on the melodic pre-history of Deprecamur te, but perhaps on something more. By saying that Benevento clung to certain archaic melodic variants while still agreeing in substance with the Carolingian melody, we are implying that the Carolingian music did not acquire its basic stylization in the north as part of a «Frankish» melodic revision, but rather that it originated in Italy and came north already fully stylized. And this may lend support to the view espoused by Stäblein and others that there were «two Roman chants»: that the melodic fabric of the Carolingian recension was not in large measure the outcome of a thoroughgoing «Frankish» stylistic overlay but represented a melodic fund that in most

---

23 An early stage of the Carolingian recension may have reached the Beneventan zone before about 838; on the date see K. Levy, «The Italian Neophytes' Chants,» *JAMS,* 23 (1970), 221, n. 100.

24 B. Stäblein, *Monumenta monodica medii aevi,* 2 (Kassel, 1970), 565–6.

25 The Beneventan neumation (Reg. 334, 65v; Napoli VI.G.34, 4; Benevento VI.34 [*PM* 15], 157) is practically identical with the 10th to 12th century neumations of Saint Gall (*PM* 1, 136; *PM* 4, 401), Picardy (*PM* 16, 45), Aquitaine (Paris lat. 903, 135), Nonantola (Rome, Casanatense 1743, 166v), and Aemilia (*PM* 18, 169v). The 13th century Worcester reading (*PM* 12, 224) is again farthest from the archetype.

respects came already stylized from Italy.[26] Yet it is a long way from a single anti-phon of peripheral, processional usage to the central repertory of proper chants for the Mass and Office, and the fact remains that each class of liturgical chant, each modal category within a class, and indeed each particular chant, has to be weighed individually in this regard. There is one final point. We have been deal-ing with an Italian chant-reading that comes down through south-central Italian, Beneventan sources. At the same time we have noted the casual attitude of the Romans about preserving their own «Urban-Roman» musical repertory. Thus it may be that what the Beneventan transmission represents is the provincial sur-vival of a neighboring Roman tradition that the Urban scribes themselves did not bother to commit to writing.

*

The main points of the foregoing are: 1. Beneventan sources preserve a slightly variant melodic reading for Deprecamur te (Fig. 2), perhaps representing an ar-chaic Italian tradition that did not filter through the Carolingian tradition (Fig. 1); 2. in that case, the Carolingian melody is likely to have been received already stylized from Italy, with little added in the way of «northern» or «Fran-kish» retouching; 3. while the preserved Italian tradition is Beneventan, the ul-timate Italian source may have been Rome. In closing, I would reemphasize the tentative nature of these proposals. Yet I would also emphasize that we are un-likely ever to have direct access to melodic readings that are older than our oldest (9th century) neumed documents. That being so, it may only be an argument of the sort traced here that can ever tell us what the fabric of the 6th to 8th century «Gregorian»-Roman chants was actually like.

---

26 The positions are summarized by Hucke in *The New Grove Dictionary*, 7, 696–7 (art.: «Gregorian and Old Roman chant»).

CHAPTER 3

Toledo, Rome, and the Legacy of Gaul

Between the late sixth and mid-ninth centuries the lengthy process unfolded that brought substantial unity to the liturgical-musical practice of the Western Church. The Roman-Benedictine liturgy of Gregory the Great was taken to England in 596–7 by the Italian-born Augustine, prior of the Monastery of St Andrew on the Caelian hill. His purpose was to substitute Roman observance for entrenched Anglo-Saxon, Celtic and Gallican rites as well as pagan customs. Yet when Augustine questioned Gregory about the variety of Christian usages he found, the pope was unwilling to offend local sensibilities and impede the Anglo-Saxons' conversion. Augustine was told to leave in place whatever of the local rites seemed desirable.[1] During the seventh and early eighth centuries an accelerating missionary activity spread the Roman liturgy through France, Germany and northern Italy. Yet wherever it arrived it became similarly intermixed with local material, and it was not until the mid-eighth century that vigorous measures were taken to impose a purer Roman usage. The change came about not through ecclesiastical initiative but through the practical politics of a pious Frankish monarch. Pepin the Short (714–68) sought to increase unity throughout his domain by imposing the Roman rite. He asked Stephen III (752–7) for clerics to teach the musical rite, and Stephen's successor Paul I (757–67) sent Roman chant books, an 'antiphonale et responsale', presumably without notation.[2] A

---

[1] 'Sed mihi placet sive in Romana, sive in Galliarum, sive in qualibet ecclesia aliquid invenisti quod plus omnipotenti Deo possit placere, sollicite eligas et in Anglorum ecclesia'; *Monumenta germaniae historica* [*MGH*], *Epistolarum. Epistolae: Gregorii I Papae Registrum*, 1 ed. P. Ewald and L. M. Hartmann (Berlin, 1887–91), p. 334.

[2] Walafrid Strabo (*c.* 804–49), *De rebus ecclesiasticis*, xxv: 'Cantilenae vero perfectiorem scientiam quam pene tota Francia diligit, Stephanus papa, cum ad Pippinum, patrem

First published in *Early Music History,* 4 (1984), 49–99. Reprinted with the permission of Cambridge University Press.

generation later, Pepin's son Charlemagne could remind the Council at Aachen in March of 789 that it was his father who 'put away the Gallican rite for the sake of unity with the Holy See and pacific concord within the Church'.[3] Despite such assurances, it was not until the early ninth century under Charlemagne's successors that the changeover to an ostensibly Roman liturgical-musical practice was substantially complete. Charles the Bald (823–77) no longer knew the Gallican practices that were native to his Frankish homeland. To hear an approximation of them, he auditioned singers from Toledo, where an old Spanish rite persisted that was recognised as a relative of the Gallican.[4]

Thus in spite of all Carolingian efforts to Romanise, certain regional repertories lingered on. The Spanish rite was one of them; the Milanese rite was another. Both musical repertories are completely preserved, though the Spanish is known only in unheighted neumes. Relics of other repertories like the Beneventan and Ravennate persisted into the twelfth century.[5] Of all the early repertories, the Gallican, situated at the centre of the politically motivated reforms, was the one most thoroughly suppressed, and it is the one about which least is known. Only a small handful of certifiably Gallican Mass prayers are preserved; liturgists rely otherwise on mixed Gregorian-Gallican usages of the eighth to ninth centuries.[6]

Caroli Magni (in primis in Franciam) pro justitia Sancti Petri a Longobardis expetenda, venisset, per suos clericos, petente eodem Pippino, invexit, indeque usus ejus longe lateque convaluit', in J. P. Migne, *Patrologiae cursus completus . . . series latina*, 114 (Paris, 1871), col. 957. Paul I: 'Direximus itaque excellentissimae praecellentiae vestrae et libros quantos reperire potuimus. Id est antiphonale et responsale', in *MGH, Epistolae Merowingici et Karolini aevi*, 1, ed. W. Gundlach (Berlin, 1892), p. 529.

3   'gallicanum tulit ob unitatem apostolicae sedis et sanctae Dei ecclesiae pacificam concordiam'; *MGH, Legum Sectio III, Capitularia regum francorum*, 1, ed. A. Boretius (Berlin, 1883), p. 61.

4   'Nam et usque ad tempora abavi nostri Pippini Gallicanae et Hispaniae ecclesiae aliter quam Romana vel Mediolanensis ecclesia divina officia celebrabant, sicut vidimus et audivimus ab eis qui ex partibus Toletanae ecclesiae ad nos venientes secundum morem ipsius ecclesiae coram nobis sacra missarum solemnia celebrarunt . . . Sed nos sequendum ducimus Romanam ecclesiam in missarum celebratione'; G. D. Mansi, *Sacrorum conciliorum nova et amplissima collectio*, 18bis (Venice, 1773), col. 730.

5   On the regional Latin repertories, see K. G. Fellerer, ed., *Geschichte der katholischen Kirchenmusik*, 2 vols. (Kassel, 1972–6), I, pp. 191ff, and the articles on Ambrosian, Beneventan, Celtic, Gallican, Mozarabic and Ravenna rites in *The New Grove Dictionary of Music and Musicians*, ed. S. Sadie, 20 vols. (London, 1980). The following conventional abbreviations are here used for chant repertories and styles: BEN – Beneventan; GALL – Gallican; GREG – Gregorian-Roman (Carolingian-Roman); MED – Ambrosian (Milanese); MOZ – Mozarabic (Old Spanish, Visigothic); ROM – Old Roman (Urban Roman).

6   A. A. King, *Liturgies of the Past* (London, 1959), pp. 123–30 (simplified introduction to the Gallican Sacramentaries).

There are two significant Gallican sources for the Lectionary,[7] yet there are only approximate ideas about certain aspects of the Mass-Ordo.[8] As for the texts and music of the chants, practically nothing is preserved in an original Gallican context. The result is that GALL remains a provocative mystery. Formerly situated at the centre of Merovingian-Carolingian power, it may hold the answer for some of the more perplexing questions that confront music historians today: the pre-history of tropes and sequences; the origins of Gregorian-Roman musical styles; and the relationship of those styles to the musical styles found at Rome.

Studies in Gallican chant during the past half-century have identified a small corpus of ostensibly Gallican pieces, surviving as hangers-on in Gregorian and other traditions.[9] They are strays – a miscellany of processional antiphons, litanies, introits, preces, graduals, alleluias, offertories, etc., lingering on the margins of the later rites. In what follows, I will attempt to expand the Gallican dossier substantially in both quantity and quality. Using evidence that is already universally available, I will make three proposals. First, that for a distinctive class of Gregorian Offertory texts, amounting to some two to three dozen pieces circulating in early Gregorian traditions, there is a likelihood of their representing originally Gallican texts. Second, that for a certain number of those same Offertory texts, the preserved Gregorian music may descend from the lost music of the Gallican Offertories. And third, that in the melodic states of some of those Gregorian Offertories, as we have them in noted versions of the tenth to the twelfth centuries, there may be represented with some exactitude the melodic states of the Gallican Offertories as they were in the later seventh century.

The standard shape of a GREG Offertory is shown in Figure 2a: this is the Offertory *Erit vobis*, for Friday in Easter Week, as it appears in an

---

[7]   A. Dold, *Das älteste Liturgiebuch der lateinischen Kirche*, Texte und Arbeiten 26–8 (Beuron, 1936); P. Salmon, *Le lectionnaire de Luxeuil: édition et étude comparative* (Rome, 1944).

[8]   E. Griffe, 'Aux origines de la liturgie gallicane', *Bulletin de littérature ecclésiastique*, 52 (1951), pp. 17–43; K. Gamber, *Ordo Antiquus Gallicanus: Der gallikanische Messritus des 6. Jahrhunderts* (Regensburg, 1965).

[9]   Paléographie Musicale, ser. I, 13 (Tournai, 1925), pp. 30ff; A. Gastoué, *Le chant gallican* (Grenoble, 1939) [=*Revue du Chant Grégorien*, 41–2 (1937–8)]; B. Stäblein, 'Gallikanische Liturgie', *Die Musik in Geschichte und Gegenwart* [*MGG*], ed. F. Blume, 16 vols. (Kassel, 1949–79), IV, cols. 1299–325; M. Huglo, 'Gallican rite, music rite, music of the', *The New Grove*, VII, pp. 113–25.

eleventh-century neumation of Novalesa in the Piedmontese north-west of Italy.[10] In their high medieval shapes, the GREG Offertories are all on this ample scale and in this moderately florid style, punctuated by occasionally lengthy melismas. An opening section designated as the *Of[fertorium]* (it will be referred to hereafter as the refrain) is followed by one to four further *V[erses]* in roughly the same style. The refrain and verses are normally related in their musical mode, and at times also in melodic details. Large-scale organisation is supplied by the repetenda, or repetendum, the final passage of the refrain, to which each verse returns as a conclusion. In *Erit vobis* the repetendum begins with the words 'in progeniis vestris' and pro-ceeds to the end of the refrain; its cue is missing after the first verse (*Dixit Moyses*) but appears after the second (*In mente habete*). Some 110 such elaborate chants appear in the modern edition of the GREG Offertories by Karl Ott. They represent practically the whole of the central repertory, though perhaps only 80% of the medieval total.[11]

Ever since the beginnings of modern chant studies, certain excep-tional features of the GREG Offertories have drawn comment. Peter Wagner remarked on the unusually wide range and virtuoso thrust of some melodies; the use of internally structured melismas; the instances of text-illustration; and the repetitions of text-phrases.[12] Wagner's discussion was amplified by Ferretti, Sidler and Johner.[13] In 1958 Apel put forward the theory that the florid melodies to which the Offertory verses were sung represented ninth-century innova-tions, supplanting earlier methods of singing the verses antiphonally to syllabic tones.[14] Apel's conjectures were countered by Steiner in 1966,[15] and disposed of convincingly in a recent study by Dyer (1982), whose conclusion seems quite correct: '[the florid] verses and not the hypothetical [syllabic] "Offertory tones", existed long before the end of the ninth century'. Dyer goes on to say: 'Obviously we cannot claim that the form in which [the Offertory melodies]

[10] Oxford, Bodleian Library, MS Douce 222 (S.C. 21796) fol. 143ᵛ.
[11] K. Ott, *Offertoriale sive versus offertoriorum* (Paris, 1935).
[12] P. Wagner, *Einführung in die gregorianischen Melodien*, I (Fribourg, 3/1911), pp. 107–13; III, (1921), pp. 418–34.
[13] P. Ferretti, *Esthétique grégorienne*, I (Paris, 1938), pp. 191–203; H. Sidler, *Studien zu den alten Offertorien mit ihren Versen* (Fribourg, 1939); D. Johner, *Wort und Ton im Choral* (Leipzig, 1940), pp. 362–84.
[14] W. Apel, *Gregorian Chant* (Bloomington, Ind. 1958), pp. 512f.
[15] R. Steiner, 'Some Questions about the Gregorian Offertories and their Verses', *Journal of the American Musicological Society*, 19 (1966), pp. 162–81.

come down to us represents a specific antiquity beyond the date of the oldest manuscripts in which they are preserved'.[16] The caution is well taken. Nevertheless, I shall endeavour to show that the existence of florid music for the Offertory refrains and verses can be pushed much further back than the oldest written sources.

In 1970 Helmut Hucke published a valuable study of the GREG Offertory texts, classifying them according to their literary sources and proposing a typology based on the performance arrangement implied by the organisation of their texts.[17] Hucke took as the basis for his classification the content of Hesbert's *Sextuplex*, as representing an authoritative consensus of the earliest GREG recensions.[18] He identified most of the text sources for some 107 Offertories that appear in the eighth- to ninth-century *Sextuplex* traditions, and he distinguished eight different classes of text-usage among them. Six of those classes, accounting for some ninety-one of the pieces, are psalmic, their texts drawn, generally verbatim, from the Psalter. A seventh class contains two Offertories whose texts are again poetic, based on canticles. An eighth class contains fourteen Offertories that are non-psalmic. As Hucke puts it, they 'do not come from the Psalms, but are taken from other biblical books'. Such texts have in common, moreover, 'that they do not follow the Bible literally, but rather summarize it, transform it, or compose a new text from biblical words'. In setting this class apart, Hucke was following in the track of Peter Wagner, who recognised its special nature when he supplied text sources for the Offertory repertory found in St Gall, Stiftsbibliothek, MS 339,[19] and particularly that of the Beuron monk Petrus Pietschmann, who, with the apparatus of the *Vetus Latina* at his disposal in 1932, gave the non-psalmic texts a full-dress treatment, laboriously tracking thirteen of Hucke's fourteen Offertory texts as precisely as was possible within the Vulgate and Old-Latin biblical traditions.[20]

The first fourteen items in Table 1 represent the fourteen non-psalmic Offertories in Hucke's list. Their liturgical assignments are

---

[16] J. Dyer, 'The Offertory Chant of the Roman Liturgy and its Musical Form', *Studi Musicali*, 11 (1982), pp. 3–30, see p. 24.

[17] H. Hucke, 'Die Texte der Offertorien', *Speculum musicae artis: Festgabe für Heinrich Husmann*, ed. H. Becker and R. Gerlach (Munich, 1970), pp. 193–203.

[18] R.-J. Hesbert, *Antiphonale missarum sextuplex* (Brussels, 1935).

[19] Wagner, *Einführung*, I, pp. 323–43.

[20] P. Pietschmann, 'Die nicht dem Psalter entnommenen Messgesangsstücke auf ihre Textgestalt untersucht', *Jahrbuch für Liturgiewissenschaft*, 12 (1932), pp. 114–30.

Table 1 *Gregorian non-psalmic offertories in Hesbert's Sextuplex*

No.	Incipit	Sextuplex (no.)	Pietschmann (no.)	Ott (page)	Text 'source' (Hucke, etc.)	Liturgical assignment (calendar order)
1	Ave Maria	5, 7bis, 33	14	13	Luke 1	4th Sunday in Advent; Wednesday in Ember Week, Advent; Annunciation
2	Sicut in holocausto	26bis, 179	10	92	Daniel 3	4th Sunday after Epiphany; 7th Sunday after Pentecost
3	Angelus Domini	79, 81, 87	13	57	Matthew 28	Easter Vigil; Easter Monday; Easter Octave
4	In die solemnitatis	84	3	61	Exodus 13	Easter Thursday
5	Erit vobis	85	1	63	Exodus 12	Easter Friday
6	Precatus est Moyses	50, 184	2	97	Exodus 32	12th Sunday after Pentecost; Thursday after 2nd Sunday in Lent
7	Oravi Deum	189	11	107	Daniel 9	17th Sunday after Pentecost
8	Sanctificavit Moyses	193	4	114	Exodus 24	18th Sunday after Pentecost
9	Vir erat in terra	196	7	122	Job 1	21st Sunday after Pentecost
10	Recordare	197	—	125	Esther 14	22nd Sunday after Pentecost
11	Domine Deus in simplicitate	100	5	159	1 Chron. 29	Dedication (Pantheon: 13 May)
12	Oratio mea	135	8	164	Job 16	Vigil St Lawrence (9 Aug.)
13	Elegerunt apostoli	148bis	16	161	Acts 6	St Stephen's Rib (9 Sept.)
14	Stetit angelus	157	17	170	Rev. 8	St Michael (29 Sept.)
15	Audi Israel	0	—	—	non-bibl., plus Ps. 80	5th Sunday before Advent
16	Viri Galilei	101bis, 102, 103	15	172	Acts 1	Vigil of Ascens; Ascension; Sunday after Ascension
17	Factus est repente	106	—	—	Acts 2	Pentecost
18	Benedictus sit Deus	172bis	6	81	Tob. 12	Trinity

those of Hesbert's *Sextuplex*, and the indications of their text sources represent those of Wagner, Pietschmann and Hucke. On the basis of the liturgical assignments, Hucke concluded that these Offertories 'represent a more recent layer within the whole Offertory tradition'.[21] So far as it goes, his conclusion is unexceptionable. The pieces are generally assigned to feasts of minor rank or apparently post-Gregorian entry to the Roman calendar: Fourth Sunday in Advent; Fourth Sunday after Epiphany; Seventh Sunday of the Pentecost series; weekdays within the Octave of Easter; last Sundays of the Pentecost series; Dedication of the Pantheon; Vigil of St Lawrence.[22] In arriving at his conclusion, however, Hucke left out of consideration four other non-psalmic Offertories that appear among the *Sextuplex* traditions. They are the last four items in Table 1: nos. 15–18. For no. 15, *Audi*, and no. 18, *Benedictus sit*, the liturgical-historical conclusions are no different: *Audi* is assigned to the Fifth Sunday before Advent, in effect the last Sunday of the Pentecost series; *Benedictus sit* is for Trinity, a feast that takes hold in GREG books only during the ninth century. But for the two remaining Offertories there are more prominent liturgical assignments. Each one appears at a major old feast. *Viri Galilei* (no. 16) is assigned to Ascension Thursday as well as to its Vigil and Octave. *Factus est repente* (no. 17) is an alternative Offertory assigned to Pentecost. There is a good deal to be said about each of these pieces.[23] But at the face-value of the *Sextuplex* liturgical assignments, it would seem that any blanket conclusions about the historical background of this text-category need to be carefully considered, and that the non-psalmic Offertories as a class may represent something more than simply 'a more recent layer'.

Some years before Hucke's classification of the Offertory texts appeared, certain observations by Giacomo Baroffio were published that have a direct bearing on the question. In his Heidelberg dissertation of 1964, dealing primarily with the MED Offertories, Baroffio noted that the GREG Offertory *Sanctificavit Moyses* had a

---

[21] Hucke, 'Die Texte der Offertorien', p. 203.

[22] On the datings (often hypothetical): Hesbert, *Sextuplex*, pp. xxxvff; A Chavasse, 'Les plus anciens types du lectionnaire et de l'antiphonaire romains de la messe', *Revue Bénédictine*, 62 (1952), pp. 3–94; Apel, *Gregorian Chant*, pp. 56–74 (based chiefly on Hesbert and Chavasse); A. Chavasse, *Le sacramentaire gélasien* (Tournai, 1958), *passim*; J. Deshusses, *Le sacramentaire grégorien*, i (Fribourg, 1971), pp. 50ff.

[23] Hesbert, *Sextuplex*, pp. LXV-LXVII; also note 81, below.

relationship with the MOZ Sacrificium (the Mozarabic 'Offertory')
Sanctificavit Moyses that went beyond a thoroughgoing identity of the
texts to some apparent parallels in musical substance.[24] Baroffio
repeated this observation in 1967, and added two others, again
involving MOZ Sacrificia with apparently close musical relations to
Offertories in other rites. Of the Offertory *Oravi Deum*, he remarked
about the MOZ and GREG versions, that they agree in astonishing
fashion. And of the Offertory *Stetit angelus*, he remarked about the
MOZ and MED versions that there was repeatedly a very close
relationship traceable.[25] Unspectacularly presented, even tucked
into footnotes, Baroffio's observations have yet to draw the attention
they merit. My own involvement with such 'international relations'
among Offertory families goes back to the autumn of 1966 when, as
yet unaware of Baroffio's work, I made some of the same observations, and added the case of the Offertory *Erit vobis*, which has
apparently 'close' textual-and-melodic correspondences between
MOZ and GREG. I have continued to ponder these linkages, and so
indeed has Baroffio, for he has commented on them during the past
decade, in formulations that seem to me on just the right track. In
1980, for the entry 'Offertory' in *The New Grove Dictionary*: 'a
systematic examination of Mozarabic documents might reveal
greater Mozarabic-Gallican penetration into the Roman tradition
than is at present accepted'; and already in 1972: 'it is sometimes
possible to "reconstruct" an Offertory, at least its text and general
structure, representing an earlier form than that transmitted by any
single preserved tradition.'[26] Nevertheless, a central point in defining the historical position of these Offertories has yet to be made. It is
that our two kinds of evidence – the category of non-psalmic
Offertory texts distinguished by Pietschmann and Hucke, and the
international relationships of Offertory music identified by Baroffio

---

[24]   G. Baroffio, *Die Offertorien der ambrosianischen Kirche* (Cologne, 1964), pp. 29, 64.
[25]   'die Fassungen . . . in erstaunlicher Weise entsprechen . . . mehrfach eine sehr enge
melodische Verwandschaft . . . spürbar'; G. Baroffio, 'Die mailändische Überlieferung
des Offertoriums *Sanctificavit*', *Festschrift Bruno Stäblein*, ed. M. Ruhnke (Kassel, 1967), p. 1,
n. 6.
[26]   *The New Grove*, XIII, p. 515; 'é talora possibile "ricostruire" un offertorio, almeno per
quanto riguarda il testo e la struttura generale, risalendo ad una forma più antica di quella
tramandata da un'unica tradizione', in 'Osservazioni sui versetti degli offertori
ambrosiani', *Archivio Ambrosiano*, 22 (1972), p. 57; also in 'Le origini del canto liturgico
nella chiesa latina e la formazione dei repertori italici', *Renovatio* (1978), no. 1, p. 47: 'si
osservano indubbie e certo non casuali affinità tra la versione gregoriana e ispanica . . .
come nel caso dell'offertorio . . . *Oravi Deum*'.

– should in fact be connected: each GREG or MED Offertory that has an apparently 'close' musical relationship with a cognate Sacrificium in the MOZ repertory is based upon a non-psalmic text.

Clearly enough, it is MOZ that occupies a central position in this complex of materials. So far, I know of seven MOZ chants that have 'musical' or textual relationships with Offertories of the GREG or MED traditions. They are listed in Table 2. In nos. 1–4, the relationships are 'musical' as well as textual; in nos. 5–7, only texts are involved. Of the seven chants in Table 2, all have non-psalmic texts, and five of them (nos. 1–4, 7) have already appeared in Table 1 as non-psalmic Offertories in the GREG *Sextuplex*. In speaking of 'musical' relationships with MOZ, one must indulge in an obvious fiction since the MOZ repertory is preserved only in staffless neumes.[27] The reader can judge the nature of the relationships by examining Figures 1 to 3, which have comparative materials for the first three Offertories in Table 2: in Figures 1a and 1b, the GREG and MOZ chants for no. 1, *Oravi Deum*; in Figures 2a and 2b, those for no. 2, *Erit vobis*; in Figures 3a and 3b, for no. 3, *Sanctificavit Moyses*. The MOZ neumations are those of the north Spanish Antiphoner of León, which was copied in the later tenth or eleventh century.[28] To simplify the comparison, the GREG versions are also presented in neumes, those of eleventh-century Novalesa.[29]

A glance at the parallel Spanish and Italian neumations makes it clear that these are not identical melodies. Yet a careful comparison of corresponding elements of text shows that again and again there are correspondences of syllabic/melismatic densities, and even some implied correspondences of melodic directions. Putting this in perspective, the MOZ and GREG neumations suggest musical relationships that are closer in detail than comparable neumations would be between parallel GREG and MED or GREG and ROM chants, where we know that a substantial musical relationship actually exists.[30] In

[27]   D. M. Randel, *An Index to the Chant of the Mozarabic Rite* (Princeton, 1973): the indispensable inventory. A handful of MOZ chants preserved in heighted palimpsest Aquitanian neumes are transcribed in C. Rojo and G. Prado, *El canto mozárabe* (Madrid, 1929).

[28]   León, Archivo Capitular, codex 8; *Antifonario visigótico mozárabe de la catedral de León, edición facsimíl*, Monumenta Hispaniae Sacra, Serie litúrgica 5/II (Madrid, 1953), fols. 238ᵛ, 178, 305; edition of text by L. Brou and J. Vives, Monumenta Hispaniae Sacra, Serie litúrgica 5/I (Madrid, 1959); L. Brou, 'Le joyau des antiphonaires latins', *Archivos Leoneses*, 7 (1954), pp. 7–114.

[29]   Oxford, Bodleian Library, MS Douce 222, fols. 152ᵛ, 143, 153.

[30]   Paléographie Musicale, Ser. I, 2 (1892), pp. 6–9: Dom Mocquereau's pathbreaking comparison of GREG-ROM-MED traditions for the Gradual *A summo caelo* and Introit *Resurrexi*.

Table 2 *International Offertories: Moz texts with Greg/Med parallels*

No.	*Moz* text	*Moz* liturgical	Text source	*Greg* text	Table 1 (no.)	*Greg* liturgical	*Med* text	*Med* liturgical	'Close' musical relationship
1	Oravi Deum	Jerome	*Daniel*	Oravi Deum	7	Dominical	—	—	MOZ–GREG
2	Erit hic vobis	Easter Friday	*Exodus*	Erit vobis hic	5	Easter Friday	Erit vobis	Pentecost	MOZ–GREG
3	Sanctificavit Moyses	Dominical	*Exodus*	Sanctificavit	8	Dominical; Dedication	Oravit	Dedication	MOZ–GREG
4	Stetit angelus	Dominical	*Matthew*	Stetit	14	Michael	Stetit	John Evangelist	MOZ–MED
5	Isti sunt	Lent–V	*Leviticus*	—	—	—	Haec dicit	Lent–V	—
6	Curvati sunt	Ascension (Responsory)	—	cf. Proc. Ant.: Cum audisset	—	Palm Sunday	Curvati	Sunday after Ascension	—
7	Alleluia. Elegerunt apostoli	Stephen	*Acts*	Elegerunt	13	Stephen	—	—	—

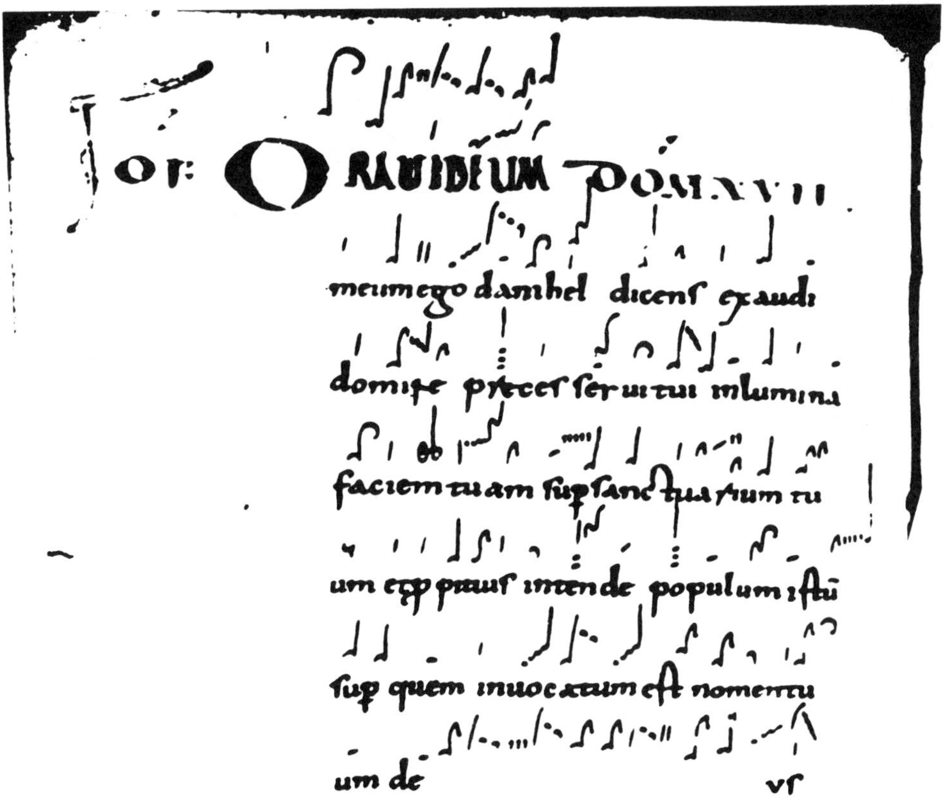

Figure 1a Offertory, *Oravi Deum*: refrain (Oxford, Bodleian Library, MS Douce 222, fol. 152ᵛ)

Figure 1b Sacrificium, *Oravi Deum*: refrain (León, Archivo Capitular, Codex 8, fol. 238ᵛ)

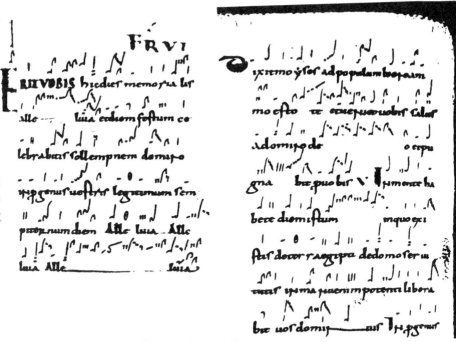

Figure 2a Offertory, *Erit vobis hic*: refrain and two verses (Oxford, Bodleian Library, MS Douce 222, fols, 143ᵛ–144ʳ)

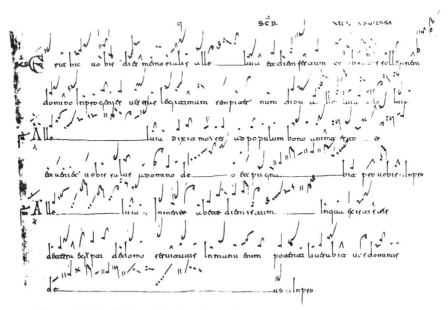

Figure 2b Sacrificium, *Erit hic vobis*: refrain and two verses (León, Archivo Capitular, Codex, 8, fol. 238ᵛ)

what follows, however, the emphasis will not be placed on such 'musical' parallels with MOZ. Instead, it will be on the substance of the verbal texts, and on their liturgical and historical background. In the long run, the several kinds of evidence – textual, liturgical, historical and 'musical' – will complement one another and tell us some things worth knowing about the early development of the Latin Offertories.

Scholars who until now have wrestled with the text sources for the non-psalmic Offertories have come to generally frustrating conclusions. They have recognised that such texts are often biblical centos – selections strung together out of original context; also that the chant wording often disagrees with the Vulgate. Ever since Pietschmann in 1932 examined the full spectrum of GREG non-psalmic Mass texts and was in many cases unable to pinpoint precise biblical sources, the view has prevailed that such texts represent lost, pre-Vulgate translations.[31] Baroffio put this recently for the Offertories: 'one or another of the archaic "old Latin" translations of parts of the Bible . . . may be earlier than the 5th century'.[32] That may be correct for certain of our Offertories. Yet a close examination of our seven 'international' texts in Table 2 shows something else as well: that a different understanding of the nature of the texts leads to a better comprehension of their origins.

Oravi Deum (Table 2, no. 1) serves in MOZ as the Sacrificium for St Jerome. In GREG, the same refrain is assigned by the *Sextuplex* to the Seventeenth Sunday after Pentecost, though in a tenth-century central Italian tradition it is for the Twenty-second Sunday.[33] The apparently close musical relationship between MOZ and GREG (which can be assessed in Figures 1a and 1b) was commented upon by Baroffio, who found that they agree in astonishing fashion.[34] Table 3a shows the text of the MOZ-GREG refrain along with the Vulgate source identified by Pietschmann and Hucke. In fact, the *Book of Daniel* supplies the basis for the chant text, but there are significant differences. The readings of the Vulgate correspond with those of our earliest Spanish and Gallican lectionaries (the Liber Commicus and

[31] Pietschmann, 'Die nicht dem Psalter entnommenen Messgesangsstücke'; P. Alfonzo, *I responsori biblici dell'ufficio romano* (Rome, 1936).
[32] 'Offertory', *The New Grove*, XIII, p. 515.
[33] Rome, Biblioteca Vallicelliana, MS B.8 (from Norcia), fol. 312ᵛ: in the archaic 'Roman Sections', an alternative at *Domin. Va post Sancti Angeli*.
[34] See note 25, above.

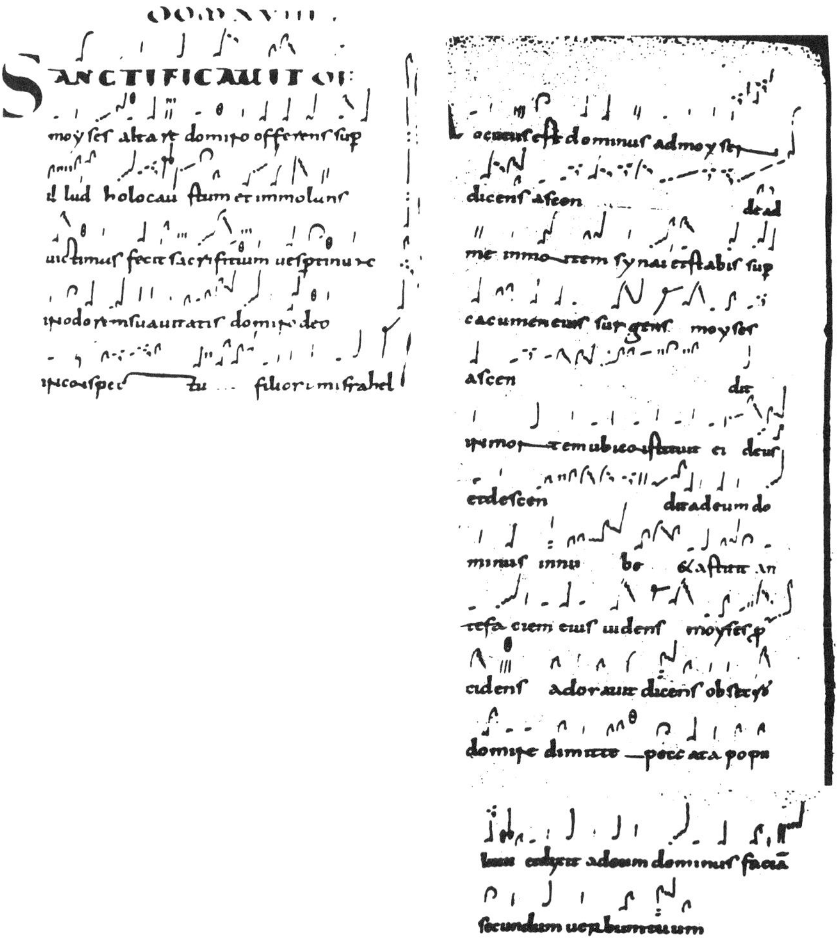

Figure 3a Offertory, *Sanctificavit*; refrain and two verses (Oxford, Bodleian Library, MS Douce 222, fols, 153ʳ–154ᵛ) (cont. on p. 64)

the Lectionary of Luxeuil, copied in the seventh to eighth century), so that we may be dealing with a pre-Vulgate translation.[35] Yet an inspection of the parallel biblical and chant texts in Table 3a suggests a different explanation. For one thing, the chant does not use all of the biblical material; there are ellipses and conflations:

[35]   Pietschmann, *op. cit.*, pp. 126 ff; *Liber Commicus, edición crítica* by J. Perez de Urbel and A. Gonzalez y Ruiz-Zorrilla, I (Madrid, 1950), p. 202; P. Salmon, *Le lectionnaire de Luxeuil*, p. 82.

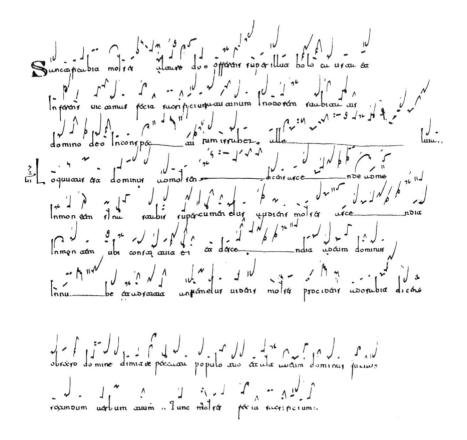

Figure 3b Sacrificium, *Sanctificavit*: refrain and two verses (León, Archivo
Capitular, Codex 8, fol. 305^r–305^v) (cont. on p. 64)

clause G ('Et propitius intende populum istum') compresses four
biblical clauses (18a–d) into one. And then the chant text alters the
Bible in ways that no simple translation would have done: in clause
B, the chant substitutes 'ego Daniel dicens for the biblical 'et
confessus sum et dixi' (4b); the point was to identify the speaker
within the chant text, something unnecessary in the fuller biblical
context. These two cases tell us that the compiler of the chant text
was less concerned with adhering to strict biblical order and ver-

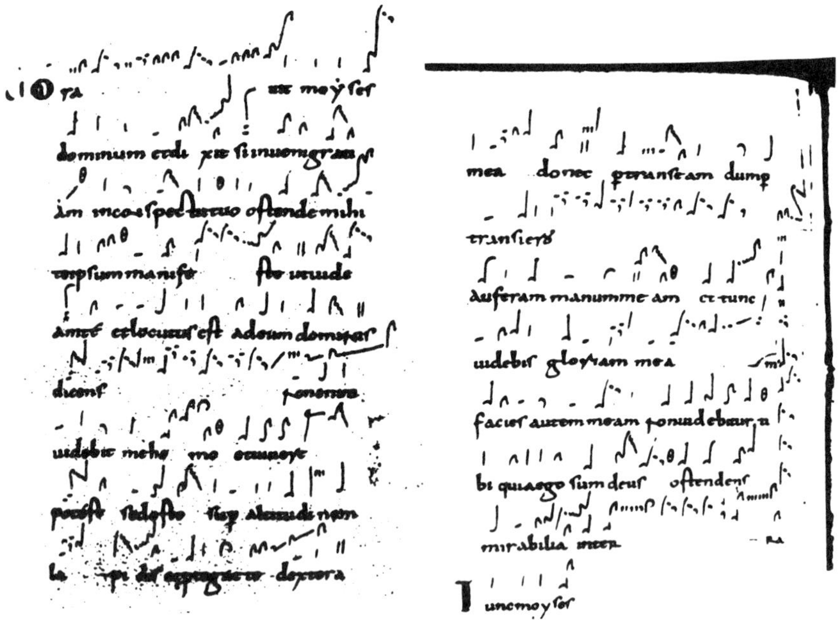

Figure 3a (cont.)

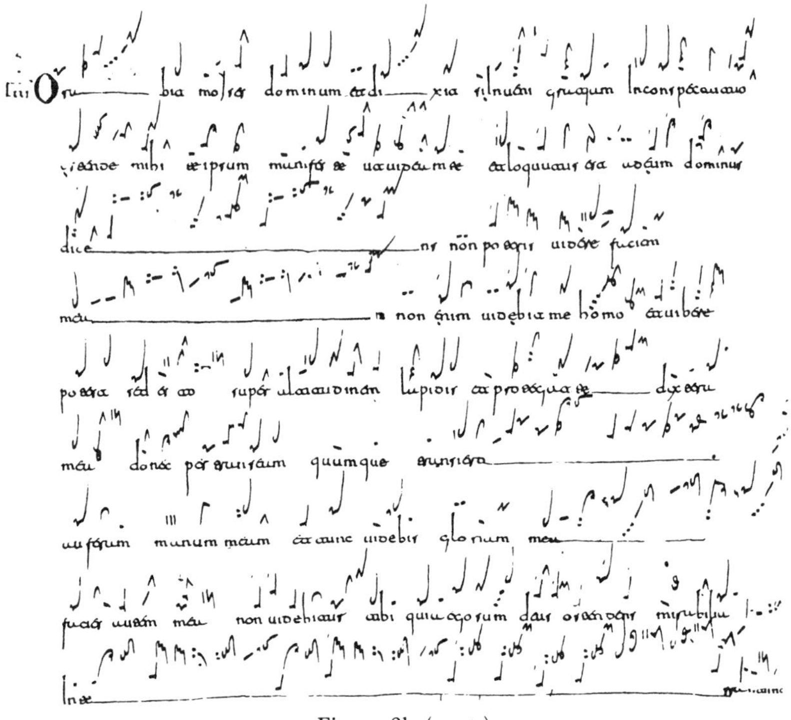

Figure 3b (cont.)

Table 3a *Offertory, 'Oravi Deum': refrain*

Vulgate clause (*Daniel* 9)	Vulgate text	Chant clause	Chant text ($Moz^1 \cong Greg^2$)
4a	Et oravi Dominum Deum meum	A	Oravi Deum meum
4b	et confessus sum et dixi	B	ego Daniel dicens
17a	Nunc ergo exaudi, Deus noster	C	Exaudi Domine
17b	orationem servi tui et preces eius	D	precem[3] servi tui
17c	et ostende faciem tuam	E	inlumina faciem tuum
17d	super sanctuarium tuum	F	super sanctuarium tuum
17e	quod desertum est, propter temetipsum		
18a	Inclina Deus meus, aurem tuam et audi,	G	REPETENDA: Et propitius intende populum istum
18b	aperi oculos tuos		
18c	et vide desolationem nostram		
18c	et civitatem		
18e	super quam invocatum est nomen tuum	H	super quem invocatum est nomen tuum Deus.
18f	neque enim in justificationibus nostris, etc.		

Notes:
[1] León, 238^v.
[2] Ott, *Offertoriale*, p. 107.
[3] Douce 222: *preces*.

biage than with shaping a text in language that was clear and concise. And that is enough to suggest the likely reason for the procedure – that the text of *Oravi* was destined from the outset to be a vehicle for musical setting, a chant 'libretto'. As further examples of this literary practice appear, the additional argument will unfold that a text of this economical sort was probably not tailored simply for syllabic music, where the numbers of syllables excised by the librettist would scarcely affect the musical design, but rather for a more elaborate style of chant – a style perhaps not dissimilar in melismatic density to what is before us in our MOZ and GREG Offertories.

For the moment, the refrain of *Oravi* has suggested that its text was designed as a 'libretto'. That suggestion is reinforced by the texts of its verses (Table 3b). In the MOZ verses, the author suppresses Vulgate verses 20b–d, with resultant tightening. Then clauses K, N and S draw on biblical clauses that are taken artfully out of sequence, which is unlikely in a pure Bible translation. The verses of *Oravi* also tell us something more, for the GREG verses reveal similar tailoring operations with respect to the Vulgate, but while they cover partly the same biblical materials, they treat them differently. MOZ clauses JKL correspond to GREG clauses κλμ; MOZ clauses O and QR correspond to GREG νξ. Thus where the identity of the MOZ-GREG refrains (Table 3a) suggests a straightforward transmission from either GREG to MOZ or MOZ to GREG, the differences between the verses, which are to some extent mutually exclusive, suggest that the verses circulated independently of the refrains, and that the whole historical situation was more complicated. In effect, we must be dealing with at least one other branch of our textual-musical Offertory tree, a lost branch that was closer than either MOZ or GREG to the trunk of that tree.

Oravi Deum has led us to suppose there was another tradition besides MOZ and GREG. Now *Erit vobis* (Table 2, no. 2), our second MOZ Offertory with 'international relations', expands the scope of the evidence by adding MED as a third regional tradition. *Erit vobis* is sung in both GREG and MOZ on Friday of Easter Week, and that close liturgical correspondence is paralleled in the close agreement between the GREG and MOZ texts and (apparently) music, extending now beyond the refrain to both of the verses (Figures 2a and 2b). *Erit vobis* in MED is the Offertory for Pentecost, a more prominent assignment than in MOZ-GREG.[36] Yet apart from some minor textual variants, the MED text agrees with MOZ and GREG in the wording of the refrain and first verse, but then has nothing to correspond with the MOZ-GREG second verse. *Erit vobis* also exemplifies the typical musical relationship between MED and GREG; it is not of the 'close' sort apparent between MOZ and GREG, but of the broad sort limited to modal and melodic generalities. The nature of the text relationships can be seen in Table 4, which shows the closest Vulgate parallels as well as two Old Latin versions adduced by Pietschmann.[37] Upon comparing the chant text with the possible text sources, Pietschmann observed 'einige Auslassungen'. Yet a close look shows that *Erit*, like *Oravi*, is not bound to the biblical-patristic wordings. *Erit* again compresses, substitutes and rearranges. Clauses I and J condense biblical verses 13–14a; clauses N and O represent a similar compression of verses 3e–h, bringing the text to a pithy close; the 'enim' added to clause N serves as a useful intensifier in the shortened text. The likeliest rationale for such operations is again that we have a 'libretto', tailored from the outset to be a text suitable for musical setting – and again, perhaps an originally florid setting. Pietschmann may have been correct in his conjecture that the underlying biblical version was not the Vulgate: 'der Text ist . . . sicher altlateinisch', and it may follow that the original music for which the libretto was formulated was composed at some time before the Vulgate became fixed in the communal memory.

Erit vobis has added MED as a third branch of our Offertory tree. Yet the MED branch is apparently no closer to the trunk of that tree than MOZ or GREG. Where *Oravi Deum*, with its MOZ and GREG verses, which are partly the same and partly different (Table 3b), told us that neither MOZ nor GREG could be the direct source for the other, now *Erit vobis* has MOZ and GREG in agreement while MED is partly independent. Still, the MED *Erit* is not the likely source for the MOZ-GREG *Erit*, since it lacks their second verse. Thus MED may turn out to be a textual-musical derivative of MOZ or GREG, yet is not likely to be the 'lost branch' we spoke of earlier. There is a further argument, on

36 *Antiphonale missarum . . . mediolanensis* (Rome, 1935), p. 256; M. Magistretti, *Manuale ambrosianum . . . saec XI* (Milan, 1904), p. 273.
37 Pietschmann, *op. cit.*, p. 114; St Ambrose, *Epist. XXIII*, 19 (Migne, *Patrologiae . . . latina*, 16, col. 1077); Pentateuch fragment, fifth to sixth century, Munich, Bayerische Staatsbibliothek, Clm 6225 (E. A. Lowe, *Codices latini antiquiores*, IX, 1959, no. 1250), ed. L. Ziegler, *Bruchstücke einer vorhieronymianischen Übersetzung des Pentateuch* (Munich, 1882).

Table 3b *Offertory, 'Oravi Deum': verses*

Vulgate clause (*Daniel* 9)	Vulgate text	*Moz* clause	*Moz* verse text (single verse)	Vulgate ref.	*Greg* clause	*Greg* verse text	Vulgate ref.
20a	Cumque adhuc loquerer et orarem	J	Quum effunderem precem meam in orationem	20a	ϰ	VERSE 1: Adhuc me loquentem	20a/21a
20b	et confiterer peccata mea				λ	et orantem et narrantem peccata mea	20b
20c	et peccata populi mei Israel				μ	et delicta populi mei Israel	20c
20d	et prosternerem preces meas						
20e	in conspectu Dei mei	K	in conspectu Domini Dei mei	20e			
		L	pro peccato populi Israhel	20e			
20f	pro monte sancto Dei mei	M	et pro loco sancto eius	20f			
		N	in tempore sacrificii	21e			
21a	Adhuc me loquente in oratione						
21b	ecce vir Gabriel	O	Gabriel	21b	ν	VERSE 2: Audivi vocem dicentem mihi	21b/22a
21c	quem videram in visione a principio						
21d	cito volans tetigit me	P	cito pervolans tetigit me	21d			
21e	in tempore sacrificii vespertini (cf. N)						

Table 3b (*cont.*)

Vulgate clause (*Daniel* 9)	Vulgate text	*Moz* clause	*Moz* verse text (single verse)	Vulgate ref.	*Greg* clause	*Greg* verse text	Vulgate ref.
22a	Et docuit me et locutus est mihi dixitque:	Q	et locutus est michi dicens	22a			
22b	Daniel, nunc egressus sum ut docerem te	R	Daniel (cf. U)	22b	ξ	Daniel, intellege verba quae loquor tibi	22b/c
22c	et intelligeres				→	→	→
23a	Ab exordio precum tuarum egressus est sermo	S	vir desideriorum	23c			
		T	ab initio obsecrationis tuae	23a			
23b	ego autem veni ut indicarem tibi	U	ego egressus sum et veni ut dicam	22b/23b	o	quia ego missus sum ad te	23b
23c	quia vir desideriorum es (cf. S)						
23d	tu ergo animadverte sermonem						
23e	et intellige visionem						
Daniel 10: 13c	Et ecce Michael unus de principibus primis venit in adiutorium meum				π	nam et Michael venit in adiutorium meum	Daniel 10: 13c/21c

Table 4 Offertory, *'Erit vobis'*

Vulgate clause		Vulgate text	Old-Latin texts	Greg clause	Greg texts[2]	Moz[3]–Med[4] variants
Exodus 12:	14a	Habebitis autem	Et erit dies hic vobis	A	REFRAIN: Erit vobis hic	MOZ–MED: hic vobis
	14b	hunc diem in monumentum	memorabilis et solemnis	B	dies memorialis. Alleluia.	
	14c	et celebrabitis eam sollemnem Domino	et diem festum agetis cum Domino	C	Et diem festum celebrabitis solemnem Domino	
	14d	in generationibus vestris	in progenies vestras	D	REPETENDA: In progenies vestris	MOZ–MED: vestras
	14e	cultu sempiterno	legitimum sempiternum diem[1]	E	legitimum sempiternum diem	
				F	Alleluia (3 times)	MOZ: (2 times)
Exodus 14:	13a	Et ait Moyses ad populum		G	VERSE 1: Dixit Moyses ad populum	MOZ–MED: Alleluia. Dixit
	13b	nolite timere		H	bono animo estote	
	13c	state et videte magnalia Domini		I	et veniet vobis salus a Domino Deo	MED: adveniet
	13d	quae facturus est hodie				
	13e	Aegyptios enim quos nunc videtis				
	13f	nequaquam ultra videbitis in sempiternum				
	14a	Dominus pugnabit pro vobis		J	et pugnabit pro vobis	
	14b	et vos tacebitis				

Table 4 (cont.)

Vulgate clause	Vulgate text	Old-Latin texts	Greg clause	Greg texts[2]	Moz[3]–Med[4] variants
Exodus 13: 3a	Et ait Moyses ad populum:	Et dixit Moyses ad populum:			
3b	Mementote diei huius	In mente habete diem hunc	K	VERSE 2: In mente habete diem istum	MED: no VERSE 2; MOZ: Alleluia. In mente
3c	in qua egressi estis de terra Aegypto	in quo existis de terra Aegypti	L	in quo existis de terra Aegypti	MOZ: qua
3d	et de domo servitutis	de domo servitutis	M	de domo servitutis	
3e	quoniam in manu forti	in manu potenti	N	in manu enim potenti	
3f	eduxit vos Dominus	eduxit nos Dominus	O	liberabit vos Dominus	MOZ: Dominus Deus
3g	de loco isto	hinc			
3h	ut non comedatis fermentum panem	et non edetur fermentum[5]			

Notes:
[1] Ambrose, *Epistolae XXIII*, 19 (Migne, *Patrologiae . . . latina*, 16, col. 1077).
[2] Douce 222, fol. 143.
[3] León, fol. 178.
[4] *Antiphonale missarum . . . mediolanensis*, p. 256.
[5] See note 37.

liturgical grounds, that makes MED seem an offshoot of a lost branch. We have noted that *Erit vobis* in MED is sung at Pentecost while in MOZ and GREG it is at Easter Friday. The text itself suggests a feast of major importance: 'This day shall be unto you a memorial . . . you shall keep it a feast to the Lord throughout your generations; you shall keep it a feast by an ordinance for ever'. At its own word, it sounds more like a Pentecost (MED) or perhaps Easter chant than it does one for Easter Friday (MOZ and GREG). Now, it is difficult to suppose that MED selected as its Pentecost Offertory a chant that served a lesser function elsewhere. It is more likely that the MED assignment reflects a Pentecost or perhaps Easter assignment in a lost branch of our Offertory tree. GREG and MOZ may have known that same Pentecost or Easter Offertory as venerable material, deprived of its earlier function by historical or liturgical change, yet worthy of preservation. Already committed to their own provisions for Pentecost or Easter, they (separately or perhaps jointly) found a place for it on the Easter weekday. In any event, the liturgical assignments for *Erit vobis* lead us to suppose that it was an Offertory for Pentecost and/or Easter in the lost branch of the tradition. And from the constellation of geographical and liturgical indications – now involving Spain, the Carolingians and Milan – there is some reason to place that lost branch in Gaul.

The third MOZ Offertory with a GREG or MED parallel is *Sanctificavit Moyses* (Table 2, no. 3). Its situation is much like that of *Erit vobis*: the three branches MOZ, GREG and MED are represented, and the neumes again suggest a close linkage between the GREG (Figure 3a) and MOZ (Figure 3b) melodies. *Sanctificavit* in MOZ serves as a dominical Offertory, with a prominent assignment to the Fourth Sunday in Lent.[38] The GREG *Sextuplex* gives it a lesser place, the Eighteenth Sunday after Pentecost, though the GREG Cantatorium of St Gall (eleventh century) has it for the Roman feast of the Dedication,[39] and the Dedication is also its assignment in MED.[40] The text is a dramatisation of the momentous dialogue between Moses and the Lord on Mount Sinai, comprising in its MOZ and GREG versions a refrain with repetenda and two verses. MOZ and GREG are nearly identical:

[38]   Randel, *An Index*, p. 468.
[39]   Paléographie Musicale, ser. II, 2 (1924), pp. 95–115.
[40]   *Antiphonale missarum . . . mediolanensis*, p. 333; Magistretti, *Manuale ambrosianum*, p. 365.

OFFERTORY, SANCTIFICAVIT (MOZ)

REFRAIN:	Sanctificabit Moyses altare Domino offerens super illut holo-causta, et inferens[a] victimas
REPET.:	Fecit sacrificium matutinum[b] in odorem suabitatis Domino Deo in conspectu filiorum Israhel. Alleluia.[c]
1ST VERSE:	Loquutus est Dominus ad Moysen dicens:

ascende ad me in montem Syna; stabis super cacumen eius;

Audiens,[d] Moyses ascendit in montem ubi constituit ei Deus

Et descendit ad eum Dominus in nube et adstitit ante faciem eius.

Videns, Moyses procidens adorabit dicens:

Obsecro Domine, dimitte peccata populo tuo

Et ayt[e] ad eum Dominus:

Faciam secundum verbum tuum.

REPET.:	Tunc Moyses fecit sacrificium . . .
2ND VERSE:[f]	Orabit Moyses Dominum et dixit:

Si inveni gratiam in conspectu tuo

ostende mihi teipsum manifeste ut videam te.

Et locutus est ad eum Dominus dicens:

Non poteris videre faciam meam.[g]

Non enim videbit me homo et vibere potest.

Sed esto super altitudinem lapidis,

Et protegat te dextera mea donec pertranseam.

Quumque transiero[h] auferam manum mean

Et tunc videbis gloriam mea[m]

Quia ego sum Deus ostendens mirabilia in terra.

REPET.:	Tunc Moyses . . .[i]

GREG and MED: [a]GREG: *immolans*. [b]GREG: *vespertinum* (cf. MED in note i, below). [c]GREG omits *Alleluia*. [d]GREG: *surgens*. [e]GREG: *dixit*. [f]MED: REFRAIN begins [g]*Non poteris . . . meam*, in MOZ and MED, lacking in GREG. [h]GREG-MED: *Dum pertransiero*; MED: VERSE begins. [i]MED REPET: *Tunc Moyses fecit sacrificium matutinum . . .*

The MED Offertory consists of just the second verse and the repetenda. Yet insofar as it uses the same text, the MED version shows a broad relationship of musical substance with GREG. Various biblical verses have been proposed as sources for this text, the most precise identifications being those of Baroffio.[41] But Pietschmann, who devoted four pages to an analysis of the literary sources, recognised that the biblical parallels were quite far removed: 'dieses Offertorium mit seinen Versikeln ist eine freie Komposition von

[41] 'Die mailändische Überlieferung', p. 2: *Ex.* 33: 12–13, 20–3; *Ex.* 29: 41–2.

Exodus-stellen'.[42] In fact, the text bears all the marks of a tightly crafted musical libretto, with the three preserved versions going back perhaps to some further source. MED can be derived from MOZ or even from GREG, though with its truncation and rearrangement of their ampler versions its transmission may be independent.

The fourth MOZ Offertory in Table 2 is *Stetit angelus*. Again the three branches MOZ, GREG and MED are represented, but now the spectrum of relationships is much different. The close linkage of text and (putatively) of music is here between MOZ and MED, and GREG is in a corner, only partly related in text, showing no hint of musical relationship with MOZ, showing nothing even of the usual broad musical relationship with MED. *Stetit angelus* in MOZ is the Sacrificium for the Fourth Sunday after the Easter Octave; in GREG, it is the Offertory for the Archangel Michael; in MED, it is for St John the Evangelist.[43] The fullest text is that of MOZ, consisting of a refrain and two verses, based on memorable passages from *Revelations* 8 and 5. In its Old Spanish musical dress this spacious creation must have taken over ten minutes to perform.

OFFERTORY, STETIT ANGELUS (MOZ)[a]

REFRAIN: Stetit angelus super aram Dei, habens turabulum aureum
et date sunt ei supplicationes multe ut darent de orationibus
   sanctorum
ad altare coram domino quod est ante tronum
et ascendit fumus supplicationum de manu angeli
REPET.: In conspectu Dei. Alleluia, Alleluia, Alleluia.
1ST VERSE: Vidi librum in dextera Dei sedentis supra tronum
scriptum intus et retro signatum signis septem
et audivi angelum fortem praedicantem vocem magnam
Quis dignus est accipere librum aut videre signa eius?
Nec quisquam poterat neque in caelo, neque in terra, neque
   sub terra
   aperire librum aut prospicere illum
Et ego flebam multum quod nemo dignus inventus esset
   qui aperiret librum aut videre illum,
Et dixit mici unus ex senioribus:
Ne fleberis, Ecce vicit Leo de Tribu Iuda, radix David,
   aperire librum et septem signa eius
REPET.: In conspectu . . .

[42] Pietschmann, *op. cit.*, p. 119.
[43] MOZ: Randel, *An Index*, p. 469; León Antiphoner, fol. 194. GREG: Hesbert, *Sextuplex*, nos. 157, 188*bis*. MED: *Antiphonale missarum . . . mediolanensis*, p. 420; Magistretti, *Manuale ambrosianum*, p. 71.

2ND VERSE: Vidi in medio throni et in medio quattuor animalium et
      seniorum
      Agnum stantem quasi occisum, habentem cornua septem et
        oculos septem
      qui sunt septem spiritus Dei missi per orbem terrarum
      Et venit et accepit librum de dextera, sedentis in trono,
        et quum accepisset librum, quattuor animalie et seniores
        prostraverunt
        se ante agnum
        habentes singuli citharas aureas et fialas plenas odoramen-
        tis supplicationum
      Et cantabant canticum novum dicentes:
      Dignus es accipere librum et solvere signa eius
      Quoniam occisus es et redemisti nos Domine sanguine tuo.
REPET.:   In conspectu . . .

ªLeón, fol. 194

MED transmits the text of the MOZ refrain and first verse with slight variants, but has nothing of the second verse. GREG has only parts of the refrain in common with MOZ and MED, then for its verses turns to Psalm 137, which is the source of the entire Michael Offertory at Rome (*In conspectu angelorum*). The texts of the MOZ, MED and GREG refrains are compared in Table 5. There can be no doubt that a close reading of *Revelations* 8: 3–4 lies behind all three forms of the refrain, but the specific wording does not seem to depend on the Vulgate; nor is there dependence on the Vulgate in the wording of the two verses, which go back ultimately to *Revelations* 5. An old translation surely lies behind this chant text, and if it could be found we might come close to the origins of our Offertories. But Pietschmann, with the *Vetus Latina* apparatus at hand, remained puzzled by the text,[44] and it would seem that no literary trace of such an Apocalypse translation survives.

Whatever the underlying biblical text, it is clear that with *Stetit angelus*, as with our other chants, a libretto-style tailoring has taken place. None of the following seems to represent a simple New Testament version: Vulgate 3ab, 'Et alius angelus venit et stetit', is reduced to refrain clause A, 'Stetit angelus'; Vulgate 4b, 'de oration-ibus sanctorum', ought to come between refrain clauses H and I, but

Table 5 Offertory, 'Stetit angelus': refrain

Vulgate clause (Revelations 8)	Vulgate text	Moz¹–Med² text	Greg³ text
3a	Et alius angelus venit	A Stetit angelus	a Stetit angelus
3b	et stetit ante altare	B super aram Dei	b juxta aram templi
3c	habens turibulum aureum	C habens turabulum⁴ auream	c habens thuribulum aureum
			c′ in manu sua
3d	et data sunt illi incensa multa	D et date sunt ei supplicationes multe	d et data sunt ei incensa multa
3e	ut daret de orationibus sanctorum omnium	E ut darent⁵ de orationibus sanctorum	
3f	super altare aureum	F (MOZ): ad altare coram Domino⁶	
3g	quod est ante thronum Dei	G quod est ante tronum	
4a	Et ascendit fumus incensorum	H et ascendit fumus supplicationum	e REPETENDA: et ascendit fumus aromatum
4b	de orationibus sanctorum	I de manu angeli	
4c	de manu Angeli	J REPETENDA: in conspectu Dei	f in conspectu Dei
4d	coram Deo	K Alleluia (3 times)	g Alleluia.

Notes:
1 León, fol. 194.
2 *Antiphonale missarum . . . mediolanensis*, p. 420.
3 Ott, *Offertoriale*, p. 170.
4 MED: thuribulum.
5 MED: daret.
6 MED: ad altare Dei.

is omitted, evidently as inessential; in GREG, clause c′, 'in manu sua', provides a useful clarification but has no Vulgate, MOZ or MED analogue. *Stetit angelus* thus confirms the view that none of our three preserved traditions was the direct source for any of the others. The possibility of MOZ or GREG as source was already foreclosed by the irreconcilable differences between the verses of *Oravi Deum*. And though the close relationship between MOZ and MED for *Stetit angelus* suggests a direct dependency, that is poorly supported by our other cases, where MOZ and GREG are 'musically' related while MED is in a corner. In short, there is every reason to continue looking beyond MOZ, GREG and MED.

Stetit angelus is the last of the four MOZ Offertories in Table 2 (nos. 1–4) having 'musical' as well as text relationships with Offertories of other rites. There are three further MOZ chants with 'international' Offertory relationships in Table 2, but these involve correspondences only of text, not of music; and in each case only two of our liturgical branches are represented: no. 5, *Isti/Haec* (MOZ-MED); no. 6, *Curvati* (MOZ-MED); and no. 7, *Elegerunt* (MOZ-GREG).

Between the MOZ Sacrificium *Isti sunt dies* and the MED Offertory *Haec dicit Dominus* (Table 2, no. 5) there are relationships of text and liturgical function. Both Offertories are assigned to the Fifth Sunday in Lent – the Sunday before Palm Sunday.[45] The texts are based on *Leviticus*, but the literary formulations are not bound to specific biblical phraseology or order, and they evidently represent another case of a libretto made up for the purpose of chant. Both the MOZ and MED versions consist of a refrain and two verses, yet their relationship is far from straightforward (Table 6). MOZ contains all the text clauses of MED plus three others: A, G and P. And the order differs in ways indicating that MOZ cannot be derived from MED (which, as usual, is less complete), while MED cannot be directly derived from the MOZ formulation. They appear to represent different derivations from a common source.

Curvati sunt celi (Table 2, no. 6) stands alone among our seven MOZ texts in being not a Sacrificium but a Responsory refrain for MOZ Ascension Matins. In MED, the same distinctive literary formulation, which has no traceable biblical or patristic sources, serves as the

[45] MOZ: Randel, *An Index*, p. 463; León antiphoner, fol. 144. MED: *Antiphonale missarum . . . mediolanensis*, p. 143; Magistretti, *Manuale ambrosianum*, p. 161; Paléographie Musicale, ser. I, 5–6, p. 208.

Table 6 *Offertory*, 'Isti sunt' (*Moz*) – 'Haec dicit' (*Med*)

Clause	Moz text[1]	Clause	Med text[2]	Clause	Vulgate text (*Leviticus* 23)
A	REFRAIN: Isti sunt dies quos devetis custodire temporibus suis			4a	Hae sunt ergo feriae Domini sanctae
				4b	quos celebrare devetis temporibus suis
B	quartadecima die ad vesperum pascha Domini est			5a	quartadecima die mensis
				5b	ad vesperum phase Domini est
C	et in quintadecima			6a	et quintadecima die mensis huius
D	REPETENDA no. 1: Sollemnitatem celebrabitis altissimo Deo vestro			6b	sollemnitas azymorum Domini est
E	VERSE 1: Loquutus est Moyses filiis Israhel dicens:			34a	Loquere filiis Israel
F	In die octabo venturo sumite vobis ramos palmarum			39d	die primo et die octavo erit sabbatum,
				39e	id est requiem
				40a	sumetisque vobis die primo
				40b	fructus arboris pulcherrimae
				40c	spatulasque palmarum
G	Et exultate in conspectu Domini			40f	et letabimini coram Domino Deo vestro
H	et secundum legem quam vobis precepit				
(D)	REPETENDA no. 1: Sollemnitatem etc.				
J	VERSE 2: Haec dicit Dominus	J	REFRAIN: Haec dicit Dominus	23	Locutusque est Dominus ad Moysen dicens
K	erit vobis sabbatum memorabile	K	erit vobis sabbatum venerabile	24c	erit vobis sabbatum memoriale
L	et vocabitur sanctum	L	et vocabitur sanctum	24e	et vocabitur sanctum
M	et offeretis ad vesperum olocaustomata	M	et offeretis ad vesperum holocaustomata vestra	25b	et offeretis holocaustum Domino

Table 6 (*cont.*)

Clause	Moz text[1]	Clause	Med text[2]	Clause	Vulgate text (*Leviticus* 23)
N	quia in die illa	N	REPETENDA no. 2: Quia in die illa	28b	in tempore diei huius
O	propitietur vobis salvator vester	O	propitiabitur vobis salvator noster	28c	quia dies propitiationis est
P	et in omnibus generationibus			28d	ut propitietur vobis Domine Deus vester
(D)	REPETENDA no. 1: Sollemnitatem etc.	E	VERSE 1: Locutus est Moyses filiis Israel dicens:		
		B	Quarto decimo die ad vesperum pascha Domini est		
		C	et in quintodecimo		
		D	REPETENDA no. 1: Solemnitatem celebrabitis altissimo Deo		
		(N/O)	REPETENDA no. 2: Quia in die etc.		
		F	VERSE 2: In die octavo venturo sumite vobis ramos palmarum		
		H	et secundum legem quam precepi vobis		
		(D)	REPETENDA no. 1: Solemnitatem etc.		
		(N/O)	REPETENDA no. 2: Quia in die etc.		

Notes:
[1] León, fol. 144.
[2] *Antiphonale missarum . . . mediolanensis*, p. 143.

Offertory for the Sunday after Ascension and the Vigil of Pentecost.[46] Huglo pointed to this MED-MOZ relationship in 1956, asking, 'esistette un intermediaro gallicano?'[47] He returned to it in 1972, observing that the climactic sixth line, 'Quantus est iste, cui Throni et Dominationes occurrent!' appears within an otherwise unrelated context, that of the GREG processional antiphon for Palm Sunday, *Cum audisset populus*, for which there are indications of Gallican origin.[48] There is no apparent relationship between the MED, MOZ and 'GALL' music for this line.

OFFERTORY, CURVATI SUNT (MED)

(1) Curvati sunt celi
(2) dum calcaret capita nubium creator astrorum
(3) et dum ascenderet caelos Dominator omnium
(4) terrore[a] concussus est numerus Angelorum,
(5) laudantium[b] et dicentium:
(6) Quantus sit[c] iste cui Throni et Dominationes occurrent![d]
(7) Hallelujah, hallelujah.[e]

MOZ RESPONSORY: [a]*tremore.* [b]*clamantium.* [c]*est.* [d]*occurrunt.* [e]MOZ adds VERSE (*Psalm* 23: 10) and REPET.: *Cui Throni, etc.*

The last of the seven 'international' chants in Table 2 is the Offertory *Elegerunt apostoli*, for St Stephen Protomartyr. This again links the text-usages of MOZ and GREG.[49] *Elegerunt* circulates widely in GREG traditions of France, Germany and Italy, and for some time it has been considered a prime example of a 'Gallican' chant surviving within Gregorian traditions.[50] Among the arguments for its GALL origin are the melodic expansions on the second syllable (*-le*) of its Alleluias (where normal GREG-ROM usage places such expansions on the final *-a*); the use of the pes stratus in its notation (a podatus with an ornamental oriscus appended to the second pitch), a neume-form apparently limited to chants originating north of the Alps;[51] and its transmission as the Stephen Offertory in West Frankish regions,

---

[46] MOZ: Randel, *An Index*, p. 249; León Antiphoner, fol. 199[v]. MED: *Antiphonale missarum . . . mediolanensis*, p. 246; Magistretti, *Manuale ambrosianum*, pp. 244, 271.
[47] M. Huglo and others, *Fonti e paleografia del canto ambrosiano* (Milan, 1956), p. 125.
[48] Huglo, 'Altgallikanische Liturgie', p. 226; Baroffio, *Die Offertorien*, p. 23.
[49] MOZ: Randel, *An Index*, pp. 309, 458; León Antiphoner, fol. 74[v]. GREG Ott, *Offertoriale*, pp. 161–3.
[50] Paléographie Musicale, ser. I, 15 (1937), p. 165.
[51] Huglo, 'Altgallikanische Liturgie', p. 228; E. Cardine, 'Sémiologie grégorienne', *Études Grégoriennes*, 11 (1970), p. 131.

instead of the Offertory *In virtute tua*, which is more at home in Italianate GREG traditions. A Gallican origin for *Elegerunt* is indicated by the *Sextuplex*, which has it only in the Senlis manuscript (later ninth century, Île-de-France) at the local feast of St Stephen's Rib on 9 September.[52] In MOZ traditions, *Elegerunt* is the Sacrificium for the main Stephen Mass at León, and at San Millán de la Cogolla it appears with the same music as the Sono of the Stephen Office.[53] Apart from minor variants, the text of the GREG refrain *Elegerunt* and its verse *Surrexerunt* are identical with the MOZ refrain and single verse.[54] The texts are a patchwork account of St Stephen's life and martyrdom, drawn from *Acts* 6 and 7. From every indication, this is another 'libretto' meant for musical setting. And MOZ and GREG are closely related in their use of the same distinctive literary formulations.

OFFERTORY, ELEGERUNT APOSTOLI (MOZ)

REFRAIN: Alleluia.[a] Elegerunt apostoli Stephanum levitam
        plenum fide et Spiritu Sancto
        quem lapidaberunt Iudei
REPET.: Orantem et dicentem:
        Domine Ihesu, accipe spiritum meum. Alleluia.[b]

VERSE: Surrexerunt autem quidam ex Iudaeis
        disputantes cum Stephano
        et non poterant resistere Spiritui Sancto
        qui loquebantur:
        Viderant[c] faciem eius tanquam faciem Angeli
        et occurrentes[d] cum[d] lapidibus caedabant eum.[e]
REPET.: Orantem . . .

GREG OFFERTORY: [a]omits. [b]REPET. begins with *Domine Ihesu*. [c]*Viderunt*; also *et videntes*. [d]omits. [e]adds *Alleluia*.

The list of seven MOZ 'international' chants in Table 2 is now complete. In case after case, we have seen biblical texts condensed, interpolated, transposed, paraphrased, with the apparent aim of producing texts suitable for musical setting, perhaps even for florid setting. In four cases, the MOZ neumes suggest correspondences with either the GREG or MED music. Now it is time to consider the

52   Hesbert, *Sextuplex*, no. 148 bis; p. CVI.
53   Madrid, Real Academia de la Historia, MS *Aemil.* 30, fol. 129.
54   Ott, *Offertoriale*, pp. 161f; Ott published two other GREG verses not found in MOZ, *Videbant faciem* and *Positis autem genibus*.

background of this situation. I stated at the outset that a 'Gallican' theory of origin seemed best to fit the facts, but before addressing this directly, let me review some of the other possibilities.

Little has been said so far about Rome. Yet with a usage as widespread and apparently archaic as this one, it is perhaps natural to think first of Rome. Our non-psalmic Offertories, based on texts that in some cases go back to pre-Vulgate translations, may be relics of an ancient Offertory type that once flourished at Rome but was displaced by the psalmic Offertories that have prevailed there since at least the later eighth century. The supplanted Roman usage would survive more tranquilly in Spain and Lombardy. It may be recalled in this connection that the early Spanish liturgy is itself supposedly Roman in origin, and that it remained Roman or Roman-African until the invasions of the Iberian peninsula during the fifth century.[55] Nevertheless there are obstacles to the theory of Roman origin. One is that the non-psalmic Offertories are so poorly represented in the Roman musical rite. Of the nearly one hundred Offertories in ROM, a bare dozen are non-psalmic, and just as in GREG they are assigned to late and minor feasts. Moreover, the ROM version is sometimes less complete than the corresponding GREG version (as in *Oravi Deum*, where the verses are lacking), and there is no case where ROM transmits a substantially fuller text than GREG.[56] In matters of musical substance as well, ROM goes its own way. There are no close musical relationships with MOZ or MED of the sort that appear between MOZ and GREG (for *Oravi*, *Erit* and *Sanctificavit*) or between MOZ and MED (for *Stetit*). In short, there is every indication that the sphere of Roman influence was at some remove from the central network of non-psalmic Offertories.

The case is slightly better for GREG as an ostensible representative of Roman practice. GREG is closely tied to the international complex in its music, and it contains some examples that are not found at Rome (among them, the 'Gallican' *Elegerunt apostoli*). Yet we have encountered arguments that render GREG origin doubtful: the slim representation of non-psalmic Offertories (at most, 20% of the ten to twelve dozen GREG Offertories are of this type); liturgical assign-

---

55 M. Righetti, *Storia liturgica*, I (Milan, 1950), p. 139.
56 ROM in Vatican, Biblioteca apostolica vaticana, lat. 5319, transcribed in B. Stäblein and M. Landwehr-Melnicki, *Die Gesänge des altrömischen Graduale*, Monumenta Monodica Medii Aevi 2 (Kassel, 1970), pp. 255–415; inventory by P. F. Cutter, *Musical Sources of the Old-Roman Mass* (American Institute of Musicology, 1979).

ments that are late and secondary; and the text situations of *Oravi* and *Stetit*, which practically oblige us to reckon with further branches of the tradition.

Turning to MED, the case for origins is perhaps stronger. Non-psalmic Offertories are in the majority there (forty-six of eighty-two pieces), and they occupy prominent positions such as Christmas, Easter, Ascension and Pentecost.[57] Even so, MED has the mark of a borrower, not a lender. Its texts are generally less complete than those of MOZ (*Erit, Sanctificavit, Stetit* and *Isti*). And its musical traditions may be less 'authoritative' than those of GREG, to judge from the three cases of apparently close musical relationship between GREG and MOZ as opposed to the single case (*Stetit angelus*) of such relationship between MED and MOZ.

Among our preserved repertories, the likeliest source is MOZ: a traffic in Offertories that went from Spain to the Carolingian north, to Milan, ultimately to Rome. The non-psalmic Offertories represent the norm in MOZ, accounting for nine-tenths of the twelve dozen Sacrificia, and supplying nearly all the important feasts of the Spanish calendar.[58] Still, a theory of MOZ origin does not explain the conflicting verses of *Oravi Deum*, which point to a further source than either MOZ or GREG. And MOZ lacks representatives of certain Offertories such as *In die, Precatus est Moyses* and *Oratio mea* (Table 1, nos. 4, 6, 12), which are likely representatives of the same practice.[59]

The remaining theory of origin is Gallican: that some or all of our non-psalmic Offertories are Gallican relics which at various times, by various routes and with varying textual-musical integrity made their way into the preserved liturgies. This seems the most plausible explanation for our network of chants. Yet the absence of certifiably Gallican texts and music makes it almost impossible to confirm. The chief sources of information concerning the Gallican Mass are two 'Epistles' ascribed to St Germanus of Paris (*d.* 576), which evidently represent the use of a Burgundian church (perhaps Autun) in the seventh or early eighth century.[60] From the first Epistle one learns that the Gallican Offertory, there called the Sono, was 'sung during the procession of oblation'; that it was sung 'dulci melodia' (perhaps

[57]   Baroffio, *Die Offertorien*, pp. 22ff.   [58]   Randel, *An Index*, pp. 457–76.

[59]   Additional MOZ Sacrificia may have been contained on the final folios of the León Antiphoner, which breaks off incomplete (fol. 306) among the Dominical Offertories.

[60]   J. Quasten, *Expositio antiquae liturgiae gallicanae* (Münster, 1934); K. Gamber, *Ordo antiquus gallicanus* (Regensburg, 1965); Migne, *Patrologiae . . . latina*, 72, p. 92.

an indication that the music was more than a simple syllabic setting); and that it 'takes its origin from the Lord directing Moses to make silver trumpets' ('praecepit dominus Moysi ut faceret tubas argenteas quas levitae clangerent', etc.).[61] Concerning this last provision, it may be observed that the author tends to use biblical or quasi-biblical passages as points of departure for mystagogic explanations of the Mass functions. Nevertheless, this may hint at the nature of the Gallican Offertory. A number of the non-psalmic Offertories in MOZ, MED and GREG have texts where the Lord speaks to Moses, Abraham or Noah; or Moses addresses Aaron or the people of Israel; or the angel Gabriel addresses Daniel. In Table 2, *Oravi Deum, Erit vobis, Sanctificavit Moyses* and *Isti sunt/Haec dicit* have passages of that sort. There is a further hint about the Gallican Sonus in a remark of Ordo Romanus xv, whose author relates it to the Gregorian Offertory.[62] There may also be 'Gallican' symptoms in the sometimes dramatic style and the centonate, paraphrase construction of our Offertory texts. Similar features have been pointed out in the texts of the Gallican Lectionary and Sacramentary. The Wolfenbüttel Lectionary, oldest of the surviving Gallican liturgical books (early sixth century, southern French), contains pericopes assembled in centonate fashion from a variety of biblical sources, with the original wording at times paraphrased, and the underlying texts in some cases pre-Vulgate.[63] Certain Gallican-style Prefaces in the Bobbio Missal (eighth century; south-eastern Gaul or north Italian *Gallia transpadana*) contain paraphrases of sermons by Sts Augustine, Maximus and Ambrose.[64] At the beginning of this century, Duchesne gave a classic formulation of the differences between Gallican and Italianate prayer styles: the Gallican – ample, oratorical, rich in imagery; the Italianate – simple and concise.[65]

[61] Gamber, *op. cit.*, p. 19.
[62] 'Et post hoc statim clerus canit offerenda, quod Franci dicit sonum'; M. Andrieu, *Les ordines romani du haut moyen âge*, III (Louvain, 1951), p. 123. On the interpretation, see *ibid.*, pp. 74–5, and J. Dyer, 'The Offertory Chant of the Roman Liturgy', p. 15, n. 45.
[63] Wolfenbüttel, Herzog-August-Bibliothek, Cod. Weissenb. 76; A. Dold, *Das älteste Liturgiebuch der lateinischen Kirche* (Beuron, 1936); King, *Liturgies of the Past*, p. 123; E. A. Lowe, *Codices latini antiquiores*, 9 (Oxford, 1959), no. 1392.
[64] Paris, Bibliothèque nationale, MS lat. 13246; A. Wilmart and others, eds., *The Bobbio Missal*, Henry Bradshaw Society, 53, 58, 61 (London, 1917–24); King, *Liturgies of the Past*, pp. 128f; Lowe, *Codices latini antiquiores*, 5 (1950), no. 653.
[65] L. Duchesne, 'Sur l'origine de la liturgie gallicane', *Revue d'Histoire et de Littérature Religieuses*, 5 (1900), p. 37: 'La composition ample, oratoire, imagée des formules gallicanes . . . si différentes de la simplicité et de la concision romaine'.

This was seen as well by Bishop, who described the early Roman rite as 'sober and restrained', and by Jungmann, who found the Gallican 'style of prayers . . . much more involved, long-winded, sentimental'.[66] Such differences appear between the psalmic Offertory texts (presumably Roman) and the non-psalmic texts (presumably Gallican).

There may be a further indication of the Gallican origin of our texts in the historical relationship between Spain and Gaul, where it is established that Gallican liturgical usages commingled with those of Spain. During the seventh century, Spain and Aquitanian Gaul were politically connected within the West Gothic kingdom. A well-known edict of the Fourth Council of Toledo in 633 speaks of 'a single order of prayer and chanting for all of Spain and Gaul'.[67] Certain MOZ chants – among them Preces and the processional antiphon *Introeunte te* – have been identified as examples of Hispanic-Gallican usage.[68] Hence it would not be surprising if some other MOZ chants, like the Offertories in Table 2, were to represent merged traditions.

In sum, the most plausible origin for our international network of non-psalmic Offertories is a Gallican or mixed Mozarabic-Gallican usage, and an important next step would be a systematic exploration of the preserved MOZ repertory with a view to identifying any Gallican residue. That laborious work remains largely to be done. Yet there is already in the external history of the Mozarabic rite, a bit of information that may fill in our historical picture. Liturgical historians tell us that the early rites of the Iberian peninsula owed something to Roman and north African usages, but that the 'Mozarabic' rite that has ultimately come down is largely a creation of seventh-century Toledo, the capital of the Visigothic kingdom. There are accounts of early liturgical activity under Petrus of Lerida (fifth to sixth century), Leander of Seville (*d.* 599) and John of Saragossa (*d.* 631). Conantius of Palencia (*d.* 639) 'was attentive and foresighted in the disposition of ecclesiastical offices, newly provid-

66   E. Bishop, 'The Genius of the Roman Rite', *Weekly Register* (May 1899), repr. in *Liturgica historica* (Oxford, 1918), pp. 4f; J. A. Jungmann, *The Early Liturgy to the Time of Gregory the Great* (London, 1959), p. 228.
67   'Unus igitur ordo orandi atque psallendi nobis per omnen Hispaniam atque Galliam'; P. Labbe and G. Cossart, *Sacrosancta concilia*, v (Paris, 1671), col. 1704.
68   M. Huglo, 'Les "preces" des graduels aquitains empruntées à la liturgie hispanique', *Hispania Sacra*, 8 (1955), pp. 361–83; Huglo, 'Source hagiopolite d'une antienne hispanique pour le Dimanche des Rameaux', *Hispania Sacra*, 10 (1957), pp. 367ff.

ing many chant melodies'. Above all there was the activity of three successive Toledan bishops of the seventh century: Eugenius II (*d.* 657), Idelphonsus (*d. c.* 680) and Julian (*d.* 690).[69] It was during their times that liturgical provisions were made for feasts as prominent as Maundy Thursday and the Ascension, which prompted Cardinal Mercati to remark that, such being the case, 'it will have to be carefully considered whether we may venture to assign to an earlier date many other *missae* of less important days'.[70] Thus the Hispanic liturgy was significantly augmented during the later seventh century. Yet from other indications it appears that within a generation after Julian's death in 690 that liturgy was essentially complete. The Muslim conquest of the Iberian peninsula in 711–12 drove numbers of ecclesiastics from their homes, often bearing treasured possessions. An evident refugee of the latter sort was the Orationale of Verona, the oldest surviving Hispanic liturgy book, which journeyed from its place of origin in the province of Tarragona in north-east Spain to Verona in northern Italy, arriving there in the later eighth century.[71] The manuscript can be roughly dated between *c.* 700 and 732: the former date on paleographical grounds, the latter on the supposition that the reconquest of Tarragona in 732 obviated further need for its migration. An Orationale is by design a prayer-book that makes no provision for musical texts. Yet in this exemplar the original scribe saw fit to enter the text-incipits of some 800 musical items that are associated with the main content of prayers. There are cues for responsories, antiphons, 'alleluiatic' antiphons and verses. These correspond so well with the full liturgy in noted MOZ antiphoners of the tenth to the twelfth centuries that it has been argued that the whole musical repertory of MOZ was in existence at the time of the Orationale.[72] To the extent that one can build upon that argument, the texts of our MOZ Offertories would themselves exist by the early eighth century. Furthermore, the supposed GALL Offertories upon which the MOZ chants are based must also be in existence before that time. There is one additional speculation along this line. In view of the original musical destination of the Offertory

[69] The documents are excerpted by M. Ferotin, *Liber mozarabicus sacramentorum* (Paris, 1912), pp. xvf.

[70] G. Mercati, 'More "Spanish Symptoms" ', in Bishop, *Liturgica historica*, p. 206.

[71] J. Vives, *Oracional visigótico* (Barcelona, 1956), pp. xiiiff.

[72] L. Brou, 'L'antiphonaire visigothique et l'antiphonaire grégorien du VIIIe siècle', *Anuario Musical*, 5 (1950), pp. 3ff.

'libretto' texts, and in view of the apparently 'close' musical relationships between four MOZ Sacrificia and their cognate GREG or MED Offertories, the possibility exists that something like the music jointly transmitted by the MOZ-GREG and MOZ-MED pairs of the tenth to twelfth centuries was already in existence in later seventh-century Gaul.

The case for Gallican origin is now essentially complete. It has focused on the seven MOZ chants for which there are music and/or text parallels among the GREG and/or MED Offertories (Table 2). Before concluding, it will be useful to return to the eighteen non-psalmic Offertories of the GREG *Sextuplex* (Table 1) that were my point of departure, and consider their origins in the overall perspective of the surviving musical families. Table 7 summarises the relationships of text and music between the eighteen *Sextuplex* Offertories and ROM, MED and MOZ.

GREG and MED have eight texts in common, six of them showing the broad similarity in modal-melodic substance that often links the two repertories. Liturgical historians remain undecided about the origins of the Milanese rite. There are theories of Roman origin, and others that view Milan as the centre for an archaic Gallican liturgy, perhaps influenced from the Syriac-Greek East.[73] Concerning the parallel MED and GREG chants, it has been supposed that where the music is related, the material came to Milan from Rome.[74] This must now be questioned for those MED non-psalmic Offertories that have MOZ counterparts (*Erit vobis*, *Sanctificavit Moyses* and *Stetit angelus*), and perhaps for some others found in MED and GREG though not in MOZ (*Angelus Domini*, *In die solemnitatis*, *Precatus est Moyses*, *Oratio mea* [*Exaudita est*] and *Audi Israel*). Both *Angelus Domini* and *In die solemnitatis* are assigned to Easter weekdays by GREG-ROM; and so is *Erit vobis*, which has a MOZ counterpart. These three Easter weekday Offertories may represent a unified historical layer. *Precatus est Moyses* has a long, dramatic text, running to a refrain and two verses in GREG, with an assignment to a minor occasion (the Twelfth or Eleventh Sunday after Pentecost). In MED, the same materials are

[73] Righetti, *Storia liturgica*, pp. 144ff; P. Borella, *Il rito ambrosiano* (Brescia, 1964), pp. 35ff.
[74] Borella, *Il rito ambrosiano*, pp. 451ff, summarises the positions; exceptions are raised by Huglo, *Fonti e paleografia*, pp. 117–37; and by Baroffio, *Die Offertorien*, and in 'Offertory', *The New Grove*, XII, p. 515.

Table 7 Gregorian non-psalmic Offertories (Sextuplex): relationships with Rom, Med and Moz

No.	Incipit	Greg	Ott[1]	Rom	MMMA[2]	Med	AMM[3]	Moz	León[4]	Note
1	Ave Maria	✓	13	✓	404					5
2	Sicut in holocausto		92							
3	Angelus Domini	✓	57	✓	388	✓	210			6
4	In die solemnitatis	✓	61	✓	312	✓	228			7, 8
5	Erit vobis	✓	63	✓	415	✓	256	✓	178	8, 9
6	Precatus est Moyses	✓	97	✓	397	✓	121, 135, 129			10
7	Oravi Deum	✓	107	✓	300			✓	238ᵛ	
8	Sanctificavit Moyses	✓	114	✓	350	✓	333	✓	305	
9	Vir erat in terra	✓	122	✓	255					
10	Recordare	✓	125	✓	264					
11	Domine Deus in simplicitate	✓	159	✓	341			✓	119	11
12	Oratio mea	✓	164	✓	392	✓	512			
13	Elegerunt apostoli		161					✓	74ᵛ	

Table 7 (cont.)

No.	Incipit	Greg	Ott[1]	Rom	MMMA[2]	Med	AMM[3]	Moz	León[4]	Note
No.	Incipit	Greg	Ott[1]	Rom	MMMA[2]	Med	AMM[3]	Moz	León[4]	Note
14	Stetit angelus	✓	170	(✓)	356	✓	420	✓	194	7, 11
15	Audi Israel	(○✓)	—			(○✓)	Pal. Mus. 5–6, 18			12
16	Viri		172							
17	Factus est repente	✓	—					✓	210	11
18	Benedictus sit		81							

Key and notes:

□ Music may be closely related.
○ Music broadly related.
✓ Same text.
(✓) Texts only partly related.
[1] Ott, *Offertoriale*.
[2] Monumenta Monodica Medii Aevi 2 (Stäblein–Melnicki).
[3] *Antiphonale missarum . . . mediolanensis*.
[4] *Antifonario visigótico mozárabe de la catedral de León, edición facsímil.*
[5] MED Psalmellus: *Antiphonale missarum . . . mediolanensis*, p. 397; music not related.
[6] BEN has related text; see Baroffio, *Die Offertorien*, p. 32.
[7] MED: little or no musical relationship to GREG.
[8] GREG–ROM: musical relationship doubtful.
[9] GREG–MED: only traces of musical relationship.
[10] MED divides GREG among 2nd, 3rd and 4th Sundays in Lent.
[11] GREG–MOZ: texts only partly the same.
[12] MED: Responsory for 4th Sunday in Advent.

spread over three successive Sundays in Lent (Second, Fourth and Third), which led Heiming to suppose that MED borrowed its three Offertories from Rome.[75] In view of the MED-MOZ linkages for *Erit*, *Sanctificavit* and *Stetit*, a MED borrowing of *Precatus est Moyses* seems likelier to come from GALL. *Angelus Domini* is the MED Offertory for Easter. Its GREG assignments are less solemn – Easter Monday and Easter Octave, though two early GREG sources (Rheinau, which is Swiss, late eighth century; and Ottoboni lat. 313, which is from St Denis, ninth century) place it at the Easter Vigil, a Mass whose early history with respect to the Offertory is unclear.[76] The situation is like that of the MED *Erit vobis* for Pentecost. If MED borrowed *Angelus Domini* for its Easter Offertory, the presumption is that it drew upon a correspondingly prominent usage. MED ignored the GREG-ROM Easter Offertory, *Terra tremuit*. Hence the possibility that the MED *Angelus Domini* at Easter reflects a Gallican Easter usage. *Oratio mea* in GREG serves for the Vigil of St Lawrence, a relatively late addition to the calendar; the chant consists of a refrain and single verse. The MED cognate *Exaudita est oratio mea* adds a verse to the GREG text and is assigned to the more important day-Mass of St Lawrence. The traffic evidently did not go from GREG (less complete) to MED (more complete); while it may have gone the other way, it seems likelier there was a further source upon which both drew. Summing up the relationship between MED and GREG, the indications of *Precatus*, *Angelus* and *Oratio–Exaudita* tend to confirm the impressions left by *Stetit*, *Erit* and *Sanctificavit* (all of which have MOZ parallels): that a lost GALL source was involved.

For two further Offertories in Table 7 (*Domine Deus in simplicitate* and *Factus est repente*) the text parallels between MOZ and GREG are not close enough to suppose there was a common 'libretto' source. They were accordingly omitted from Table 2. *Domine Deus in simplicitate* has been the standard GREG-ROM Offertory for the Dedication since at least the tenth century. The association of the Roman Dedication feast (13 May) with the consecration of the Pantheon as Sta Maria ad Martyres took place during the early seventh century, and has attached something of a fixed date to this feast, putting it among the

---

[75] 'Offertori romani pregregoriani nella liturgia milanese', *Ambrosius* (1939), pp. 83–8; a revision of Heiming's conclusions by Baroffio, 'Osservazioni sui versetti', pp. 54–8.

[76] Hesbert, *Sextuplex*, no. 79b and p. LXI, n. 7; early Latin traditions are traced in my 'Italian Neophytes' Chants', *Journal of the American Musicological Society*, 23 (1970), pp. 183ff.

earliest additions to the Roman calendar after the death of Gregory the Great in 604.[77] Both the GREG and MOZ texts of *Domine Deus in simplicitate* are of the 'libretto' type, drawing loosely on *1 Chronicles* 29. There is the possibility of a common text formulation behind them, but they may be based independently on the same biblical passages. The Mass prayers for this feast in the Gregorian Sacramentary have been identified as of Gallican origin.[78] A similar suggestion of MOZ background has been made for the Dedication Gradual *Locus iste*.[79] This would fit with a Gallican origin for the Offertory *Domine Deus in simplicitate*. Concerning the Pentecost Offertory *Factus est repente*, there is similar uncertainty whether the GREG and MOZ texts descend from a common Offertory libretto or go back independently to the same passages in *Acts*. The GREG chant was given a detailed treatment by Hesbert, who in 1961 supposed it to be of Roman origin.[80] I will return to the question in a forthcoming article with support for the suggestions by Huglo and Baroffio that the GREG *Factus est repente* represents a survival of Gallican usage.[81]

Of the eighteen GREG Offertories in Table 7, there are six with no Roman counterparts at all (nos. 2, 13, 15, 16, 17, 18), while a seventh (no. 14) has only a partial Roman counterpart. For those Offertories one might adopt the description 'non-Roman', and for each of them there are further tokens of such origin. *Elegerunt apostoli*, we have observed, is the common example of a 'Gallican' Offertory flourishing in a GREG context.[82] *Sicut in holocausto* has a persuasive witness of its northern origin. It comes with the GREG Mass *Omnes gentes* for the Seventh Sunday after Pentecost, a Mass that the Carolingian scribe of the Blandiniensis (late eighth century) remarks 'is not found in Roman Antiphoners'.[83] *Benedictus sit* is for Trinity, a feast of largely ninth-century diffusion, its Mass-prayers attributed to Alcuin, its

---

77 Hesbert, *Sextuplex*, p. xciii: 'en 608 vraisemblablement'; J. Deshusses, *Le sacramentaire grégorien*, p. 52: 'entre les années 609 et 638'.

78 J. Deshusses, 'Le sacramentaire de Gellone dans son contexte historique', *Ephemerides Liturgicae*, 75 (1961), p. 207.

79 L. Brou, 'Le IVe Livre d'Esdras dans la liturgie hispanique et le Graduel romain "Locus iste" de la Messe de la Dédicace', *Sacris Erudiri*, 9 (1957), pp. 75–109.

80 R.-J. Hesbert. 'Un antique offertoire de la Pentecôte', *Organicae voces: Festschrift Joseph Smits van Waesberghe* (Amsterdam, 1963), pp. 59–69.

81 Huglo, 'Altgallikanische Liturgie', p. 229; Baroffio, 'Offertory', *The New Grove*, xiii, p. 515.

82 *Paléographie Musicale*, ser. i, 15 (1937), p. 165.

83 R.-J. Hesbert, 'La Messe "Omnes gentes" du VIIe Dimanche après la Pentecôte', *Revue Grégorienne*, 17 (1932), pp. 81–9, 170–9; 18 (1933), pp. 1–14; Hesbert, *Sextuplex*, no. 179.

music never taken into the ROM Graduals.[84] *Viri Galilei* and *Factus est repente*, for Ascension and Pentecost, are also non-psalmic Offertories with major liturgical assignments in the *Sextuplex*, where they conflict with the usual GREG assignments (*Ascendit Deus* and *Confirma hoc*). The explanation may be that, like *Erit vobis* and *Angelus Domini*, they were prominent GALL Offertories, sufficiently prized to be maintained on the margins of local GREG traditions where they once flourished. For the Michael Offertory *Stetit angelus*, we have seen a mixed tradition. The GREG refrain is non-psalmic, drawn from the same source (*Revelations*) as the MED and MOZ refrains, whose close relationships of text and music point to GALL origin. The GREG verses draw on Psalm 137, the text of the Michael Offertory at ROM, ignored by MED and MOZ. *Audi Israel*, for the Advent season, appears in the *Sextuplex* only in Rheinau (eighth century), though it later has GREG music that circulates narrowly.[85] In text and music it is related to the MED Responsory *Audi Israel*.[86] Since there is no ROM representative for this piece, a likely source for the shared GREG-MED material would be GALL.

Finally, the eleven non-psalmic Offertories that are common to GREG and ROM raise questions of fundamental importance. If the non-psalmic texts represent a type that was originally 'non-Roman', under what circumstances did those eleven texts gain entry to the liturgy of Rome? And if the music that was originally accommodated to the texts was also 'non Roman', why does their ROM music represent some of the same melodic substances as the GREG, MED and (apparently) MOZ music? And then, since the ROM and GREG musical versions are at times palpably related, why do the relationships show such an irregular pattern, ranging at other times to no apparent connection at all?

The likeliest answer to the first question is that the texts of this type reached Rome as accretions to Gregorian traditions, returned to the capital from the Carolingian north. There are analogies here

---

[84]   In the *Sextuplex*, it appears only in Senlis (no. 172*bis*), and not at all in the ROM Graduals: Cutter, *Musical Sources of the Old-Roman Mass*; cf. S. Baeumer, *Histoire du Bréviaire* (Paris, 1905), I, p. 427; II, p. 60.

[85]   A manuscript from Ravenna (Padua, Biblioteca capitolare, MS A. 47) can be added to the five sources (all central or north Italian) listed by Hesbert, *Sextuplex*, p. xxxvi, n.3, and W. H. Frere, *The Sarum Gradual* (London, 1895), p. LXXXIV.

[86]   Paléographie Musicale, ser. I, 5–6 (1896–1900), fol. 18; the chant does not circulate as a Responsory in either GREG (Hesbert, *Corpus antiphonalium officii*, Rome, 1963—) or ROM (Cutter, *Musical Sources of the Old Roman Mass*, including an inventory of the Office chants).

with the histories of the Sacramentary and Pontificale. A Roman Sacramentary incorporating Frankish additions reached northern Italy as early as *c.* 770 in the copy of the 'eighth-century Gelasian' Sacramentary in Rome, Biblioteca Angelica, MS 1408.[87] The late eighth-century Sacramentary of Hadrian enhanced with the *Hucusque* supplement of Benedict of Aniane, and the 'Roman-Germanic' Pontificale of Mainz, both containing northern materials, entered Roman liturgical usage between the ninth and twelfth centuries.[88] The case most familiar to music historians is the chant of the Credo, which, as Berno of Reichenau (*d.* 1048) tells us, was added to the Urban Mass shortly after 1014 at the instance of the Ottonian Emperor Henry II.[89]

Concerning the second question, we know that Roman musicians at a time between the ninth and eleventh centuries indulged in the practice of converting imported melodies to prevailing Roman style. Most obvious is the case of the *Veterem hominem* antiphons for the Epiphany Octave. These were originally Byzantine hymn-strophes which underwent textual and musical translations at Aachen in 802, being turned at Charlemagne's request from Greek into Latin, and from Byzantine into GREG melos.[90] Then the Gregorianised antiphons made their way to Rome. At whatever time they appeared, the Roman musicians were still committed to their local melodic dialect, for they made the further conversion, turning the antiphons from GREG into ROM melos.[91] The earlier Byzantine and GREG melodic shapes are still discernible beneath the ROM stylisation, but the local details represent an idiomatic Roman overlay. At some later time – by the later eleventh century, when the manuscripts begin – the Roman musicians were no longer indulging in such conversions. Among other chants, the Tracts for Holy Saturday, the Offertory *Domine Jesu Christe* and the Trisagion of Good Friday made their way

87 C. Vogel, *La Reforme cultuelle sous Pépin le Bref et sous Charlemagne* (Graz, 1965), p. 190, n. 41.

88 Deshusses, *Le sacramentaire grégorien*, pp. 47–75. C. Vogel and R. Elze, *Le pontifical romano-germanique du dixième siècle*, Studi e Testi 226–7 (Vatican City, 1963).

89 Berno, 'De quibusdam rebus ad missae officium spectantibus', cap. 2; Migne, *Patrologiae . . . latina*, 142, cols. 1060f.

90 J. Handschin, 'Sur quelques tropaires grecs traduits en latin', *Annales Musicologiques*, 2 (1954), pp. 27–60; O. Strunk, 'The Latin Antiphons for the Octave of the Epiphany', in *Recueil de Travaux de l'Institut d'Études Byzantines*, VIII: *Mélanges G. Ostrogorsky*, 2 (Belgrade, 1964), pp. 417–26; repr. in O. Strunk, *Essays on Music in the Byzantine World* (New York, 1977), pp. 208ff.

91 Vatican, Biblioteca Apostolica Vaticana, Arch. San Pietro, MS B. 79, fol. 42v; London British Library, Add. MS 29988, fol. 38v.

from Carolingian-Gregorian traditions into the noted Roman books, where they appear simply in their GREG musical dress.[92]

Concerning the third question, the irregular pattern of musical relationships between GREG and ROM, the fact is that only the Offertory *Vir erat* has a notably close musical relationship. In seven other GREG-ROM parallels (*Ave, Angelus, Precatus, Oravi, Sanctificavit, Recordare* and *Oratio*), the relationship can be described as 'fair' to 'good'. In two others (*In die* and *Erit vobis*) it is 'poor', and in one (*Domine Deus in simplicitate*) there is no apparent musical relationship at all. We have already seen that for some of these same chants there are musical relationships between GREG and MOZ or GREG and MED; yet no pattern emerges between those pairings and GREG-ROM. Thus for *Erit vobis, Sanctificavit Moyses* and *Oravi Deum*, where the GREG-MOZ musical link appears close, the linkages among the other families are mixed: for *Erit*, GREG-MED is fair, GREG-ROM is poor; for *Sanctificavit*, GREG-MED is good, GREG-ROM is fair; for *Oravi*, there is no MED representative, and GREG-ROM is at some points good.

This irregularity in the GREG-ROM relationship can be accounted for in various ways. One might suppose that ROM received its GREG materials in different transmissions, and that some of the GREG melodies we know are later or different from the GREG Offertory melodies that were the basis of the ROM chants. Corroboration may be found in the short verse-divisions of the ROM *Sanctificavit Moyses*, which do not occur in GREG traditions. Still another explanation of the irregular GREG-ROM pattern is more attractive in that it may offer a glimpse into the ROM melodic workshop. That is, the Roman musicians may have received the same GREG music we know, yet chose to treat it in various ways. As a rule, the treatment was matter-of-fact, concerned with imposing the standard ROM idioms while ignoring to a greater or lesser extent the often shapely melodic contours and the dramatic and pictorial details of the GREG versions. However, with an extraordinary composition like *Vir erat* (so the argument would run), the melodic features were so striking that the Romans troubled to preserve more of the GREG original. This lengthy emotional monologue of the afflicted Job was singled out by

---

[92] T. Klauser, 'Die liturgischen Austauschbeziehungen zwischen der römischen und der fränkisch-deutschen Kirche vom achten bis zum elften Jahrhundert', *Historisches Jahrbuch*, 53 (1933), pp. 186–7, points to comparable Roman liturgical accretions during the 960s.

Amalarius because of the rhetorical repetitions in its text.[93] *Vir erat* has neither a MED nor MOZ analogue, so that one must consider the possibility of Roman origin. But the uncommonly dramatic matter, the 'libretto' nature of its verbal formulation (Amalarius speaks aptly of the 'officii auctor') and its assignment to a later Sunday (the Twenty-first) in the Pentecost series, seem to place it among our Gallican candidates.

The network involving non-psalmic Offertories is now complete, but an over-arching question remains. Everything so far has focused on the 'non-psalmic' texts as symptoms of 'Gallican' origin. Yet, after all is said, how fundamentally do the non-psalmic minority of GREG Offertories differ from the psalmic majority? Concerning the texts themselves, the differences may be more apparent than real. To be sure, there is the tendency of the psalmic texts to use the Bible literally, while the non-psalmic texts compress, rearrange and paraphrase its verbiage. Yet such differences were to a considerable extent imposed upon the Offertory librettists by the different sorts of literary matter with which they dealt. The non-psalmic texts generally contained some kernel of story-line, and there was the need to cut the biblical narrative to musically viable proportions. With the psalmic texts, there was no scenario, no story. The psalmic essence lay in general pieties, couched in a limited repertory of verbal formulas that recur throughout the Psalter, sometimes identically, often with only minor change. The distinction of the psalmic text, then, lay in its specific verbiage, and precisely the literal wording of the Psalter was what the psalmic librettist tended to preserve. Thus in either case, psalmic or non-psalmic, the Offertory text was a 'libretto'. Similar operations of centonate selection and tailoring (minimal for the psalmic pieces) took place in both, and what differences there are between the two varieties of text can be explained by the underlying difference in literary substance. One is not constrained, therefore, to suppose that different historical or geographical origins lay behind them. A similar estimate can be obtained from the music. At a broad view of the musical styles, the psalmic Offertories are not cut of substantially different fabric from the non-psalmic ones. There are similarities in melodic contour,

---

[93] *Amalarii episcopi opera liturgica omnia*, II, ed. I. M. Hanssens, Studi e Testi 139 (Vatican City, 1948), p. 373.

melismatic density, modal behaviour; similar internally structured melismas, text-repetitions, word-illustrations.[94]

In short, neither the texts nor the music oblige us to suppose that the GREG non-psalmic Offertories had different antecedents from the psalmic ones. And in that case, the whole notion that the GREG non-psalmic pieces represent textual-musical descendents of GALL practice has at least to be re-examined, and perhaps even abandoned. In fact it is the notion, tacitly maintained so far, that the psalmic Offertories represent Roman origin, that needs to be reconsidered. Put simply, Roman origin remains probable for the bulk of the psalmic Offertory texts common to GREG and ROM, but for the music that accompanies those texts in GREG, there is a likelihood of their representing a Carolingian stylistic overlay in many cases, and wholly new 'northern' music in some. Thus the Roman psalmic texts, and doubtless some of the ROM music as well, would have gone north during the seventh to ninth centuries, there to be tailored into transalpine musical style. This is in line with the theory of GREG as representing a Carolingian stylisation, advocated by Hucke and Huglo.[95] I would observe only that the situation must be examined category by category, mode by mode, chant by chant. The likeliest GREG categories to include takeovers and conversions of 'northern' or Gallican melodies are the Alleluia verses, Offertories and processional antiphons.[96] Yet even among the processional antiphons there is a case of an archaic Italianate melos apparently transmitted intact within GREG.[97]

I can sum up only with hypotheses, not conclusions:
  (1) that many of the eighteen non-psalmic Offertory texts in the

[94] Johner, *Wort und Ton im Choral*, pp. 381–4: 'Das Offertorium und die anderen responsorialien Gesänge'.
[95] H. Hucke, 'Die Einführung des Gregorianische Gesanges im Frankenreich', *Römische Quartalschrift*, 49 (1954), pp. 172ff; Hucke, 'Gregorianischer Gesang in altrömischer und fränkischer Uberlieferung', *Archiv für Musikwissenschaft*, 12 (1955), pp. 74ff; Hucke, 'Gregorian and Old Roman Chant', *The New Grove*, VII, pp. 693ff; M. Huglo, 'Römisch-fränkische Liturgie', in Fellerer, *Geschichte*, I (1972), pp. 233ff.
[96] Processional antiphons of Gallican origin are discussed by Huglo, 'Altgallikanische Liturgie', p. 228, and 'Antiphon', *The New Grove*, I, p. 480.
[97] In 'A Gregorian Processional Antiphon', forthcoming in *Report of the Thirteenth International Congress [of the International Musicological Society, Strasbourg, 1982]*, I argue that the processional antiphon *Deprecamur te Domine*, as found in Frankish-derived sources of the tenth to twelfth centuries, may faithfully represent an Italian (Roman-Benedictine or Beneventan) melodic state of the seventh to eighth century.

GREG *Sextuplex* were fashioned from the outset as 'librettos' for musical setting;

(2) that such non-psalmic librettos represent a prevailing text-type in parts of Gaul, and from there made their way at various times and with varying integrity into MOZ, MED, GREG and ROM;

(3) that such non-psalmic Offertories were used in Gaul before *c.* 700, since they became rooted in Spain by the later seventh or early eighth century, the *terminus ante quem, c.* 700–32, supplied by the Orationale of Verona;

(4) that some of the GALL libretto-texts may have originated much earlier than the seventh to eighth century, in view of the presumptive age of some of the underlying pre-Vulgate, Old-Latin literary sources;

(5) that the GALL librettos were designed from the outset to receive, not simply syllabic music, but specifically music in florid style – the repetitions of text phrases and the economies imposed on the biblical verbiage point to melismatic intention;

(6) that some of the original GALL music may survive in MOZ, MED and GREG Offertories (particularly where two families show close musical parallels), having made its way into MOZ by *c.* 700 (see 3 above) and into GREG by *c.* 800 (as witnessed by the text-traditions of Rheinau and the Blandiniensis);

(7) that some of the original GALL music may be distantly reflected even at Rome, as in the Offertory *Vir erat*, which presumably reached ROM as a Carolingian or perhaps Ottonian import.

All of the foregoing will need careful testing before firm conclusions can be drawn. There are questions still to be asked of the *Sextuplex* Offertories (Tables 1 and 7); of the two to three dozen non-psalmic Offertories that circulate in other early GREG traditions; of the Offertories common to GREG and ROM; of those which serve crossover liturgical functions in different rites (such as the use of *Elegerunt* as both a Sacrificium and a Sono within MOZ, or of the Offertories *Curvati* and *Audi* as Responsories in MOZ amd MED);[98] of the dozen and a half surviving 'Old-Beneventan' Offertories, which like most proper texts in that tradition are non-psalmic, yet show little relationship to the complex of texts considered here; of the

---

[98] The question of 'melodic archetypes' is discussed in an important article by Thomas H. Connolly, 'Introits and Archetypes: Some Archaisms of the Old Roman Chant', *Journal of the American Musicological Society*, 25 (1972), pp. 157–74.

Latin Offertories in the enigmatic near-Eastern or north African tradition preserved in the ninth- to tenth-century fragments at Mount Sinai;[99] of the traces of a Proper Offertory-cycle in Byzantine, Slavic, Armenian and Georgian traditions, pointing ultimately to a descent from Greek traditions of fifth- to sixth-century Jerusalem.[100] Any of these avenues may open a line of argument that will oblige a radical revision of the foregoing hypotheses. Yet supposing for the moment that the thrusts and emphases set out here will prove essentially sound, then some final observations may be in order.

First, that the lost Gallican musical liturgy has been reclaimed to an unprecedented extent. Two or three dozen GREG non-psalmic Offertories may now be viewed as possible derivatives or even outright survivals of GALL Offertory texts and music, with the roster of such Gallican candidates still more abundant in MED and in MOZ. Second, the MOZ repertory takes on new interest as a potential source of GALL materials; further studies are needed, capitalising on the highly effective methods used by Brou and Randel, for whom the pre-diastematic states of the MOZ notations were no obstacles to significant discoveries.[101] Third, the enigmatic histories of the 'two Roman chants', GREG and ROM, are illumined by the identification of a GALL layer, entrenched not only among the GREG Offertories but even firmly within the liturgy of Urban Rome. Finally, our grasp of melodic pre-history is singularly expanded. An extraordinary constellation of melodic evidence permits us, at least speculatively, to reach beyond our oldest documents and grapple with approximations of the Offertory melodies as they were in earlier times.

---

[99]   E. A. Lowe, 'Two New Latin Liturgical Fragments on Mount Sinai', and B. Fischer, 'Zur Liturgie der lateinischen Hss. von Sinai', *Revue Bénédictine*, 74 (1964), pp. 252–83 and 284–97.

[100]   Byzantine and Slavic rites since the ninth century use just four chants for the Offertory or 'Cherubic Hymn'; versions and discussion in my 'A Hymn for Thursday in Holy Week', *Journal of the American Musicological Society*, 16 (1963), pp. 127ff, 158–68. A larger selection of Proper Offertory chants is found in the early usage of Jerusalem; H. Leeb, *Die Gesänge im Gemeindegottesdienst von Jerusalem (vom 5. bis 8. Jahrhundert)* (Vienna, 1970), pp. 113–24; R. Taft, 'A Proper Offertory Chant for Easter in Some Slavonic Manuscripts', *Orientalia Christiana Periodica*, 36 (1970), pp. 437–43.

[101]   L. Brou: 'Le "Psallendum" de la Messe et les chants connexes', *Ephemerides Liturgicae*, 61 (1947), pp. 13–54; 'L'Alleluia dans la liturgie mozarabe', *Anuario Musical*, 6 (1951), pp. 3–90; 'Notes de paléographie musical mozarabe [I]', *Anuario Musical*, 7 (1952), pp. 51–76. D. M. Randel: *The Responsorial Psalm Tones for the Mozarabic Office* (Princeton, 1969); 'Responsorial Psalmody in the Mozarabic Rite', *Études Grégoriennes*, 10 (1969), pp. 87–116; 'Antiphonal Psalmody in the Mozarabic Rite', *Report of the Twelfth Congress of the International Musicological Society: Berkeley, 1977* (1982), I, pp. 414–22. Also, C. W. Brockett, *Antiphons, Responsories and Other Chants of the Mozarabic Rite* (Brooklyn, 1968).

Supposing that the liturgical-musical commerce between GALL and GREG took place by the later eighth century, and between GALL and MOZ already by the later seventh century, then in the apparently close musical agreements between four MOZ Sacrificia and their cognates in GREG or MED, we may control some of the substance of those melodies as they were in Merovingian times. That is, for the first time we may be able to look back of the Carolingians, whose neumatic notations crystallised the musical liturgy for later ages, into the seventh to eighth century past, and view something of the music during the later stages of its oral transmission.

CHAPTER 4

Charlemagne's Archetype of Gregorian Chant

For Michel Huglo on his 65th birthday.

WHEN WAS GREGORIAN CHANT first written down? When were the propers of the Roman Mass and Office, which we can trace in an unbroken line from the later Carolingians to Solesmes, given their definitive neumed forms? If current wisdom is believed, the neumatic notation was not devised until the first half of the ninth century; it arose in the service of novel and ancillary chants like tropes, sequences, genealogies, Celebrant's and diaconal *ekphoneses,* theorist's illustrations, and polyphony. The central repertory of Gregorian proper chants would remain consigned to professional memories and improvisational maneuver during the early generations of the neumes' availability; its systematic neumation would not be undertaken until ca. 900. This scenario, whose origin we owe largely to Mlle. Corbin, has won wide acceptance.[1] I believe it is wrong. My aim here is to assemble witnesses to the existence of an authoritative neumed recension of the Gregorian propers ca. 800, a century sooner than is presently supposed.

To begin, we must deal with two related archetypes of Gregorian chant, one containing the verbal texts alone, the other consisting of the same core of liturgy and text plus the supplement of neumes. Inasmuch as early traditions for the Mass propers are better documented than those for the Of-

---

[1] Solange Corbin, "Les notations neumatiques en France à l'époque carolingienne," *Revue d'histoire de l'église en France* 38 (1952): 225–32; Corbin, "Les neumes," *Histoire de la musique,* Encyclopédie de la Pléiade, no. 9. (Paris, 1960), 1. 690–94; Corbin, *Die Neumen;* Vol. 1, facs. in 3 of *Paleographie der Musik nach den Plänen Leo Schrades.* (Cologne 1977), 22–42. It is also embraced by Helmut Hucke, "Toward a New Historical View of Gregorian Chant," *JAMS,* 33 (1980): 445; and by Leo Treitler: "The earliest practical notations served primarily a cueing function for celebrants reciting ecclesiastical readings and prayers. . . . The notation of antiphons, responsories, and Mass-Proper items for the cantor and schola did not begin until the tenth century"; "Reading and Singing: On the Genesis of Occidental Music-Writing," *EMH* 4 (1984): 176. For the Rutgers Symposium of 4–5 April 1986 at which the original version of my present paper was delivered, Dr. Hucke's prospectus read: "Written tradition of Western music and of chant did not exist at the time of St. Gregory the Great, and not even when Roman Chant was introduced into the Frankish Empire. It did not begin until ca. 900 . . . . Before chant was written down around 900, it was transmitted orally. To study the history of chant up to 900 is to study an oral tradition."

First published in *Journal of the American Musicological Society* 40 (1987): 1–30. Reprinted by permission.

fice, my focus will be on the Mass, although the historical situation should be a parallel for the Office.

The oldest full witnesses of the verbal texts of the Mass propers are the half dozen documents that receive a masterful edition in Hesbert's *Sextuplex;*[2] they are the first six items in Table 4.1. All are of apparent north-European origin, with dates ranging between the later eighth and later ninth centuries. A substantial consensus among them points to a standard text recension circulating in Frankish regions by ca. 800, a recension whose lost original I shall call the Carolingian Text Archetype. In one of the oldest sources, the Blandiniensis (*Bland*) (Table 4.1, No. 2, dating ca. 800), there is an annotation contrasting the manuscript's own provisions with those of Roman antiphoners known to its compiler.[3] Thus there were Italian roots reaching farther back than the Frankish sources, but no substantial relic of an eighth-century Roman text is preserved.

As for the Gregorian propers with neumes, the earliest surviving witnesses date from ca. 900, a century after those with the text alone.[4] Some of the more important of them are listed in Table 4.2. These too are in the main northern European, and there is a substantial degree of consensus, pointing to an archetype which I shall call the Carolingian Neumed Archetype. Their dates begin ca. 900. It is this distribution of the surviving sources, with text witnesses beginning ca. 800 and neumed witnesses ca. 900, that lends support to the theory that neumes were not supplied to the full Gregorian repertory until a century after the text tradition was established. In my view, the two traditions were closely linked in date and function, with both circulating around the end of the eighth century. Both would represent Charlemagne's politics of liturgical renewal and both would implement the changes that were set in motion by Charlemagne's father, Pepin, at the time of Pope Stephen II's visit to France in 754.[5]

Let me address the view that the Gregorian musical collection began later (ca. 900) than the text collection (ca. 800), by examining first what I see as its flawed rationale. It is true enough that a century-long gap separates the earliest preserved witnesses of text from those with music; and what neumations there are from the middle and late ninth century are given to new and ancillary chants—tropes, sequences, hymns, lections, Celebrants' chants, etc.—rather than to the Gregorian propers. Yet this

---

[2] *AMS.*

[3] *AMS,* no. 179 (the Seventh Sunday after Pentecost): "Ista ebdomata non est in antefonarios romanos." The situation is studied in Hesbert's "La messe 'Omnes gentes' du VIIIe dimanche après la Pentecôte et l'Antiphonale missarum romain," *RG* 17 (1932): 81–89, 170–79; *RG* 18 (1933): 1–14.

[4] Both types are surveyed by Peter Jeffery, "The Oldest Sources of the *Graduale*: A Preliminary Checklist of MSS Copied before about 900 AD," *Journal of Musicology* 2 (1983): 316–21.

[5] Cyrille Vogel, *La reforme cultuelle sour Pépin le Bref et sous Charlemagne* (Graz, 1965).

TABLE 4.1

Carolingian Text Archetype: Early Descendents (Mass books)

No.	Name	Type	Date	Origin	Presentation
1.	Rheinau	Antiphonale missarum	late 8/early 9	northern France or Switzerland	elegant
2.	Bland[iniensis]	Ant. miss.	late 8/early 9	northern Europe	elegant
3.	Monza Cantatorium	Cantatorium	late 8/early 9, or middle 9	northeastern France	purpureus, uncials
4.	Compiègne [Compendiensis]	Ant. miss.	late 9	Soissons?	deluxe
5.	Senlis	Ant. miss.	betw. 877–882	St. Denis/Senlis?	elegant
6.	Corbie	Ant. miss.	"shortly after 853"	Corbie	elegant
7.	Lucca fragment	List of chants (Advent)	late 8	Lucca?	routine

| 8. | "Monza Schwesterhandschrift" | Cantatorium | late 8/early 9, or middle 9 | northeast France | purpureus; uncials |

Notes to Table 4.1.

Rheinau (Zürich, Zentralbibliothek, Rheinau 30): see AMS, no. 2; CLA 7, no. 1019; CLLA nos. 802, 1325; LeGR, 2.155 ("8e–9e siècle"); P. Jeffery, "The Oldest Sources of the Gradual: A Preliminary Checklist of MSS Copied Before About 900 AD," *Journal of Musicology* 2 (1983): 319.

Bland[iniensis] (Brussels, Bibl. Royale, MS. 10127-44): See AMS, no. 3; CLA 10, no. 1548; CLLA, nos. 856, 1320; LeGR, 2.37 ("fin 8e/début 9e s."); Jeffery, 319.

Monza (Monza, Tesoro della Basilica S. Giovanni, Cod. CIX): see AMS, no. 1 ("8th cy."); CLLA, No. 1310 (Bischoff: "2nd third of 9th c."); LeGR, 2.77 ("début 9e"); Jeffery, 320.

Compiègne (*Compendiensis*: Paris, Bibl. nat., MS. Lat. 17436): AMS, no. 4; CLLA, no. 1330; LeGR, 2.109; J. Froger, "Le lieu et destination du 'Compendiense,'" in Ut mens concordet voci. Festschrift Eugène Cardine (St. Ottilien, 1980), 338–53 ("Soissons, late 9th century"); Jeffery, 319.

Senlis (Paris, Bibl. Ste.-Genev., MS. lat 111): AMS, no. 6; CLLA, nos. 745, 1322; LeGR, 2.113; Jeffery, 319.

Corbie (Paris, Bibl. nat., MS. lat. 12050): see AMS, no. 5; CLLA, nos. 745, 1335; LeGR, 2.105; Jeffery, 319.

Lucca Fragment (incipits list: Lucca, Bibl. capit., 490, fol. 30–31): see AMS, no. 7; CLA, 3, no. 303; CLLA, no. 1302; LeGR, 2.65 ("end of 8th c."); Michel Huglo in *Kirchenmusikalisches Jahrbuch* 35 (1951): 10–15; Jacques Froger, "Le fragment de Lucques (fin du VIIe siècle), *EG* 18 (1979): 145–55; Jeffery, 320.

"Monza Schwesterhandschrift" (Berlin, Cleveland, [and Trier]: CLLA, no 1311 (Bischoff: "2nd third of 9th c."); LeGR, 2.143 ("beg. 9th c."); Petrus Siffrin, "Eine Schwesterhandschrift des Graduale von Monza," in Ephemerides liturgicae 64 (1950): 53–81; Jeffery, 320.

Table 4.2
Carolingian Neumed Archetype: Early Descendents (Mass books)

No.	Name	Type	Date	Neume type
1.	Laon 239	Antiphonale missarum	ca. 900–930	Lorraine
2.	Chartres 47	Ant. miss.	end 9th c.	Breton
3.	Saint Gall 359	Cantatorium	early 10th c.	Saint Gall
4.	Laon fragment	Cantatorium	ca. 900	Lorraine
5.	Valenciennes fragment	Ant. miss.	end 9th c.	Breton
6.	Monza excerpt	Ant. miss.	early 10th c.	proto-Nonantolan?
7.	Albi excerpt	Ant. miss. (Processionale)	early 10th c.	proto-Aquitaine

Notes to Table 4.2.
Laon 239 (Laon, Bibl. mun., MS. 239): see CLLA, no. 1350. LeGR, 2.27 ("vers 930"); PalMus, 10 (facs. ed.).
Chartres 47 (destroyed): CLLA, no. 1351; LeGR, 2.43 ("10e s."); Michel Huglo, "On the Origins of the Troper-proser," *Journal of the Plainsong and Medieval Music Society* 2 (1979): 14 ("end of 9th c.") PalMus 11 (facs. ed.).
Saint-Gall 359 (St. Gallen, Stiftsbibliothek, Cod. 359): CLLA, no. 1315; LeGR, 2.132 ("début du 10e s."); *PalMus* ser. 2, vol. 2 (facs. ed.).
Laon fragment (Laon, Bibl. mun., 266): CLLA, no. 1313; Peter Jeffery, "An Early Cantatorium Fragment Related to Ms. Laon 239," in *Scriptorium* 36 (1982): 245–52; Jeffery (1983), 320.
Valenciennes fragment (Valenciennes, Bibl. Mun., 407): CLLA, no. 1304d; LeGR, 2.148; Jeffery (1983), 320.
Monza excerpt (Monza, Duono f-1/101): CLLA, nos. 801, 1250, 1336; Rossana Dalmonte, *Catalogo musicale del Duomo di Monza* (Bologna, 1969), 20–23, Table 7.
Albi excerpt (Albi, Bibl. mun., 44): Huglo, "La tradition musicale aquitaine. Répertoire et notation," *Cahiers de Fanjeaux* 17 (Toulouse, 1982): 253–68; Pl. 5.

fails to consider the plausibilities of survival. With representatives of Mass antiphoners as rare as they are between the eighth and tenth century, there is an obligation to consider what may have failed to survive as well as what did.

Table 4.1 has shown the chief early descendents of the Carolingian Text Archetype. Of the eight items listed there, only three—Rheinau, Bland, and Lucca—go back to the late eighth or early ninth century, thus to the period before we have actual evidence of neumes. The Monza Cantatorium and its Trier-Berlin-Cleveland sister fragments may date from that remote time, or they may (as Bischoff indicates) date only from the second third of the ninth century.[6] As for Compiègne, Senlis, and Corbie, they are of later date, originating at a time when notations are already available. Thus only Rheinau, Bland, and Lucca are surely earlier than our first sources with neumes: only these three survive as representatives of the text antiphoner during the three-quarters of a century from the late eighth through middle ninth century.

It is hazardous to assess the survival rates of Carolingian manuscripts. Yet for text antiphoners of the early period represented by Rheinau, Bland, and Lucca we have indications that they cannot have been altogether rare. A number of documents indicate the obligation of priests to know the content of the Antiphoner.[7] If each fair size church or monastic house had just a single text antiphoner, the number of copies should have mounted into the hundreds during the first century of the Carolingian ecclesiastical reform. At certain houses there were multiple copies. An inventory of 831 for Centula (St. Riquier) lists six volumes of "Antiphonarii," none of which have survived.[8] If we measure the survivors

---

[6] *CLLA*, 500ff.

[7] *a.* An edict, perhaps from the last decade of Charlemagne's reign: "Haec sunt quae iussa sunt discere omnes ecclesiasticos . . . , "it lists the Creeds, Lord's Prayer, contents of the Sacramentary, etc., and then: "9. Cantum Romanorum in nocte. 10. Et ad missa [sic] similiter; 11. Evangelium intellegere, seu lectiones libri comitis (the Gospels and Epistles); 12. Omelias dominicis diebus . . . ; 15. Scribere cartas et epistulas." *Capitularia regum francorum,* Vol. 1. MGH, *Legum sectio 2,* ed., Alfred Boretius (Hanover, 1883), 235.

b. An episcopal (?) edict to priests at a diocesan synod, probably of the early ninth century: "Ammonere vos cupio, fratres et filioli mei, ut ista pauca capitula quae hinc scripta sunt intentius audiatis. 1. Imprimis, ut sacerdos Dei de divina scriptura doctus sit . . . ; 2. Ut totum psalterium memoriter teneat; 3. Ut signaculum [the Creeds] et baptisterium [words and prayers of the baptismal service] memoriter teneat; 4. Ut de canonibus doctus sit et suum penitentiale bene sciat; 5. Ut cantum et compotum [calendar matters]; 6. Ut nullus sacerdos feminas secum habitare permittat . . . ; 7. Ut presbyteri in tabernis bibere no praesumant"; etc. These are fundamental concerns for all priests, prominent among them the memorization of the Psalter and Creed, and the knowledge of chant. MGH 1. 236–37.

c. Such prescriptions are elaborated in a capitulary of Bishop Haito of Basel (807–23) whose sixth paragraph lists the Antiphoner as a necessary volume: "Quae ipsis sacerdotibus necessaria sunt ad discendum, id est sacramentarium, lectionarius, antifonarius, baptisterium, compotus, canon penitentialis, psalterium, homeliae per circulum anni dominicis diebus et singulis festibitatibus aptae. Ex quibus omnibus si unun defuerit, sacerdotis nomen vix en eo constabit." MGH 1. 363.

d. At the Council of Rispach in 798: Paragraph 8. "Episcopus autem unusquisque in civitate sua scolam constituat et sapientem doctorem, qui secundum traditionem Romanorum possit instruere et lectionibus vacare et inde debitum discere, ut per canonicas horas cursus in aecclesia debeat canere unicuique secundum congruum tempus vel dispositas festivitates, qualiter ille cantus adornet aecclesiam Dei et audientes aedificentur." *Concilia,* Vol. 2. MGH, *Legum 3, Concilia aevi karolini,* ed. Albert Werminghoff (Hanover 1906), 199.

[8] Bruno Stäblein, *MMMA.* Vol. 2, *Die Gesänge des altrömische Graduale* (Kassel, 1979), 78*f, Note 381; the note lists further instances.

against the numbers that are apparently lost, the disappearance rate is so high that the extant text antiphoners cannot really be taken as statistical indices. They are accidents, all of which might have disappeared. They may tell us nothing about the original situation.

As for the neumed antiphoners (Table 4.2), they were doubtless fewer in number than the text antiphoners (Table 4.1). The early neumes were too small to be read by choral singers during a service, and they were un-likely to be consulted during performance by ninth-century soloists and choirmasters who still consigned much about the repertory to their mem-ories. In all, there were fewer musicians who used fully neumed proper collections than there were priests who used missals, and even fewer well-heeled individuals would have kept a noted book for the pure pleasure of ownership. The chance of survival was accordingly smaller for the neumed collections than for the text collections whose chances, we have seen, were vanishingly small.

Other factors should have increased the text collections' odds of sur-vival. The preserved descendents of the Carolingian Text Archetype tend to be attractive examples of the book creator's art. Among the Sextuplex manuscripts they range from the simple elegance of Rheinau and Bland to the *purpurei* of Monza and Trier-Berlin-Cleveland (Table 4.1, last col-umn). For the early neumed manuscripts (Table 4.2), the already poor prospect of survival was further dimmed by the fact that even when nicely executed, the pages bearing neumes rarely have the tidy attractiveness of those with text alone. And where a text antiphoner might remain useful indefinitely, requiring little change in order to be kept current, the neumed antiphoners were rendered obsolete by notational innovations of the tenth and eleventh centuries. The emergence of staff lines and clefs meant that new books were substituted, and the older ones with prediastematic neumes had little further purpose. All things considered, it is remarkable how few text antiphoners survive from the later eighth and ninth centuries. It should therefore be no surprise if there are none at all with neumes.

In evaluating the plausibilities of survival, one must also consider the ninth-century neumations of music other than Gregorian chant. As a group, these are earlier than the Gregorian neumations and that has fos-tered the theory that neumes were invented to serve other repertories than the Gregorian. Yet in most instances the survival of such strays is not at-tributable to the music itself but to the nature and content of the host man-uscript. Certain of the miscellaneous early neumations are for Celebrant's chants (Preface, Exultet), lections, etc., where survival is due to the texts, and to host Sacramentaries and Lectionaries that are exceptionally fine.[9]

---

[9] The twenty-one items in David Hiley's "Table of Extant Examples of 9th-Century No-tation" *NGD* 13. 346, *s.v.* "Notation") are the best current inventory of neumatic in-

In other cases, such as the oldest dated neumes, set to the prosula *Psalle modulamina,* or various relics of the Pentecost Greek Mass (missa graeca), the neumed entries are additions to manuscripts whose principal content is not related to the music.[10]

To sum up, the theory of the neumed antiphoners' origin a century after the text antiphoners' may be commended for its cautious reliance on the surviving evidence, but it does not stand up to scrutiny. When closely examined, there is no aspect that appears soundly based. The absence of early noted antiphoners does not validate the late scenario of Corbin, nor does it preclude the early scenario to which I now turn. Speculations have long circulated about the existence of noted recensions going back even as far as Gregory the Great, but no plausible case has yet been made.[11] I offer seven indices of the existence of an early Gregorian neumation, all pointing well back of 900, some pointing back of 800.

The first index of an early date is a matter of paleographic common sense. Around the year 900, when the first substantial witnesses of the noted Gregorian propers appear (see Table 4.2), there are already marked differences in regional ductus: the distinctive neumes of Lorraine, Saint Gall, Brittany, etc. The brilliant work of our generation's Gregorian semiologists, the "école Cardine," has affirmed the long held premise—going back to volumes 2 and 3 of the *Paléographie musicale*—that a common neumatic archetype lies behind the diverse regional manifestations. Dom Cardine calls this the "archétype d'écriture."[12] I prefer a terminological distinction between the Carolingian Neumed Archetype and its neumeless counterpart, the Carolingian Text Archetype. Yet whatever the name, the varieties of ductus ca. 900, all descendents of an authoritative archetypal neumation, render awkward the claim that "the different regional paleographic styles go back to the very beginning of neume notation."[13] It is more likely that a period of development lay between the neumed arche-

---

cunabula; some further possibilities appear in the inventory by Solange Corbin, *Die Neumen* (1977): 21–41, among them the Sélestat Lectionary (Corbin, Table 2), and the neumed Exultet in Arsenal 227 (Corbin, Table 5).

   [10] Hiley, *NGD* 13. 346, 7th, 10th, and 12th items.

   [11] Recent advocates of an 8th century or earlier date have included Higini Anglès "Gregorian Chant," *New Oxford History of Music* (1954). 2: 106–108, arguing for the time of Gregory; and Jacques Froger, "The critical edition of the Roman Gradual by the monks of Solesmes," *JPMMS* 1 (1978); 81–97. Froger correctly, as I see it, dates the archetype: " . . . we aim to restore the Gradual to the state in which it was diffused in the Carolingian Empire from the last quarter of the 8th century" (p. 82), but he attempts no justification of the dating.

   [12] Eugène Cardine "Vue d'ensemble sur le chant grégorien," *EG* 16 (1977): 174.

   [13] Helmut Hucke, "Toward a New Historical View of Gregorian Chant," *JAMS*, 23 (1980): 445.

type and its first preserved descendents. Allowing for paleographic change one can suppose an intervening half century, and perhaps much longer.

A second index of an early Gregorian neumation can be taken from the politics of the Frankish Empire whose subdivisions had begun even before the death of Charlemagne in 814. The most considerable of these came in 843 with the Treaty of Verdun, which formalized the growing split between a French West and German East. Musical consequences are recognizable in the differing states of the East- and West-Frankish sequence repertories. Among the Gregorian neumed propers there are discrepancies reflecting similar causes, but these are small while the agreements are large. Huglo observed that this points to a noted Gregorian archetype before the middle ninth century.[14]

The third index of an early date for the Carolingian neumed archetype is the reception of the Gregorian repertory in south Italy. Charlemagne took over the old kingdom of the Lombards after the capitulation at Pavia in 774, but in practice he was limited to the northern Duchy of Spoleto, and it was only ca. 787 that the southern Duchy of Benevento came under effective Carolingian control. South Italy was unlikely to have received a Frankish-Gregorian transmission before that time.[15] At the later end, Dom Hesbert has placed the arrival of Gregorian chant at Benevento before ca. 808.[16] Some time ago I pointed out that Hesbert's reasoning was sound but his date represented a faulty reading which has to be changed to before ca. 838.[17] A Gregorian musical recension would thus arrive at Benevento between ca. 787 and ca. 838, and since the neumatic details of the Beneventan readings agree with those of northern Europe, this again indicates an archetypal Gregorian recension before the middle ninth century.

The fourth index of an early noted archetype depends on the "missa graeca," the composite of Byzantine, quasi-Byzantine, and Latin musical elements which was evidently assembled for the celebration of some Frankish imperial Pentecost of the late eighth or early ninth century. Charles Atkinson has tentatively proposed the years 827–35 for the compilation.[18] I would prefer to keep it during the last decades of Charlemagne's reign, in particular between ca. 797 and 814.[19] Yet for present purposes either dating will suffice. What matters is that there are some six

---

[14] Michel Huglo, "De monodiska handskrifternas fördelning i två grupper, öst och väst," *Helsingin yliopiston käytännöllisen teologian laitos: Käytännöllisen teologian julkaisuja* (1975); 47–65.

[15] Jules Gay, *L'Italie méridionale et l'empire byzantin.* Bibliothèque des écoles françaises d'Athènes et de Rome, no. 90 (Paris, 1904), 1. 25–48.

[16] Rene-Jean Hesbert, "La tradition Bénéventaine," *PalMus* 14 (1936): 450f.

[17] Kenneth Levy, "The Italian Neophytes' Chants," *JAMS,* 23 (1970): 221, note 100.

[18] Charles Atkinson, "Zur Entstehung und Überlieferung der 'Missa graeca'," *AfMw* 29 (1982): 144f.

dozen manuscripts of the ninth through twelfth centuries with traces of this Pentecost Greek Mass.[20] They represent various regions: France, Germany, Lowlands, and England (by way of France). The exception is Italy, which has at most five sources with Greek chants, none showing any relation to Pentecost, and none originating in the Beneventan zone. It may be that the Frankish-Gregorian tradition that came to Benevento left the north at so late a time that the Pentecost Greek Mass no longer mattered enough for inclusion. Yet the Beneventan transmission occurred before ca. 838. Thus a likelier assumption is that it left the north before the elements of the Pentecost Greek Mass were annexed to the Gradual and Troper, hence at the latest by 827–35, and perhaps during the reign of Charlemagne.

The fifth index comes from the *Musica disciplina* of Aurelian of Réôme, written ca. 850.[21] Lawrence Gushee has demonstrated that Aurelian knew the neumatic notation.[22] Yet to judge from the nature of his musical citations, Aurelian may not have supplied the treatise with noted illustrations. Instead, he may have expected his specialist readers to have neumed antiphoners available for consultation. An indication of this is found in Chapter 10, 27–29, where Aurelian cites an unusual passage in two Responsory verses of the first mode:

> There is in this mode [the First Authentic] a certain phrase (*divisio*) in the Responsories of the Nocturns that I do not remember finding elsewhere in the whole repertory (*latitudinem*) of the Responsory verses, except only in the verses of these two Responsories: Resp. *Domine, ne in ira tua;* Verse, *Timor et tremor;* and Resp. *Peccantem me cotidie;* Verse, *Deus in nomine*

---

[19] Levy, "The Byzantine Sanctus and its Modal Tradition in East and West," *Annales musicologiques* 6 (1963): 36.

[20] Atkinson (1982): 120–25, provides an exhaustive inventory.

[21] *Aureliani reomensis musica disciplina*, ed. Lawrence Gushee, CSM 21 (American Institute of Musicology, 1975).

[22] Lawrence L. Gushee, "The *Musica disciplina* of Aurelian of Réôme. (Ph.D. diss., Yale University, 1963) 215: ". . .it is precisely here that we meet with phrases positively indicating the use of musical notation. For instance, we cannot take the phrase 'by the eye' *(oculo)* in the following sentence . . . as metaphorical: "' . . . since, indeed, there are some tones that have, in their inflection, very nearly the same arrangement of their verses, the tenor of the one tone will change to the other, unless they are surveyed *by the eye* [Gushee's italics] with a cautious inspection or examination at the middle or the end. This the diligent singer can easily recognize in these two tones, namely, the first plagal and the fourth plagal.'" " . . . quoniam quidem sunt nonnulli toni qui prope uno eodemque modo ordine versuum in suamet retinent inflexione, et nisi aut in medio aut in fine provida inspectione aut perspicatione antea circumvallentur oculo, unius toni tenor in alterius permutabitur. Quod studiosus cantor in his duobus tonis, videlicet plagis proti et plagis tetrardi otius valet agnoscere." I would add that in various instances Aurelian makes detailed melodic comparisons, singling out individual syllables of particular chants of the Gregorian repertory with such directions as "on the 15th syllable of . . . " (CSM 21, 119). This too indicates neumations.

tuo. Which verses, although they could have the same arrangement as the others, nevertheless, because this remained so among the ancients, so also must it remain among us, in their memory.[23]

The survey of the verse repertory that Aurelian describes— "quam non uspiam memini me in latitudinem totius responsoriorum versibus reperisse"—is unlikely to have been a scroll through a memory bank, but rather a point to point comparison of neumed chants in a reference antiphoner. When Aurelian opts to preserve the musical anomaly because it was used "among the ancients" ("apud antiquos ita mansit"), he is likely to have found the former tradition in a noted antiphoner.

Then in Chapter 13, the reader is told of a musical passage in two Gregorian Gradual verses that is "not found elsewhere in the prolixity of the whole Antiphonale" ("memini me non alicubi reperisse in prolixitate totius antiphonarii").[24] One must again conclude that Aurelian is not referring to a singer's well-stocked memory but to the prolixity of a fully noted Mass antiphoner.

My sixth index of the early date comes from the famous capitulary, or *Admonitio generalis,* addressed by Charlemagne to the Frankish clergy on 23 March 789, setting forth the guidelines of his ecclesiastical reforms. In its eightieth chapter there is the injunction to all clergy ("omni clero") that they fully learn the Roman chant which his father Pepin ordered substituted for the Gallican chant.[25] In its seventy-second chapter, addressed to "priests" ("sacerdotibus"), there is the injunction,

> . . .that there be schools for teaching boys to read. Be sure to emend carefully in every monastery and bishop's house the psalms [*psalmos*], notes [*notas*], chants [*cantus*], calendar material [*computus*], grammar(s) [*grammaticam*], and the Epistles and Gospels [*libros catholicos*]. For often enough

---

[23] "Est in hoc tono quaedam divisio in nocturnalibus responsoriis quam non uspiam memini me in latitudine totius responsoriorum versibus repperisse, nisi solummodo in versibus istorum duorum responsorium. Hi autem sunt: Resp. Domine, ne in ira tua; V. Timor et tremor, et item: Resp. Peccantem me cotidie; V. Deus in nomine tuo, qui, cum ordinem possidere queant ceterorum, tamen [quia] apud antiquos ita mansit, apud nos quoque ob eorum memoriam necesse est permanere." *CSM* 21, 88–89. I cannot say how rare this phrase is among the First Mode Responsory verses, but the two verses end identically in the readings of the Worcester Antiphoner *PalMus* 12 [1922–25] 60, 137), suggesting that the chants known to Aurelian in 850 were like the ones we know.

[24] *CSM* 21, 99. I am indebted to Professor Gushee for confirming this reading of the Valenciennes manuscript. Aurelian here cites identical verse endings of the Graduals *Tollite portas* and *Haec dies;* our later neumed traditions (*GT*, 25 and 212) once more indicate that he is talking about the chants as we know them.

[25] "Ut cantum Romanum pleniter discant, et ordinabiliter per nocturnale vel gradale officium peragatur, secundum quod beatae memoriae genitor noster Pippinus rex decertavit ut fieret quando Gallicanum tulit ob unanimitatem apostolicae sedis et sanctae Dei aeclesiae pacificam concordiam." *MGH*, ed. Alfred Boretius, 1. 61.

there are those who want to call upon God well, but because of poor texts [*inemendatos libros*] they do it poorly."[26]

The passage is often cited as a possible indication of neumes, though as yet without firm claim.[27] Within my present historical framework, Charlemagne's "notas" may perhaps be taken at face value. At issue are both the word *notas* and its context: *psalmos, notas, cantus, computus, grammaticam,* and *libros catholicos.* These are texts to be scrupulously emended for ecclesiastical establishments. We await adequate guides to Merovingian-Carolingian usage, but a sifting of available glossaries has produced no support for the view that Charlemagne's "notas" refers to notaries' shorthand signs (Tironian notes) or schoolboys' jottings about texts under study, rather than to the neumes of plainchant—which is what the context suggests: " . . . *psalmos, notas, cantus* . . . "[28]

My seventh index of an early date for the Carolingian Neumed Archetype points again to 800 and the reign of Charlemagne. It depends in part on eleventh-century evidence, hence it cannot, any more than the previous indices, lead to firm conclusions about an eighth-century Gregorian neumation. Yet it comes as close to proof as I think anything can.

Despite Charlemagne's characterization of his father's thoroughness in suppressing the old Gallican chant,[29] it appears that the process by which Gregorian chant supplanted Gallican chant in the Frankish homeland was not one of outright exchange of an existing liturgical-musical corpus for a wholly different one. Only the final stages can be traced in surviving documents, but from the amount of apparently Gallican material that

---

[26] Et ut scolae legentium puerorum fiant. Psalmos, notas, cantus, compotum, grammaticam per singula monasteria vel episcopia et libros catholicos bene emendate; quia saepe, dum bene aliqui Deum rogare cupiunt, sed per inemendatos libros male rogant. *MGH*, 1. 60.

[27] *NGD* 6. 344b, s.v. "Notation".

[28] Franz Blatt's *Novum Glossarium mediae latinitatis* (Copenhagen, 1957–present), the best compilation, begins only with the ninth century; its extensive entries under *neuma* (pp. 1231–34) and *nota* (pp. 1391–96), assembled by Anne-Marie Bautier-Regnier, are excerpted in her "A propos des sens de *neuma* et de *nota* en latin médieval," *Revue belge de musicologie* 18 (1964): 1–9. The comprehensive *Mittellateinisches Wörterbuch* (1959ff) of the Bavarian and Berlin Academies does not reach this portion of the alphabet. I have consulted Maigne d'Arnis, *Lexicon manuale* (Paris, 1860); Forcellini *et al., Totius latinitatis lexicon,* (Padova, 1864–98); Diefenbach, *Novum glossarium* (Frankfurt, 1867); Du Cange-Favre, *Glossarium mediae et infimae latinitatis* (Niort, 1883–87); A. Bartal, *Glossarium mediae et infimiae latinitatis regni hungariae* (Leipzig, 1901); F. Arnaldi, *Latinitatis italicae medii aevii* (Brussels, 1939); A. Souter, *A Glossary of Later Latin to 600 A.D.* (Oxford, 1949); R. E. Latham, *Revised Medieval and Latin Word List from British and Irish Sources* (Oxford, 1965); J. F. Niermeyer, *Mediae latinitatis lexicon minus* (Leiden, 1976); and P. G. W. Glare, *Oxford Latin Dictionary* (1982).

[29] . . . *quod beatae memoriae genitor noster Pippinus rex decertavit ut fieret quando Gallicanum tulit . . . ; MGH* 1. 61.

lingers in the Sextuplex and other early chant sources, it would seem there were preliminary editions that, for a while, perpetuated locally esteemed Gallican matter that later became obsolete. In a recent article, I outlined one such class of Gallican survivals: nonpsalmic Offertories, whose texts are centonate librettos, composed of fragments drawn from biblical or postbiblical narrative rather than the verbatim Psalter. Certain Offertories of this class (among them, *Sanctificavit, Erit hic vobis, Oravi Deum, Precatus est Moyses,* and *Vir erat*) found permanent places in the Frankish-Gregorian canon, assigned to later and lesser calendar stations, such as the final Sundays after Pentecost, or the formerly aliturgical Thursdays in Lent; eventually they were absorbed even into the Urban Roman liturgy. For others, there was a briefer regional or local survival. Some of these Gallican apocrypha, attached to the fringes of Gregorian traditions, open extraordinary perspectives on the early history of the rite.[30]

One such chant is the Pentecost Offertory, *Factus est repente.* As with other Offertories of this type, its text is a nonpsalmic libretto, centonized from passages in the second chapter of Acts. The chant has already served as the centerpiece of a discussion by Dom Hesbert, who concluded that it was both old and Roman.[31] If I return to *Factus est repente* now, it is not because I view it as Gallican rather than Roman in origin, but because evidence that was unknown to Hesbert gives it a potential role in the history of the neumed archetype.

Hesbert knew *Factus est repente* in two recensions, one northern European, the other Italo-Beneventan. In the Frankish north, its presumable homeland, he found it only in the Blandiniensis, one of the two oldest unneumed sources of the Gregorian Antiphonale missarum (Table 4.1, No. 2), a codex for which there is every indication of late eighth or early ninth century origin. *Factus* appears in Bland as an alternative to the standard Gregorian Pentecost Offertory, *Confirma hoc Deus,* whose psalmic text it follows:

> OFF. Confirma hoc Deus quod operatus es in nobis. VERSE 1. Cantate Domino psalmum dicite nomini ejus. VERSE 2. In aecclesiis benedicite Domino Deum de fontibus Israhel. VERSE 3. Regna terre cantate Deo.
>
> ITEM OFF. Factus est repente de caelo sonus tamquam advenientis in spiritu vehementis & replevit totam domum hubi erant sedentes alleluia. VERSE 1. Et repleti sunt omnes Spiritu Sancto loquentes magnalia Dei alleluia alleluia.[32]

---

[30] Kenneth Levy, "Toledo, Rome, and the Legacy of Gaul," *EMH* 4 (1984): 49–99; reprinted here as Chapter 3.

[31] René-Jean Hesbert, "Un antique offertoire de la Pentecôte: 'Factus est repente,'" *Organicae voces: Festschrift Joseph Smits van Waesberghe* (Amsterdam, 1963), 59–69.

[32] Hesbert, *AMS,* 124.

Among the Sextuplex traditions, then, *Factus est repente* has the earliest and narrowest of circulations. It seems already to be obsolescent by ca. 800. For the centuries that followed, Hesbert's search of more than six hundred Graduals and Missals uncovered no further sources from northern Europe. But it did turn up seven from Italy, all dating from the eleventh and twelfth centuries. Six of these are from the Beneventan zone and the seventh is from the Abruzzi, abutting the northern limit of the Beneventan zone. The Offertory refrain in these Italian versions has the same text as Bland; but the verse has an ampler beginning and an altered conclusion:

> ITALIAN VERSE. Et apparuerunt Apostoli dispertitae linguae tamquam ignis, seditque supra singulos eorum; et repleti sunt omnes Spiritu Sancto, et coeperunt loqui magnalia Dei. Alleluia.
>
> BLAND VERSE. Et repleti sunt omnes Spiritu Sancto loquentes magnalia Dei alleluia alleluia.

The six Beneventan versions are noted and their agreements indicate a common neumed source. Hesbert's transcription of the Beneventan *Factus est repente*, an "antique composition . . . qui, bien exécutée devait être fort belle," is based upon the ensemble of Beneventan readings seen in Example 4.1.[33]

There are two main differences between the northern text tradition of Bland and the composite southern tradition of Benevento and the Abruzzi (Ex. 4.1) One is the discrepancy in the verse texts, to which I will return. The other is the liturgical assignment. Bland prescribes *Factus est repente* as an alternate for Pentecost Sunday, appended to the standard Gregorian-Roman *Confirma hoc Deus,* while the Italian sources have *Factus* only at Thursday in Pentecost week. Hesbert found a satisfactory explanation: *Factus* was once a fixture on Pentecost Sunday but was obliged to give way to the newer Gregorian provision of *Confirma hoc;* it was preserved in the Beneventan-Abruzzese tradition by transfer to a neighboring occasion that lacked proper chants (Pentecost Thursday long remained aliturgical).[34]

Having reclaimed *Factus* to this extent, Hesbert was obliged to leave it, the available documents opening no further avenues. His conclusion that it was "An Old Offertory for Pentecost" will stand. But his supposition that it was of Roman origin should have been suspect even in 1963, when there were indications that the Gregorian recensions with which *Factus est repente* circulated were promulgated in the Frankish

---

[33] Hesbert (1963), 62–63.

[34] Hesbert (1963), 68f; it is an application of the "loi des doublets" described by Michel Huglo, *Les tonaires* (Paris, 1971), 296.

Example 4.1. Offertory, *Factus est repente*
(Beneventan versions, transcr. Hesbert)

north.[35] The chant has no analogue in the Old Roman musical repertory.[36] The class of nonpsalmic, centonate libretto Offertories that it represents now appears to be of Gallican origin.[37]

[35] Helmut Hucke, "Die Einführung des gregorianische Gesanges im Frankenreich,"
Römische Quartalschrift 44 (1954): 172–87; Michel Huglo, "Le chant 'vieux-romain': liste
des manuscrits et témoins indirects," *Sacris erudiri* 6 (1954): 96–123; Willi Apel, "The Central Problem of Gregorian Chant," *JAMS* 9 (1956): 118–27; Joseph Gajard, "'Vieux-romain' et 'Grégorien,'" *EG* 3 (1959): 7ff.

[36] Paul F. Cutter, *The Musical Sources of the Old-Roman Mass.* Musical Studies and Documents 36 (American Institute of Musicology, 1979).

[37] Levy (1984), here Chapter 3.

Despite the thoroughness of Hesbert's search, two important witnesses of *Factus est repente* eluded him. One was a noted version from the Beneventan zone, the earliest yet discovered, datable around the middle eleventh century. The other was a noted version from the Frankish homeland, datable around 1000, hence earlier than any Beneventan neumation, and a unique witness of the northern melodic practice. Singly and together, they expand the evidence so considerably that I would now venture the following four propositions:

> 1. that the Gallo-Gregorian Offertory *Factus est repente* reached south Italy from the Frankish north by ca. 800;
> 2. that *Factus* arrived as a component in a full Gregorian musical recension;
> 3. that the music of *Factus* made its journey not in an oral transmission, but fully neumed;
> 4. that the whole Gregorian recension with which *Factus* came to Italy ca.800 was itself fully neumed.

Hesbert could have encountered the new Beneventan witness only with difficulty since it was in an American collection whose resources were not included in the Solesmes documentation upon which he relied.[38] MS W. 6 of the Walters Art Gallery in Baltimore is a *missale plenum* of the middle eleventh century, written for Canosa, near Monte Gargano, in the southeast corner of the Italian peninsula. The text is executed in the Bari type of Beneventan script, and is embellished with handsome zoomorphic initials. Small in outer dimensions (19 × 12 cm.), the manuscript contains the prayers, lections, and chants for the principal feasts of the Temporale and Sanctorale, but it lacks the bulky provisions for the numbered Sundays and seasonal weekdays. It may have served a prosperous cleric for portable use.[39]

The version of *Factus* in the Walters Missal makes three important contributions to our dossier. First, it is the only Beneventan version in staffless neumes, hence the earliest witness of the Italian recension (see Fig. 4.1). Second, it is assigned, not as in all other Beneventan manuscripts, to Pentecost Thursday, but to Pentecost Sunday itself. This appearance in the southeastern Beneventan zone, which tends to be more conservative than the western regions, confirms the Offertory's archaic assignment to Pentecost, which otherwise is found only in the eighth-ninth century Blandiniensis. Third, the Canosa missal supplies this confirmation in most striking fashion, for it does not prescribe *Factus est repente* merely as an alternative to the standard Gregorian *Confirma hoc* (which is the situation already in *Bland*); *Factus* stands here as the sole Offertory for Pentecost.

---

[38] It was listed by Huglo (1971): 194, note 2.

[39] Full edition and commentary by Sieghild Rehle, *Missale beneventanum von Canosa* Textus patristici et liturgici, Fasc. 9 (Regensburg, 1972).

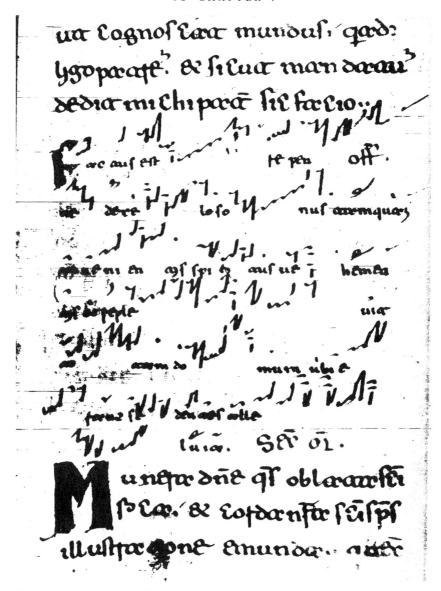

Figure 4.1. Canosa Missal (f. 152)

These three points are the basis of my first proposition—that *Factus est repente* reached South Italy ca. 800. In brief, the Canosa Missal, with *Factus* as its sole Pentecost Offertory, would represent an earlier stage of the Gregorian tradition than any other known: a stage before the psalmic Offertory *Confirma hoc* became fixed at Pentecost, hence a stage even before Bland, where *Confirma hoc* is installed as the Pentecost Offertory and the nonpsalmic *Factus est repente* is relegated to alternate status. Bland, as we know, dates from ca. 800.

My second proposition is that the full Gregorian repertory reached Italy at the same time as *Factus est repente*. It seems doubtful that this obsolescent Gallican Offertory journeyed to Italy in an isolated transmission of an individual chant; more likely it came installed as the Pentecost Offertory in a full Gregorian Mass antiphoner. Thus whatever can be said about the early date of *Factus* in the Canosa Missal should apply as well to the whole transmission with which it came. We shall soon see decisive support for this.

My other new witness of *Factus est repente* is a unique northern neumation, found in the Gradual Troper of Prüm, Paris, lat. 9448, copied around 1000 (see Fig. 4.2). This manuscript has long been recognized as one of the best sources of the Gradual and Troper, yet in recent inventories it has curiously been slighted. It was omitted from the Solesmes census of Graduals and plenary Missals for the critical edition of the Roman Gradual, evidently because it was classed as a Troper.[40] It was omitted from Husmann's census of Tropers for opposite reasons.[41] Nevertheless Paris 9448 was described by Gautier in 1886 and it has often been used since.[42] The failure of its neumation for *Factus est repente* to draw Hesbert's attention must be attributed to a simple oversight.

The Benedictine abbey at Prüm was located just forty-five miles south of Charlemagne's birthplace and capital at Aachen. Founded in 710, it enjoyed many benefices and visits from Frankish kings and it remained prominent for centuries. During the 890s its abbot was Regino, whose writings are among the era's most informative on music theory; and it was from Prüm in 1008 that the monk Bernhard, himself a commentator on liturgy and music, was called to the abbacy of Reichenau by the Emperor Henry II. The abbey's cultural pretensions around 1000 can be gauged from this "magnifique manuscrit" (Gautier), with splendid full page illuminations embellishing a text that is rich in liturgical and musical archaisms.

Among the latter is its Offertory *Factus est repente*. Since Prüm represents the same northern region as Bland, it is no surprise to discover Bland's pro-

---

[40] *Le Graduel Romain, Édition critique.* Vol. 2, Les sources (Solesmes, [1957]).

[41] Heinrich Husmann, *Tropen-und Sequenzenhandschriften.* Ser. B, vol. 5: 1 of *Répertoire international des sources musicales.* (Munich, 1964), 110 (". . .dem berühmten Prümer Graduale").

[42] Léon Gautier, *Histoire de la poésie liturgique au moyen age: Les Tropes.* (Paris, 1886), 1:123. Margaretha Rossholm Lagerlöf, "A Book of Songs Placed upon the Altar of the Saviour Giving Praise to the Virgin Mary and Homage to the Emperor," G. Iversen, ed., Research on Tropes, Konferenser 8. Kungl. Vitterhets Historie och Antikvitets Akademien (Stockholm, 1983), 125–78, is an amply illustrated art historical study.

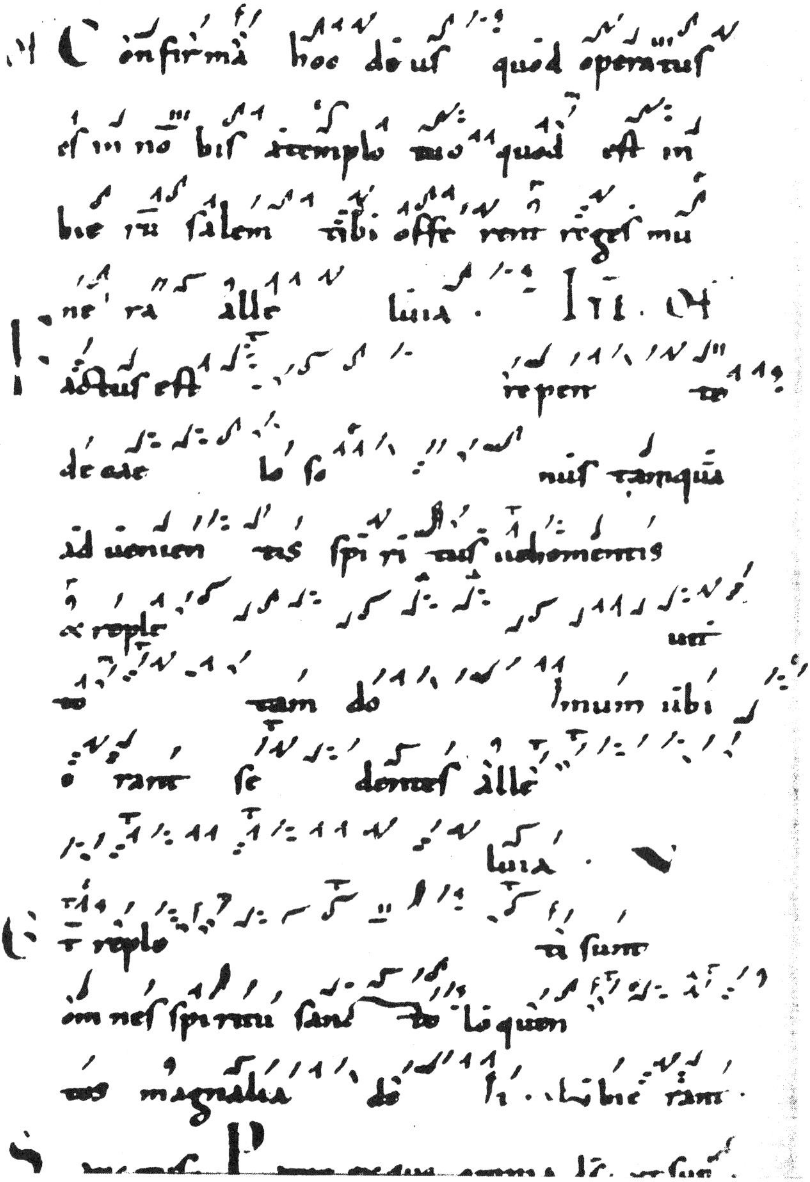

Figure 4.2. Prüm Gradual-Troper (f. 51)

visions reproduced. Prüm's Pentecost Offertory is the standard Gregorian *Confirma hoc* without verses. Immediately following, and again designated as an alternate ("Item Of[f]"), there is the apocryphal *Factus est repente* with verse *Et repleti sunt omnes,* both texts just as in Bland. Prüm also has *Factus* cued at the Pentecost Octave, another mark of its former prominence.

At the outset, Prüm answers an important question. I have spoken of the apocryphon *Factus est repente* as a Frankish import to Benevento, basing this on the Gallican style of its nonpsalmic, centonate libretto text. Yet until now only the Italian melodic reading has been known, and there was no way of telling whether the material that traveled south from Gaul to Italy included music as well as text, or whether the melody in the Beneventan sources was simply a local and later composition. The Prüm manuscript sets doubt to rest. A comparison of its neumation (Fig. 4.2) with that of Canosa (Fig. 4.1), or with Hesbert's generic Beneventan transcription (Ex. 4.1), shows that for the refrain both the text and music are the same.

I will return to this melody and subject its northern and southern readings to close scrutiny. Before that, however, one further observation about my proposed pre-Bland or early transmission of *Factus* to Benevento. Inasmuch as the oldest Italian witness (the Canosa missal) dates from the eleventh century, there can be no assurance that the music did not come south during the later ninth, tenth, or early eleventh century. Yet in the Frankish north, the Gallican-style *Factus est repente* had reached obsolescence as the Pentecost Offertory by ca. 800; it barely survived among the Sextuplex sources, with only Bland transmitting it as a hanger-on; Prüm in its way confirms the narrowness of northern survival by mirroring the provisions of Bland. Thus there were few local traditions using *Factus est repente* even ca. 800, and presumably still fewer kept on using it through the ninth and tenth centuries. One of those was the source for Benevento, whose verse differs from that of Bland-Prüm. That transmission is likelier to have reached Benevento in the late eighth or early ninth century (the time of Bland or earlier), when the repertory of Offertory refrains and verses was richer in Gallican holdovers, rather than later, when the entrenchment of the standard Gregorian canon had narrowed the options. Furthermore, if one supposes there was a late (ninth to eleventh century) transmission of *Factus* to Benevento, one must explain why the standard Offertory *Confirma hoc* should have been disregarded at a time when there was no longer an apparent liturgical warrant for any other Pentecost Offertory than that same *Confirma hoc.* Thus a late transmission of *Factus* to Benevento remains possible, but less likely than an early transmission, at a time before Bland, when *Factus* would still flourish as a Pentecost Offertory in the Gallo-Frankish north.

My third proposition is that when the music of the *Factus* refrain reached Benevento ca. 800, it arrived not in an oral transmission, but neumed. Under normal conditions of evidence there should be no way for documents of the eleventh century to tell us how singers of the eighth-ninth century practiced their craft, no way to assure us that they relied on neumations rather than fashioning their chants through the exercise of memory and improvisational skills. With *Factus,* an extraordinary constellation of evidence points to a noted tradition ca. 800. Now let me return to my earlier statement that the Prüm and Beneventan melodies for the Offertory refrain are the same, and inquire how far this sameness extends. An answer can be taken from Figure 4.3, where the melisma "et replevit" of the refrain is shown in the readings of Prüm (Fig. 4.3a), Benevento 6.34 (Fig. 4.3c), Benevento 6.39 (Fig. 4.3d), and Hesbert's composite Beneventan transcription (Fig. 4.3b). The neumations are close enough to indicate a common written source. There are agreements of pitch groupings into compound neumes. There is the uncommon neume, *pes stratus* (a podatus plus oriscus), which is considered a symptom of a Gallican or imported chant.[43] This appears three times in the Prüm version of the melisma; in Benevento 6.34 and 6.39, each of the three instances is resolved as a podatus plus simplex, replacing the final oriscus with punctum shapes; but in the earlier Canosa missal (which abbreviates its "et replevit" melisma, retaining only the beginning and end; see Fig. 4.1), the first of the pes stratus is nevertheless translated with an oriscus; and vestiges of an oriscus in other Beneventan neumations are reflected in Hesbert's transcription. These agreements in detail indicate that Prüm and Benevento descend from the same noted formulation. Their common neumatic origin offers support for my third proposition, that the melody of *Factus* arrived in Italy neumed.

There is further support for this in my fourth proposition, that the melody of *Factus* reached Benevento in a full Gregorian neumed recension. I have already suggested that *Factus* would not have journeyed from the north as an isolated chant, but rather as part of a complete repertory. Thanks to a sharp-eyed observation by Dom Hesbert, this can be given solidity and extended to show that the transmission entailed the use of neumes.

Hesbert's analysis of his newly restored Pentecost Offertory disclosed a melody that was almost entirely independent of the rest of the Gregorian repertory. But at one small passage in the refrain, at the word 'repente,' Hesbert identified the musical fabric of *Factus est repente* with that of the Gre-

---

[43] Eugène Cardine, "Semiologie grégorienne," *EG* 11 (1970): 131; However the pes stratus, in addition to its appearances in Gallican chants and Frankish sequences (see Michel Huglo, "Römisch-fränkische Liturgie," Karl-Gustav Fellerer, *Geschichte der katholischen Kirchenmusik* Vol. 1 ([Kassel, 1972], 228 and 238), is common enough in early English and central Italian collections of the Gregorian propers. In a future paper I will consider the possibility that this neume was applied to the full Gregorian repertory in early west Frankish traditions.

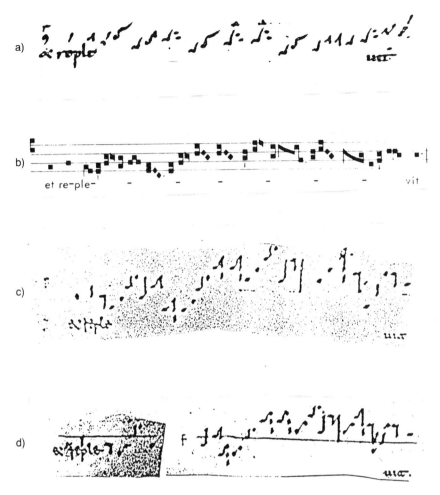

Figure 4.3. Melisma "et replevit" a) Prüm; b) transcription; c) Benevento 6.34; d) Benevento 6.39

gorian Offertory *Angelus Domini* at the words *de celo*.[44] The parallel is shown in Fig. 4.4.[45] The situation is not unusual: a centonate formula appearing in different contexts of text and music and at points far removed in the Gregorian Mass book. There is an underlying logic, since the two Offertories are based on nonpsalmic, centonate libretto texts (*Angelus Domini* draws on Matthew 28), and both represent the G-plagal mode of this Gal-

[44] Hesbert (1963): 64.

[45] Fig. 4.4a: *Graduale sacrosanctae romanae ecclesiae* no. 696 (Paris, Tournai, Rome, 1952), 246. Fig. 4.4b: see Fig. 4.1, above.

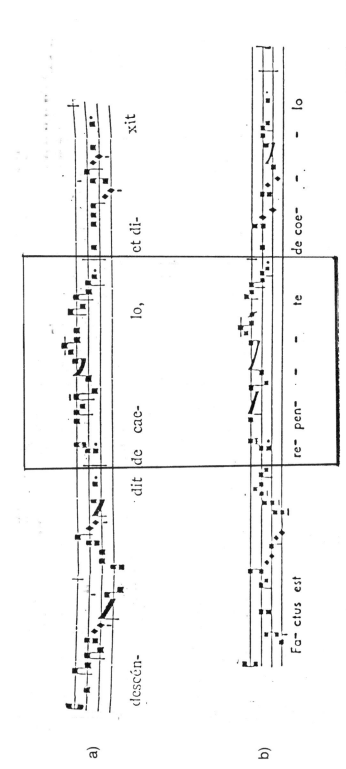

Figure 4.4. Centonate contexts of "de celo" and "repente"

lican liturgical-historical type. However, there is a significant difference. Where *Factus est repente* is an apocryphon of restricted preservation, *Angelus Domini* found a regular place in the Gregorian canon; it appears in five of the Sextuplex manuscripts, assigned to Holy Saturday, Easter Monday, and the Easter Octave;[46] it settled as the standard Gregorian Offertory for Easter Monday. This carries an uncommon historical potential. For if *Factus* and *Angelus* should be closely related in the neumation of their centonate "de celo/repente" formula, then what we have learned about the early history of *Factus est repente* should apply as well to the history of *Angelus Domini*. And what we learn about the neumation of *Angelus* should in turn apply to the full Gregorian recension with which it circulated.

Figure 4.5 compares the neumation of our two melismas: four selected regional neumations of the "de celo" melisma in Figure 4.5a (the left hand column), and the two regional neumations of the "repente" melisma in Figure 4.5b (the right hand column).[47] In Figure 4.5a[1] ("de caelo") the readings of Lorraine and Saint Gall accompany the square-note version of the *Editio vaticana* as reproduced in the *Graduale Triplex*. To judge from the quilisma in the opening figure, from the oriscus as penultimate pitch, and from the general agreements in neumatic disposition and melodic detail, it appears that Lorraine and Saint Gall descend from the same written archetype. But so does Prüm (Fig. 4.5a[2]), whose neumation is close to that of Saint Gall, as well as the twelfth-century south Italian neumations of Benevento 6.34 (Fig. 4.5a[3]) and its eleventh-century forerunner, Benevento 6.33 (Fig. 4.5a[4]). In 6.34 a scandicus is substituted for the ornamental opening quilisma figure of Lorraine, Saint Gall, and Prüm; but the quilisma survives in Benevento 6.33. Thus there is a common written source behind the neumations of *Angelus Domini* in tenth-eleventh century traditions of the Frankish north and Benevento. As for the melisma "repente" of the Offertory *Factus est*, a comparison of the surviving neumations (Prüm and Benevento) in Figure 4.5b confirms what Figure 4.3 leads us to expect: that behind these two recensions there is also a common neumation.

Do the archetypal neumations for these two melismas themselves turn out to be the same? Looking first at the readings of Prüm, the neumations of "de celo" (Fig. 4.5a[2]) and "repente" (Fig. 4.5b[2]) are substantially identical. If minor variants between the Prüm neumations leave doubt about their underlying identity, they are removed by the readings of Benevento, for in

[46] *AMS*, nos. 79b, 81a, 87. In light of its paschal assignments and the concordance of its libretto text with a musically related Offertory of the Milanese rite for Easter Sunday (*Antiphonale missarum mediolanensis* [Rome, 1935]: 210), *Angelus Domini* may descend from a Gallican Easter Offertory, just as *Factus* would from a Gallican Pentecost Offertory.

[47] Fig. 4.5a[1]: *Graduale triplex* (Solesmes, 1979), 218; 4.5a[2]: Paris 9448, 36; 4.5a[3]: Benevento 6.34, 132; 4.5a[4]: Benevento 6.33, 84. Fig. 4.5b[1]: Hesbert (Ex. 4.1); 4.5b[2]: Paris 9448, 51 (Fig. 4.2); 4.5b[3]: Benevento 6.34, 192; 4.5b[4]: Baltimore, Walters 6, 152 (Fig. 4.1).

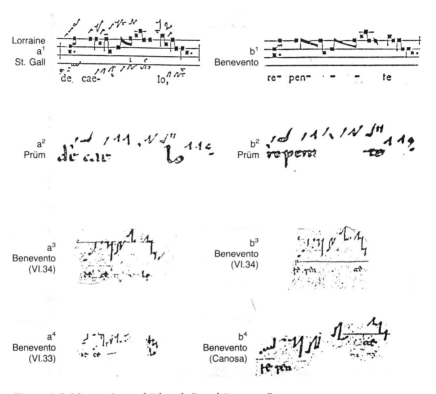

Figure 4.5. Neumations of "de celo" and "repente"

Benevento 6.34, 6.33, and the Canosa Missal (Figs. 4.5a³, 4.5b³, 4.5a⁴, 4.5b⁴), the neumations of "de celo" and "repente" are precisely the same.

That being the case, my fourth proposition receives substantial support. There is no good way to explain the exact neumatic correspondence in Prüm and Benevento of two contextually unrelated melismas occupying isolated corners of the Gregorian Mass book other than by supposing that what brought their two Offertories (*Angelus Domini* and *Factus est repente*) from the Frankish north to southern Italy was a precisely neumed, editorially homogenized recension of the full Gregorian repertory: in short, a neumed archetype whose existence can now be placed with some assurance around the year 800.

My aim has been double: to give greater substance to the concept of the Carolingian neumed archetype of Gregorian chant and to make a hundred year adjustment in its date, setting it back from ca. 900, where it has settled in recent opinion, to shortly before 800, in the middle of Charlemagne's reign. In my view, the neumatic notation is likely to have been employed during the later eighth century in effecting the changeover from Gallican to Gregorian musical repertories and the authoritative neumation of the Gregorian propers, whose descendents we know in the *Editio vaticana*, would be a fruit of Charlemagne's Carolingian renaissance. I have no firm proofs. Short of a dated early neumation or a dated description of early neumatic practice, it is difficult to imagine what form such proof could take. Instead, I have a variety of indices which point to the middle ninth and late eighth centuries as times when the noted Gregorian edition existed. Each index has some shortcoming. Concerning the varieties of neumatic ductus ca. 900: I cannot prove that the regional neumations began in a common ductus and then evolved differently, but that is likelier than for them to have differed from the start.[48] Concerning the divisions of the Empire during the earlier ninth century, the arrival of Gregorian chant at Benevento before 838, and the compilation of the *missa graeca* during the last decades of Charlemagne's reign: neither the specific dates nor the connections with the Gregorian repertory are firm. Concerning the discussions by Aurelian of Réôme (ca. 850) and the reference to "notas" in Charlemagne's *Admonitio generalis* (789): the odds are that these describe neumed proper collections, but neither instance is conclusive. As for my final index, the apocryphal, Gallican Pentecost Offertory, *Factus est repente* and its centonate relationship with the Paschal Offertory *Angelus Domini*: this should remove many doubts concerning the early circulation of the Carolingian Neumed Archetype, yet the possibility remains that Benevento received its melody for *Factus est repente* after the date, by ca. 800, which the early obsolescence of the *Factus* Offertory has led me to infer. Thus each of my indices has weaknesses; yet each also has strengths. Taken together, they make a considerable case for the neumed archetype, the ancestor of our later Gregorian recensions, as a product of the same fertile decades around the turn of the ninth century that saw the revised Carolingian editions of the sacramentary, homiliary, lectionaries, tonary, etc.[49]

---

[48] I will consider certain merits of the "common beginnings" theory in "On the Origin of Neumes," Chapter 5.

[49] There is no adequate current survey. *Cf.* Cyrille Vogel, "La reforme liturgique sous Charlemagne," *Karl der Grosse: Lebenswerk und Nachleben* (Düsseldorf, 1965): 2. 217–32; Vogel, *La reforme cultuelle sous Pépin le Bref et sous Charlemagne* (Graz, 1965); Erna Patzelt, *Die karolingische Renaissance* (Graz, 1965). For the Sacramentary, the situation is amply covered in the editions of the Gregorian and Gellone sacramentaries by Jean Deshusses: *Le sacramentaire grégorien* 2 vols., Spicilegium friburgense: (1971 and 1979); *Liber sacramentorum gellonensis* (2 vols., Corpus christianorum, Series latina, 159, 159A (Tournai, 1981). For the Tonary, we have the masterful *Les Tonaires* (Paris, 1971) of Michel Huglo; also Walther Lipphardt, *Der karolingische Tonar von Metz* (Münster, Westfallen, 1965).

I have gone to some length in this exercise because the challenge is more than one of marshalling arguments for a difficult proof. The consequences go beyond a mere century's revision in a medieval date. The new historical perspectives that emerge from my revised chronology bear on three central issues in Gregorian chant. Concerning the origin of neume species, my framework offers musical paleographers a sounder basis for projecting the pre-history of tenth-eleventh century neume species than they have had before. Concerning the interrelations of oral and written practice, if my case for the Gregorian propers being crystallized in neumes ca. 800 is correct, then various assertions about the effects of oral and improvisational techniques on Gregorian melodies during the ninth through eleventh centuries will need fundamental review.[50] Concerning the relationship between the Old Roman and Frankish musical repertories, if my claim holds that the neumes were employed in the process of shaping the Gregorian recension during the later eighth century, then it may be asked whether some of the musical content of the *antefonarios romanos,* known to the compiler of Bland ca. 800, was not at that time cast in neumatic form. That is, how much of the Gregorian musical substance that advocates of the *frankische Überlieferung* have been explaining as an essentially northern stylistic overlay actually represents the Frankish melodic footprint? May the bulk of the Gregorian repertory not be attributable instead to large-scale appropriations of Roman melodies, with but minor northern retouchings and supplementations, the latter chiefly among the Alleluias and Offertories?[51] On each of these issues—the early history of neumes, the symbiosis of oral and written practice, and the genesis of the Old Roman and Gregorian melodies—much remains to be said. I will return to them in further chapters devoted to the emergence of Gregorian chant.

---

[50] Leo Treitler, "Homer and Gregory: The Transmission of Epic Poetry and Plainchant," *The Musical Quarterly* 60 (1974), 333–72; Helmut Hucke, "Toward a New Historical View of Gregorian Chant," *JAMS* 33 (1980), 437–67; Leo Treitler, "Oral, Written, and Literate Process in the Transmission of Medieval Music," *Speculum* 56 (1981), 471–91.

[51] See Hucke, "Gregorian and Old Roman Chant," in *NGD*, 6. 696–97; Treitler (1981): 474.

CHAPTER 5

On the Origin of Neumes

How did Latin neumes begin? And what developments lie between those beginnings and the first plentiful documents of neuming which date from about 900? A long line of speculations has failed to produce generally credited answers to these questions.[1] Figure 1 shows a stemma by Joseph Froger that can serve as orientation to the problem.[2] This does not address ultimate origins. Its 'original' is the archetypal neumation of the Frankish–'Gregorian' mass propers, a lost formation compiled some time after neumatic beginnings. It goes on to the regional neume-species of 900, all ostensible out-growths of that archetype: *Ept* – German; *Cla* – north Italian; *Clu* – Cluny; *Dij* – Burgundian; *Den* – St Denis; *Lan* – Lorraine or 'Metz'; *Mur 3* – St Gall or 'Alammanian'; *Cha* – Breton; *Alb* – Aquitanian; *Ben* – south Italian/Beneventan. Between the unknown 'original' and the multiple neume-species around 900 an obscure evolution takes place. There is, in Froger's words, 'une sorte de nuée opaque. . . [une] zone brumeuse'.

The dates and places of the developments are similarly clouded. R.-J. Hesbert's *Sextuplex* in 1935 supplied an approximate shape of the Carolingian text-archetype of Gregorian chant – of the words without music – circulated in Frankish domains during the later eighth century.[3] For the corresponding musical archetype – the texts plus neumes – no comparable shape has emerged. Spanish scholars like to speak of neumes going back as far as Gregory the Great.[4] Yet

---

[1] S. Corbin, 'Neumatic Notations', *The New Grove Dictionary of Music and Musicians*, ed. S. Sadie, 20 vols. (London, 1980), xiii, p. 128: 'There have been many hypotheses concerning the origin of neumes, none of which has been completely satisfactory in all respects.'

[2] *Le graduel romain: Édition critique par les moines de Solesmes*, iv: *Le texte neumatique*, 2: *Les relations généalogiques des manuscrits* (Solesmes, 1962), p. 92.

[3] R.-J. Hesbert, *Antiphonale missarum sextuplex* (Brussels, 1935).

[4] G. M. Suñol, *Introduction à la paléographie musicale grégorienne* (Paris, 1935), pp. 30ff; H. Anglès, 'Gregorian Chant', in *New Oxford History of Music*, ii: *Early Medieval Music up to 1300*,

First published in *Early Music History*, 7 (1987), 59–90. Reprinted with the permission of Cambridge University Press.

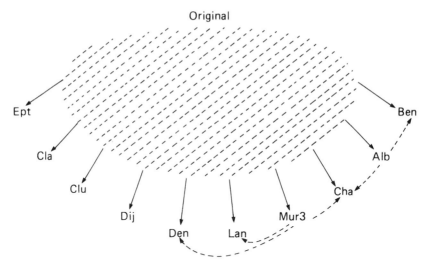

Figure 1   The stemma of Joseph Froger (1962)

the prevailing opinion is that of Solange Corbin, who saw the neumes as an invention of the earlier ninth century for the purpose of recording ancillary and novel music like lections, celebrants' chants, tropes, sequences and polyphony, while the central repertory of Gregorian propers remained consigned to oral transmission until about 900.[5] Eugène Cardine cautiously endorsed this late application of neumes to the Gregorian corpus and placed the collection's origin 'between the Rhine and the Seine'.[6] Corbin's view has also been adopted by Helmut Hucke and Leo Treitler, whose claims that oral-improvisatory techniques continued to shape Gregorian melodic transmissions of the ninth century and beyond it helps to support.[7]

ed. Anselm Hughes (London, 1954), pp. 106ff; R. Costa, 'Acotaciones sobre la antigüedad de la notación musical en occidente', *Anuario Musical*, 36 (1981), pp. 39–67.

[5]   S. Corbin, 'Les notations neumatiques en France à l'époque carolingienne', *Revue d'Histoire de l'Église en France*, 38 (1952), pp. 226–8; *idem*, 'Les neumes', in *Histoire de la musique*, I: *Encyclopédie de la Pléiade*, I (Paris, 1960), pp. 690–4; *idem, Die Neumen, Paläographie der Musik nach den Plänen Leo Schrades*, I/3 (Cologne, 1977), pp. 22–42; see also J. Froger, 'L'édition critique de L'*Antiphonale missarum* romain par les moines de Solesmes', *Études Grégoriennes*, 1 (1954), p. 156; J. Hourlier, 'L'origine des neumes', *Ut mens concordet voci: Festschrift E. Cardine*, ed. J. B. Göschl (St Ottilien, 1980), p. 360.

[6]   E. Cardine, 'Vue d'ensemble sur le chant grégorien', *Études Grégoriennes*, 16 (1977), p. 174.

[7]   H. Hucke, 'Toward a New Historical View of Gregorian Chant', *Journal of the American Musicological Society [JAMS]*, 33 (1980), p. 445: 'Through the studies of Solange Corbin it has become evident that the neumes are of Carolingian origin. They were developed in France

However the Corbin–Hucke–Treitler views have encountered resistance. Michel Huglo has ventured, in light of the close connections between the East and West Frankish branches of the noted tradition, that a Carolingian neumed archetype existed before the Carolingian *divisio imperii* of the mid-ninth century. That would disqualify something of Corbin's late dating and the arguments that depend on it.[8] Huglo has also subscribed to an origin of neumes as far back as 800.[9] I have myself addressed the issue of chronology in a recent paper titled 'Charlemagne's Archetype of Gregorian Chant'. What is proposed there is the existence of a Carolingian–Gregorian neumed recension a full century earlier than has been supposed. It puts the neumes in wide use during the later eighth century, with copies of an authoritative noted archetype of the Frankish–Gregorian propers circulating around the end of that century.[10] A corollary of this earlier date for the neumed archetype is a revised conception of the early written transmission: the melodies of the Gregorian mass propers were crystallised under Charlemagne in an authoritative neumed recension that left no substantial licence for oral-improvisational manoeuvre.

In the present paper, the focus shifts from chronology to the neumes themselves – to their nature and ways of transmitting the

in the ninth century. . . Perhaps neumes were developed and used at first for theoretical demonstrations, and only occasionally employed to notate a particular melody or to give a musical explanation here or there in a parchment manuscript.' For Treitler, 'the earliest practical notations served primarily a cueing function for celebrants reciting ecclesiastical readings and prayers. . . The notation of antiphons, responsories, and Mass-Proper items for the cantor and schola did not begin until the tenth century. . . In the beginning the principal tasks of notations for text collections were to indicate qualitative aspects of performance and to help the singer to adapt his melodic knowledge to the texts before him. They were thus practical notations, and they were tools for an oral tradition'; 'Reading and Singing: On the Genesis of Occidental Music-Writing', *Early Music History*, 4 (1984), pp. 176–7. Treitler speaks elsewhere of 'the fact that the Gregorian Chant tradition was, in its early centuries, an oral performance practice. . . The oral tradition was translated after the ninth century into writing. But the evolution from a performance practice represented in writing, to a tradition of composing, transmission, and reading, took place over a span of centuries'; in 'The Early History of Music Writing in the West', *JAMS*, 35 (1982), p. 237.

8 M. Huglo, 'De monodiska handskrifternas fördelning i två grupper, öst och väst', *Helsingin yliopiston käytännöllisen teologian laitos: Kätännöllisen teologian julkaisuja*, 3 (1975), pp. 47–65.

9 M. Huglo and C. Durand, 'Catalogue de L'Exposition des manuscrits notés de Saint Benoit sur Loire', *Les sources en musicologie* (Paris, CNRS, 1981), p. 172: 'La notation musicale. . . a été conçue, à l'origine, vers l'an 800/830.' Huglo formerly accepted the Corbin view: 'On the Origins of the Troper-Proser', *Journal of the Plainsong and Mediaeval Music Society*, 2 (1979), p. 13: 'Towards the end of the ninth century, when the notation of the complete repertory *in integro* was undertaken. . .'.

10 K. Levy, 'Charlemagne's Archetype of Gregorian Chant', *JAMS*, 40 (1987), pp. 1–31.

Gregorian melodies. I will propose fresh scenarios for three early stages of neumatic practice: 1. ultimate origins; 2. 'Charlemagne's archetype'; 3. the neume-species *c.* 900. Stages 1 and 2 are 'prehistoric' in that no neumes survive from their times. Only for stage 3 are there actual neumes. The evidence is spotty, and my results cannot pretend to be more than conjectures.

I. ORIGINS: THE TWO METHODS OF NEUMING

Various explanations of neume origins are now in circulation.

a. Accents. Most often encountered is the theory that the 'accents' of late Classical antiquity – the Alexandrian 'ten prosodic signs': acute, grave, circumflex etc. – were the principal factors in origins.[11] Generally speaking, an acute accent would enter musical service as the indicator of a higher pitch than the one preceding; a grave accent, of a lower pitch; a circumflex, of a succession of higher and lower pitches. With the addition of some nuance signs like the quilisma, oriscus and liquescences, the system would be complete.[12] Advocates of this 'accent theory' tend to cite a south German statement of *c.* 1000 (Vatican City, Biblioteca Apostolica Vaticana, MS Pal. lat. 235) that 'the notational sign called the neume comes from the accents'.[13]

b. Byzantine–Greek models. Latin neumes are also explained as derivatives of Byzantine notational practice.[14] The Byzantine *oxeia* and *bareia* reproduce the Alexandrian acute and grave accents, so this amounts to a variant of the accent theory. Since the premises of Byzantine notational usage differ in part from those of the West and

[11] I. von Müller, *Handbuch der klassischen Altertums-Wissenschaft*, I: *Einleitende und Hilfs-Disziplinen* (Munich, 1892), pp. 307ff.

[12] C. E. H. de Coussemaker, *Histoire de l'harmonie au Moyen Age* (Paris, 1852), pp. 149ff; P. Bohn, 'Das liturgische Rezitativ und dessen Bezeichnung in den liturgischen Bücher des Mittelalters', *Monatshefte für Musikgeschichte*, 19 (1887), pp. 29ff; concerning later discussions, see Corbin, *Die Neumen*, pp. 19–21.

[13] *De accentibus toni oritur nota quae dicitur neuma*; P. Wagner, *Einführung in die gregorianischen Melodien*, II (2nd edn, Leipzig, 1912), p. 355.

[14] The notion of Greco-Byzantine origin, going back to Riemann (*Studien zur Geschichte der Notenschrift* [Leipzig, 1878], p. 112), has been revived by C. Floros (*Universale Neumenkunde* [Kassel, 1970], II, pp. 232ff), whose theories should be approached with a caution indicated for the Latin notations by M. Huglo in *Revue de Musicologie*, 58 (1972), pp. 109–12, and for the Byzantine notations by M. Haas, 'Probleme einer "Universale Neumenkunde"', *Forum Musicologicum*, 1 (1975), pp. 305–22.

the origins of the Byzantine system have yet to be established, this theory is unsatisfactory.

c. Cheironomy. The explanation, given currency by André Mocquereau, is that musical neumes were written counterparts of choirmasters' hand-gestures, tracing melodic trajectories during performance.[15] The late-medieval testimony is assembled by Huglo, who judiciously refrains from an endorsement.[16]

d. Punctuation-signs and language-usage. The theory that neumes were signs that were earlier used as text-punctuation comes ultimately from Bohn and Thibaut.[17] Certain stylised forms that are employed as editorial markings and punctuations (question marks, commas, colons) in the literary texts and liturgical recitations of a given Carolingian region may in fact find use in the same region as neume-shapes for the quilisma, oriscus etc. The shapes of the punctuation-neume doublets differ so much from region to region that such local correspondences can scarcely reflect a common origin. The theory is nevertheless a point of departure for Treitler, who links the overall phenomenon of neume-origins to the Carolingian usage of text and language: 'The rise of music-writing is associated with the normalisation of the Latin language and its script, with the spread of writing and literacy, and with language-pedagogy. . . The strongest factors [in neume-origins] relate to the development of language in speech and writing and to the theory and pedagogy of language.'[18]

e. Ekphonetic notations. Related in part to the Byzantine theory of origins and in part to that of punctuation and language is the derivation of Latin neumes from the ekphonetic notations used in Byzantium between the ninth and fifteenth centuries to regulate the delivery of scriptural lections and ceremonial texts. This theory,

---

[15]   Paléographie Musicale, series I, 1 (1889), pp. 96ff.
[16]   'La chironomie médiévale', *Revue de Musicologie*, 49 (1963), pp. 153–71; the theory is rejected by Hucke, 'Die Cheironomie und die Entstehung der Neumenschrift', *Die Musikforschung*, 32 (1979), pp. 1–16.
[17]   Bohn, 'Das liturgische Rezitativ', pp. 45ff; J.-B. Thibaut, *Monuments de la notation ekphonétique et neumatique de l'Église latine* (St Petersburg, 1912), *passim*.
[18]   Treitler, 'Reading and Singing', pp. 186–208, cf. pp. 206–7; the same view is featured in his 'The Early History of Music Writing in the West', pp. 269ff, and 'Die Entstehung der abendländischen Notenschrift', *Die Musikforschung*, 37 (1984), pp. 259–67.

which also received its impetus from Thibaut, has found little support in scientific studies by later Byzantinists.[19]

f. Eclectic theories. Inasmuch as none of the existing theories by itself explains notational origins, there have been composites of two or three of them. A recent formulation by Dom Cardine combines elements of the accent, punctuation and cheironomy theories:

> *The Origin of Neumes.* The first scribes of Gregorian melodies employed signs that were already used with literary texts, retaining essentially their original signification or modifying this in an analogous sense. [*Accent-theory*:] The acute and grave accents of the grammarians were by nature suited to distinguish high and low notes: hence *virga* and *tractulus*. [*Punctuation*:] Certain abbreviation signs were used because of the finesse of their design, to represent sounds that were lightly repeated: hence *stropha* and *trigon*. Contraction signs were used for sounds particularly bound up with their neighbours: *oriscus*. The interrogative sign was chosen as the figure for a vocal phenomenon that lay close to the rising melos of an interrogative phrase: the *quilisma*. . . [*Cheironomy*:] The basic intention of the system was to translate the melody as gesture and fix the gesture as written sign. A neume is a gesture 'inked' upon the parchment.[20]

Coming as it does from the doyen of musical Gregorianists – at the beginning of Cardine's masterful *Sémiologie grégorienne* – this commands respect, and in fact it embodies a significant kernel of truth. Yet if the simple suggestions that I now put forward come at all close to the mark, then the existing explanations of neume origins may be set aside. Neither accents nor punctuation and language nor

[19] Thibaut, *Origine byzantine de la notation neumatique de l'Église latine* (Paris, 1907); *idem, Monuments de la notation ekphonétique et hagiopolite de l'Église grecque* (St Petersburg, 1913); C. Höeg, *La notation ekphonétique* (Copenhagen, 1935); M. Haas, *Byzantinische und slavische Notationen, Palaeographie der Musik*, 1/2 (Cologne, 1973), pp. 213–16; G. Engberg, 'Ekphonetic Notation', *The New Grove Dictionary*, vi, pp. 99ff.

[20] '*L'origine dei neumi.* I primi scrittori delle melodie gregoriane utilizzarono dei segni già usati nei testi letterari, conservando essenzialmente il loro significato originale o modificandolo in un senso analogo. L'accento acuto e grave dei grammatici era già per sua natura adatto a distinguere le note alte dalle note basse: virga e tractulus. I segni di abbreviazione furono usati, a causa della finezza del loro disegno, per rappresentare i suoni leggermente ripercossi: stropha e trigon. I segni di contrazione furono attribuiti ai suoni particolarmente legati a quelli vicini: oriscus. Il punto interrogativo fu scelto per raffigurare un fenomeno vocale affine alla modulazione ascendente della frase interrogativa: quilisma. . . Alla base del sistema si trova l'intenzione di tradurre una melodia mediante il gesto e di fissare il gesto per mezzo dei segno grafico. Infatti il neuma è un gesto "inchiostrato" sulla pergamena.' E. Cardine, *Semiologia gregoriana* (Rome, 1968), pp. 4–5. A similar omnibus is proposed by Dom Hourlier in his retrospective 'L'origine des neumes', p. 359: 'L'origine des neumes se trouve donc dans l'arsenal de signes autres que les lettres, dont dispose le copiste d'un text littéraire au ixe siècle.'

ekphonetic neumes would be relevant. The Byzantine theory, a variant of the accents theory, merely avoids the issue. Only cheironomy will be seen to play a role in early neumatic developments, but with no bearing on ultimate origins.

How did neumes begin? My first undertaking is to dispose of a notion that has enjoyed a broad though largely tacit support. It is that all of the oldest neumes represent a single 'original' development. In its place I offer the notion of two separate developments representing two distinct 'methods' or approaches to the process of neumation. For the moment these are designated Type 1 and Type 2. Type 1 is the earlier, Type 2 the later, and only Type 1 would put us in touch with neumatic origins. Let me make no mystery about this. The documents are well known and the fundamental observations were made long ago in a provocative study by Handschin. Type 1 is represented by the handful of surviving specimens that have so far been labelled as specimens of the 'St Amand' or 'Palaeofrank' notation. Type 2 comprises all other early Latin neume-species.

The study of the Palaeofrank notation began in the 1950s when Handschin and Jammers independently focused on an archaic neume-species found in a small number of examples from north-east France and north-west Germany.[21] Shortly thereafter, Hourlier and Huglo amplified the discussion and supplied a comprehensive inventory of sources.[22] There have been more recent discussions of the enigmas posed by the Type 1/Palaeofrank notations, but the state of the question has seen little advance beyond the formulations of the 1950s.[23]

The views of Hourlier and Huglo were summarised in a stemma which – like that of Froger in Figure 1 – amounts to a comprehensive projection of the origin of neume-species. It is reproduced in Figure 2.[24] All the regional families again descend from a single lost

[21] J. Handschin, 'Eine alte Neumenschrift', *Acta Musicologica*, 22 (1950), pp. 69–97; Handschin, 'Zu Eine alte Neumenschrift', *ibid.*, 26 (1953), pp. 87–8; E. Jammers, *Die Essener Neumenhandschriften der Landes- und Stadt-Bibliothek Düsseldorf* (Ratingen, 1952); Jammers, 'Die paläofränkische Neumenschrift', *Scriptorium*, 7 (1953), pp. 235–59, reprinted in Jammers's *Schrift Ordnung Gestalt*, ed. E. Hammerstein (Berne, 1969), pp. 35–58, which also contains (pp. 70–87) his fertile but erratic 'Die Entstehung der Neumenschrift'.

[22] 'Notation paléofranque', *Études Grégoriennes*, 2 (1957), pp. 212–19.

[23] Stäblein, *Schriftbild der einstimmigen Musik* (Leipzig, 1975), pp. 27 (historical stemma), 28–9, 106–8; S. Corbin, *Die Neumen*, pp. 75–81; L. Treitler, 'The Early History of Music Writing in the West', pp. 263ff; *idem*, 'Reading and Singing', pp. 148ff.

[24] 'Notation paléofranque', p. 218.

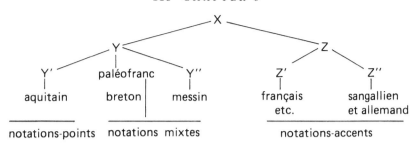

Figure 2   The stemma of Jean Hourlier and Michel Huglo (1957)

archetype, the Hourlier–Huglo 'X', Froger's 'original'. But Figure 2, by taking the Palaeofrank branch into account, improves on the stemma of Froger, for whom the Palaeofrank documents were an obstacle in the path of a critical edition of the Gregorian Gradual, hence were ignored. In Figure 2, the Palaeofrank branch has an early position among the mixed neumes (*notations mixtes*), between the accent-neumes (*notations-accents*) of the central French and German species on the one hand, and the point-neumes (*notations-points*) of the Aquitanian species on the other. Also grouped with these mixed notations, though later in time than the Palaeofrank and perhaps its direct descendants, are the neume-species of Brittany and Lorraine ('messin'). Omitted for reasons of space are the Italian notations, 'dont la carte est extrêmement complexe', which are generically close to the 'notations-accents' and derive from the same single archetype 'X'.

In Figure 3, I offer an altogether different representation of neumatic beginnings. Instead of a single written original from which all Latin neumes organically descend, I propose a stemma of three branches that coexist during a period of some centuries. The oldest branch is not written at all. It is memory: a melodic tradition of the Gregorian propers that was – as I shall say – 'concretised' in professional memories at the time written processes began. This remembered, reified melodic tradition went on to nourish two written branches during the early centuries of neumatic transmission.

Various issues raised by my stemma will be considered as the discussion unfolds. To begin, there is the position of the Palaeofrank species. This appears, not as the outgrowth of a single, all-inclusive neumatic development, but as an original written tradition that was different in method and distinct in genealogy from all the other neume-species. One gauge of this Type 1/Palaeofrank independence can be taken from the geography of the sources. Handschin pointed out that the documents of Palaeofrank notation represent by and large the same regions in which the neume-species of Metz became dominant during the later ninth and tenth centuries. The archaism of the Palaeofrank species led him to suppose a chronological succession in which the Metz species (one might with Corbin now say the Lorraine species) supplanted the Palaeofrank in this central region of the Carolingian empire. Handschin suggested for the Palaeofrank the alternative name of 'pre-Metz' notation.[25]

Liturgical and repertorial considerations now lead to a related conclusion. Previous siftings of the Palaeofrank materials give the impression that what is extant amounts to a mere scattering of music lying mainly outside the Gregorian tradition. However a careful examination suggests that a complete recension of the Gregorian mass propers once existed in Type 1/Palaeofrank neumes. Table 1 reproduces the inventory of sources compiled by Hourlier and Huglo. Altogether there are some twenty items, dated between the mid-ninth and the eleventh or twelfth centuries.[26] In the column headed 'Foliation' there are no complete Type 1/Palaeofrank collections, only fragments and marginalia. In the column headed 'Description', the neumed entries can be seen as a miscellany of classical texts (Horace: nos. 6, 9), Old Testament lections (Lamentations: no. 14), Carolingian music theory (Aurelian: no. 16; tonary – Noaeane: no. 19), Carolingian ceremonial and liturgical music (*missa graeca*, Laudes regiae, litany: nos. 4, 15, 8), trope and sequence (nos. 2, 13, 18), Gregorian office propers (All Saints and Requiem: nos. 1 and 20), and Gregorian mass propers (nos. 3, 5, 11). Of the twenty items, then, only five are devoted to the central Gregorian repertory, and of these the office chants lie partly outside the standard corpus since the formula for All Saints (no. 1) was a Carolingian accretion.[27] Turning to the mass chants, the neumations seem to be limited to marginalia in two sacramentaries (nos. 3 and 5) plus additions to some eight folios of a missal at Paris (no. 11). On closer inspection, however,

[25] 'Eine alte Neumenschrift', p. 94; 'Zu Eine alte Neumenschrift', p. 88.
[26] 'Notation paléofranque', p. 216.
[27] Hesbert, *Antiphonale missarum sextuplex*, p. cix, n. 1; M. Huglo, *Les tonaires* (Paris, 1971), p. 32.

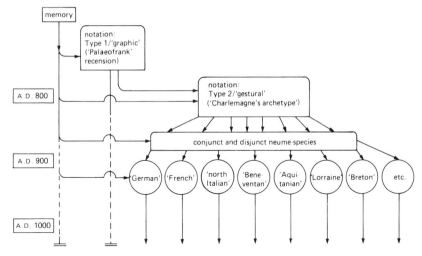

Figure 3   Gregorian propers: three-branch stemma

these three sources suggest a much richer picture of the Palaeofrank mass neumations.

The two sacramentaries now at Düsseldorf were written in northeast France. They are prayer books, not intended for musical entries. But as often happens with good-sized exemplars of the sacramentary and lectionary, additions have been made to the ample margins.[28] Among them are some four dozen chants of the mass proper with Type 1/Palaeofrank neumes, either noted in full or simply as incipits.[29] Among these are calendar-entries for the first, second and fourth weeks in Advent, for the last three days of Holy Week, and for the feasts of St Michael, the Holy Cross, and some others spread through the year. The selection may at first appear random, but the presence of the Advent Sundays, the First Sunday among them, and the wide selection of feasts suggests the possibility of a comprehensive neumed cycle.

There is support for this in Paris lat. 17305 (Table 1, no. 11), a full missal of the tenth (or perhaps ninth) century, again copied in northeast France.[30] Here the musical texts were part of the original plan,

[28] Jammers, *Die Essener Neumenhandschriften*, pp. 11ff, gives detailed indications of the contents.
[29] I am greatly indebted to Dr G. Karpp, Head of the Manuscript Division of the University Library at Düsseldorf, and Dr H. Finger of that institution, for their extreme kindness in facilitating my consultation of the two sacramentaries.
[30] *La notation musicale des chants liturgiques latins*, Paléographie Musicale, series II, 3 (Solesmes,

Table 1 *Inventory of Palaeofrank manuscripts (after Hourlier and Huglo)*

No.	Source	Foliation	Description	Date (century)	Provenance
1	Douai, Bibliothèque Municipale, 6	136	Office of All Saints	9th–11th	Marchiennes
2	Douai, Bibliothèque Municipale, 246	guard sheet	troped *Benedicamus Domino* settings	11th	Anchin
3	Düsseldorf, Landes- und Stadtbibliothek, D.1	marginalia	mass antiphons	9th–10th	Korvey
4	Düsseldorf, Landes- und Stadtbibliothek, D.2	6, 203	*missa graeca*	10th	Korvey
5	Düsseldorf, Landes- und Stadtbibliothek, D.3	marginalia	mass antiphons	11th	Cologne
6	Leiden, Bibliotheek der Rijksuniversiteit, P.L. 28	(cf. Paris 9792)	fragment from Horace		Beauvais
7	Paris, Bibliothèque Nationale, fonds lat. 2291	10, 12ᵛ, 14ᵛ	incipit+doxology	9th	St Amand
8	Paris, Bibliothèque Nationale, fonds lat. 2717	2ᵛ, 128ᵛ	marginalia and litany		St Amand
9	Paris, Bibliothèque Nationale, fonds lat. 9792		fragment from Horace		Beauvais
10	Paris, Bibliothèque Nationale, fonds lat. 15614	105	missal	12th	Soissons
11	Paris, Bibliothèque Nationale, fonds lat. 17305	9–16	incipit	11th	northern France
12	Paris, Bibliothèque Nationale, fonds lat. 17306	58, 176–	alleluia melismas	11th	Amiens
13	Paris, Bibliothèque Nationale, n. acq. lat. 1618	91	Lamentations	10th–11th	St Bénigne?
14	St Omer, Bibliothèque de la Ville, 666	17ᵛ	Laudes regiae	9th?	St Bertin
15	Valenciennes, Bibliothèque Municipale, 107	28	Aurelian of Réome	early 12th	St Amand
16	Valenciennes, Bibliothèque Municipale, 148	71ᵛ, 72, 84	pen trial	end of 9th	St Amand
17	Valenciennes, Bibliothèque Municipale, 150	36	trope *Quem vere*	end of 9th	St Amand
18	Valenciennes, Bibliothèque Municipale, 294	19	Noeane	early 12th	St Amand
19	Valenciennes, Bibliothèque Municipale, 337	42	Requiem, Alleluia, responsory	11th	St Amand
20	Valenciennes, Bibliothèque Municipale, 399	1, 7, 208		11th	St Amand

although no neumes were intended since horizontal space was not left for melismas. Nevertheless, another four dozen chants of the Gregorian proper have had a Type 1/Palaeofrank neumation of at least their incipits squeezed into the cramped interlinear space. The Paris missal's neumed repertory complements that of the Düsseldorf sacramentaries. Filling out the Advent–Winter calendar are the vigil and three masses for Christmas Day as well as the saints' days of Christmas week (Stephen, John, Holy Innocents, Silvester). Later on, the Type 1 noted entries become rarer as an initial determination to neume the entire cycle seems to give out. But there are notations for proper mass chants of the Second Sunday after Christmas, of Tuesday in the Fourth Week of Lent, Easter Thursday, Pentecost, the Second Sunday after Pentecost, and the April feast of Tiburtius and Valerianus. The combined repertories of the Paris and Düsseldorf manuscripts amount to some eight dozen items of the mass proper noted in Type 1/Palaeofrank neumes. They represent minor as well as major feasts that are distributed through the liturgical cycles of temporale and sanctorale. All this suggests a full Type 1/Palaeofrank neumation. It would exist within the same territory of north-east France that by the end of the ninth century was the domain of the Lorraine neume-species.[31]

Thus we have one region with two neumations, one earlier, one later. Why were there two successive neumations of the Gregorian mass-propers in the Carolingian heartland? For an answer, I turn to the notations themselves, where I have to substantiate my claim that two different types or methods of neuming were involved.

Figure 4 shows the opening incises of the introit *Dum medium silentium* for the Second Sunday after Christmas. The notation is Type 1/Palaeofrank, after the Paris missal (see also Figure 5).[32] This assortment of dots, strokes and twists scarcely differs from that in other neume-species. A two-pitch ascent can be noted here, as in

1963), Pl. 1, has a facsimile of fol. 15ᵛ, col. A. Handschin considered this source only in his added remarks of 1953, and he recognised its significance only in part: 'Ein ganz liturgisches Gesangbuch mit dieser Notation besitzen wir nicht. Das wichtigste Dokument, ist wohl das Missale Paris 17305.' 'Zu Eine alte Neumenschrift', p. 87. His death two years later prevented a promised return to a fuller study.

[31] J. Hourlier, 'Le domaine de la notation messine', *Revue Grégorienne*, 30 (1951), pp. 96–113, 150–8; certain Palaeofrank witnesses are included here (pp. 106–7) under their older Solesmes designation of 'notation de Saint Amand'.

[32] Paris lat. 17305, fol. 16; the diplomatic transcription and square-note resolution in Figure 5 are those of Corbin's *Die Neumen*, pp. 78–9.

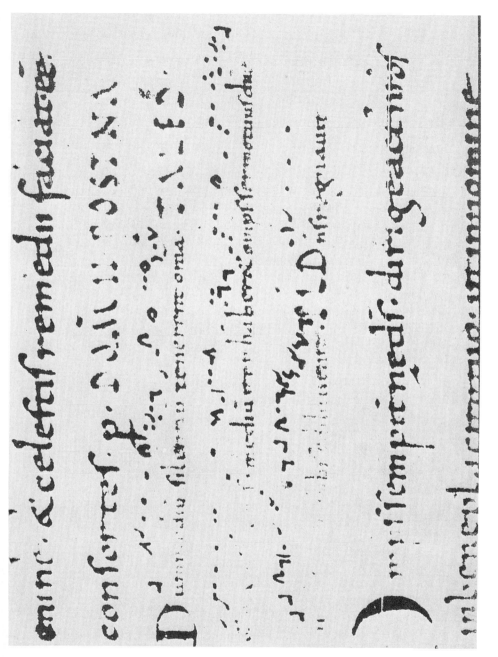

Figure 4   Type 1/Palaeofrank notation: opening of the introit *Dum medium silentium*, from the missal Paris, Bibliothèque Nationale, MS fonds lat. 17305

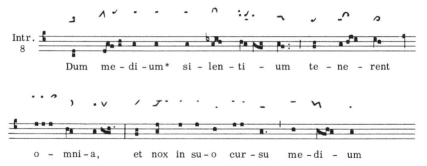

Figure 5   Opening of the introit *Dum medium silentium* (after Corbin) (cf. Figure 4)

most Type 2 species, with two dots, the second placed higher and to the right of the first, as on the final two pitches of silen-*ti*-um. Yet the two-pitch ascent in Type 1/Palaeofrank can also take the special form of a diagonal that combines the two dots into a single upward-angled stroke, as on the last two pitches of *me*-dium, on *te*-nerent, or on *et* nox. That is a departure from general Type 2 practice. Something similar is seen in the succession of three pitches, lower–higher–lower, which in Type 1/Palaeofrank can take the unusual form of a half-circle open to the bottom, as on si-*len*-tium.

Further instances of such unusual forms are found in Figure 6a (see also Figure 7), which shows the introit *Ad te levavi* for the First Sunday of Advent in the notation of the Düsseldorf Sacramentary D.1.[33] The neumatic ductus of Düsseldorf differs from that of the Paris missal, but the Type 1 anomalies are again present: the single-stroke podatus on *le*-vavi, *a*-ni-*mam*, and con-*fi*-do; the semicircular torculus on ne-*que* and ir-*ri*-deant. The familiar names for the Type 2 neumes (clivis, torculus, etc.) have little chance of being 'original' or applying to Type 1. They are of apparent Alammanian origin, and appear to have arisen no earlier than the eleventh century, with no likely connection to the first stages of neuming.[34]

To fathom the notational anomalies, one should also approach them from the other direction. How do the neume-species of Type 2 differ from Type 1? Figure 6b shows a generic Type 2 notation for the same passage of the introit *Ad te levavi*. Where Type 1's low–high–low sequence, found on *neque* and *irrideant*, is the down-turned half-circle,

---

[33]   Stäblein, *Schriftbild*, 107, from which Figure 7 is taken, reproduces the full page, Düsseldorf D.1, fol. 126ᵛ.
[34]   M. Huglo, 'Les noms des neumes et leur origine', *Études Grégoriennes*, 1 (1954), pp. 58, 67.

Ad te le - va - vi *   a - ni - mam me - am :

De - us me - us   in te con - fi - do,

non   e - ru - be - scam : ne - que   ir - ri - de - ant   me

in - i - mi - ci   me - i :

Figure 6   The introit *Ad te levavi*, (a) in Type 1/Palaeofrank notation as in the sacramentary Düsseldorf, Landes- und Stadtbibliothek, MS D.1; (b) in Type 2/ Alammanian notation

the Type 2 torculus in each instance prefaces the arc with an opening flourish: first a downward stroke, then upward, then arching down again; Type 1 lacks the initial downward stroke. Similarly with the succession of two pitches in ascent, or podatus: Type 1 can accomplish this with an ascending diagonal (as on *le*-vavi) while Type 2 again adds an opening flourish: a downward stroke for the low starting pitch, turning to an ascent for the higher ending. Similarly

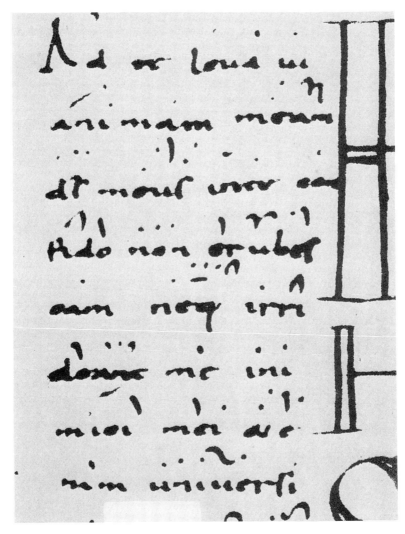

Figure 7 The introit *Ad te levavi* (cf. Figure 6)

with the succession of two descending pitches, or clivis: Type 1 can accomplish this with a downward diagonal (as on *me*-us, confi-*do*, *e*-rubescam etc.), but Type 2 prefaces the descending stroke with a small introductory flourish. However it is with the single pitches in isolation that the fundamental differences in procedure between the two types are clearest. Figure 8 compares the basic shapes of punctum and virga along with those of torculus, podatus and clivis.

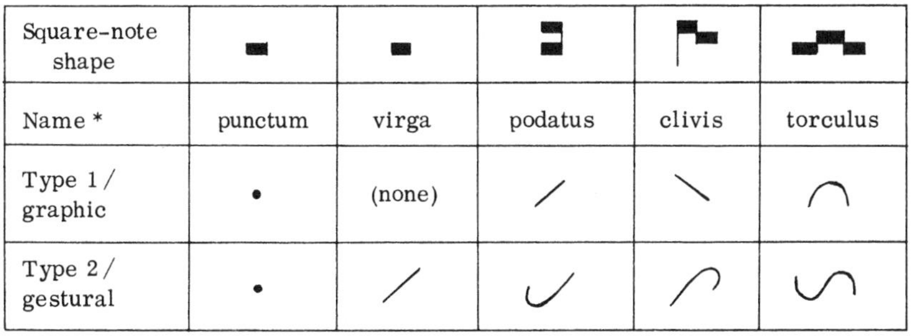

Square-note shape	▬	▪	⬙	⌐▬	▬▬
Name *	punctum	virga	podatus	clivis	torculus
Type 1 / graphic	•	(none)	/	\	⌒
Type 2 / gestural	•	/	∪	⌐	⌣⌒

*Applies only to Type 2.

Figure 8   Simple neumes, Types 1 and 2

In Type 2 there are two basic options for neuming an isolated pitch: for one that is unemphatic or lies relatively low, there is the plain dot or punctum; for one that is emphasised or lies relatively high, there is the ascending diagonal or virga. The Type 1 notation lacks that option: an ascending diagonal – the virga shape of Type 2 – in Type 1 signifies a two-pitch ascent or podatus.

The roster of Type 1 Palaeofrank signs, like that of all other neume-species, is made up of dots and strokes, single and combined, conveying information about melodic outlines and phrasings; there are rounded shapes indicating liquescence and melodic nuance; and there are altered and special shapes indicating diverse lengths.[35] Yet in the situations just seen, Type 1/Palaeofrank stands apart. It has the rising diagonal for the two-pitch ascent, a Palaeofrank option for the podatus, lacking the customary initial stroke. It has the dome-shaped torculus, lacking an initial stroke. And it has the descending diagonal for the clivis, again lacking the initial stroke. In each instance the Palaeofrank uses fewer strokes – its scribes have been more economical in translating the melodic substance onto the page. These procedural curiosities have been noticed by every student of the notation, but the explanations that have emerged are inconclusive. The stumbling-block may lie in supposing there was a single

[35] S. Corbin, in *Die Neumen*, 77, and in the neume-table accompanying her article 'Neumatic Notations' (*The New Grove Dictionary*, xii, p. 131), makes a distinction between a 'hypothetical archetype' of the Palaeofrank notation (as mirrored perhaps in Paris 2291) which lacked quilisma, oriscus, and liquescent punctum, and a 'surviving form' of the Palaeofrank (as in Paris 17305) which added such signs. Handschin argued long ago, with regard to the same manuscripts she cites, that this distinction lacks sufficient basis ('Zu Eine alte Neumenschrift', pp. 87–8).

development behind all the early neumations: in supposing that the Palaeofrank represents the same notational-methodological premises as the rest. I suggest instead that the economical behaviour of the Type 1/Palaeofrank notation is the symptom of a quite different process. What Type 1 offers is a chart of pitch-positions where each element of the melos, whether it appears on the page as part of a ligature or as a separate sign, is treated as a positioned point. Even the variety of curvatures used to signify 'ornamental' neumes (quilisma, oriscus, apostrophus) and liquescence are explainable in this way – as simple written analogues of the vocal nuances. If there is one word that describes this relationship between sound and sign it would be 'graphic'. In what follows, I shall suggest this rationale for the Type 1 notation by substituting 'graphic' for the designation 'Palaeofrank'. It accounts for the behaviour of the Type 1 notation: each sound, plain or nuanced, is given a positioned, simply descriptive shape.

Yet what of the Type 2 method? It has those 'extra' strokes at the beginnings of its podatus, torculus etc. And in some Type 2 species, the difference between relatively lower and higher pitches may be indicated by the option of dots or strokes, which is not available in Type 1. My proposal is that such features mark the Type 2 notation as no longer a chart of inert pitches, of abstract melodic positions (the method of Type 1), but as a chart showing analogues of up-and-down intervallic motion. The Type 2 neumes in essence reflect the contours of melodic flow: they show general melodic 'gestures'. Where I have described Type 1's exact plotting of pitch-loci and nuances as graphic, I would describe the Type 2 method, with its analogues of melodic flow, as 'gestural'. To this I would add that here and only here would one of the traditional theories of neumatic origins seem to apply: the theory of cheironomy. As Cardine put it, 'a neume is a gesture "inked" upon the parchment'.[36] But, in my projection, the cheironomy of Cardine's inked gestures has no bearing on Type 1, no link to ultimate neumatic origins. It applies only to the revised notations of Type 2.

If the dichotomy of graphic and gestural methods is provisionally accepted, some further questions arise. Why were there two notational methods? Why two successive 'editions' of the Gregorian propers, an earlier one utilising a graphic method and then a revision

---

[36] Cardine, *Semiologia gregoriana*, p. 5.

substituting a gestural method? My answer may open a long-sought window on neumatic origins. The Type 1/graphic's one-to-one renderings of pitch-position and nuance would suit the conditions of an initial transfer of chants from oral delivery to written record. One can imagine a commission charged with the responsibility of producing a pilot neumation, turning to the method of Type 1/graphic, for establishing a first conversion from oral performance and some rounds of editorial change – whether simple retouches or more ambitious revisions. As for the Type 2/gestural method, its shapelier analogues of intervallic motions suggest a different set of conditions. Type 2 would be useful for choirmasters and singers who reproduced the repertory. The gestural diagrams were more vivid as representations of melodic flow, they rendered the chants more memorable for those who sang, they supplied visual paradigms that were easily convertible into hand and arm motions for those who guided singers. In short, where the Type 1/graphic neumes produced as it were a scholarly or scientific text, the Type 2/gestural neumes produced a 'performing edition'.

These identifications of the Palaeofrank method as graphic and original have been approached by earlier discussions, which do not, however, reach their full systematic and historical implications. In 1930, Paolo Ferretti, the clear-headed analyst of Gregorian centonate and accommodative processes, turned his attention to the origins of notation and in a few paragraphs outlined a theory of neume-origins that comes close to the views suggested here. For Ferretti, the full roster of neumatic signs grew from just five *radicaux* – 'root' signs. The five were well chosen: the acute and grave accents plus the three nuance-signs apostrophus, oriscus and quilisma. Ferretti interpreted all other pitch signs as *dérivés*, elaborations and combinations of the radicals, which were the *générateurs*.[37] The grip of the accent-theory is still there, as is the supposition that a single system underlies all Latin neumes. Ferretti's theory is eclectic, and he addresses only neumes of Type 2. Yet by narrowing the field to these particular roots he approximated what may be seen as the basic graphic premise of an original Type 1 notation.

Handschin's discussion of Palaeofrank neumes comes still closer. 'Might this be the notation used in France before the Roman singing masters arrived, before the Carolingian dynasty?' 'The principle of

---

[37]   Paléographie Musicale, series I, 13 (1930), pp. 66–8.

this notation is clear: the pitch-height corresponds to the higher or lower placement on the parchment.' 'Let us say: this might be the ideal diastematic notation, just like one that resolves everything into dots.' 'For our neume-type we can scarcely conceive of a point of departure other than a purely musical one, basically independent of speech.'[38]

Recently, David Hiley prefaced a summary of current theories about neumatic origins with a remark indicating dissatisfaction with all of them: 'it might be argued that the functional demands on the notation system were sufficiently strong to initiate development without drawing upon any pre-existing system'.[39] Hiley did not elaborate, but it is a practical explanation of this sort that I have advanced, and will now try to situate within the historical context of my three-branch stemma (Figure 3).

I have suggested some of the background for my two neumatic methods by assigning to Type 1/graphic the status of original neumes. The pre-history of Type 1 is difficult to assess. Its elementary processes may be age-old. Its survivals into the tenth or eleventh century, well after Type 2/gestural became established, suggest that Type 1 was previously well entrenched. Inasmuch as significant events – among which I count the invention of neumes – are more likely to reflect significant than trivial causes, the origins of Type 1 may reach back to Gregory the Great, under whom an authoritative revision of the Antiphonale seems to have been issued.[40] Isidore of Seville's statement that 'sounds perish . . . because they cannot be written down' has been an obstacle to putting musical neumes in

---

38   'Wäre dies etwa diejenige Notation, welche im Frankenreich im Gebrauch war, bevor die römischen Gesangsmeister ins Land kamen, also vor der Karolingerdynastie?' ('Eine alte Neumenschrift', p. 76). 'Das Prinzip dieser Neumenschrift ist klar: dem Tonhöhen-Grad entspricht die höhere oder tiefere Ort auf dem Pergament' (*ibid.*, p. 78). 'Sagen wir: sie *könnte* [Handschin's italics] die ideale diastematische Neumenschrift sein nicht weniger als eine solche, die alles in Punkte auflöst (*ibid.*, p. 81). 'Es ist kaum anders denkbar, als dass wir für unseren Neumentypus einen grundsätzlich *von der Sprache unabhängigen* [my italics], einen rein musikalischen Ausgangspunkt annehmen müssen.' (*ibid.*, p. 82). However Handschin, like Ferretti, was bound to the concept of a single origin for all the neume-species, and ultimately to the derivation of neumes from accents: 'Die Ableitung der Neumen von den Akzenten, die ich nicht abgelehnt, sondern nur eingeschränkt haben möchte . . .' (*ibid.*, p. 83).

39   Article 'Notation', § III, 1 (iii) [Western Plainchant], *The New Grove Dictionary*, XIII, p. 345.

40   C. Callewaert, 'L'oeuvre liturgique de S. Grégoire', *Revue d'Histoire Ecclésiastique*, 33 (1937), pp. 306–26; K. Gamber, *Codices liturgici latini antiquiores*, 2nd edn (Freiburg Schweiz, 1968), pp. 492ff.

Gregory's time. A recent revaluation of the statement may leave a 'Gregorian' notation again tenable.[41] But a likelier occasion for the first neumes would be the revision of the liturgy that was set in motion by the Frankish monarch Pepin during Pope Stephen II's visit to France in 753–4.[42] The conversion of Frankish church music from Gallican to Roman use may have brought about the Type 1/graphic method during the decades following. It remains open whether the neumes were actually a Frankish invention or a cooperative Italo-Frankish or even an earlier Italian one.

As for the change from the Type 1/graphic method to the Type 2/gestural with its enhanced support for memorisation and performance, the genesis of the gestural method may be linked to the promulgation of the authoritative Frankish–Gregorian neumed antiphoner – the antiphoner I would call 'Charlemagne's archetype' and date *c.* 800.[43] Whatever the specifics of chronology, the conversion from graphic to gestural need not have taken much time. Differences in musical substance are slight between the two recensions, and the notational modifications required could have been accomplished in weeks rather than years.

With this my general proposals concerning neume-origins are complete, but some related issues need consideration. One is the importance accorded under existing theories of origin to the distinction between accent-neumes, which set the chant-melos mainly in ligatures (as in the Alammanian neume-species), and point-neumes, which set much of it as separate dots (as in the Aquitanian and Breton species). This dichotomy of accents–points is deeply embedded in earlier theories of neume-origins, and it retains its importance in the projection of Hourlier and Huglo (see Figure 2).[44] Because the Palaeofrank notation must be classed as a point notation, it raises a problem for advocates of the accent theory who are obliged to explain why a point notation should be more archaic than the earliest one with accents. However, Handschin recognised much of the inadequacy of the accents/points:

[41] R. Costa, 'Acotaciones'. Isidore's wording: 'Nisi enim ab homine memoria teneantur soni, pereunt, quia scribi non possunt'; *Isidori hispalensis episcopi etymologiarum sive originum*, ed. W. M. Lindsay, I (Oxford, 1911), lib. III, xv, p. 2.

[42] C. Vogel, *La réforme culturelle sous Pépin le bref et sous Charlemagne* (Graz, 1965).

[43] 'Charlemagne's Archetype', *JAMS*, 40 (1987), pp. 1–31.

[44] A classic exposition of the theory is given by Ferretti in Paléographie Musicale, series I, 13, pp. 62ff.

One might come to a basically different distinction between neume-types than the usual one of stroke vs. point neumes, *neumes-accents* vs. *neumes à points superposés*. The criterion is perhaps not that of connected or separated ductus, but rather that in one case the tone is expressed as a *position* on a vertical scale while in the other it is expressed as a rising *stroke*.[45]

In my scheme (Figure 3), the accent/point dichotomy has no connection at all with neumatic origins – with the Type 1/graphic method. It involves only the neume-species of the Type 2/gestural method. For the nomenclature of accents and points, with its implied endorsement of the accent theory of origins, I would substitute the more neutral designations of ductus as being either conjunct or disjunct, where 'conjunct' represents the species which make liberal use of ligatures, and 'disjunct' those which tend to resolve the melodic motions into separate signs. My illustrations of Type 2 notation (Figures 6b and 8) have taken the shape of a generic conjunct ductus, and in the next part of this paper I shall consider the neumation of Charlemagne's archetype and offer reasons for supposing that this original of the Type 2 recension had such a ductus. However, the gestural rationale would underlie all Type 2

---

[45]   'Man könnte daher zu einer anderen Grundeinteilung der Neumentypen gelangen als die übliche: Strich und Punktneumen, neumes-accents et neumes à points superposés. Das Massgebende ist vielleicht nicht die verbundene oder getrennte Schreibung, sondern dies, dass im einen Fall der Ton nur durch einen *Ort* der Vertikaldimension, im anderen auch durch eine aufsteigende *Strecke* dargestellt ist.' *Acta Musicologica*, 22 (1950), p. 80. Accents and points, however, play a continuing role, as in recent theorisings by Treitler ('The Early History of Music Writing in the West', pp. 237–79; and 'Reading and Singing', pp. 135–208). The neo-nomenclature of 'iconic' and 'symbolic' scripts used in the former (p. 254) comes down to the old accents and points. Treitler's 'A' or 'symbolic' scripts are the neume-species 1–6 and 11–12 of the table adapted (*ibid.*, p. 246) from Corbin's *Neumen*, beginning of the Anhang: 1. St Gall; 2. England; 3. Burgundy; 4. Chartres; 5. Nevers; 6. Normandy; 11. Catalan; 12. Bologna; all have been conventionally classed as accent-neumes. Treitler's 'B' or 'iconic' scripts are neume-species 7–10 of Corbin's table: 7. Lorraine–Messine; 8. Palaeofrankish; 9. Breton; 10. Aquitanian; of these, the Lorraine, Breton and Aquitanian notations have been conventionally classed as point-neumes. The grouping of the Palaeofrankish neumes with them perpetuates the conception that Handschin in 1950 undertook to correct. Concerning the priority of accents or points, Treitler sums up: 'Is an historical development vis-à-vis symbolic and iconic writing discernible? In the present state of our knowledge we cannot give chronological priority to one or the other notational mode. Specifically, we do not know whether the Paleofrankish and early Aquitanian scripts, on the one hand, or the Germanic ones, on the other, were the earliest ones in use. . .' ('The Early History of Music Writing in the West', p. 254). In a curious statement two years later he abandoned the issue of origins: 'The question was left open [in 1982] whether the first notations were predominantly symbolic or iconic. Now we can answer: "both." The notations of the treatises are predominantly iconic. The practical notations began as predominantly symbolic systems. Which of the two had actual temporal priority is not a question of the greatest historical import' ('Reading and Singing', pp. 177–8).

notations, and it would be as much a part of the species with disjunct
ductus – of the 'notations à points superposés' of Brittany, Occitaine,
Lorraine, Nonantola etc. – as it is of the conjunct species of St Gall,
Burgundy, central Italy etc. Some of the disjunct species, like that of
Lorraine, have clear indications of an underlying conjunct basis, as
can be gauged from the tabulations of Laon and St Gall neumations
in the *Graduale triplex*.[46] In some other disjunct species, enough
cursive patterns remain to document an underlying gestural method
and conjunct conception. Early specimens of Aquitanian notation
show more traces of conjunct ductus than later ones.[47] The indications are rarer for the disjunct species of Brittany and Nonantola.
Yet even if the gestural impulses are resolved to the point where they
are no longer manifest on the page, the rationale would remain: each
dot, tractulus, uncinus, apostrophus etc. in the disjunct species of
Type 2 would represent, not a fixed pitch-locus as in Type 1/graphic,
but a point of arrival or departure, a node or target, in a continuity of
gestural intervallic motions.

A second issue regarding Type 1 is its survival into the tenth
century and beyond.[48] Why should an older, graphic method persist
after a newer, gestural method was established around 800? One
answer may be that most examples of Type 1 are not excerpted from
standard recensions like those of the Mass and Office Antiphoners,
which tended to impose the newer notational method. The classical
texts, tropes, sequences, and elements of the *missa graeca* (Table 1,
nos. 2, 4, 6, 7, 9, 13, 18),[49] may be seen as occasional or private
jottings that readily continued in the older system. The theoretical
entries (nos. 16 and 19) were destined for consultation, not performance, which would have lessened the impulse to put them in the
performance-orientated Type 2 neumes. As for the mass and office

---

[46] *Graduale triplex seu graduale romanum . . . ornatum neumis laudunensibus (cod. 239) et sangallensibus* (Solesmes, 1979).
[47] Corbin, *Die Neumen*, Taf. 19 (Paris, Bibliothèque Nationale, MS fonds lat. 1240; tenth century) and Taf. 20 (Paris, Bibliothèque Nationale, MS fonds lat. 903; eleventh century) with neumations for the Improperia; M. Huglo, 'La tradition musicale aquitaine. Répertoire et notation', *Liturgie et musique (ixe – xive s.)*, Cahiers de Fanjeaux 17 (1982), Pl. v, showing processional antiphons in the 'ninth-century' neumation of Albi, Bibliothèque Municipale, MS 44.
[48] The datings are given in the Hourlier–Huglo table (see Table 1 above).
[49] On the *missa graeca*, C. Atkinson, 'Zur Entstehung und Überlieferung der "Missa graeca"', *Archiv für Musikwissenschaft*, 39 (1982), pp. 113–45; the Type 1 neumations (as in Düsseldorf D.2 and Vatican City, Biblioteca Apostolica Vaticana, MS Reg. lat. 215) would reflect the original dictation, compilation etc.; the change to Type 2 would come as the material began to spread.

propers (nos. 1, 3, 5, 11, 20), these again are miscellaneous additions, compressed within margins and between lines of manuscripts that were not intended for neumes. They would reflect the practicality of conservative scribes, clinging to the space-saving Type 1 'graphics' for what amounted to personal memoranda.

Another in this miscellany of Type 1 issues is the variety of ductus and origins of the preserved documents. So long as the 'Palaeofrank notation' is viewed as just one regional style among a number of such styles, the differences raise problems. But if Type 1 is viewed as a 'method' that was applicable at different times and places, it is reasonable for the surviving specimens to show the palaeographic and geographical diversity they do.

A final issue is the occasional appearance among the Type 1 neumes of Type 2 features: a 'gestural clivis' instead of a graphic descending diagonal, etc. Such departures from systematic rigour are likely to be the lapses of scribes who were customary notators in Type 2.

II. 'CHARLEMAGNE'S ARCHETYPE' AND THE EVOLUTION OF NEUME-SPECIES

From the first stage of Latin neumes, that of origins, I turn now to the second and third stages. The second focuses on the Frankish–Gregorian archetype: the lost 'original' of Froger's stemma (Figure 1), the 'X' of the Hourlier–Huglo stemma (Figure 2), the model collection of Gregorian mass propers in Type 2/gestural neumes that I would date to the end of the eighth century and identify as 'Charlemagne's archetype'. The third stage concerns the transformations of the written Gregorian tradition from that archetype through Froger's 'zone brumeuse' to the point where our first substantial documents of neuming appear – the neume-species of c. 900 (see Figure 1). The essential point is, what kind of neumation did the archetype have: what single model can account for the palaeographic variety of the neume-species? It is here that Dom Cardine and his cohort of Gregorian semiologists have been most vulnerable. The failure to define an archetypal neumation capable of generating the multiplicity of neume-species has clouded their impressive findings. In my view, the semiologists are correct in supposing that there was an authoritative neumed archetype behind the neume-species of 900. Yet a number of factors need to be redefined and freshly combined in order to clarify the development. There are six points to my presentation. The first three address the rationale of the lost archetype: 1. an earlier date; 2. a conjunct, nuance-poor archetype; 3. a memory-resident, concretised melos. The last three consider the emergence of the neume-species: 4. an eroding memory and supplemented notation; 5. copying from dictation; and 6. a 'gestural mind-set'. Some of the points will be relatively familiar, others will be more novel. Taken together, they may explain the hitherto obscure neumatic shape of the archetype and the problematic descent of the neume-species.

1. An earlier date. In beginning this paper I stated that many recent suppositions about neume origins are based on Mlle Corbin's assertion that the earliest Frankish–Gregorian neumed collections were compiled only *c.* 900, and the distinctive neumatic ductus of St Gall, Lorraine, Aquitaine, Brittany etc., which first appear about that time, stand at or near the beginning of the noted Gregorian tradition.[50] In a companion paper, I have argued that a neumed Gregorian archetype was in existence as early as *c.* 800, promulgated as 'Charlemagne's archetype' – as a central factor in the Frankish strategy of liturgical-musical unification.[51] In the present paper I have suggested this was the first major application of gestural neuming. An advantage of setting the Gregorian neumation earlier is that it allows a full century for the palaeographic evolution of the neume-species, which is awkward to explain if neumation itself begins only around 900.[52]

2. A conjunct, nuance-poor archetype. Yet the questions remain. What sort of neumation did Charlemagne's archetype have? What single palaeographic model can account for the diversity of shapes and techniques around 900? Let me begin with two suggestions. First, that the archetypal neumation had a conjunct rather than a

---

[50] See notes 5–7 above; also Hucke, 'Toward a New Historical View of Gregorian Chant', p. 445: 'the different regional paleographic styles go back to the very beginning of neume notation'.

[51] 'Charlemagne's Archetype'.

[52] Lawrence Gushee observed long ago, 'It is also possible that diverse styles of notation had already evolved between 850 and 900.' 'The Musica disciplina of Aurelian of Réôme' (PhD dissertation, Yale University, 1963), p. 257.

disjunct ductus: the tendency was to dispense the melos in ligatures, as in the Alammanian species, rather than resolve it into separate points, as in the Lorraine and Breton species. To this extent I would endorse the basic choice by Dom Froger in his edition of the *Graduel romain*, whose sample chants for the first Advent mass show a substantially Alammanian ductus.[53] My second suggestion is that the archetypal neumation was not 'nuance-rich' (amply provided with specifiers of rhythmic and melodic detail) but 'nuance-poor' (sparing in such provisions). This accords less well with Froger's samples or with a long line of received opinion. Ever since the first arguments concerning the relative authority of archaic Gregorian neumations,[54] the prevailing assumption has been that the earlier neumations were more lavish in specifications of melodic nuance and rhythmic detail while the later ones became progressively impoverished.[55] The nuance-rich neume-species, in particular the Alammanian, are favoured for their wealth of pitch-specifiers and nuance-indicators – strokes (*episemata*), modified shapes (liquescences etc.), 'Romanus letters', and *coupures* (neumatic disjunctions indicating rhythmic values). As found in such exemplars as the cantatorium St Gall, Stiftsbibliothek, MS 359 (*c*. 900) and the gradual Einsiedeln, Stiftsbibliothek, MS 121 (*c*. 1000), these describe the Gregorian melodic substance in impressive detail.[56] The traditions of Lotharingia, Brittany, Ile-de-France, Aquitaine and Italy have received less attention because of their lesser quotients of detail. The results are apparent in the Paléographie Musicale, which operated for half a century before an Italian mass-book was reproduced in facsimile; in the Solesmes *Graduale* of 1908, which relied on the Alammanian readings for most of its rhythmic and melodic detail; and in Froger's sample reconstructions for his 'édition critique'.

Yet when all is said, these fine points of performance practice may indicate quite another evolution of the early notations. Time and again in singing through the *Graduale triplex* one comes upon the

[53] *Le graduel romain. Édition critique*, IV/2: *Le texte neumatique: Les relations généalogiques entre les manuscrits*, pp. 69–86.

[54] Froger, 'L'édition critique de l'*Antiphonale missarum* romain', pp. 151f.

[55] Dom Cardine makes essentially this point: 'On constate en effet d'une façon générale que les manuscrits sont en accord entre eux pour noter les particularités les plus fines, d'autant mieux qu'ils sont plus anciens. . .'; in 'A propos des formes possibles d'une figure neumatique: le pes subbipunctus dans les premiers manuscrits sangalliens', *Festschrift F. X. Haberl*, ed. F. A. Stein (Regensburg, 1977), p. 68.

[56] Paléographie Musicale, series II, 2 (1925) and 4 (1896).

Alammanian neumes describing a particular nuanced melodic situation with a particular array of explicative signs while for the same situation the Lorraine neumation has a different, partly conflicting notational array.[57] Since the underlying melodic substance is the same, down to the fine points, a reversal of the accepted historical sequence is worth considering: instead of a nuance-rich archetype whose wealths of specifiers progressively erode, a nuance-poor archetype – a spare neumatic skeleton – whose basic specifications are then diversely clarified. The notion of a nuance-poor archetype is not without precedent, much of it again being anticipated in Handschin's discussion of the Palaeofrank notation.[58] Its provisions would, as I see this, include the factors of liquescence, quilisma, oriscus and their compounds; also the distinctions between longer and shorter durations of single pitches as expressed by points, their elongations, and *strophici*. These are all used by the Type 1/graphic notations. By the same reckoning, a nuance-poor archetype would not include *episemata* or *coupures*, whose diffusion is localised, and there would be few if any auxiliary letters.[59]

To my earlier proposal that the Type 2/gestural archetype had a conjunct rather than a disjunct ductus, I would thus add that it had a nuance-poor rather than a nuance-rich neumation. Once the historical perspective is adjusted, it is not surprising if corroborative indications should appear. I have shown signs of a conjunct, nuance-poor archetype in the close agreements of detail between the archaic, nuance-poor neumations of Prüm and Benevento for the offertories *Factus est repente* and *Angelus Domini*.[60] Moreover, a survey of tenth- and early eleventh-century copies of the mass-antiphóner suggests that the majority of surviving early neumations were close reflections of a conjunct, nuance-poor archetype. Dom Froger in 1962 offered

---

57   For a simple instance, Cardine, *Sémiologie grégorienne*, Ex. 32; for others, many pages of the *Graduale triplex*.
58   'Diese "gregorianische" Neumensippe scheint sich tatsächlich in ihren frühesten erhaltenen Vertretern wenig um rhythmische Ausdrucksmöglichkeiten zu kümmern. Im 9. und 10. Jh. dringen dann umgekehrt in die "gregorianischen" Neumenschriften teilweise rhythmische Elemente ein. . .'; 'Eine alte Neumenschrift', p. 82. The position is picked up in a recent review of Göschl's *Semiologische Untersuchungen* by Hartmut Möller: '. . . die vorherrschende Sichtweise, dass diese hochdifferenzierte Notation den zeitlichen Ausgangspunkt für die frühdeutsche Neumenschrift bildet verdient . . . eine Überprüfung'; *Die Musikforschung*, 38 (1985), p. 69.
59   Cardine's classic exposition of *coupures* in *Sémiologie grégorienne*, ch. 9, is based on St Gall procedures.
60   Levy, 'Charlemagne's Archetype'; the discussions of Figs. 4 and 6.

ten sub-families as the bases for his critical edition of the Gregorian Gradual (see Figure 1 above). Most of the ten have nuance-poor neumations. Their origins reach from Arras, Ile de France, Dijon and Epternach in the Frankish north, through Ravenna, Abruzzi, Umbria and the Beneventan zone in the Italian south.[61] They are not just provincial copies, from places where nuances might casually slip away, since among their origins are such bulwarks of Carolingian cultural orthodoxy as Corbie, St Denis, Tours and Prüm. And they are not just late copies, since the Mont Renaud manuscript is likely to have received its neumes still during the tenth century, some generations after the earliest nuance-rich copies (St Gall 359 and Laon, Bibliothèque Municipale, MSS 266 and 239).[62]

3. A memory-resident, concretised melos. Thus the written means for specifying melodic detail may differ from one copy to the next, but the fine points of melodic substance are constant. How was the melodic integrity maintained? The safeguard was memory. Huglo put this long ago: 'l'invention de la notation neumatique. . . . facilita l'effort de mémoire, sans le supprimer totalement.'[63] Cardine has spoken of 'la pensée du compositeur telle qu'elle était conservée dans la mémoire du premier notateur'.[64] Yet if the acknowledgement of the memory factor is widespread, a certain emphasis remains to be drawn from it concerning the nature of the melos it preserved. This is that the minimally pitch-specific, minimally nuance-indicative neumations of the nuance-poor archetype were viable transmitters

[61] Le graduel romain. Édition critique, IV/2, p. 64; the chief witnesses of the 'écriture sangallienne' (Gal 1, Mur 3, Bab, and Gal 2) and 'messine' (Lan) would count as nuance-rich. But for Froger's other species the neumes fit that description to a much lesser degree or not at all. Froger dropped the north Italian manuscript Milan, Biblioteca Trivulziana, D. 127 in a subsequent presentation, reducing the number of sub-families to nine: 'The Critical Edition of the Roman Gradual by the Monks of Solesmes', Journal of the Plainsong and Mediaeval Music Society, 1 (1978), pp. 85–6. I would retain this Civate missal as a reflection of the nuance-poor original, and add to the list other early copies such as Cambrai, Bibliothèque Municipale, MS 75(76) (Arras); Paris, Bibliothèque Nationale, MSS fonds lat. 9434 (Tours), 18010 (Corbie) and 9448 (Prüm); Baltimore, Walters Art Gallery, MS 11 (Forlimpopoli–Ravenna); Vatican City, Biblioteca Apostolica Vaticana, MSS Vat. lat. 4770 (Abruzzi) and Vat. urb. lat. 560 (central Italy).
[62] Paléographie Musicale 16: L'Antiphonaire du Mont-Renaud (Solesmes, 1955); on the origin and date of its notation: Le graduel romain, II (1957), 157, and the remarks by M. Huglo in JAMS, 32 (1979), p. 556. Concerning the earliest nuance-rich sources there is the important article by P. Jeffery, 'An Early Cantatorium Fragment Related to MS. Laon 239', Scriptorium, 36 (1982), pp. 245–52.
[63] 'Les noms des neumes', p. 53.
[64] Cardine, 'A propos des formes possibles d'une figure neumatique', p. 61.

of the Gregorian melos because that melos was imprinted in all its fullness upon professional memories. The church musicians who opted for the inexact aides-mémoire of staffless neumes – for skeletal notations that ignored exact pitch-heights and bypassed many nuances – were content with incomplete representations of melodic substance because the full substance seemed safely lodged in memory. This simple calculus of notation and memory says that the Gregorian chants from their first neumation were no longer 'improvised' – that few if any options were left for the strategies and vagaries of individual performers. The chants were concretised, reified entities, recognisable in their specific melodic dress, integrally stored and reproducible from memory.

4. An eroding memory and supplemented notation. Then the back-up memories began to fail. The written technology that became the partner of memory, by its availability and exercise rendered memory more fallible. Enterprising scribes might have responded to the inadequacies of the authorised neumation from the start by devising improvements in specifying pitch, nuance and duration – improvements for the sake of system itself. But more purposeful efforts to increase written specifity would have been a response to increasing concern for the integrity of the melodic tradition. The neume-species c. 900 would represent a century's-worth of notational tinkerings, carried out in different ways at different places, and with particular zeal at proud schools like those of Laon and St Gall.[65]

5. Copying from dictation. Yet there may be more to the diversity of neume-species. Our preserved neumations of the Gregorian mass propers are in most cases simple duplications of a written model. Reflecting ultimately the notational shapes in Charlemagne's arche-type, they were recorded from a direct viewing of that original or one of its descendants. But it was also possible to take copies from dictation. A setting-down of heard sounds was a natural process for musicians, the way any musical text was originally established. It offered the possibility of speed and convenience, with simultaneous

[65] Carolingian Laon is the focus of Peter Jeffery's 'An Early Cantatorium Fragment' and of recent studies by John J. Contreni: *The Cathedral School of Laon from 850 to 930: Its Manuscripts and Masters* (Munich, 1978); *Codex Laudunensis 468: A Ninth-Century Guide to Virgil, Sedulius, and the Liberal Arts* (1984).

duplications from a single, perhaps difficultly accessible exemplar.[66] One can imagine two parallel tracks for the Gregorian musical transmission. On the one hand, an authorised neumation whose conjunct, nuance-poor shapes were scrupulously reproduced, sign by sign. On the other hand, 'dictation'. Carolingian and Ottonian musicians sang the chants in order to convey their full melodic substance. Master musicians had to accompany the neumed exemplars, repeating phrase by phrase so that others could learn. Musicians journeying to Carolingian centres would have been instructed in this way, and in some instances the actual writing-down of the chant may have resulted from such melodic dictation rather than from visual replication. The dictation removed the scribe from the shapes on the page, and with that distancing from the palaeographic model there may have been a freedom to personalise the neumatic shapes.

6. A gestural mind-set. There may be still another factor behind the palaeographic variety of the neume-species. I return here to the two fundamental neume-types – Type 1/graphic and Type 2/ gestural, which I have distinguished, not as styles or ductus but as processes or methods. Now the promulgators of the Type 2 noted archetype supplied a model that was gesturally conceived. My point is that the gestural method itself may have encouraged a bypassing of the model's specific neume-shapes in favour of neumations that were continuously fresh 're-gesturings' of the well-remembered Gregorian melos. Each step in the writing process, each notational act, each ligature, each neume set down, would be the manifestation of a gestural impulse. Each Type 2 neumation – from the Carolingian original through its network of descendants – would be executed, not merely as the copy of a written model but in an overriding sense as the active realisation of the method. The resulting neumations would reflect personal and local choices as to what was notationally accurate and vivid. It may be from the vitality of

66 W. Wattenbach, *Das Schriftwesen im Mittelalter* (4th edn, Graz, 1958), pp. 421ff, gives indications and contra-indications of dictation as a factor in copying texts. Professor Robert Snow, with whom I have been privileged to discuss this issue, believes dictation had a significant role in the process of neuming. It has a role in the familiar iconographic topos of the dove dictating the Sacramentary or the Antiphoner to Pope Gregory who then dictates to a scribe; this is dealt with by B. Stäblein, ' "Gregorius Praesul", der Prolog zum römischen Antiphonale', *Musik und Verlag: Festschrift K. Vötterle*, ed. R. Baum and W. Rehm (Kassel, 1968), pp. 554f, with further observations by L. Treitler, 'Homer and Gregory', *The Musical Quarterly*, 60 (1974), pp. 337–44.

this gestural mind-set that some of the variety in tenth- and eleventh-century neumations flows.[67]

I have offered fresh scenarios for three early stages of neume history: 1. ultimate origins; 2. the Frankish–Gregorian noted mass-book *c.* 800; and 3. the emergence of neume-species *c.* 900. Concerning ultimate origins, instead of a single development embracing all neumatic incunabula, I suggest two distinct developments: an earlier one of Type 1/graphic neumes whose aim was to describe pitch-positions; and a later one of Type 2/gestural neumes whose aim was to describe intervallic flow. Type 1/graphic is documented in the scattered vestiges of the Palaeofrank notation. Its principle would be to provide simple visual analogues of pitch-loci. Thus it was useful for establishing a written text and for editorial modifications. It may reflect the processes of church musicians engaged in a first conversion of chants from oral dictation to neumatic record. And this would dispose of all prior theories that have derived neume-origins from prosodic accents, Byzantine melodic notations, punctuation-signs, language-usage, cheironomy, ekphonetic notations, and combinations of these. The Type 2/gestural neumes would represent a different method, incorporated in the lost Carolingian archetype of Gregorian chant: Charlemagne's archetype, the Frankish *editio princeps* from which the main line of surviving neumed propers descends. This gestural method aimed to produce charts that were vivid as memory aids and easily animated as hand-and-arm motions for guiding performance. It is only to the Type 2/gestural notation that one of the traditional neumatic etiologies would apply – the notion of cheironomy – but with no link to origins.

The dates and places of these developments remain obscure. Graphic neumes may reach back to Gregory the Great or farther, but they are likely to be a Frankish or cooperative Roman–Frankish innovation of the 760s or 770s, occasioned by Pepin's substitution of the Roman chant for the Gallican. The gestural neumes would

[67] The neumes transmitting the ninth–eleventh-century repertories of Hispanic chant all seem to represent the same Type 2/gestural origins as those for the Gregorian–Roman chants. Despite their differences in appearance, the two major varieties of Spanish notation, those with vertical ductus, representing mainly the northern regions of the peninsula, and those with horizontal ductus, representing Toledo and the south, may descend from a common adoption of Carolingian notational practices that would have reached Galicia, Asturias or the Spanish March by the earlier ninth century; see my 'Old-Hispanic Chant in its European Context', *Congreso Internacional: España en la Musica de Occidente, Salamanca, 1985*, ed. I. Fernández de la Cuesta (Madrid, 1987), I, pp. 1–16.

follow during the 770s to the 790s. The gestural recension could replace the graphic in a very short time.

As for my second and third stages – the transition from Charlemagne's archetype of *c.* 800 through Froger's 'zone brumeuse' to the neume-species of *c.* 900 – the proposal is that the Type 2/gestural neumes of *c.* 800 were not yet nuance-rich (laden with auxiliary indications of pitch, rhythm and other performance details), but instead were nuance-poor, with a minimum of details. Inasmuch as the melodic and rhythmic auxiliaries take different forms in different neume-species, and are to some extent in conflict as to system, the notational enrichments are likely to be additions to an archetype that was itself sparse in detail. The many nuance-poor copies of the tenth and eleventh centuries would thus be viewed as faithful replications of a nuance-poor original rather than degradations of one that was nuance-rich. The neumators who supplemented the skeletal early notations drew on professional memories where the substance of the chants remained crystallised for some generations after the neumed transmission began. A further reason for the diversity of the neume-species around 900 may be the practice of taking copies from dictation; and perhaps as well an inherent licence of the gestural method which encouraged scribes to personalise the mimetics of chant notation and shape their own gestural forms.

These proposals depend to a considerable extent on the distinction between two methods of neuming, graphic and gestural. That is something for which I cannot offer independent support. Yet if the conjectures about the nature and purpose of the two methods are not altogether wide of the mark, then the early developments of neumatic notation stand illumined in ways that have not previously seemed possible. In the gestural rationale that I suggest for the archetypal Carolingian–Gregorian neumation of the late eighth century, there is an explanation of the diversity of ductus and procedure that mark the earliest noted collections *c.* 900. And in the graphic rationale that I suggest for the neumatic development prior to the gestural, there is the chance of a clarification still farther back. With the graphic neumes one may reach the murky border between oral and written transmissions, where the process can be discerned by which Latin church melodies were first converted to written record.

CHAPTER 6

On Gregorian Orality

C<small>AN ONE LOOK BACK AT THE BEGINNINGS OF PLAINCHANT</small> and see an unwritten melos behind the musical substances that are profiled in early neumes? Viewing orality by way of the written record has long had an appeal. When Peter Wagner and Paolo Ferretti described florid Gregorian Tracts as realizations of "psalmodic" frameworks, the oral, improvisatory element was already basic to their conception of melodic origins.[1] For the nineteenth century's pioneers in plainchant history, this was not yet so. The Mass and Office Propers in preserved neumations were taken to be faithful copies of authoritative written models that were established under Gregory the Great. This view was encouraged by John the Deacon's Life of Gregory, which hinted at an exemplar of Gregorian times preserved at the Lateran during the later ninth century,[2] and by other Carolingian mythmakers who alluded to a "Gregorian" antecedent for the chanted propers in trope-like

---

[1] Peter Wagner, *Einführung in die Gregorianischen Melodien*, vol. 3, *Gregorianische Formenlehre* (Leipzig: Breitkopf und Härtel, 1921), x: "Ihr Stil: freiere psalmodieähnliche Variationen. . . ." Paolo Ferretti, *Estetica gregoriana, ossia Trattato delle forme musicali del canto gregoriano*, vol. 1 (Rome: Pontificio Istituto di Musica Sacra, 1934), 132–39.

[2] The text (2.6) does not imply neumes: "Lateranensis . . . ubi usque hodie lectus ejus, in quo recubans modulabatur, et flagellum ipsius, quo pueris minabatur, veneratione congrua cum authentico Antiphonario reservatur . . ."; Jacques Paul Migne, *Patrologiae Cursus Completus . . . Series Latina*, vol. 75 (Paris: Garnier, 1862), col. 90. J. L. F. Danjou, who first drew attention to the Gradual-Tonary of Saint-Bénigne of Dijon (Montpellier, Faculté de Médecine, MS H. 159), described it as "un des Antiphonaires notés au commencement du IXe siècle, ou par un des clercs que Charlemagne avait fait étudier à Rome, ou par un des chantres que le pape Adrien avait envoyés en France, lesquels avaient sous les yeux l'exemplaire noté de la main même de saint Grégoire, exemplaire qu'on voyait encore au Xe siècle à Saint-Jean-de-Latran"; cited in *Paléographie musicale*, vol. 7 (Solesmes: Imprimerie Saint-Pierre, 1901), 9–10 after *Revue de la musique liturgique*, December 1847. The Belgian Jesuit Louis Lambillotte, who in 1851 edited a diplomatic facsimile of the Cantatorium, Saint Gall 359, believed "dans ce monument unique, nous possédons véritablement l'oeuvre de Saint Grégoire"; he supposed that particular manuscript was copied ca. 790, after "l'Antiphonaire autographe de Saint Grégoire"; *Antiphonaire de Saint Grégoire. Facsimile de manuscrit de Saint-Gall*, 2nd ed. (Brussels: CH.-J.-A. Greuse, 1867), 10.

First published in *JAMS*, 43 (1990), 185–227. Reprinted by permission.

encomia that preface some early musical collections.[3] The association of "Gregory" with neumed plainchant needed revision as it became clear that the surviving noted documents were much later than the sixth–seventh centuries. In place of the written "Gregorian" original, the notion took hold of an unwritten transmission between the melodies' conception and their writing-down. This was not readily acknowledged, in part because it raised knotty historical and theological problems, but in part because specialists for a long while had enough else to occupy them. Oral-improvisational issues were set aside as they analyzed the received Gregorian versions for their modal behavior and melodic structure, pondered the origin of the neumes, and debated the nature of rhythmic and microtonal nuances.

Issues of orality reached the surface at the International Congress of Sacred Music held at Rome in 1950. Eugène Cardine reported there on the projected Benedictine *édition critique* of the Gregorian Mass Propers, and he declared that between the music's origin and its conversion to neumes there lay a stage of oral transmission.[4] Walter Lipphardt spoke of "Kernmelodien," and a "lebendige Improvisations-kunst," which he identified with the "Italian South," contrasting it with the more sculptural shapes he saw as the products of a northern "fränkischen Tradition."[5] Lipphardt's notions of improvisatory art and Frankish tradition were stimulated by Bruno Stäblein's paper delivered at that same Congress, reviewing the relationship between the Old Roman and Gregorian repertories.[6] With this, the link between melodic origins and musical notation was cut, and in its place stood the questions concerning oral transmission that have since been high on specialists' agendas. Contributions came from Hucke (begin-

---

[3] "Gregorius praesul . . . qui . . . conposuit hunc libellum musicae artis scolae cantorum"; in the Monza Cantatorium, fol. 2, ed. René-Jean Hesbert, *Antiphonale Missarum Sextuplex* (Brussels: Vromant, 1935), 2; Bruno Stäblein, "'Gregorius prae-sul,' der Prolog zum römischen Antiphonale," in *Musik und Verlag: Karl Vötterle zum 65. Geburtstag* (Kassel: Bärenreiter, 1968), 537–61; Michel Huglo, *Les livres de chant liturgique*, Typologie des sources du moyen âge occidental. Directeur: L. Genicot. Fasc. 52 (Turnhout: Brepols, 1988), 81, 101–21.

[4] Eugène Cardine, "De l'édition critique du Graduel," in Higini Anglès, ed., *Atti del Congresso Internazionale di Musica Sacra* (Rome, 1950; reprint, Tournai: Desclée, 1952), 190: "la notation musicale . . . ayant fait son apparition vers la fin du IXe siècle sous forme de neumes . . . nous n'aurons pas là le livre primitif sous sa forme matérielle, puisque la notation musicale était alors inconnue."

[5] Walter Lipphardt, "Gregor der Grosse und sein Anteil am römischen Antipho-nar," in *Atti del Congresso Internazionale di Musica Sacra*, 248–54.

[6] Stäblein, "Zur Frühgeschichte des römischen Chorals," in *Atti del Congresso Internazionale di Musica Sacra*, 271–75.

ning in 1953),[7] Apel (1956),[8] Levy (1963),[9] Cutter (1967),[10] and
Connolly (1972).[11] Already in 1957, Ferand added the perspective of
a specialist in improvisation.[12] Then Nettl in 1974 examined the
nature and scope of improvisatory practice with an ethnomusicolo-
gist's rigor. At one end of Nettl's spectrum lay free, ecstatic deliveries
of a sort imaginable at ultimate beginnings: music that is the outcome
of "unpremeditated, spur of the moment decisions." At the other end
lay a melos that is essentially fixed and memorized, with only a
narrow margin for embellishment: the singers are "performing a
version of something."[13] Much of plainchant doubtless began as freely
improvised oral delivery, and much of it may have remained near that
freer end of the improvisatory spectrum throughout its oral transmission. It may only have been the availability of neumes that rendered
the fixing of melodic shapes a practicality. Yet it may also be that
some chants during the purely oral stage went from the freely
improvisatory toward more calculated methods of melodic production. Events during a stage prior to notation are by their nature

[7] Helmut Hucke, "Musikalische Formen des Offiziumsantiphonen," *Kirchenmusikalisches Jahrbuch* 37 (1953): 7–33; idem, "Zur Entwicklung des christlichen
Kultgesangs zum Gregorianischen Gesang," *Römische Quartalschrift* 48 (1953): 172–85;
idem, "Improvisation im Gregorianischen Gesang," *Kirchenmusikalisches Jahrbuch* 38
(1954): 5–8.
[8] Willi Apel, "The Central Problem of Gregorian Chant," this JOURNAL 9 (1956):
118–27; idem, *Gregorian Chant* (Bloomington: Indiana University Press, 1958), 324
and 511, dealing with the second-mode tracts and "skeleton melodies."
[9] Kenneth Levy, "The Byzantine Sanctus and its Modal Tradition in East and
West," *Annales musicologiques* 6 (1958–63): 52–59; idem, "The Trisagion in Byzantium
and the West," *Report of the Eleventh Congress of the International Musicological Society,
Copenhagen, 1972*, ed. Henrik Glahn, Søren Sørenson, and Peter Ryom (Copenhagen:
Wilhelm Hansen, 1974), 761–65.
[10] Paul F. Cutter, "The Old-Roman Chant Tradition: Oral or Written?," this
JOURNAL 20 (1967): 167–81; idem, "Oral Transmission of the Old-Roman Responsories?," *The Musical Quarterly* 62 (1976): 182–94.
[11] Thomas H. Connolly, "Introits and Archetypes: Some Archaisms of the Old
Roman Chant," this JOURNAL 25 (1972): 157–74.
[12] Ernest Ferand, "Improvisation," *Die Musik in Geschichte und Gegenwart*, vol. 6
(Kassel: Bärenreiter, 1957), cols. 1096–1100. "Das melismatische Singen, später in
den responsorischen Formen des greg. Gsg. bevorzugt, weist improvisatorische Züge
in besonders reichem Masse auf . . . Spuren der Improvisationspraxis sind in den
meisten Formen des greg. Gsg. nachweisbar oder zumindest zu vermuten . . ." (col.
1098).
[13] Bruno Nettl, "Thoughts on Improvisation: A Comparative Approach," *The
Musical Quarterly* 60 (1974): 1–19; cf. 3; also Nettl's "Types of Tradition and
Transmission," in *Cross-Cultural Perspectives on Music*, ed. Robert Falck and Timothy
Rice (Toronto: University of Toronto Press, 1982), 3–19.

"probably irrecoverable," as David Hughes has put it,[14] but in what follows I will venture such a recovery.

Questions of plainchant orality continued to be dealt with by a narrow circle of specialists until a series of papers by Leo Treitler and Helmut Hucke, begun in 1974, brought them to broader musicological attention.[15] Treitler's and Hucke's proposals are concerned with four subject-areas. One is the date of the Gregorian corpus's conversion to neumes; in agreement with Solange Corbin, they put this about 900.[16] Two is the rationale of the early neuming technique; they find this largely in Carolingian punctuation practice.[17] Three is the nature of melodic production after the introduction of neumes; along with Ferand and van der Werf, they envisage oral-improvisational practices that were "reconstructive" or "reimprovisational," continuing during the first two or three centuries of the noted transmission.[18] My own views on each of these have been rather

---

[14] "Evidence for the Traditional View of the Transmission of Gregorian Chant," this JOURNAL 40 (1987): 377.

[15] Recent positions appear in the "Communication" by Treitler in this JOURNAL 41 (1988): 566–75, and in Hucke's "Gregorianische Fragen," *Die Musikforschung* 41 (1988): 304–30, particularly 326–30; these contain responses to criticisms that were launched in my "Charlemagne's Archetype of Gregorian Chant," this JOURNAL 40 (1987): 1–30, and by David Hughes in "Evidence for the Traditional View of the Transmission of Gregorian Chant." Hughes has further remarks in two "Communications": this JOURNAL 41 (1988): 578–79, and 42 (1989): 435–37.

[16] Solange Corbin, "Les notations neumatiques en France à l'époque carolingienne," *Revue d'histoire de l'église en France* 38 (1952): 226–28; idem, "Les neumes," in Roland Manuel, ed., *Histoire de la musique*, Encyclopédie de la Pléiade, no. 9 (Paris: Gallimard, 1960), vol. 1, 690–94; idem, *Die Neumen*, Palaeographie der Musik nach den Plänen Leo Schrades, vol. 1, sect. 3 (Cologne: Arno Volk-Verlag, 1977), 22–42; Treitler, "Reading and Singing: On the Genesis of Occidental Music-Writing," *Early Music History* 4 (1984): 176; Hucke, "Toward a New Historical View of Gregorian Chant," this JOURNAL 33 (1980): 445. In "Oral, Written, and Literate Process in the Transmission of Medieval Music," *Speculum* 56 (1981): 474–75, Treitler states, "Before the tenth century the tradition of Western art music was an oral tradition."

[17] Treitler, "The Early History of Music Writing in the West," this JOURNAL 35 (1982): 237–79; idem, "Reading and Singing: On the Genesis of Occidental Music Writing," 135–208; idem, "Die Entstehung der abendländischen Notenschrift," *Die Musikforschung* 37 (1984): 259–67; Hucke, "Die Anfänge der abendländischen Notenschrift," *Festschrift Rudolf Elvers*, ed. Ernst Herttrich and Hans Schneider (Tutzing: H. Schneider Verlag, 1985), 271–88.

[18] Ferand, "Improvisation," col. 1099: "Die Unbestimmtheit der Neumenschrift, zumindest in ihren Anfängen, ist in dem Umstand begründet, dass die so aufgezeichneten Gesänge selbst keine eindeutigen festen Gebilde waren, sondern lediglich mehr oder weniger in Umrissen gegebene Melodieskelette, die von den Sängern in vielfach veränderter Gestalt improvisatorisch immer wider neugefasst wurden." Treitler speaks of Gregorian chant in a similar vein: "The oral tradition was translated after the ninth century into writing. But the evolution from a performance practice represented in writing, to a tradition of composing, transmission, and reading, took

different, and they are already spelled out to some extent in earlier papers.[19] My focus now is on the fourth area, concerning the nature of the melos before neumes were introduced, and the relation between the vanished oral and the written versions that we have. This is the most significant of the areas, and the most challenging, in that it addresses the substance of the prehistoric melos and the basis for forming opinions about it. In Treitler's and Hucke's conceptions, good access to the oral states is had by way of the preserved written states, and what these reveal are improvisational practices that were relatively free. The Gregorian melodies arose from "the continuity of performance."[20] The preserved versions are witnesses of "a performance practice represented in writing,"[21] "documentations of a performance practice,"[22] "frozen improvisations";[23] they offer "trans-

---

place over a span of centuries. . . . The act of writing was thus a kind of performance analogous to singing out, and the written score served as an exemplification of the song, to be taken more as a model for performance than as a blueprint"; "The Early History of Music Writing," 237. He supplies this process with the name of "reconstruction": "a repeated process of performance-composition—something between the reproduction of a fixed, memorized melody and the extempore invention of a new one. I would call it a reconstruction; the performer had to think how the piece was to go and then actively reconstruct it according to what he remembered"; in "'Centonate' Chant: übles Flickwerk or E pluribus unus?," this JOURNAL 28 (1975): 11. Hendrik van der Werf gives this the name "reimprovisation"; *The Emergence of Gregorian Chant: A Comparative Study of Ambrosian, Roman, and Gregorian Chant* (Rochester: the Author, 1983), vol. 1, part 1, *A Study of Modes and Melodies*, 164–66; "the tradition according to which a given melody was reimprovised for every occasion, including even the act of copying it . . . ; the persistence of the unheighted neumes in places like Sankt Gallen is testimony to the continued interest in reimprovisation. It made no sense to notate precisely melodies which one knew to vary from one year to another and from one singer to the next"; ibid., 165.

[19] On the nature of the melos after neumes ("reimprovisation"), in my "Communication" to this JOURNAL 41 (1988): 576; on the date of the Gregorian neumation, in "Charlemagne's Archetype of Gregorian Chant"; on neumatic etiology, in "On the Origin of Neumes," *Early Music History* 7 (1987): 59–90.

[20] Treitler, "Homer and Gregory: The Transmission of Epic Poetry and Chant," *The Musical Quarterly* 60 (1974): 346.

[21] Treitler, "The Early History of Music Writing in the West," 237.

[22] Hucke, "Toward a New Historical View of Gregorian Chant," 453–54; the refrains of two Gregorian responsories "are not different, individual melodies in a strict sense. They are 'documentations of a performance practice.'" In Hucke's "Die Anfänge der Bearbeitung": "Das Stammrepertoire des Gregorianischen Gesangs ist Aufzeichnung aus mündlicher überlieferung"; in *Bearbeitung in der Musik. Colloquium Kurt von Fischer zum 70. Geburtstag*, ed. Dorothea Baumann, *Schweizer Jahrbuch für Musikwissenschaft*, Neue Folge, 3 (1983): 16.

[23] Hucke, "Der übergang von mündlicher zu schriftlicher Musiküberlieferung im Mittelalter," in *Report of the Twelfth Congress of the International Musicological Society, Berkeley, 1977*, ed. Daniel Heartz and Bonnie Wade (Basel: Bärenreiter, 1981),

parent" images of bygone oral deliveries.[24] In light of earlier discussions of orality, reaching back to Cardine's and Lipphardt's declarations of 1950, these assertions are not altogether novel, so that an occasional tone of discoverer's fervor that is evident in them is a bit surprising. Treitler's recent "Communication" has it: "what is striking is the resistance to a serious confrontation with the reality that at some time in history, no matter how far back one wants to push it, the Western musical heritage goes back to an oral tradition that left its mark and that is never entirely out of the picture as a factor in musical practice."[25] That protests too much. The question has long been, not whether oral elements survive, but how much oral there is, and how one goes about making its identification. Some of the Gregorian neumed versions may represent faithful recordings of bygone oral-improvisational deliveries; they may be "transparent" witnesses of the oral past. Others may represent only the last stages in a multi-stage process where compositional and editorial additions that entered during prior written stages now obstruct the view.

What promised to be a major support for conjectures about oral melodic behavior was the analogy, introduced by Treitler in 1974, between Gregorian chant and the works of Balkan epic bards. Plainchant stood to be illuminated by the practice of ancient Homer and of the modern Serbian-Macedonian "singers of tales" whose productions were analyzed in the comparative literary studies of Parry and Lord.[26] The link of "Homer and Gregory" catches the fancy, but apart from both of them once being "oral," there is little basis for crossover. The improvisatory flights of Gregorian plainchant took place in the medium of music; those of epic bards in the medium of words; and what Parry and Lord dealt with were the verbal texts. For plainchant, the texts come verbatim from Scripture (or sometimes Patristic literature), and are not results of improvisatory elaboration. The improvisations that produced the bardic texts also differ in

---

180–90. "In der schriftlichen überlieferung von Solostücken ist, beispielsweise in den Tractus und in den Gradualienversen, eine Vortragspraxis eingefroren worden" (p. 180).

[24] Treitler, "Communication" in this JOURNAL 41 (1988): 575: "No matter how uniform the written transmission is, and even if we regard it exclusively as a product of copying faithfully from one source to another, it is transparent to the oral tradition that was its ultimate source."

[25] Treitler, "Communication," 575.

[26] Albert B. Lord, *The Singer of Tales* (Cambridge: Harvard University Press, 1960); also Lord's summary, "Oral Poetry," in Alex Preminger, et al., *Princeton Encyclopedia of Poetry and Poetics* (Princeton: Princeton University Press, 1965), 591–93.

character from those of the plainchant melos. For the epic, the verbal basis is the stichic one-liner; in Homer, the dactyllic hexameter. Epic continuities are built up in a succession of such short repeated formations. In modern epic there is a tendency for the music to conform to the shapes of the repeating one-liners;[27] a similar conformity is projected for Homeric music, operating under hexametric constraints.[28] Freer melismatic, "improvisational" elaborations of the sort that may have contributed to the shaping of florid Gregorian chants have no counterpart in epic at all. Then too, the improvisers of epic were soloists. There are solo Gregorian chants that display a marked improvisational thrust, as was recognized in Wagner's description of Tracts as "psalmodie-ähnliche Variationen."[29] Yet in Gregorian responsorial chants, the solo passages are often linked in style and substance to the choral passages. For the choral deliveries of a Gregorian *schola cantorum*, considerable predetermination and coordination must be supposed. Such improvisational flights as are generated in a "process of oral composition through performance"[30] would find little place.[31]

[27] James A. Notopoulos, *Modern Greek Heroic Poetry* (Ethnic Folkways Library Album FE 4468, New York, 1960) discussed examples of the techniques; see also Stathis Gauntlett, *Rebetika Carmina Graeciae Recentioris: A Contribution to the Definition of the Term and the Genre rebetiko tragoudi through Detailed Analysis of its Verses and of the Evolution of its Performance* (D. Phil. diss., Oxford University, 1978; Athens: Denise Harvey, 1985), 61: "the processes of improvised oral composition appear to have been expedited by the large degree of uniformity which exists in the metrical and strophic specifications of these verses. . . . This widespread uniformity would have secured considerable flexibility in combination of couplets from different cycles and scope for the interchange of melodies between cycles."

[28] Giovanni Comotti, *Music in Greek and Roman Culture* (Baltimore: Johns Hopkins University Press, 1989), 14: "the hexameter poetry of the rhapsodes, recited rather than sung, such as the great Homeric epics (the *Iliad* and the *Odyssey*)." For the lyrics of Sappho, "the melodic sequences on which these songs were modulated had evidently a very simple structure that conformed to the metrical figures of the poetic text"; ibid, 21.

[29] Wagner, *Einführung in die Gregorianischen Melodien*, vol. 3, *Gregorianische Formenlehre*, 353.

[30] Treitler, "'Centonate' Chant," 12.

[31] This difficulty is acknowledged by Treitler in the ultimate footnote to his initial paper. His apparent response is to question the antiquity of the Gregorian antiphonal and responsorial Propers ("Homer and Gregory," 371–72, n. 22): "One question will surely have arisen in the minds of thoughtful readers of the present essay: all of my inferences have been about 'the singer,' whereas we think of the performance of the antiphonal and responsorial chants of the Mass and Office as involving choirs. Does this not make the hypothesis of oral composition inapplicable to all but the small minority of chants for soloists, such as the tracts on which I have mainly based the foregoing analysis? Not at all. I shall briefly mention the most important considerations. (a) The hypothesis is meant to apply only through the eighth century at the

Apart from the questionable fit between "Homer" and "Gregory," the more fundamental trouble with such projections about orality is that they are based on what amounts to a single witness. Gregorian chant reaches us in a remarkably uniform state. Hundreds of manuscripts of the ninth through thirteenth centuries represent a tradition that was established by Carolingian musicians under a mandate to impose a single authoritative usage in their realm. This unity of tradition has been underscored by David Hughes.[32] What matters here is that other musical versions are generally lost. The Gregorian text that comes down is a unique source which is not "oral" and "early" but "written" and "late." Efforts to identify oral elements through analysis of its fabric are bound to remain, as they were with the "psalmodic" designations of Wagner and Ferretti, exercises in personal intuition.

*   *   *

For surer indications of an oral state one wants better evidence. Something like this may be obtained from cases of parallel readings or "multiples." Where two or more plainchants (generally representatives of different liturgical families) share the same texts and ritual functions, and also some amount of modal-melodic substance, their music in common may represent an earlier "oral" formulation. Dom Mocquereau made comparisons of this sort a century ago, paralleling the Gregorian, Milanese, and Old-Roman versions of the Introit

---

latest for the Gregorian tradition; for the Old Roman, speculation can be of only the most tentative sort, pending more systematic study. (b) The first testimony we have of antiphonal choral singing is given by Amalarius of Metz, who wrote in the ninth century; earlier than that there is anecdotal evidence of refrain singing by the congregation, and of responsorial singing by a choir. (c) In principle, refrain singing is not as such in conflict with the practice of oral composition. This question reminds us in general of how very much in the dark we remain about the place of the choir in the early history of plainchant." To deny the existence of the eighth-century Proper repertory (the repertory in Hesbert's Sextuplex) this way seems less than convincing, as does Hucke's response to the same question in "Der übergang von mündlicher zu schriftlicher Musiküberlieferung im Mittelalter," 180–90; cf. 182.

[32] "Evidence for the Traditional View of the Transmission of Gregorian Chant," 398: "The extreme stability of the basic tradition is obvious enough. An ideal example of this is the transmission of the Alleluia Dies sanctificatus . . . ; here a complex melismatic tune recurs virtually unchanged in source after source and texting after texting. For an equally convincing and more accessible instance of stability one may leaf through the pages of the *Graduale Triplex* (Solesmes: Abbaye Saint-Pierre, 1979) noting how rarely the readings of Lan and Mur 3 disagree."

Resurrexi and the Gradual *A summo caelo*.[33] Stäblein made use of similar comparisons in 1950 in launching the current round of speculations about Old Roman chant.[34] Recently, Dom Claire has used multiples to seek out archaic modality and the "corde-mère" of certain modes;[35] Alberto Turco, to consider the "marche vers l'Octoéchos" of certain antiphons;[36] Terence Bailey, the links among Ambrosian, Old Beneventan, and Roman repertories;[37] van der Werf, the existence of "parent melodies."[38] I have used multiples to address archaic states of the anaphoral chants, of the Easter-vigil mass, and the Trisagion.[39] In 1984, I pointed to multiples found in Old-Hispanic, Gregorian, and Ambrosian traditions as indications that certain Proper chants that are first preserved in neumes of the tenth through twelfth centuries had assumed much of their eventual melodic shape by about 700.[40]

For multiples to be of use in viewing oral states, they must meet certain conditions. The neumations should be relatively early, as close as possible to the time of oral transmission. They should be different enough to be seen as the fruits of independent acts of writing, and not as outgrowths of a common written model. Yet their melodic substances should be alike enough to suggest some of the musical physiognomy of an ultimate oral source. These conditions are not easily met. The written versions tend to be late: a Gregorian witness may go back to the later ninth or tenth century, but the counterpart Old Roman, Milanese, Beneventan, or Ravennate witnesses may begin only with the eleventh or twelfth century. The influence of one written version upon another cannot be discounted: the neumed Gregorian version may have been the model for the others. Then too,

---

[33] *Paléographie musicale*, vol. 2 (Solesmes: Imprimerie Saint-Pierre, 1891), 6–9.

[34] Stäblein, "Zur Frühgeschichte des römischen Chorals," 271–75. A recent contribution is Stefan Klöckner's "Analytische Untersuchungen an 16. Introiten im I. Ton des altrömischen und des fränkisch-gregorianischen Repertoires hinsichtlich einer bewussten melodischen Abhängigkeit," *Beiträge zur Gregorianik* 5 (1988): 3–95.

[35] Jean Claire, "L'Evolution modale et les répertoires liturgiques occidentaux," *Revue grégorienne* 40 (1962): 196–210, 229–45; idem, "La psalmodie responsoriale antique," *Revue grégorienne* 41 (1963): 7–29; idem, "Les répertoires liturgiques latins avant l'Octoéchos," *Études grégoriennes* 15 (1975): 1–181 and supplement.

[36] "Les répertoires liturgiques latins," 177–221; also his "Melodie-tipo e timbri modali nell' Antiphonale romanum," in *Studi Gregoriani* 3 (1897): 191–241.

[37] Terence Bailey, *The Ambrosian Alleluias* (London: The Plainsong and Mediaeval Music Society, 1983), 53–60.

[38] van der Werf, *The Emergence of Gregorian Chant*, vol. 1, part 1, 110.

[39] Levy, "The Byzantine Sanctus and its Modal Tradition in East and West," 7–67; idem, "The Italian Neophytes' Chants," this JOURNAL 23 (1970): 181–227; idem "The Trisagion in Byzantium and the West," 761–65.

[40] "Toledo, Rome and the Legacy of Gaul," *Early Music History* 4 (1984): 49–99.

when plainchants travel they tend to take on the stylistic features of the regions where they settle. The first things obscured by a new stylization are the surface details of what went before.

Some years ago, I examined a situation that met these conditions unusually well. It was a case of what I now propose calling "close multiples." For the processional Antiphon *Deprecamur te Domine*, there is a "Gregorian" pedigree perhaps better than that for any other chant. Through citations in Bede and the *Vita* of St. Augustine of Canterbury it can be traced to the Roman liturgical environment under Gregory the Great.[41] There are four medieval versions of its music. All are in the protos with finals on D. The Old Roman and Milanese versions are independent in their melodic details. Of the other two, one is a widely-circulated "Carolingian" version, and one appears only in the Beneventan zone. They have musical substances that are often identical although their neumations may be independent. This offers a possible window on an oral stage. The closer their agreement, the sharper the view through that window.

This notion was advanced tentatively for *Deprecamur*. Now there may be a stronger case of close multiples with the Offertory *Elegerunt apostoli*. This chant for St. Stephen Protomartyr has often been cited as a Gallican relic surviving in a Gregorian liturgical environment.[42] I have lent support by observing that *Elegerunt*'s text is not a verbatim excerpt from the Psalter (as is the case with most Gregorian offertories), but a patchwork of "non-psalmic" phrases drawn from *Acts* 6 and 7. Texts of this "centonate-libretto" sort are the norm among the florid Hispanic Offertories. Inasmuch as *Elegerunt* serves as a basis for florid Offertories in both the Mozarabic and Gregorian rites, it represents a class of "international" chants for which a Gallican antecedent can be supposed.[43]

Among the earliest Gregorian documents, *Elegerunt* finds only a marginal place. In Hesbert's collection of old unnoted Mass Propers it

---

[41] Levy, "A Gregorian Processional Antiphon," *Schweizer Jahrbuch für Musikwissenschaft*, Neue Folge, 2 (1982): 91–102.

[42] *Paléographie musicale*, vol. 15 (Solesmes: Imprimerie Saint-Pierre, 1937–53), 165: "d'origine gallicane"; Michel Huglo, "Altgallikanische Liturgie," in Karl Gustav Fellerer, *Geschichte der katholischen Kirchenmusik* (Kassel: Bärenreiter, 1972), vol. 1, 226; Huglo, "Gallican Rite, Music," in *The New Grove Dictionary of Music and Musicians* (London: Macmillan, 1980), vol. 7, 116–17; Giacomo Bonifacio Baroffio and Ruth Steiner, "Offertory," in ibid, vol. 13, 515.

[43] Levy, "Toledo, Rome and the Legacy of Gaul," 80–87; Hucke's "Die Texte der Offertorien," in *Speculum Musicae Artis: Festgabe für Heinrich Husmann*, ed. Heinz Becker and Reinhard Gerlach (Munich: W. Fink, 1970), 193–203, has a useful source-identification and classification of Gregorian offertory texts.

appears only in a usage of St. Denis, assigned to a rare Stephen feast on September 9 that is of likely Gallican origin.[44] Most of the regional Italian usages, including the oldest tradition of Rome, have as their Stephen-Offertory a psalmic text (generally *In virtute tua*) for which an Italianate origin seems likely.[45] By the middle ninth century, however, *Elegerunt* was included in a neumed recension of the Gregorian Propers that received wide European circulation. Example 1 shows its opening refrain in a reading that is common to French, German, Italian, and English sources. The reading here is that of the Gradual-Tonary of Dijon, compiled ca. 1025, whose "bilingual" notation—coupling neumes with pitch-letters—makes it the earliest pitch-specific witness for the Mass Propers.[46]

There are many medieval copies of this version, which found its way into the modern Vatican Gradual.[47] That all the copies descend from a single *campo aperto* neumation is indicated by the melismas on (1) "Elegerunt," (3) "plenum," and (6) "lapidaverunt," whose fourfold pitch-repercussions tend to be launched by a *pes stratus* (marked with asterisks in Example 1). Vestiges of this distinctive neume appear in the Abruzzi, Emilia, Ravenna, the Piedmont, Normandy, Sarum, Einsiedeln-St. Gall, and perhaps Schaffhausen.[48] Such agreements in

[44] Hesbert, *Antiphonale Missarum Sextuplex*, CVI and no. 148bis; see Huglo, "Gallican Rite," 116.

[45] *In virtute tua* is the Stephen Offertory at Rome; Stäblein, *Monumenta Monodica Medii Aevi*, vol. 2 (Kassel: Bärenreiter, 1970), 631; Paul F. Cutter, *Musical Sources of the Old-Roman Mass*, Musical Studies and Documents, vol. 39 (American Institute of Musicology, 1972), 412.

[46] *Paléographie musicale*, vol. 8 (Solesmes: Imprimerie Saint-Pierre, 1901–5), 267; the B-flats indicated by the manuscript's alphabetic notation are placed above the staff in the transcription; on the manuscript, see Michel Huglo, "Le tonaire de St. Bénigne de Dijon," *Annales Musicologiques* 4 (1956): 7–18; Finn Egeland Hansen, ed., *H159: Montpellier: Tonary of St. Benigne of Dijon*, (Copenhagen: Dan Fog Musikforlag, 1974); Huglo, review of Hansen, *The Grammar of Gregorian Tonality*, this JOURNAL 37 (1984): 416–24.

[47] The Vatican edition is reprinted along with the Saint Gall neumation in the *Graduale Triplex*, 634; *Elegerunt* appears with its complement of verses in the *Offertoriale* edited by Carolus Ott (Tournai: Desclée, 1935), 161–63, and in an amplified reprint of the latter by Rupert Fischer, *Offertoires neumés avec leurs versets d'après les manuscrits Laon 239 et Einsiedeln 121* (Solesmes: Abbaye Saint-Pierre, 1978), 161–63.

[48] Abruzzi: Biblioteca Vaticana, lat. 4770, fol. 5; Emilia: Rome, Angelica 123, fol. 33 (*Paléographie musicale*, vol. 18 [Solesmes: Imprimerie Saint-Pierre, 1969]); Ravenna: Baltimore, Walters Art Gallery, W. 11, fol. 18; the Piedmont: Novalesa, Oxford, Bodleian Library, Douce 222, fol. 109; Normandy: Paris, Bibliothèque Nationale, lat. 10508, addition to fol. 3; Sarum: (W. H. Frere, ed., *Graduale Sarisburiense* [London: B. Quaritch, 1894], pl. 16); Einsiedeln?: Einsiedeln 121 (*Paléographie musicale*, vol. 4, [Solesmes: Imprimerie Saint-Pierre, 1894], pl. 35); Schaffhausen?: (*Paléographie musicale*, vol. 3, [Solesmes: Imprimerie Saint-Pierre, 1892], pl. 130).

Example 1

"Vulgate" *Elegerunt*

a wide spread of East and West Frankish sources speak for an original neumation that circulated before the *divisio imperii* of the 840s.[49]

Turning to *Elegerunt*'s musical substance, there are noteworthy features in the three upward sweeps of an octave from C to C, which are apparent highlightings for the three key words (1)"Elegerunt,"

---

[49] See Huglo, *Les Livres de chant liturgiques*, 84, on the musical consequences of this division.

(6)"lapidaverunt," and "spiritum." Another response to text-meaning may be seen in the intonation-like figure given to the hortatory "Domine" in line eight. There are some exact melodic correspondences, the most extensive of them involving the pattern K^{Vg}, which appears in lines three and six on "plenum" and "lapidaverunt." This contains two formulaic elements, a and b, which appear elsewhere in different melodic contexts.[50] Element a, with the four-fold pitch-repercussions launched by the *pes stratus*, is also found in line one on Ele-*ge*-runt, and a vestige of it is perhaps seen in line nine on "spi-*ri*-tum" (a'). Element b is also found in line eight on "Domi-*ne*." Then there is the cadential element m^v, which closes lines six and nine. Such correspondences give this expansive G-mode melody a particular "form."

At the time the authoritative Carolingian-Gregorian repertory was neumed,[51] the pressures for musical-liturgical uniformity were so great that the Gregorian Mass Propers generally reach us in a single melodic version. *Elegerunt* is unusual in having perhaps half a dozen different musical versions spread among Frankish sources of the tenth through twelfth centuries. The version in Example 1 enjoyed the widest circulation and longest life, and for that reason it will be called here the "Vulgate" *Elegerunt* (V). The others will be called "minority" versions.

There is an important minority version in sources from the Aquitaine (version A); it is the only *Elegerunt* found in that region. Example 2 shows it in the reading of an eleventh-century Gradual of Toulouse whose notation is the characteristic "disjunct" neume-species ("notations à points superposées") of the French southwest.[52] Some other Aquitainian manuscripts transmit this same reading with minor variants. All apparently descend from a single neumatic archetype.[53]

---

[50] On uses of formulaic, "centonate" materials, see my introduction to "Plainchant" in *The New Grove Dictionary of Music and Musicians*, vol. 14, 804–5.

[51] On the question of date, see my "Charlemagne's Archetype of Gregorian Chant," 1–30.

[52] London, British Library, Harleian 4951, fol. 136. On "disjunct" and "conjunct" styles of neumation, see my "On the Origin of Neumes," 79–81.

[53] The reading of Paris, Bibliothèque Nationale, lat. 903 can be seen in *Paléographie musicale*, vol. 13 (Solesmes: Imprimerie Saint-Pierre, 1925), pl. 23; there are related readings in Paris, Bibliothèque Nationale, lat. 776, fol. 15v; Paris, Bibliothèque Nationale, lat. 780, fol. 10; Paris, Bibliothèque Nationale, nouv. acq. lat. 1177, fol. 9v. On the Aquitanian family of Graduals, see Huglo, "Gradual," *The New Grove Dictionary of Music and Musicians*, vol. 7, 605–6.

Example 2

"Aquitanian" *Elegerunt*

A comparison of the melodies in Examples 1 and 2 shows that a basic musical stock is common to both. Each chant, however, exhibits particular turns of phrase, and these are distinctive and systematic enough to qualify each one as a separate stylization.[54] The Vulgate's

---

[54] Charlotte Roederer has pointed to a similar case with the "Aquitanian" and "Gregorian" processional Antiphon, *Stetit/Stabat angelus ad sepulcrum*; "Can We Identify an Aquitanian Chant Style," this JOURNAL 27 (1974): 75–99.

three ascents from the low C have Aquitanian counterparts, but on (1) "Elegerunt," Aquitaine rises only to pitch b, while on (6) "lapidaverunt" and (9) "spiritum" it reaches the d, then turns back with a direct descending fifth skip to g that has no Vulgate counterpart. Each chant also has a different scheme of internal repetitions and melodic references. Where the Vulgate's (6) "lapidaverunt" reproduces its music on (3) "plenum" (Pattern K), and where at both those points the Vulgate has fourfold repercussions launched by a *pes stratus* (element *a*, which also appears on (1) "Elegerunt"), the Aquitanian version ignores the Vulgate's melodic identities, but offers other identities of its own. The Aquitaine version of Pattern K (K^{Aq}) in line six reappears at the end of line nine, and the concluding element m^{Aq} (in lines six and nine) also appears by itself at the end of line eight. In the Vulgate, these points are only roughly related. There is also a parallel involving element n^{Aq} in the first and third of Aquitaine's lines for which the Vulgate has no real counterpart. These differences in style and layout mark Aquitaine as a musical formulation that is somehow independent of the Vulgate.[55]

Further light on the Aquitaine version is cast by a twelfth-century version from Auxerre, to the north of Burgundy. Unlike the "disjunct" neumatic ductus of Aquitaine, the Auxerre notation is "conjunct," and its neumes are disposed on a cleffed staff.[56] But the melodies are practically the same. Example 3 is the transcription of Auxerre, with the manuscript original shown in Figure 1.[57] It is not clear whether Aquitaine's disjunct neumes and Auxerre's conjunct neumes reflect independent neumations, or whether they both go back to a common neumation employing a conjunct ductus, with their differences attributable in part to Aquitaine's early turn (during the ninth century) toward disjunct neumes, and in part to variants that entered Auxerre's tradition during its lengthier passage from *campo aperto* neumes to the staff. For present purposes it will suffice to consider Aquitaine and Auxerre as representatives of a single neumatic formulation, while giving preference to Aquitaine because of its greater age and number of witnesses.

Still another melody for *Elegerunt* is found in the Beneventan zone of south Italy (version *B*). It is the only *Elegerunt* that appears there,

[55] The Alleluias that complete the refrains are not considered here. They tend to represent musical traditions separate from the rest, differing among minority versions as well as among branches of the Vulgate tradition; along with the verses that follow the *Elegerunt* refrain, they offer substantial avenues for further study.

[56] See my "On the Origin of Neumes," 76–86, for the designations "conjunct" and "disjunct" as substitutes for "accent" and "point" neume-species.

[57] Paris, Bibliothèque Nationale, lat. 10511, fol. 154.

Example 3

"Auxerre" *Elegerunt*

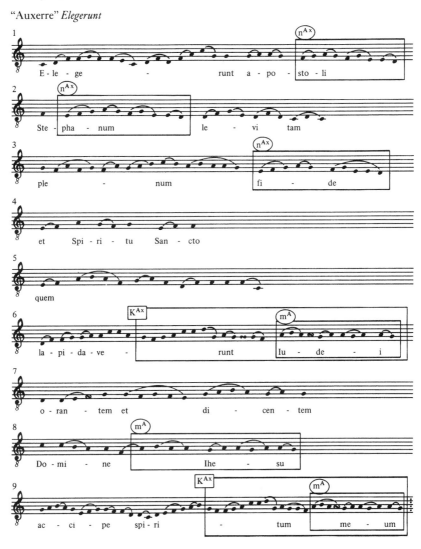

and all copies descend from a single *campo aperto* neumation whose earliest witnesses are Benevento VI.33 and Walters 6 (a Missal of Canosa), both written during the eleventh century. The Canosa neumation is shown in Figure 2.[58] The chant itself is transcribed in

---

[58] Benevento, Biblioteca Capitolare, VI.33, fol. 4; facsimiles in *Paléographie musicale*, vol. 20 (Solesmes: Imprimerie Saint-Pierre, 1983).

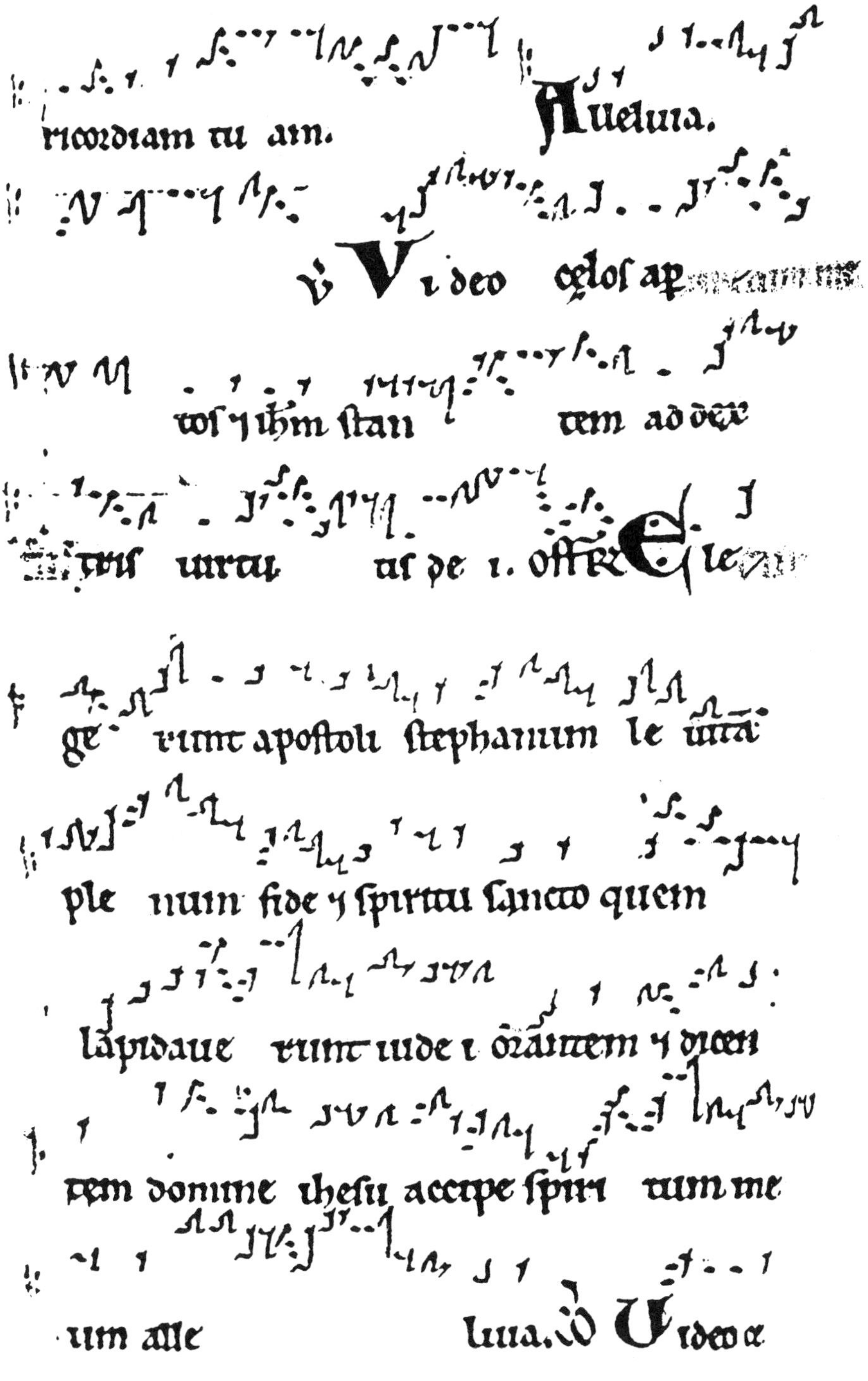

ricordiam tu am. Alleluia.

V. Video celos ap[erto]s

tos 7 ihm stan tem ad dex

tris uirtu as pe i. offrc Elege

ge runt apostoli stephanum le uita

ple num fide 7 spiritu sancto quem

lapidaue runt iude i oramtem 7 dicen

rem domine thesu accipe spiri tum me

um alle luia. d Videa

Figure 1. Auxerre Alleluia *Video celos* and Offertory *Elegerunt*.

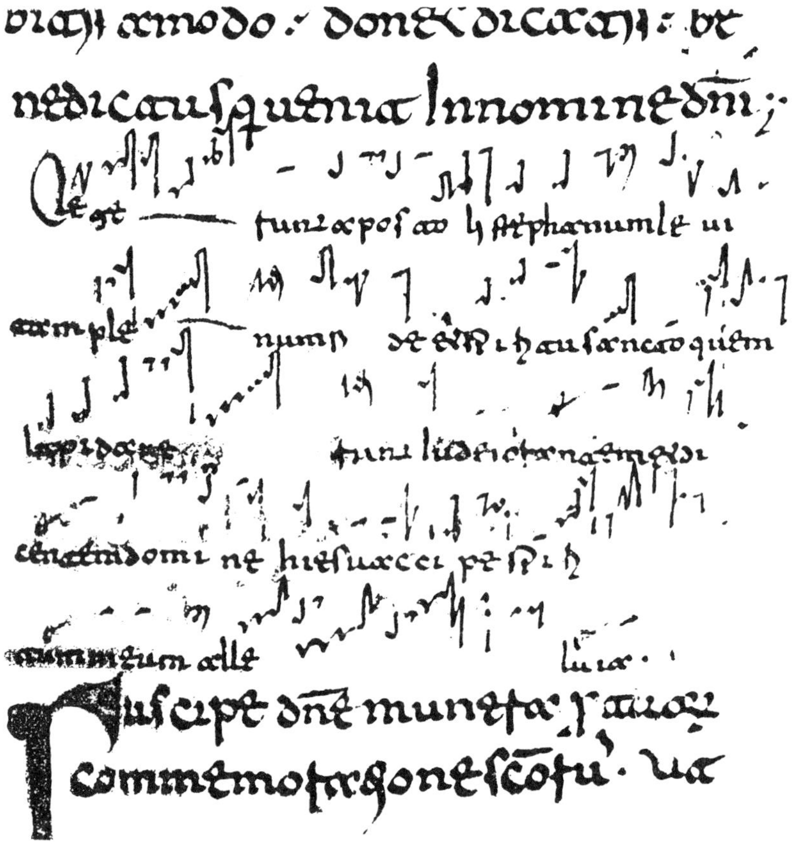

Figure 2. Beneventan Offertory *Elegerunt*.

Example 4 after the twelfth-century staffed version of Benevento
VI.34.[59] This Beneventan *Elegerunt* shares many of its modal and
melodic features with the Vulgate and Aquitaine versions, and it is
often quite close in musical particulars to one or the other of them.
But it is not really identical with either. There are the same upward
sweeps on (1) "Elegerunt," (6) "lapidaverunt," and (9) "spiritum," but
the departure-point for "spiritum" is not the low C as in the others but
the d above it. Benevento's use of pattern K^B mirrors the exact
melodic correspondences of the Vulgate's pattern K^{Vg} on (3) "plenum
fide" and (6) "lapidaverunt Iudei." Yet it ignores the Aquitaine-
Auxerre correspondences between the pattern Ks in lines six and
nine. Its melodic substance for this pattern also differs from that of the
Vulgate, although it is almost identical with that of Aquitaine-

[59] *Paléographie musicale*, vol. 15, fol. 22.

Example 4

"Beneventan" *Elegerunt*

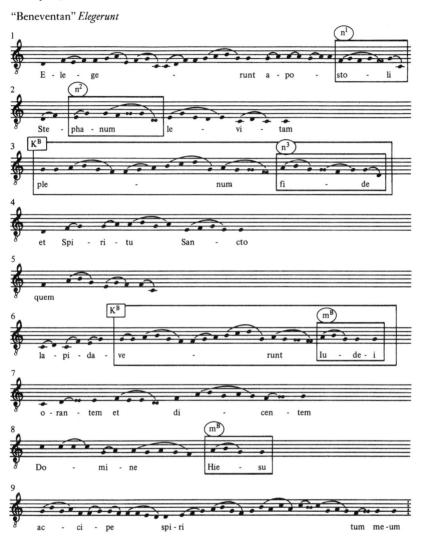

Auxerre. Benevento's three *n*-figures in lines one, two, and three reflect the placement of element n^{Aq} in Aquitaine, but the Aquitanian music is the same in all three instances, while the Beneventan music is not. Benevento corresponds with the Vulgate in one aspect of its larger "form," the parallel pattern Ks in lines three and six, yet it maintains its own stylistic profile. In other formal and melodic aspects it is close to Aquitaine, but again somewhat separate. In the end, the written Beneventan version cannot be seen as either the model or the derivative of the Vulgate or Aquitaine. It is found only in south Italy, but in view of the melodic substance that it shares with the Vulgate and Aquitaine, its ultimate origin should like theirs be sought north of the Alps, on the native ground of its centonate-libretto, "Gallican"-style text. The Beneventan version may have reached south Italy in an early recension of the Carolingian Mass Propers, arriving there by the beginning of the ninth century.[60]

A further perspective on this comes from England. In much the way that Auxerre expands the picture of the Aquitanian version, so that of Benevento is expanded by a version written in the eleventh-century staffless neumes of southwest England which appears in both of the Winchester tropers as well as the Kentish Gradual-Troper Cotton Caligula A.14.[61] I know of no staffed example. The three English readings have a common neumatic model. The neumation of the younger Winchester troper (dating from about 1050?) is seen in Figure 3.[62] A musical relation to the Beneventan version seems possible, closer at the start, with differences increasing toward the end. Benevento and Kent may be outgrowths of a version that once circulated in central or northern France. It probably got to south Italy by about 800; concerning the "Anglo-Saxon" version one can only say that it was at Winchester by about 1000.[63]

Now there are three (and perhaps as many as five) different musical traditions for *Elegerunt*: the Vulgate, Aquitaine-Auxerre, and Benevento-Kent. They share a good deal of melodic substance but differ in their neumation and in aspects of their musical style and

[60] Levy, "Charlemagne's Archetype of Gregorian Chant," 11–27; the introduction of Gregorian chant to south Italy is discussed in Thomas Forrest Kelly, *The Beneventan Chant* (Cambridge: Cambridge University Press, 1989), 18–25.

[61] Cambridge, Corpus Christi College, 473, fol. 14v; Oxford, Bodleian 775, fol. 116v; London, British Library, Cotton Caligula A. 14, fol. 5 (*Paléographie musicale*, vol. 3, pl. 180). Heinrich Husmann, *Tropen und Sequenzenenhandschriften*, Répertoire international des sources musicales, vol. B V¹ (Munich: G. Henle Verlag, 1964), 154–55 suggests Canterbury as the origin of the Caligula troper; Alejandro Enrique Planchart, *The Repertory of Tropes at Winchester* (Princeton: Princeton University Press, 1977), vol. 2, 21, describes it as a fragment of an Anglo-Saxon troper from ca. 1050.

[62] Oxford, Bodleian 775, fol. 116v.

[63] Susan Rankin gives indications that Corbie was a source for English neumed traditions; "Neumatic Notations in Anglo-Saxon England," in Huglo, ed., *Musicologie médiévale: Notations et séquences. Actes de la Table Ronde du C. N. R. S. à l'Institut de Recherche et d'Histoire des Textes: 6–7 septembre 1982* (Paris: Centre Nationale de la Recherche Scientifique, 1987), 130–31. *Elegerunt* is the sole Offertory to appear in the Bodleian copy with a full noted refrain and verse; all other Offertories have a cue for the refrain followed by the neumed verses; this should make it an addition, perhaps to the Offertory cycle once it was in England, or perhaps to the parent French cycle before it went to England.

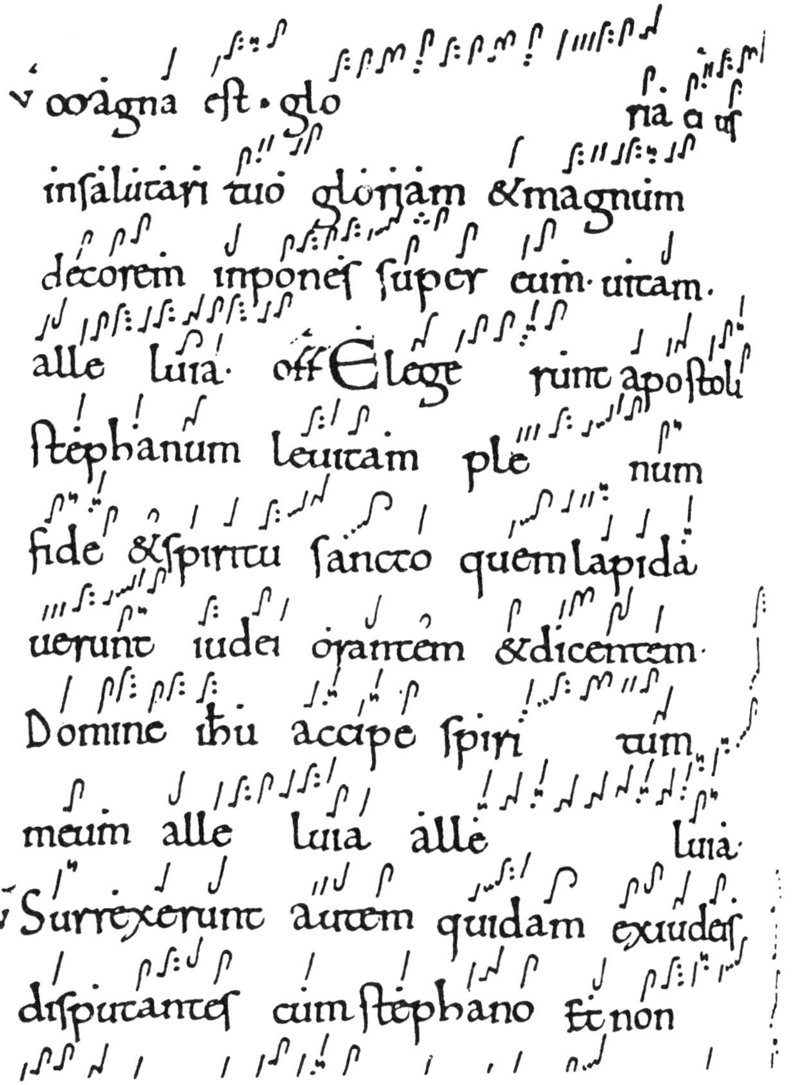

Figure 3. Anglo-Saxon Offertory *Elegerunt*.

form. Some other minority *Elegerunts* survive only in *campo aperto* neumes, so their melodic substance remains out of reach. The most significant is a "Northern" version, found in eleventh-century Paris (the tradition of Saint Denis) and Arras (Cambrai 75).[64] The reading of Arras is shown in Figure 4.

[64] Paris, Bibliothèque Nationale, lat. 9436, fol. 72 (St. Denis usage); Cambrai, Bibliothèque Municipale, 75 (76), fol. 35v.

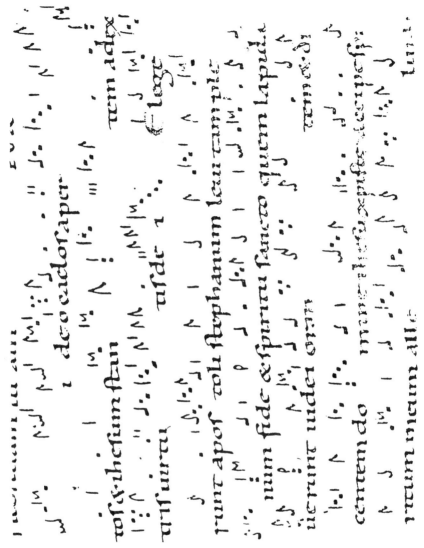

Figure 4. "Northern" Alleluia *Video celos* and Offertory *Elegerunt*.

A similar and perhaps identical version (the neumes are not clear) is found in the archaic "Paleofrankish" notation of Paris MS lat. 17305, dating from the later ninth or tenth century. [65] Of all the *Elegerunts*, this one, representing a region extending from Paris through the Franco-Belgian north, stands closest to the Carolingian heartland. It is

[65] Paris, Bibliothèque Nationale, lat. 17305, fol. 14v; on the "graphic" rationale of the "Paleofrank" notation, see my "On the Origin of Neumes," 70–79.

unique in its short melismatic expansion on the word (7)"orantem," and in adding the word "Christe" after (8)"Domine Jesu." Its staffless neumes indicate none of the internal melodic correspondences that serve to relate the Vulgate, Aquitaine, and Beneventan versions.

Traces of other minority *Elegerunts* appear on a leaf of Arsenal MS 1198, where fragments of the text are entered in an eleventh-century French hand; the first three entries bear neumes.[66] The first may be the Vulgate; the second and third do not seem to agree with other known versions.

Finally, there is an Old-Hispanic *Elegerunt*, representing the mixed Gallican-Mozarabic liturgical background from which this Offertory must have sprung. It survives only in staffless neumes of the Hispanic "northern" notational style: as a Sacrificium or Mass Offertory in the tenth-century Antiphoner of Leon, and as a Sono of the Office in the eleventh-century "Liber misticus" of San Millán de la Cogolla, now at Madrid.[67] An apparent parallel between its sixth and ninth lines may reflect the melodic correspondences found between those same lines in the Frankish versions, but no further relationships are apparent.

*   *   *

With this, the dossier of *Elegerunts* is complete. In addition to the neumed version that remained in isolation on the Iberian peninsula, there were no fewer than four "Gallo-Gregorian" versions in Carolingian liturgical regions during the ninth through twelfth centuries. If the cognate *Elegerunts* at Aquitaine and Auxerre, at Benevento and Anglo-Saxon England, and at Paris-Arras and the "Paleofrank" North, are reckoned as separate, there were as many as seven. Whether four or seven, the number is large for a text of the Gregorian Proper when for most texts only a single chant survives. Now the question is, why does *Elegerunt* have so many?

[66] Paris, Bibliothèque de l'Arsenal, ms. 1198, fol. 14v; Solange Corbin (with Madeleine Bernard), *Répertoire de manuscrits médiévaux contenant des notations musicales*, vol. 3, *Bibliothèques parisiennes* (Paris: Centre National de la Recherche Scientifique, 1974), 38 and pl. VII.

[67] Facsimile in *Antifonario visigótico mozárabe de la Catedral de León*, vol. 1, Monumenta Hispaniae Sacra, Serie litúrgica, vol. 5 (Barcelona and Madrid: Consejo Superior de Investigaciones Científicas, 1959), fol. 74v; Madrid, Academia de la Historia, MS 30, fol. 129; Don M. Randel, *An Index to the Chant of the Mozarabic Rite* (Princeton: Princeton University Press, 1973); Levy, "Old-Hispanic Chant In Its European Context," in *España en la Música de Occidente* (Madrid: Ministerio de Cultura, 1987), vol. 1, 3–14.

The simplest explanation would be that despite their manifest differences, the minority melodies are not independent formulations, but instead are decayed readings of the written Vulgate. Erosions of melodic integrity are not uncommon among Gregorian readings of the tenth century and later. They result from a weakening bond between the *campo aperto* neumes, in which the chants were first recorded, and the memories of singers upon which the early, incomplete neumatic records depended for essential information, mainly about pitch, that they left out. In a centuries-long development, singers' memories went their own way and differing opinions about pitch-levels and details of melodic contour became encrusted in local written traditions. The differences between the Vulgate and minority *Elegerunts* may be attributable to such decay. Yet if they are, one should expect to find similar traces of decay among other Offertories in the same regional recensions. But that does not happen. The differences elsewhere do not approach those among the *Elegerunts*. In the Aquitaine tradition, nearly all other Offertories agree quite well with the mainline Gregorian readings that are represented in early, carefully neumed witnesses like Laon 239, Chartres 109, and St. Gall 339. That is so with Offertories based on psalmic texts, like *Ad te Domine, levavi*,[68] representing a putative Roman type where stricter musical conformity might be expected; but it is also so with *Angelus Domini*,[69] whose text is a "non-psalmic libretto" of the same "Gallican" type as *Elegerunt*, making it a likelier candidate for comparable melodic discrepancy. The same also applies to the Offertories in the Auxerre tradition, where neither *Ad te levavi* nor *Angelus Domini* departs significantly from the standard Gregorian neumation. What differences there are represent the time and place, as can be judged from the proximity of Auxerre's reading of *Ad te levavi* to that of a contemporary one from nearby Nevers, as published by van der Werf.[70] The minor differences are of an order that would seem a normal consequence of the centuries of regional transmission that intervened between the promulgation of the Carolingian neumed recension and these descendents. Much the same can be said of the Offertories in the Beneventan recension, where both *Ad te levavi* and *Angelus Domini* are in the main line of *campo aperto* neumations,[71] and so also of the

---

[68] *Paléographie musicale*, vol. 13, fol. 2.

[69] *Paléographie musicale*, vol. 13, fol. 155.

[70] Paris, Bibliothèque Nationale, nouv. acq. lat., 1235, fol. 9v; van der Werf, *The Emergence of Gregorian Chant*, vol. 1, part 2, 166–78.

[71] *Ad te levavi*, Benevento VI. 34 (*Paléographie musicale*, vol. 15), fol. 1v; *Angelus Domini*, Benevento VI.34 (*Paléographie musicale*, vol. 15), fol. 132.

Anglo-Saxon and "Northern" (Paris-Arras-"Paleofrank") recensions. In sum, casual melodic decay does not account for the differences in *Elegerunt*'s multiples.

If not decay, then perhaps there was a more purposeful process of "reimprovisation" or "reconstruction," of the kind recently proposed by van der Werf, Treitler, and Hucke as explanation for differences among Gregorian readings?[72] The notion is that the early neumations did not represent fixed melodic entities. Instead they were points of reference and departure for scribes and singers who during some early centuries of the written transmission continued to exercise age-old improvisatory freedoms. The variant *Elegerunts* would result from taking one of the neumed versions—perhaps the Vulgate—as the point of departure for elaboration. Yet the melodic variants in mainline Gregorian chants that have been interpreted as the outcome of active reimprovisatory endeavor seem better explained by the passive processes of notational and melodic "decay" just described. The differences between readings are of a minor order, turning on a particular choice of pitch or reciting tone, or on the altered contour of a small melodic group. They show up in versions noted on the staff, and so are at a considerable remove in time and notational technique from the *campo aperto* neumes that lay at the root of the tradition. Concerning the general run of Gregorian variants, it seems to me that David Hughes was quite correct in observing that "the inference to be drawn is not that the melody was composed anew by improvisation at each performance, but rather that certain kinds of details were somewhat flexible."[73] With the *Elegerunts*, the variants are more substantial than elsewhere, so that they more than any others might be identified as the results of reimprovisatory operations. Yet they differ enough among themselves in neumation, style, and form (different text-syllables paired with different melodic substances) that it is difficult to see any one of them as the melodic generator of any of the others. They are likelier to represent three independent written formulations.

Two further assumptions in the theories of "decay" and "reimprovisation" also need review: one, that the Vulgate was the oldest *Elegerunt*; the other, that it began as the most authoritative version. Neither of these can be sustained. The Vulgate became the majority

---

[72] See note 18.

[73] "Evidence for the Traditional View of the Transmission of Gregorian Chant," 398; instead of considering the melodic details "somewhat flexible," however, I would prefer to say that local memories turned "somewhat fallible."

version, and it reaches us as the authoritative version. In the agreement of its neumations in the Carolingian East and West, there is also the mark of its attachment to a mainline Gregorian recension that circulated before Charlemagne's empire underwent its major political division during the 840s. Yet each of the minority traditions (Aquitaine, Benevento, "Northern," and Old Hispanic) has a claim to considerable antiquity. Each goes back to a formulation in staffless neumes, and the archaic "Paleofrankish" neumation for Paris-Arras-"North" bids to be more ancient than any of the rest. In this company, the Vulgate need not be the oldest, nor the one that at the outset stood first among equals.

What may be a better explanation of *Elegerunt*'s multiples would begin with their identification as the musical favorites of different Gallican regions. The geography is clear for Aquitaine/Auxerre, which appears in adjacent zones of the French southwest and Burgundy. It is similarly clear for Paris-Arras-"North," which has a habitat closer to the Carolingian heartland. Inasmuch as the cognate versions in outlying Benevento and Kent have the same Gallican-style (centonate-libretto) text as all the other *Elegerunts*, and also the same basic modal-melodic substance as Aquitaine-Auxerre and the Vulgate, they should represent still another Gallo-Carolingian region. And that should also be the case for the Vulgate. In light of the generalities of musical style that link the Vulgate version with the main line of standard Gregorian Offertories, to narrow its origin by means of the other regional *Elegerunts* should help to focus the search for the pocket of editorial activity—still a prime mystery—where the authoritative Carolingian musical corpus received its definitive melodic and neumatic shaping.

Now if the *Elegerunts* were the musical favorites of different Carolingian regions, the question can be asked, whether they were long-established in those regions, or creations that came relatively late? There are reasons for seeing them as the relics of old and entrenched Gallican traditions. The parallel Eastern and Western neumations for the Vulgate *Elegerunt* have indicated that this version was circulated by the middle of the ninth century. For the others, a number of hypothetical situations would explain their survival. An authoritative Gregorian repertory might arrive without an *Elegerunt* at a place that had its own favorite version, which was then annexed to the arriving repertory. Or an authoritative Gregorian repertory might arrive with the Vulgate *Elegerunt* at a place that had its own favorite, and the import was rejected and supplanted by the local one. Or an authorized Gregorian repertory might arrive with the Vulgate at a place that did not want any *Elegerunt*, and the import was ignored, local use continuing (or taking up) with some other Stephen Offertory like *In virtute tua* or *Posuisti*. Each of these situations gives the local versions a certain age and autonomy. The most interesting case would be where the local favorite replaces the arriving Vulgate; this is something to which I will return.

Yet it must already be apparent that the *Elegerunts* promise better than most other cases of multiples. Their differences in neumation, style, and form speak for writings-down that took place independently. Since three of them (the Vulgate, Aquitaine-Auxerre, and Benevento-Kent) share modal-melodic materials, the substance that they share must have a common source, and if their neumations were originally as separate and independent as they seem to be, then that source itself was likely to be oral. There is a remote chance that some archaic written formulation, perhaps cast in a Hellenistic-derived alphabetic or symbolic notation, transmitted a melodic shape that was the common source. But there is no indication that such notations were used to record large amounts of Latin plainchant before neumes, and there is no apparent reason for *Elegerunt* to receive special treatment.

Now the *Elegerunts'* status as regional favorites helps support the notion of their ultimate oral existence. If they were latter-day melodic creations, of the later ninth through eleventh centuries, this would come at times when the Gallican traditions whose regional flowerings they seem to represent were overshadowed by the authoritative Carolingian-Gregorian tradition. Once the Gregorian was established in a region, the chances for fresh musical essays with *Elegerunt's* Gallican-style text greatly diminished. What the multiples suggest instead are earlier times of continuing Gallican vigor, times when the conversions to neumes reflect a climate where local rites still flourish. All four of the main Carolingian traditions (Vulgate, Aquitanian, Beneventan, Northern) are therefore likely to exist by the later eighth century, perhaps in written form already at that time, and in a purely oral form perhaps much farther back.

What began as the possibility that the *Elegerunts* had oral antecedents has now turned into what seems a likelihood. In that case, there is yet another set of questions to address. They concern the relationship between the oral and written melodic states: in brief, to what extent do the neumed versions of these sometime Gallican favorites perpetuate the substances of oral deliveries that went before? For the three Elegerunts that survived long enough to reach pitch-specific notations, an answer comes from their relationships as "close multi-

Example 5

Elegerunts V, A, and B

ples." Aquitaine, Benevento, and the Vulgate are exceptional in the amounts of melodic detail they share. Their musical differences have been considered above in connection with Examples 1–4. Each was seen as having a distinctive melodic style, a particular set of internal parallels, and an independent neumatic disposition. Now it is their proximities that are important, and these can be judged in Example 5. There are ample agreements of detail on corresponding syllables, words, and phrases. They run throughout, and they are particularly

Example 5 (*continued*)

notable in the segments of fabric that are not tied into form-building parallels, as in the agreements on (2)"levitam," (5) "quem," and (9) "accipe." Earlier I gave as a reason for converting a minority version to neumes the desire to sustain a local favorite in the face of the arriving Vulgate. Yet the Vulgate differs in only small ways from the minority versions. The local musicians must then have set considerable store in the small differences. In rejecting the Vulgate's similar details, they were insisting on their own preferences; they were recording them with care. In effect, they have left accurate transcriptions of the local oral deliveries.

Example 5 (*continued*)

If *Elegerunt*'s close multiples tell us this much, they also do one thing more. They answer a question about the nature of the melos during oral transmission. Did a considerable improvisatory license persist throughout the purely oral phase, or was there a turn toward more calculated methods of melodic production? These multiples say that the oral melos became stable and remembered. There is no better explanation of the musical ties between *Elegerunt*'s independently neumed regional recensions than as parallel outgrowths of a melodic formulation that before neumatic fixing acquired a fixed, memorized profile.

Speculative this is, and speculative it is bound to remain. Yet an oral *Elegerunt* that was the source for the written ones seems to have been "memorized," not "improvised." In Nettl's spectrum of improvisatory processes, its singers were no longer "improvising upon something," they were "performing a version of something."[74] At face value, this applies only to a single chant, and it is one whose lineage is not Gregorian but Gallican. Alongside it can perhaps be placed the processional Antiphon *Deprecamur te Domine*, another case of close multiples, whose lineage is properly Gregorian. This might end here, with the two isolated cases, but consideration must also be given to the general correspondences in musical style that link these two chants with others in their categories of Gallican Offertories and Gregorian processional Antiphons. The Vulgate *Elegerunt* is related to Offertories of its distinctive text-type (non-psalmic, centonate librettos) in the Carolingian-Gregorian recension,[75] and to the general style of the Gregorian Offertories. Similarly, *Deprecamur te*, in its manifestations as "Carolingian" and Beneventan close-multiples, is related to other processional Antiphons of presumable Italic origin that circulate with the main Gregorian collection. In this way, suppositions about a memorized melos during later oral stages can be extended to considerable portions of both those major repertories.

In the end, the question is one of memory: of how sizable a role it played during oral transmission, and how plausible that role would be. It has long been presumed that there was a significant reliance on memory in the stage before neume writing began, and that this was carried over into the relationship between singers' memories and the techniques of *campo aperto* neuming that was the essence of the early written transmission.[76]

[74] Nettl, "Thoughts on Improvisation," 9.

[75] Such as *Angelus Domini*; according to *Paléographie musicale*, vol. 15, 167, it lends formulas to *Factus est repente*.

[76] Dom Cardine wrote of a time when "la notation n'était pas encore inventée: la mélodie des textes chantés était entièrement confiée à la mémoire"; "Vue d'ensemble sur le chant grégorien," *Études grégoriennes* 16 (1977): 173. Similarly Huglo has written of "les mélodies du répertoire liturgique conservées dans toutes les mémoires," and of an early neumed stage when the tradition, "reste essentiellement basé sur la mémorisation" (p. 34); "Tradition orale et tradition écrite dans la transmission des mélodies grégoriennes," in *Studien zur Tradition in der Musik. Kurt von Fischer zum 60. Geburtstag*, ed. Hans Heinz Eggebrecht and Max Lütolf (Munich: Musikverlag Katzbichler, 1973), 31–42; cf. 35, 34. Huglo accurately distinguished three stages: an early one of pure oral tradition based on memorization; a mixed one, where memory received the support of campo aperto neumes; and then a stage where the pitch-specific notation released the singers from dependence on memory.

Concerning memory-use after neumes were introduced, the nature of the neumes speaks for a considerable input from memory. These give precise details of duration and delivery with figures like the tractulus, episema, liquescences, oriscus, and quilisma (using their later Germanic names).[77] They show information about pitch less well; there are accurate charts of ups, downs, and repetitions, but there is little or nothing about pitch-levels and interval-widths. Inasmuch as the factors of length and ornament are represented in detail, it can scarcely be that just the pitch choices were left to the vagaries of "re-improvisational" or "reconstructive" performers.[78] It must rather be that the musicians who devised the economical neumatic system of graphing melodic events considered the specifics of pitch to be secure enough in professional memories to sustain this somewhat casual treatment by the early neumes. Essential to the system, therefore, was a dependence on memory for much of the information about pitch. At the point when the repertory was cast in neumes the singers' memories were stocked with the full complement of melodic information.[79]

Turning to the purely oral deliveries of a prior stage, it may be that the lack of a handy written means for consolidating and reviewing compositional decisions kept plainchant deliveries near the free end of the improvisatory spectrum throughout their oral transmission. Singers may have wanted it that way, as something that gave scope to their operations. Yet it may also be that the memory-usage that was the partner of the early *campo aperto* neumes was itself the continuation of a usage during a prior, purely oral stage. The close multiples of *Elegerunt* and *Deprecamur* have suggested this in their own way. It can also be observed that if the developers of the *campo aperto* system were engaged in first-time fixings of melodic substances that until then were produced as freely-improvised deliveries, they might have been less willing to consign as much of the fruit of their labors to memory as they did. The neumes in fact supply about the level of support one would expect for professional musicians whose memories were already practiced in handling an essentially concretized repertory.

[77] Michel Huglo, "Les noms des neumes et leur origine," *Études grégoriennes* I (1954): 53–67.
[78] See note 18.
[79] Jacques Handschin put this with characteristic clarity: "je ungenauer die Notierung, um so mehr müssen wir die alten Sänger ästimieren, die mit einer so rudimentären Gedächtnisbeihilfe die Melodien richtig zu singen vermochten." *Musikgeschichte im Überblick* (Lucerne: Raber, 1948), 128.

Another sign of a turn toward fixity in later oral stages may be seen in the nature of certain melodies. Within the written repertory's assortment of styles and procedures there are obvious distinctions to be made. For some kinds of melos, the chances of memorized oral antecedents are greater, with others less. For florid soloists' chants where the fabric is an apparent elaboration of a "psalmodic" framework, the techniques of free, improvisational delivery may have prevailed throughout oral transmission; the versions fixed by the Carolingian neumators may be faithful images of former improvisational deliveries. On the other hand, for chants where "centonate" processes have a role, the situation may be different, and to some extent this affects the assessment of "psalmodic" chants where there is a considerable centonate component. Centonate chants have fabrics that are more or less densely woven with short formulas and patterns which may reappear in other contexts and combinations throughout an extensive repertory. Where there is a substantial centonate input, the chance of free improvisatory survival is lessened. The ultimate origins of centonate procedures may lie in age-old improvisatory techniques where select melodic elements were "hot-wired" in from volatile, artful memories. Yet in such fine-tooled creations as the fifth-mode Graduals or eighth-mode Tracts, the neumed entities that appear on ninth- and tenth-century parchment are likely to incorporate considerable amounts of compositional and editorial tinkerings that entered during written stages. For such musical texts there are analogies in the realm of ancient literary epic. But they are not with the *Iliad* or *Odyssey*. They are with such poetry as the *Aeneid*, which is replete with archaic, epic-type gestures, but whose deployment of those gestures is the result of a cooly calculated written process.

Taken together, the deliberate centonate constructions and the florid psalmodic elaborations amount to only a small part of the repertory. For the large bulk of plainchant, the conditions of oral delivery may have been still different. The rationale for most Gregorian chants lies in distinctive melodic profiles, in formulations that are unique as to melodic detail.[80] In Byzantine chant there is a parallel usage, and even a name for the phenomenon. The chants are called "idiomela," that is, "distinctive," "unique," "original" melodies. Hundreds of chants may draw their basic materials from a common fund of conventional modal-melodic gestures, but each of them is turned

---

[80] Thus Hubert Sidler characterized the Gregorian Offertories as unique in their shapes, both as to melody and structure; *Studien zu den alten Offertorien mit ihren Versen* (Fribourg: Verlag des Musikwissenschaften Instituts der Universität, 1934), 7.

out as a distinct melodic entity, with singular twists given to the familiar gestures. Each chant is notable for those twists. This says that the idiomelic chants were by nature "memorable," and since for many of them the written tradition goes back to the earliest noted states, there is the chance of a memorability reaching farther back. A further indication of this may be seen in another common feature of idiomelic repertories: certain pieces emerge as favorites and become musical models to which new texts are accommodated. In the Byzantine terminology again, a uniquely-profiled *idiomelon* becomes a prototype or generator *automelon*, the basis for imitated melodies or *prosomoia*. Automelic chants are generally cut of the same stylized cloth as the idiomelic chants that make up the bulk of their particular category. But the automela were so well fixed in choristers' and congregational memories that in earlier hymn-books they rarely appear with neumes. It was sufficient to identify the model by its text-incipit and supply the fresh text. Automelic prototypes and their adaptations are also common in the West, with their most familiar examples among the Gregorian Alleluias, as in the type *Dies sanctificatus*.[81] The Byzantine musicians persisted longer in relying on memory, so that most of the model-melodies and even many of the adaptations were transmitted without neumes until after the fall of the Empire in the fifteenth century. The Latin musicians turned sooner to the regular neuming of both models and adaptations, so that even in the oldest neumed Graduals and Antiphoners the imitated versions are written out. Yet the Eastern and Western practices have in common that where the idiomelic chants with their distinctive profiles were by nature simply "memorable," the automelic chants were by nature "remembered" and "memorized." With these respected models, the chance that memorability reaches back of the earliest neumings is good. The role taken by prototypes and adaptations in filling out the Gregorian roster of the later eighth century indicates a similar role for verbatim memory during a prior oral stage.[82]

---

[81] K.-H. Schlager, *Thematischer Katalog der ältesten Alleluia-Melodien* (Munich: Walter Ricke Verlag, 1965), 38–39; there are recent discussions of the practice by M. Huglo, "Antiphon," *The New Grove Dictionary of Music and Musicians*, vol. 1, 473–76; Huglo, "Gradual," vol. 7, 603; Jean Claire, "Les formules centons des *alleluia* anciens," *Études grégoriennes* 20 (1981): 3–4 and 12 pages of charts.

[82] Prototypes and their imitations are well represented among the Latin Offertories, as in the group that includes *Viri Galilei* where five texts are accommodated to the same melody; Baroffio and Steiner, "Offertory," vol. 13, 516. Of particular interest is the Offertory *Posuisti* for St. Gorgonius of Metz, with music based on the

From diverse viewpoints (close multiples, neumatic technique, idiomelic-automelic practice) an image of the later oral transmission has emerged in which much of the melos was memorized rather than freely improvised. There have long been common-sense reasons for supposing this was the case, but it has never been taken so near to proof. Now the final point to be considered is that of plausibility. Were the memories of church singers without the support of musical notations capable of managing the amounts of melodic substance that this implies? The eighth- and ninth-century Gradual contained about 560 chants: 70 Introits, 118 Graduals, 100 Alleluias, 18 Tracts, 107 Offertories, and 150 Communions.[83] The figure can be expressed in hours in performance, and so as a function of tempo. Something can be inferred about Carolingian plainchant tempos from the nuance-rich neumations of the Gregorian Mass Propers that are found in manuscripts like Saint-Gall 359 and Laon 239. If the scribes took pains to indicate such details of length and ornament, it was because the niceties were supposed to be manifested in performance, and the deliveries must have gone at a pace moderate enough to allow those effects to be heard. Estimates of duration can be based on present-day performances, where Introits take about 3 minutes each (much of the time for the psalm-tone and repeated Antiphon); Graduals about 3½ minutes; Alleluias with verse about 2 minutes; Tracts, 5; Offertories with verses, 8; Communions, 2 to 3. A tally that may run generously high would put the aggregate for the late-eighth-century Mass Propers at about 35 hours of moderately-paced music, the largest single segment (about 14 hours) going to the Offertories and their verses. Comparisons with other musical repertories are bound to be misleading, with different conditions (polyphonic, instrumental, written, sound-recorded, etc.) always involved. For the thirty-five hours of "memorable" plainchant, a corresponding portion of Beethoven's output would be the symphonies, sonatas, and quartets; of Wagner's output, the canon of ten mature dramas minus one, as from *Tannhäuser* through *Parsifal*. Wagner is the better comparison, with music that is text based and often moderate in pace.

The figures for the Mass Propers need to be augmented by those for the Office, where the first full Antiphoner with neumes (dating from about 1000) contains about six hundred Greater Responsories, a

---

Offertory *Angelus Domini; Posuisti* may have been compiled soon after the translation of the saint's body to Metz around 754; Hesbert, *Antiphonale Missarum Sextuplex*, CVI and no. 148bis.

[83] Huglo, *Les livres de chant liturgique*, 102.

number that tends to increase rapidly thereafter as the availability of pitch-specific notations rendered fresh compositional essays more practical.[84] The Antiphoner's calls on the Carolingian singer's memory would be limited, however, by the considerable amounts of stereotyped matter in the refrains and verses of the Greater Responsories, and by the thousands of Office Antiphons that are modeled on between four and five dozen melodic prototypes. At another rough estimate, the Antiphoner would add thirty-five or forty hours of distinctive melos, so that, in a provisional tally of the music of the Gregorian Propers, about 800 might come to seventy-five or eighty hours of memorized matter. This would correspond to the selection of Beethoven's instrumental works plus the full Wagnerian canon.

In a final accounting, there would be further reductions. Although prototype melodies are less common among the Mass chants than those for the Office, they are well represented among the Graduals and Offertories, in addition to the Alleluias mentioned above. It must also be supposed that among the psalmodic chants and the centonate chants there was, for the diverse reasons already given, less dependence on fixed-memorized matter than among the idiomelic chants. That further lightens the burden of Carolingian memory.

* * *

In a recent paper I proposed as a major accomplishment of Carolingian liturgists during the later eighth century the shutting-down of what remained of improvisatory freedom in the "Gregorian" plainchant environment; it was done through the promulgation of an authoritative melodic repertory whose substances were concretized in neumes.[85] In the present paper I have tried to look behind the introduction of neumes toward a stage where transmission was entirely unwritten. The true face of plainchant orality will never be revealed, and efforts to view it, by whatever means, are bound to remain speculative. From the rare situation examined here it appears that substantial amounts of Latin plainchant while still in oral transmission acquired the status of song stored in memory. The argument depends on "close multiples," where a chant survives in parallel readings that are musically related but notationally independent. For the Offertory *Elegerunt apostoli* there are three versions

---

[84] Paul F. Cutter, "Responsory," *The New Grove Dictionary of Music and Musicians*, vol. 14, 759.
[85] "Charlemagne's Archetype of Gregorian Chant," 1–30.

(Aquitainian, Beneventan, and "Vulgate") that evidently represent the melodic preferences of different Gallican-Carolingian regions. There is a chance they were taken out of the oral state and put into writing at a relatively recent time, perhaps during the later ninth through eleventh centuries; or even that they were fashioned as fresh compositions in the medium of neumes at that time. Yet the local Gallican traditions that *Elegerunt*'s multiples represent were by then largely obsolete because of the spread of the Gregorian musical usage through Carolingian liturgical dependencies during the later eighth to early ninth centuries. It is likelier therefore that the regional versions existed at earlier times of continuing Gallican vigor, and perhaps at times before neumes. Despite the apparent independence of their written traditions, the three musical substances are very much alike, and that adds the thrust to their testimony. In the narrow range of differences between them can be guaged the precision with which the locally-prized oral deliveries were recorded. More than that, in order for them to emerge so much alike from the independent processes of transmission, the "oral" substance that they shared must itself have had the shape of a whole, remembered melody. This may apply only to the Gallo-Gregorian offertory *Elegerunt*, for which an unusually rich documentation survives. Yet arguments of liturgical-musical analogy suggest extending its application to large parts of the early repertory. If some of this is granted, it would seem worthwhile to seek out and analyze other cases of close multiples. It is by their means, and perhaps their means alone, that we may gain a clouded window on the oral past.

CHAPTER 7

Abbot Helisachar's Antiphoner

IN 781, CHARLEMAGNE placed Louis the Pious, then age three, on the throne of Aquitaine. He would remain there until 814 when he succeeded his father at Aachen. On the move north, Louis took two southern councillors with him. The better known is Benedict of Aniane (c. 750–821), an abbot and theologian to whom recent opinion ascribes authorship of the *Hucusque* prologue to the supplement to Hadrian's Sacramentary, which was formerly ascribed to Alcuin.[1] Lesser known is Helisachar (Elisagarus), a sometime abbot of S. Albinus of Angers, who for awhile would serve as archchancellor in the emperor's palace. Two documents of Helisachar's liturgical activity have come down to us. A letter, attributed to him by Dom Morin, prefaces a supplement to Alcuin's Epistolary.[2] Another letter, addressed to the archbishop Nidibrius of Narbonne, describes a revision of the office antiphoner that Helisachar undertook during the early years of Louis' reign. This was dated ca. 814–22 by Edmund Bishop, who twice published it after an apparently unique, tenth century source. Bishop, in 1886, dealt summarily with the letter's content concerning the verse texts of responsories;[3] his remarks were extended in a posthumous paper whose chief purpose was to show that Alcuin was the author of the *Hucusque*.[4]

Helisachar's textual and liturgical points have been examined at length by Morin and Bishop, but there are musical matters that deserve a closer

[1] Jean Deshusses, "Le Supplément au Sacramentaire grégorien: Alcuin ou S. Benoît d' Aniane?," *Archiv für Liturgiewissenschaft* (1965): 48–71; Deshusses, *Le sacramentaire grégorien, Édition comparative.* Vol. 1 of *Le sacramentaire, le supplément d'Aniane (Spicilegium friburgense)*, ed. G. Meersseman and A. Hänggi (Friburg, Switzerland: 1971) 68–70, 351–53.

[2] Germain Morin, "Une rédaction inédite de la préface au supplément du Comes d'Alcuin," *Revue bénédictine* 29 (1912): 341–48.

[3] "Ein Schreiben des Abts Helisachar," *Neues Archiv der Gesellschaft für ältere deutsche Geschichtskunde* 11 (Hanover, 1886), 564–68; London, British Library, Harl. 2637, fols. 53v–55r.

[4] "A Letter of Abbat (sic) Helisachar," *Liturgica Historica: Papers on the Liturgy and Religious Life of the Western Church* (Oxford, 1918), 333–48; Helisachar's text was republished, in Bishop's transcription, by E. Duemmler, *tomus V Epistolae Karolini Aevi*, vol. 5 MGH, vol. 3, ed. E. Duemmler (Berlin, 1899), 307–309.

Portions of this chapter were first published in *Journal of the American Musicological Society* 48 (1995): 171–72, 177–84. Reprinted by permission.

look, for the letter touches on the state of the Gregorian melodies three-quarters of a century before there are surviving neumed witnesses. One question has to do with melodic status: were Gregorian chants by this time settled as fixed musical entities—remembered melodies; or was there still latitude for improvisational input and options with regard to pitch? Another question has to do with the transmission medium: did this remain unwritten, that is, were the singers' deliveries produced by way of improvisations and purely oral memories, or was there by ca. 820 a support for memory in the form of neumes? Further, when the music came to be written down, was this accomplished in organized fashion, under a central authority at some particular place and time; or were there dispersed initiatives at scattered places?

The letter starts out recalling a time when Helisachar and his episcopal colleague were at Aachen. Together they attended Matins services where certain things about the responsories seemed in need of improvement.[5]

(1) Reverentissimo meritoque venerando Nidibrio, Narbonensis aecclesiae flore virtutum exornato archiepiscopo, Helisachar inutilis et omnium exiguus in Domino Deo aeterna prosperitatis salutem.

(1) To the most reverend, venerable Nidibrius, archbishop of the church of Narbonne, adorned with the flower of virtues, Helisachar, unworthy and paltry, sends greetings in the Lord eternal.

(2) Meminisse credimus sanctam paternitatem vestram, quod dudum quando apud Aquasgrani palatium me offitium palatinum, vosque propter ecclesiastica dirimenda imperialis iussio obstringeret, et frequenter una nocturnis horis ad divinum celebrandum offitium conveniremus, animumque nostrum sacrae scripturae lectio serenum efficeret;

(2) I think you will recall that some time ago when palace affairs constrained me to Aachen and imperial order brought you there to settle ecclesiastical matters, we were often together at the celebration of the night office. There the readings left us serene in spirit,

(3) sed ut referre solebatis responsoria auctoritate et ratione carentia, versusque qui in quibusdam responsoriis a nostris vestrisque cantoribus inconvenienter aptabantur, animum vestrum magna ex parte obnubilarent,

(3) but you were much puzzled by certain responsories which were, as you said, lacking in authority and sense; and by verses which, as sung by my singers and yours, were in certain cases improperly accommodated (to the repetenda of the refrains).

[5] Bishop proposes Christmas 814 for the events described in the letter; *Liturgica historica*, 336–37.

The talk is of texts, not music. There are chants that are "auctoritate et ratione carentia"; some are built upon nonbiblical texts; others use biblical centos (see 7 below). These are more susceptible to alteration than texts based on familiar Scripture, and though they are not rejected (see 23 below), they tend to need correction. Helisachar is also concerned with "versus qui . . . inconvenienter aptabantur," which are of two sorts: those with different literary sources than the refrains to which they are attached (see 12 below), and those where the sense connection between verse end and repetendum beginning is garbled. Unlike the Roman practice, which has the entire refrain repeated after the verse, the Cisalpine practice (perhaps originating in Gaul and then carried over to the Carolingian-Gregorian) rejoins the refrain at its middle, so that the adjustment of a lead-in word or two may be needed so that the wording makes sense.[6] Such adjustments had musical dimensions; an appropriate melodic fit was needed between the responsory's end and the truncated refrain. Helisachar's concern here may be exclusively textual (though see 24 below).

(4) mihi imperando iniunxeritis, ut adhibito sollerti studio pro captu ingenii in divinarum scripturarum pratis versus convenientes indagarem, et in responsoriis auctoritate et ratione refertis, congruis in locis aptarem.

(4) you enjoined me to use skill and ingenuity, seeking out suitable verses in the repertory of Holy Scripture, and fitting them appropriately to their responsories.

(5) Sed licet hoc negotium vires meas excedere, meamque insipientiam tale quid nullo modo posse iudicaverim, non praesumpsi tamen omittere quin id quod vestra sanctitas imperaverat summa cum devotione exequerer, fisus in illius gratuita misericordia qui potens est per inutilem et exiguum servum vestro sancto desiderio satisfacere, et quod vestrae devotioni et meritis debebatur meae quoque imperitiae administrare.

(5) Though this matter exceeds my ability, and my dullness is such that I should not be a proper judge, yet I would not presume to neglect but rather to carry out with greatest dedication what your reverence asked, trusting in the ready mercy of Him who is able to satisfy your wish by the means of your inept and humble servant, and supplement my lack of skill in what is owed to your devotion and merit.

---

[6] The linkage of verse endings with repetendum is mentioned by Amalar of Metz (c. 780–850), sometime bishop of Trier, in the so-called *Prologus de ordine antiphonarii* (written probably in 831–34): "Notandum est necessarium nobis esse ut alteros versus habeat noster antiphonarius quam romanus, quoniam altero ordine cantamus nostros responsorios quam Romani. Illi a capite incipiunt responsorium, finito versu, nos versum finitum, informamus in responsorium per latera eius, ac si facimus de duobus corporibus unum corpus. Ideo necesse est ut hos versus queramus, quorum sensus cum mediis responsoriorum conveniat, ut fiat unus sensus ex verbis responsorii et verbis versus"; in *Amalarii episcopi opera liturgica omnia*, ed. Ioanne Michaele Hanssens, vol. 1 of Studi e Testi, vol. 138 (Vatican City, 1948), 362; see also Amalar's *Liber de ordine antiphonarii*, vol. 3 of Studi e Testi, 55.

(6) Adgrediens itaque hoc opus, aggregatisque hinc inde antiphonariis cantoribusque, adhibita etiam librorum copia et peritis lectoribus, coepimus diligenter concordiam probare antiphonariorum.

(6) Taking on this task, and gathering antiphoners and singers here and there, and also some other books and skilled readers, I began diligently to test the agreement among the antiphoners.

The gathering of antiphoners and singers anticipates more specific musical operations to come.

(7) Sed quamquam in gradali cantu qui solummodo auctoritate sanctarum scripturarum nitet minime discordare possent, in nocturnali tamen qui sive ex auctoritate divina seu ex sanctorum patrum dictis compositus extat, paucissimi in unum concordare reperti sunt;

7) Among the mass chants (*in gradali cantu*) that depend on the sole authority of Holy Scriptures, they could scarcely disagree; but in the night office, which either rests on divine authority or on writings of the holy fathers, few were found to agree.

(This is not quite accurate about the mass texts, which include sources outside of Scripture, although the office antiphoners have more such texts.

(8) quoniam quaedam in eis scriptorum vitio depravata, quaedam imperitorum voto ablata, quaedam etiam sunt admixta.

(8) certain things in them are distorted by writers' errors, others by the mistakes of the unskilled, and some are due to inappropriate combinations.

(9) Unde liquido patet quod antiphonarius bene apud urbem Romanam ab auctore suo editus in nocturnalibus officiis, ab his quos supra memoravimus magna ex parte sit violatus.

(9) From which it is clear that the antiphoner of the night office, which was properly edited by its author at Rome, has been considerably corrupted by those just mentioned.

(10) Quamquam igitur ab his qui capacitatis ingenio pollent facile queant approbanda eligi et improbanda reici, propter simplices tamen minusque capaces modis omnibus imperiis vestris parendum fuit.

(10) Although those who are capable can easily choose what is good and reject what is bad, for the simpler and less able, in every way it was necessary to obey your injunction.

(11) Collatione ergo antiphonariorum celebrata eorumque lectione diligenter approbata, utque magna dissonantia perspecta est, antiphonas et responsoria quae erant auctoritate et ratione carentia, quae etiam digne in Dei laudibus cantari nequibant, respuimus.

(11) A careful collation of the antiphoners and their readings having been made, and great disagreements seen, those antiphons and responsories which were lacking in authority and reason, and were accordingly unfit for singing in praise of God, were rejected.

(12) Ea vero quae auctoritate plena sunt locis suis ordinavimus, eisque ex eadem auctoritate amminiculante eorundem librorum copia versus congruentissimos iuxta capacitatem ingenii nostri adscivimus, ut videlicet iuxta sanctionem vestram, unde responsorium erat, inde etiam conveniens foret et versus.

(12) Those however with full authority have been put in their proper place. And to them, with the help of a number of the same books, I assigned (according to my judgement) a number of congruent verses so that, as you prescribed, the verse came from the same place as the responsory.

Helisachar's observations to this point may concern only the verbal texts. He approves for entry certain antiphons and responsories that have non-biblical and perhaps cento texts; they may conform with the Roman edition mentioned in 9.

(13) Erant sane quaedam antiphonae vel responsoria auctoritate plena et in Dei laudibus decentia quae neque a nostris neque a vestris cantoribus sciebantur.

(13) Now there were some antiphons and responsories having full authority and suitability for the praise of God [as to their texts], which were not known [as to their music] either by my own singers or by yours.

(14) Unde nostri fuit studii quosdam melodiae artis magistros advocare, a quibus vestri nostrique ea avidissime didicere.

(14) Wherefore I sought out certain masters of the art of melody from whom they did eagerly learn them.

(15) Ita vero res divina amminiculante gratia successit, ut quod auctoritas et ratio vindicabat in eodem opere poneretur, et quod deerat plurimorum documento suppleretur;

(15) And so it came about, with divine grace helping, that what authority and good sense approved was placed in that same work, and what was missing was supplied on the basis of multiple sources.

With 13–15 he turns to the music. These antiphons and responsories were suitable for inclusion as regards their verbal texts; the words might have been entered as they stood. What prevented it was that the melodies were unknown to the local singers; entry into the antiphoner depended on having the melodies. What was missing was musical and Helisachar looked around for musicians who could supply the music. There are three possibilities, one for each of the scenarios set out in Chapter 1. The late independent scenario would have the external musicians supply crystallized melodies that were lodged solely in singers' memories without neumes. The reimprovisational scenario would have the missing matter come as improvisational strategies, partly dependent on memory. The early archetype scenario would see the missing matter ("quod deerat"), and what justified the written inclusion ("in eodem opere poneretur"), as fixed melodic matter that was lodged verbatim in memories with the support of neumes. That is what seems to be suggested by Helisachar's involvement of practical musicians in making diligent comparisons of the antiphoner's content ("aggregatisque hinc inde antiphonariis cantoribusque, adhibita etiam librorum copia et peritis lectoribus, coepimus diligenter concordiam probare antiphonariorum") (6); now, in assembling his antiphoner, he has managed, " . . . ut quod auctoritas et ratio vindicabat in eodem opere poneretur, et quod deerat plurimorum documento suppleretur (15)." This speaks for accurate (written?) documentation rather than singers' improvised or remembered deliveries.

(16) quodque vitio scriptorum, insolentia cantorum, aliquibus in locis depravatum erat aut quorundam imperitorum demptum vel additum fuerat, artis studio corrigeretur limaque rectitudinis poliretur.	(16) And what because of writers' error or singers' inexperience was in some place faulty, or had something taken away or added by some unskilled person, is corrected by the exercise of art and polished with the file of accuracy.

This can be seen as corrections made to written substance. "Vitio scriptorum" and "insolentia cantorum" have led to errors in the written antiphoner ("aliquibus in locis depravatum erat") which are now corrected through the "exercise of art and polished with the file of accuracy" ("artis studio corrigeretur limaque rectitudinis poliretur)." What calls forth the artful, corrective exercise may be not the verbal texts, but the accurate rendering of melodic details. The errors so scrupulously handled in this definitive manner may be dealt with in the medium of neumes.

(17) Quia ergo hoc opus vestra iussione peractum vestraeque devotioni est dedicatum, etsi non illis quibus forte non placebit, nostris tamen vestrisque cantoribus precipue necessarium humiliter exoro, ut a paternitate vestra benigne suscipiatur et in Dei laudibus devotissime utatur.	(17) This work is accomplished at your direction and dedicated to your piety, and though it may chance not to please everybody, it is necessary to my singers and yours. I humbly ask that your fatherly eminence favorably receive it and devotedly apply it in the praise of God.
(18) His vero quibus animo sedet ad diligenter transcribendum hoc opus commodate.	(18) Be favorable to those of a mind to diligently transcribe this work.
(19) Fastidiosis autem et ingratis ad reprehendendum potius quam ad discendum paratis minime pandite.	(19) Be little receptive to the scornful and ungrateful who are ready rather to criticize than to learn.

(20) Eos itaque quibus commodatum fuerit deposcite, ut nihil ex eo demant, nihil in eo addant vel mutent; quoniam iuxta beati Hieronimi sententiam nihil profuit emendasse libros, nisi emendatio librariorum diligentia conservetur.

(20) Therefore require of them who shall take this on to subtract naught from it, nor add nor change; since in the judgment of the blessed Jerome it avails naught to emend books unless the emendation is preserved by the diligence of copyists.

(21) In praefato namque opere si quippiam quolibet modo non humilitatis, sed mordacitatis voto reprehendi potest, sciatur potius id simplici dissimulatione actum quam neglegentia aut imperitia pretermissum;

(21) If in the aforesaid work anything of whatsoever sort is blamed as an act of cleverness rather than humility, know that this was done by simple carelessness rather than negligence or lack of skill;

(22) quoniam oportebat quod multorum longo et devotissimo usu in divinis cultibus detritum erat, nostro etiam silentio potius comprobari quam presumptione aliqua tangendo preiudicari.

(22) for it was fitting that what was ingrained in churchly practice through the long and assiduous use of many, be approved by our silent acquiescence rather than presumptiously altered.

(23) Quicquid namque in eo ordinatum sanctitas repperit vestra, nisi neglegentia rursus aut incuria depravatum fuerit, nihil reor repperiri posse quod non in Dei laudibus aut auctoritate sicut premissum est sacra, aut sanctorum patrum dictis compositum, aut multorum usu pia devotione longo iam tempore vindicatum, decenter assumi potest.

(23) Whatever your sanctity finds set forth therein, except again it was spoiled by neglect or oversight, I think nothing can be found that cannot be justified by sacred authority, as has been said; or composed in works of the holy fathers; or supported by longtime use of many in pious devotions.

(24) Quia autem sicut premisimus nostris vestrisque cantoribus hoc opus oportunum esse iudicavimus, oportet ut sive ab his sive ab illis summopere observetur, quatinus versus convenienter positi atque ordinati secundum artis cantilenae modum honeste canantur et in responsoriorum convenientibus locis aptentur.

(24) Because, as we have said to our own and to your singers, we have judged this work to be useful, it must be absolutely followed by mine and yours so that the verses, suitably placed and ordered in the manner of the melodic art, may be properly sung and accommodated to the appropriate places in the responsories.

Helisachar approaches a close and returns to music. The injunction that verses be "suitably placed" ("convenienter positi") may concern only the texts; though what occasions it may be that accommodations between repetenda and verses involve music as well as text, and they are problematic chiefly in their musical dimension.[7] The stricture that verses be "ordered in the manner of the melodic art and properly sung" ("*ordinati secundum artis cantilenae modum honeste canantur*") again suggests musical substance that may be entering the antiphoner in the form of neumatic profiles.

(25) Quapropter necesse est, qui ad melodiae artis normam decoremque compositi sunt, et cantoribus magnum documentum et, ut ita dixerim, quendam ducatum in eadem arte prebent, bene intelligantur;	(25) Wherefore it is necessary that the things which are composed in accord with the norm and esthetic of melodic art and which, I might also say, offer to singers a major exemplar of that art, be well understood;
(26) ut his bene notis nullatenus in quoquam ab eiusdem artis auctoritate oberretur.	(26) so you will note well in this that nothing in any way strays from the authority of that art.

The antiphoner is put together "in accord with the norm and esthetic of the melodic art" ("ad melodiae artis normam decoremque compositi sunt)." The resulting compilation is "a major exemplar of that art" ("*quendam ducatum in eadem arte prebent*)." Helisachar admonishes that "nothing in any way strays from the authority of that art." This suggests again that the responsories and antiphons gaining entry are there, not just as edited verbal texts, but as texts fitted with accurately outlined melodies.

---

[7] Amalar of Metz knew Helisachar's work on the revised antiphoner, and he may also have known this letter:

laboravit et sudavit sacerdos Dei Elisagarus, adprime eruditus, et studiosissimus in lectione et divino cultu, necnon et inter priores primus palatii excellentissimi Hludovici imperatoris. Non solum ille, sed et quoscumque de eruditis ad se potuit convocare, in praesenti negotio sudaverunt . . . . Hoc prospexit memoratus vir et gloriosus presbyter Elisagarus, qua de re certavit ut ex diversis libris congregaret versus convenientes responsoriis, quos nos et alii multi cupiunt frequentare in nocturnali officio. *Amalarii episcopi opera liturgica omnia*, 1. 362–63.	"Helisachar, priest of the Lord and foremost among those in Emperor Louis' palace, who was first class in his knowledge and dedication to the divine service, labored and sweated over this project. Not only he but also other specialists he could call in sweated . . . . He reviewed all this and struggled to collect out of various books verses suitable to the responsories that we and many others cherish in the night office.

On its face, this concerns the texts, but the "*labor*" and "*sudor*" suggest something more than choosing verses, adjusting word discrepancies between verses and responsories, and whipping a handful of nonbiblical texts into shape. These had musical dimensions, and some of this work may be due to neuming.

(27) Sancta deus Trinitas te mei memorem in sua sancta militia prolixo tempore conservet, honorabiliter venerande et venerabiliter honorande pater.	(27) May God and the Holy Trinity long conserve you in remembering me among his saintly host, honorably venerable and venerably honorable father.

Helisachar uses the prose style of a high official communicating with an ecclesiastical peer. His language is laced with epistolary flourishes, and it falls short as to musical specifics. Still, a century before the first surviving neumed antiphoners, he can be seen gathering singers and antiphoners together, and making detailed comparisons among antiphons and responsories. The chants he is dealing with are fixed in their verbal details, and he insists on their accurate copying. The insistence on accuracy may carry over to the melodies, which can also be seen as fixed entities. Their musical details are likely committed to verbatim memory and there are indications that they were accurately depicted in neumes. Thus in some responsories, Helischar has texts that are suitable as to literary source and correct enough in verbiage to warrant entry in his antiphoner. But before they can be entered in the volume he must have their music, and since local musicians do not know the melodies, he seeks others who can supply the missing musical element; only then are the pieces entered (13–15). The insistence on accuracy suggests that what those other musicians supplied were remembered melodies, something more specific than mere recollections of how improvised deliveries should go. It remains open whether the melodic information was carried by professional memories alone, or by memories that had neumatic profiles for support. Yet again, when Helisachar speaks of "writers' error" ("vitio scriptorum") and "singers' inexperience" ("insolentia cantorum") causing faults ("aliquibus in locis depravatum erat") that are rectified by the "exercise of art and polished with the file of accuracy" ("artis studio corrigeretur limaque rectitudinis poliretur") (16), "he appears to be discussing written musical substance. This suggestion of music writing is maintained when he goes on to describe the resulting antiphoner as compiled, "ad melodiae artis normam decoremque (24)." With its details correctly rendered, it is a musical entity—"a major exemplar of melodic art" ("quendam ducatum in eadem arte) (25)." Nothing says outright that the Gregorian propers ca. 820 bore neumes, but the implication is strong that in Helisachar's time this went without saying.

CHAPTER 8

Aurelian's Use of Neumes

ABBOT HELISACHAR'S letter to Nidibrius of Narbonne (Ch. 7) has indications that the Gregorian chants known to both of them ca. 820 were already settled in musical details: fixed and specific, down to fine points of melody, with no scope for improvisatory flights, or even for minor variants. With this go indications that the melodic substances at that time were already, as a matter of course, receiving a record in neumes. Helisachar's letter, written in a high churchman's prose style, does not get down to musical details. Now a closer look may be had from the *Musica disciplina* of Aurelian of Réôme, written perhaps two or three decades later in roughly the same ecclesiastical milieu.[1] The basic questions are the same: were the melodies stabilized and well-remembered, or open to improvisational variability; and was there recording in neumes?[2] Aurelian's painstaking descriptions of particular musical details also let us consider the stability of the melos between his time and that of the first preserved neumings, ca. 900.

In his nineteenth chapter, Aurelian takes up a musical detail found in two Responsories: " . . . in the Responsory *Magi veniunt ab oriente*, on the twenty-second syllable, that is '-tes' of 'dicentes,' the melody does not curve through a twisting inflection (*anfractus inflexionum*) because another syllable follows directly with a melodic winding-around (*circumvolvitur*); it would be absurd for that same melodic motion to be repeated on successive syllables, with no pause or other syllable in between. In the Responsory *Iste est qui ante Deum magnas virtutes operatus est*, however, on the eighteenth syllable, that is 'est,' there is a circumvolution (*circumvolutionem*—a two-pitch ascent) as well as a circumflexion (*circumflex-*

---

[1] *Corpus Scriptorum de Musica*, vol. 21 (American Institute of Musicology, 1975), ed. Lawrence Gushee. The treatise has long been supposed to be written ca. 840–850; it can be put a generation later through a link with Aurelien, archbishop of Lyon, 876–95 (Gushee, *CSM*, 14); another argument suggesting the last quarter of the ninth century is pointed out by Michael Bernhard, "Textkritisches zu Aurelianus Reomensis," *Musica Disciplina* 40 (1986): 49–61.

[2] Recent answers have been in the negative; thus Leo Treitler, "Reading and Singing," *EMH* 4 (1984): 161: "Aurelian certainly knew the chant tradition as an oral tradition, and he wrote his treatise with the presumptions, habits, and expectations that implies . . . . The *Musica disciplina* is a treatise for singers in an oral tradition. It is the first and last of its kind."

ionem: a two-pitch descent); that is so because between this syllable and the one that winds around after it there is the syllable 'et,' which has an acute accent (*acutus accentus:* a two-pitch ascent) that separates the two melodic turns."[3]

What Aurelian is saying in this roundabout way can be seen in Example 8.1.[4] The two Responsories draw their music from a common fund of G-plagal materials; they are sometimes the same, sometimes different. At this point they differ only in a detail: they share the common cadential antipenult in column V; but in column W, where *Iste est* has a twisting inflection with four pitches, *Magi veniunt* has just two pitches; then they have identical torculus wind-arounds in column Y. Aurelian remarks about the discrepancy in column W that successive melodic curvatures would not be appropriate to the style. *Iste est* avoids them with its extra syllable in column X; but *Magi veniunt,* lacking that syllable, has its curvature in column W limited to just the two pitches. In simple terms, *Iste est* has made a subtle accommodation for its extra syllable in column X.

Two points are worth making. First, the Gregorian melos Aurelian describes is absolutely fixed and specific. A single syllable, even a single pitch or two, was a matter of concern to the editor of the chant. Second, the musical details that are here described in labored prose are exactly the same details that turn up in the eventual neumed sources ca. 900. Clearly, the melodies were entities with fixed details in Aurelian's time, and they retained their musical fixity between then and the first surviving neumings.

Again in Chapter nineteen, in a passage to which Handschin first drew attention,[5] Aurelian describes a similar case involving two Passion Week Responsories that differ on an even slighter detail:

"In the first responsory (*Erue a framea Deus animam meam*), the melody that is made on the tenth syllable, a-, is borne around slowly (*tractim*) and

---

[3] " . . . in hoc responsorio: *Resp. Magi veniunt ab oriente,* vicesima secunda eiusdem responsorii syllaba, videlicet '-tes' ut 'dicentes,' ideo non incurvatur per anfractus inflexionum quia protinus altera subsequitur syllaba quae circumvolvitur. Ideoque absurdum esset si iteraretur duplatio modulationis in duabus syllabis, nulla interiacente morula vel qualibet syllaba. In hoc autem responsorio: *Resp. Iste est qui ante Deum magnas virtutes operatus est,* idcirco octavadecima syllaba, scilicet "est," circumvolutionem ac circumflexionem recipit, quia inest inter hanc et illam ea quae post circumvolvatur, id est 'et,' atque in ipsa fit acutus accentus quae has duas distinguit modulationes"; *Aureliani reomensis Musica Disciplina,* ed. Lawrence Gushee, vol. 2 of *CSM,* 128.

[4] The Responsories *Iste est* (Common of Confessors) and *Magi veniunt* (Epiphany) appear, as Aurelian describes, in Hartker's Antiphoner (*Pal Mus,* ser. 2, vol 1 *Antiphonaire de l'office monastique transcrit par Hartker:* MSS Saint-Gall 390–391 [Solesmes, 1900], 378 and 74); accurate staff transcriptions appear in *Liber responsorialis . . . juxta ritum monasticum* (Solesme, 1895), 199, 208, and 76–7.

[5] Jacques Handschin, "Eine alte Neumenschrift," *AcM* 22 (1950): 72.

Example 8.1. Responsories *Iste est* (Common of Confessors) and *Magi veniunt* (Epiphany).

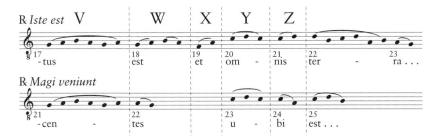

with a long curve because it is immediately followed by another vowel or syllable, -ni-, and only then does that other sound occur which is begun with an undulant and flexible voice (*vinola flexibilique voce*). In the second responsory, *De ore leonis libera me Domine,* on the ninth syllable, -ra, the melody is not thus lengthened with a turning-around (*circumflexe*), but is shortened, because a syllable is lacking that follows the sound of the syllable which precedes it, and the syllable that receives the undulant sound (*vinolam*) follows directly."[6]

This is illustrated in Example 8.2.[7] Again, the music has been shaped to accommodate one syllable more or less, and Aurelian explains the process in terms of avoiding successive melodic curves. Thus *Erue a framea,* with its additional syllable in column Y can indulge in the *podatus*-curvature in column X,[8] while *De ore leonis,* lacking the additional syllable, avoids successive curves by having a *virga* in that column. In Hartker's antiphoner, ca. 1000, the melisma in column W that is described by Aurelian as being "borne around slowly," in fact starts out with an *episema* and *tractulus,* both indicators of slowing. Then the melisma in column Z

---

[6] "In priori quidem ea melodia quae fit in decima syllaba, videlicet 'a-,' tractim prolixoque anfractu, idcirco circumfertur, quia ilico ab altera excipitur vocali, seu syllaba, scilicet '-ni-,' et rursus altera sonoritas habet ubi vinola flexibilique initietur voce. In secundo vero responsorio, ideo in [nona] eiusdem syllaba, hoc est '-ra,' non tam circumflexe protra[h]itur vocis concentus, sed corripitur, quia deest syllaba que antecedentis excipiat in se sonoritatem atque protinus subsequitur haec quia vinolam recipit vocem"; *CSM* vol. 21, 121–22.

[7] *Pal Mus,* ser. 2, vol. 1, 167.

[8] Aurelian's descriptions do not use the familiar neume names (clivis, podatus, torculus, quilisma, etc.), which evidently were not yet systematized; Michel Huglo, "Les noms des neumes et leur origine," *EG* 1 (1954): 53-67. It should be emphasized that his descriptions are of melodic motions rather than of neume forms: his ad hoc verbiage cannot be taken as a technical vocabulary for neuming.

Example 8.2. Responsories *Erue a framea* and *De ore leonis*

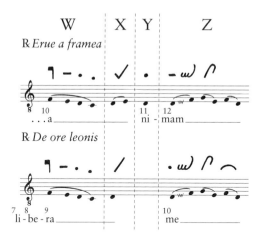

that Aurelian describes as "begun with a caressing and flexible voice (*vinola flexibilique voce*)," appears with a *quilisma* (Fig. 8.1).[9]

Once again, the music Aurelian knows is fixed, down to fine nuances, and the precise melodic details he describes turn up in the eventual neumed sources. His focus on little turns and twists, and their appearance in a spectrum of regional tenth century neumings, adds further weight to the view that the ninth-century Gregorian transmission had no license for singers' improvisations or freedom of pitch choice. These are isolated bits of four Responsories, and in a statistical sense hardly an adequate sampling of the full repertory. Yet in the logic of plainchant transmission, such unremarkable bits as these, which might be culled from anywhere in the repertory, say that the great bulk of the music was already quite stable and accurately transmitted in Aurelian's time.

Now the question is, what kept the melodic details so resistant to change? Was it memory alone—was that an adequate vessel for the considerable accumulation of fixed melos? Or did memory have, indeed, did it have to have, the support of music writing? The common answer to this has been that the Gregorian repertory in Aurelian's time was not neumed, for he would have used neumes if they were available, obviating the cumbersome verbal descriptions of melodic details. On the other hand, the original redaction of Aurelian's treatise contained neumed examples, in two instances he says they are being used, and that is reflected in the single surviving early copy of his treatise (the ninth century Valenciennes MS 148), where a number of illustrations are supplied with Paleofrank

---

[9] *Pal Mus* ser. 2, vol. 1 (1900) 167.

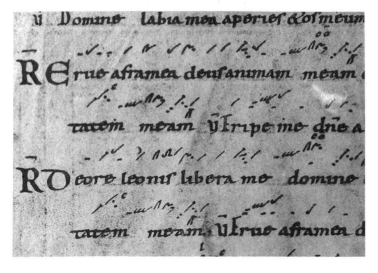

Figure 8.1. Hartker's Antiphoner: *Erue a framea* and *De ore leonis*

neumes.[10] However those are, by and large, for chants that were not normally noted in early antiphoners: *noeane* formulas and verses at the introit (there is one responsory verse that might regularly be neumed).[11] Aurelian's avoidance of neumes for the bulk of his Gregorian citations may say that he expected his readers to have neumed antiphoners available for consultation.

Something further along this line can be gathered from an observation in Chapter 13 concerning the verse *Quis ascendet in montem,* of the Gradual *Tollite portas principes:*

> Note also that the melody of the verse that occurs before the first complete phrase, which ends on 'Domini,' I do not remember finding elsewhere in the whole length of the antiphoner than here and in the verse of the Easter responsory *Haec dies,* in its verse *Confitemini Domino.*[12]

A similar remark is found in Chapter 10:

> There is among the night responsories of this mode a certain passage that I do not remember finding elsewhere in the whole repertory of responsory

[10] *CSM,* vol. 21, 121–22.

[11] Lawrence Gushee, "The Musica Disciplina of Aurelian of Réôme" (Ph.D. diss., Yale University, 1963), 244–59.

[12] "Notandum praeterea quia istius modulatio versus ante primam distinctionem totam quae finit in "Domino" memini me nonalicubi repperisse in prolixitate totius antiphonarii, nisi hic et in versu paschalis festivitatis responsorii, Grad. Haec dies, in eiiusdem versu, Confitemini Domino"; *CSM,* vol. 21, 99.

verses, except in the verses of the two responsories: *Domine, ne in ira tua* and *Peccantem me cotidie.*"[13]

Such relationships between isolated spots in the repertory might have been produced by a search through, so to speak, an oral memory bank. Yet with spots that are so distant and agreements that are so precise, it seems likelier that memory was abetted by a run of eye and hand through gatherings of leaves that bore neumatic notations. Worth notice is Aurelian's way of pinpointing melodic details, not just by citing the supporting word or syllable, but by a deliberate countdown to that syllable's number in the text (thus an "eighteenth" or a "twenty-second" or syllable, as in Exx. 8.1 and 8.2). This suggests a document that is being fingered and a visual inspection of noted music.

Aurelian refers on occasion to musical usages of earlier times. In Chapter 10, he mentions an unusual feature that is shared by the first-mode responsories *Domine, ne in ira tva* and *Peccantem me cotidie*: " . . . these could have the same arrangement as the others, but since the ancients had it this way, it must remain so with us, in their memory."[14] There is a similar reference in Chapter 12 to " . . . a particular division at the end of the verse, as in the Responsory *Declara super nos*, with Verse *Declaratio sermonum tuorum*, which certainly comes from the ancients."[15] An acquaintance with melodic details of times past may have been based simply on oldtimers' memories, including his own. But in light of the other indications of neumatic use, the access to earlier musical states may have depended on archivings in noted form.

Conjectures about ninth century melodic states and notational usage come down in the end to matters of memory. Aurelian supplies a perspective in Chapter 19, when in discussing the memory capacities of ordinary singers, he lists the chants they ought to know.

> Anyone may be called by the name of singer; but, unless I'm mistaken, he can't be called perfect unless he has implanted by memory in the sheath of his heart the melody of the verses of all the modes, and the differences, both of the modes and of the verses of the antiphons, introits, and responsories.[16]

[13] "Est in hoc tono (Mode 1) quaedam divisio in nocturnalibus responsoriis, quam non uspiam nemini me in latitudine totius responsoriorum versibus repperisse, nisi solummodo in versibus istorum duorum responsoriorum (Domine, ne in ira tua and Peccantem me cotidie)"; *CSM*, vol. 21, 88-89.

[14] "qui, cum ordinem possidere queant ceterorum, tamen apud antiquos ita mansit, apud nos quoque ob eorum memoriam necesse est permanere"; *CSM*, vol. 21, 89.

[15] "Praeterea quedam exceptis his in fine versus est divisio, ut in hoc: Resp. Declara super nos; Versus. Declaratio sermonum tuorum, quod utique ab antiquis tractum est"; *CSM*, vol. 21, 94.

[16] "Porro autem etsi opinio me non fefellit, licet quispiam cantoris censeatur vocabulo, minime tamen perfectus esse poterit, nisi modulationem omnium versuum per omnes tonos,

He surely has in mind the psalm tones attached to antiphons and introits—music so familiar that it was rarely supplied with neumes in early
antiphoners; also the *differentiae* that link antiphon beginnings with
psalm tone endings, perhaps as well the standard verse tones for responsories, which were sung by soloists but had choral connections that would
concern ordinary singers; neither of these was regularly neumed in early
antiphoners. He is unlikely to have had in mind the soloists' responsory
verses with more elaborate, independent melodies. Yet even at a generous
reading that takes some of these into account, what is remarkable about
Aurelian's reckoning of the "by heart" obligation of Carolingian singers—
in theca cordis memoriter insitam—is that it comes to so little. The great
bulk of proper melodies, the mainline Gregorian corpus of mass and office chants, made no real claim on such memories.

Yet that compilation of precisely fixed Gregorian melodic shapes had
to be on tap somewhere. It was in choirmasters' memories. Every ninth
century establishment that mounted Gregorian singing needed at least one
specialist who knew all of the dozens of hours' worth of proper melodies
by heart. That meant verbatim control of melodic substances which were,
as Aurelian's pinpoint citations indicate, quite fixed and finely nuanced.
All ninth century choirmasters bore this obligation. Among them perhaps
were some who could have managed such encyclopedic control without
the help of written memoranda, but it is hard to imagine their number
was very great.

How formidable the challenge to memory was can be judged from an
observation of Guido of Arezzo's in the early eleventh century. By that
time, fully neumed Gregorian collections had long been the rule; yet the
technology of neumatic writing, and with it the nature of the Gregorian
melodic transmission, remained much as it was at the time of the first surviving antiphoners, ca. 900, and indeed as it seems already to have been
in the times of Aurelian and Helisachar. That Gregorian transmission represented a coupling of verbatim memory, where the full melodic substances were stored, and staffless neumes, whose accurate outlinings of
the melodic substance supplied memory with an indispensable support.
The well-stocked memories and the precise neumatic outlines had need of
one another; neither could work by itself. Then Guido advocated an improved technology that reduced the memory quotient. He took pride in
comparing his cleffed staff lines with what there was before:

> for if at present those who have succeeded in gaining only an imperfect
> knowledge of singing in ten years of study intercede most devoutly before
> God for their teachers, what think you will be done for us and our helpers,

---

discretionemque tam tonorum, quam versuum antiphonarum seu introituum, nec ne responsoriorum in theca cordis memoriter insitam habuerit"; *CSM*, vol. 21, 118.

who can produce a perfect singer in the space of one year, or at the most in two?[17]

Now if Guido's contemporaries, with the help of neumes, took ten years to memorize the repertory, then memorizing it without neumes was a manifest impossibility. This would be scarcely less true for the ninth century than for the eleventh. The Carolingian-Gregorian repertory (reckoned from the content of Hesbert's *Sextuplex* and *CAO*), was not that much smaller then the repertory in Guido's time.[18] As Helisachar and Aurelian make clear, the melodies they knew were precisely fixed; details were matters of concern, and there was no lessening of memory obligation with the improvisatory options. For the ninth century choirmaster, if neumes were used, the burden was close to what brought the eleventh century apprentice master to that ten year extremity. If neumes were not used, then the burden seems unsustainable.

Aurelian's setting-out of musical details, coupled with Helisachar's insistence on accuracy, should lay to rest any notion that improvisation was a continuing option in the ninth-century Gregorian melodic transmission. Both authors describe a melos that was fixed, down to fine details. Aurelian's descriptions also reveal a melos that is exactly the same as the one found eventually in neumed versions. In addition Aurelian uses neumes when he wants to. If he chooses to do without them for some purposes in his treatise, that would be because he knew that his readers, all trained musicians, had neumed antiphoners available for consultation.

[17] Oliver Strunk, *Source Readings in Music History* (New York: W. W. Norton, 1950), 122; *Epistola Guidonis Michaeli Monacho De ignoto cantu* (written ca. 1030): "...ut quos ego et omnes ante me summa cum difficultate ecclesiasticos cantus didicimus . . . nam si illi pro suis apud Deum devotissime intercedunt magistris, qui hactenus ab eis vix decennio cantandi imperfectam scientiam consequi potuerunt, quid putas pro nobis nostrisque adiutoribus fiet, qui annali spatio, aut si multum, biennio perfectum cantorem efficimus?"; *GS*, 2. 43b.

[18] *AMS* Hesbert, *Corpus antiphonalium officii* vol. 1–6 (Rome, 1963-79).

CHAPTER 9

Plainchant before Neumes

THE MELODIC SUBSTANCES of Gregorian chant can be traced with some certainty to ca. 900 when the first surviving antiphoners with neumes were made. Those early neumings lack precision about pitch height and interval width. They are, however, exact enough about duration and ornament so that, despite the approximate profilings of pitch motions, they can be seen to represent music that was quite fixed, down to fine details, and meant to sound the same on every occasion. The melodic fixity was a likely outcome of the ecclesiastical reforms overseen by Pippin and Charlemagne in the later eighth century. During earlier times, the transmission probably went without notation and the nature and substance of the melos can only be guessed.

There might be various relationships between the unneumed and neumed states. Some of the music, as noted, may accurately mirror prior aural deliveries. Some may have been altered during written editorial operations on the way to a final neumed version, making antecedents less clear. Some of it may have originated in compositional initiatives where neumes were used, thus giving no access to an earlier state. In what follows, four different classes of chant will be considered, each having something of its own behavior, and each reflecting perhaps a different process of aural generation, or, a different path from aural to notational delivery.

1. remembered melodies,
2. accommodated melodies,
3. psalmic matrices,
4. centonate compilations.

1. *Remembered melodies: idiomela.* The large majority of eighth century Gregorian chants can be seen as having attained, before notation, the fixity of remembered melodies. Much of their musical substance was drawn from familiar modal-melodic materials that were lodged in a communal memory. But each chant had distinctive musical touches that set it apart from the others in its class, and each was recognized as a distinctive, memorable entity. Byzantine musical usage has a name for this, calling such chants *idiomela*. An *idiomelon* is a remembered song, a tune in its own right. In the eighth-tenth century Gregorian mass repertory surveyed in

Hesbert's *Sextuplex*,[1] most of the chants would seem to have been idiomela, including most introits, offertories (with verses), and communions, as well as many graduals and alleluia verses.

An obvious symptom of idiomelic music is to have text meaning reflected in musical substance; this is rare among Gregorian chants,[2] where
the factors that make for uniqueness and memorability are almost always
abstractly musical. Differences that seem slight today were enough to lend
a chant idiomelic distinction. Thus the D-mode offertories *Stetit angelus*
and *Viri Galilei* share much musical substance but are independent, idiomelic melodies.[3]

There is a common sense line of speculation about such chants. With in-
dividuality as their nature, they start out in relatively free improvisations;
through liturgical repetition they become firmed in memory; and at an
eventual writing-down, the well-remembered aural melos is highly enough
prized to be accurately recorded. The neumed versions of idiomelic chants
would reflect with some faithfulness the prior memorized substance.

Light is thrown on the aural status of idiomelic chants by instances of
close multiples, such as those examined in Chapters 2, 3, and 6. These
amount to a single chant that has come down through independent dictations and neumings in different regions. The melodic result remains
much the same everywhere, pointing to a common, memorized aural state
behind the same, yet different, written states. Yet that the written readings are not quite the same, says that memories without neumatic support
were not adequate to effect exact recall. The idiomelic chants before
neuming were well-remembered, not verbatim-remembered.

The Carolingian musical reformers were so thorough in suppressing archaic local variants that surviving close multiples are rare. Still, those already discussed have represented the classes of processional antiphons
and offertories, and examples can be drawn from other classes, particularly alleluia verses. Taken together, their testimony indicates a considerable presence of idiomelic chants in Gregorian aural states. The bulk of
the repertory, before it reached neuming, would have been fixed, remembered melody.

2. *Accommodated melodies: the idiomelic-automelic-prosomoiac syndrome.* A second class, linked to the idiomelic class, contains the model
melody or automelic-prosomoiac chants. In most plainchant repertories,
certain favorite melodies are singled out and have fresh texts applied to

---

[1] R.-J. Hesbert, *AMS* (Brussels, 1935).

[2] Dominicus Johner, *Wort und Ton im Choral*, 2nd edition (Leipzig, 1953), 435ff; Willi
Apel, *Gregorian Chant* (Bloomington: IN 1958), 301ff.

[3] These are readily comparable in *Tonaire des pièces de la Messe: selon le Graduale triplex
et l'Offertoriale triplex* (Solesmes, 1991) Offertoires, 5, 13 and 4, 11; also Carolus Ott, *Offertoriale sive versus offertoriorum* (Tournai, 1935), 170, 172.

them. Again there is a Byzantine nomenclature; an idiomelic chant that is used as a model is called an *automelon* (or generative melody); and the result of applying a fresh text to the model melody is a *prosomoion* (or imitation). The chants that serve as models in general have much the same style and technique as the others in their idiomelic class and what sets them apart is their status as favorites. There are familiar examples of the Gregorian automelic-prosomoiac practice among graduals of the *Justus ut palma* type, where a large number of texts, many assigned to landmark dates of the liturgical calendar, are set to the same melodic model.[4] It is not clear which, if any, particular chant was the original model.[5] Automelic-prosomoiac accommodations are also a major presence among Gregorian alleluias (as with the *Dies Sanctificatus* type),[6] and to a lesser extent in other classes. The considerable presence of the automelic syndrome in the earliest surviving repertories lends support to the view, previously put forward, that much of the Gregorian musical repertory attained the status of well-remembered melos before it was neumed. More than that, there is some likelihood that the neumators-editors, because they were dealing with favorite tunes, inclined to record them accurately. Again, the relationship between unneumed melodic states and their neumed successors was presumably close.

3. *Psalmic Matrices.* A third, less abundant class of Gregorian chants contains those built on the psalmic matrix. These have a more substantial musical basis than the general modal melodic pool from which most idiomelic substances draw. The role of preexistent material suggests a different relationship between aural and notational states. Psalm poetry itself is built of complementary half-lines, and in its plainchant dress there is the tendency to mirror those verbal shapes while adding some further conventions. An opening hemistich may start out musically with an intonation formula, go on to a reciting tone, then perhaps a flexion within the recitative, and a medial cadence. A closing hemistich may start with a second intonation, then a reciting tone (generally at the same pitch level as before), another optional flexion, and a final cadence. Example 9.1 shows the disposition of some of these elements in the syllabic psalmody which complements Gregorian introits of the G-authentic mode; the accommodation here is to Psalm 94:1.[7]

---

[4] Peter Jeffery, "The Lost Chant Tradition of Early Christian Jerusalem," *Early Music History* 11 (1992): 173 n. 45, sums up the bibliography on this group.

[5] Silvius von Kessel, "Original oder Adaptation," *Beiträge zür Gregorianik* 18 (1994): 15–74.

[6] Karl-Heinz Schlager, *Thematischer Katalog der ältesten Alleluia-Melodien*, vol. 2 (Erlanger Arbeiten zur Musikwissenschaft, ed. by Martin Ruhnke, (Munich, 1965), 86-7 (Mel. 38).

[7] The *Liber Usualis*, No. 801, (Tournai, 1953) 15–16, gives an ampler version, adapted to the Lesser Doxology.

Example 9.1. Introit Psalmody, G-authentic

Psalm 94:1a

Ve - ni - te ex - ul - te - mus Do - mi - no

Psalm 94:1b

ju - bi - le - mus De - o sa - lu - ta - ri no - stro

Elements of this same psalmic matrix can be observed in example 9.2, another G-authentic setting, now in the more florid dress of an alleluia verse. The Vatican edition provides a single verse for this alleluia refrain, but medieval sources add a further verse with much the same kind of musical fabric. Example 9.2 shows a twelfth-century reading of the two verses.[8] For chants of this psalm-matrix class, just as for those of the idiomelic-automelic-prosomoiac classes, there doubtless were improvisational beginnings. Yet where the idiomelic chants would turn toward melodic fixity while still aurally transmitted, the psalmic class, because of its familiar, more substantial musical basis, might hold on to improvisatory generation for a longer time—even so long as the transmission remained neumeless. The aural focus would be on the tensions between the familiar matrix and its improvisational realization rather than on the replication of a particular melodic version and thus on the exercise of artistry that produced the version. When it came to recording in neumes, the transcribers would respect the persistent improvisational orientation as best they could by accurately recording a particular aural-improvisational delivery. That would make the noted versions relatively clear windows on the unwritten past.

This view of improvisatory traits continuing until the time of writing-down finds support in the ostensibly improvisational behavior of some other florid settings of Psalm 94. Example 9.3[9] shows the same psalmic matrix underlying the Gregorian verses in example 9.2, but given different melodic spins in the Milanese rite, with the same two verses, and again as Mass alleluias in the G-mode.

[8] Karl-Heinz Schlager, *Alleluia-Melodien I, bis 1100,* vol. 7 of *MMMA,* ed. Bruno Stäblein, (Kassel: Bärenreiter, 1968), 529–30.

[9] *Antiphonale missarum juxta ritum sanctae ecclesiae mediolanensis* (Roma: 1935), 292–93; cf. *Pal Mus* 6, 321; *New Oxford History of Music,* Vol. 2, *Early Medieval Music up to 1300,* ed. Dom Anselm Hughes (Oxford, 1954), 131ff, *MGG* 6, 1391; Michel Huglo, et al., *Fonti e paleografia del canto ambrosiano* vol. 7 of *Archivio Ambrosiano.* (Milan, 1956), tables 8a and b.

Example 9.2. Gregorian Alleluia verses

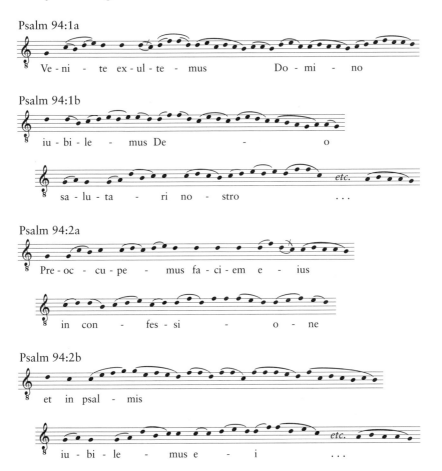

Psalm 94:1a

Ve - ni - te ex - ul - te - mus   Do - mi - no

Psalm 94:1b

iu - bi - le - mus De   o

sa - lu - ta - ri no - stro   *etc.*   ...

Psalm 94:2a

Pre - oc - cu - pe - mus fa - ci - em e - ius

in con - fes - si - o - ne

Psalm 94:2b

et in psal - mis

iu - bi - le - mus e - i   *etc.*   ...

Something like this can also be ventured about the Old Roman mass alleluia settings of Psalm 94 (vv. 1 and 2), seen in example 9.4.[10] Modal categories are not made explicit at Milan and Rome, as they are by the tonaries that distill Carolingian-Gregorian usage. But these Roman verses share the same G-authentic area as the rest.

Much the same can be said of the alleluia verses sung at the Divine Liturgy in the Byzantine tradition of Hagia Sophia at Constantinople. They are transmitted in the anthology of florid soloists' music named the Psaltikon, whose noted exemplars reach back to the thirteenth century,

[10] Bruno Stäblein and Margareta Landwehr-Melnicki, *Die Gesänge des altrömischen Graduale Vat. lat. 5319* vol. 2 of *MMMA* (Kassel, 1970), 201.

Example 9.3. Milanese Alleluia verses

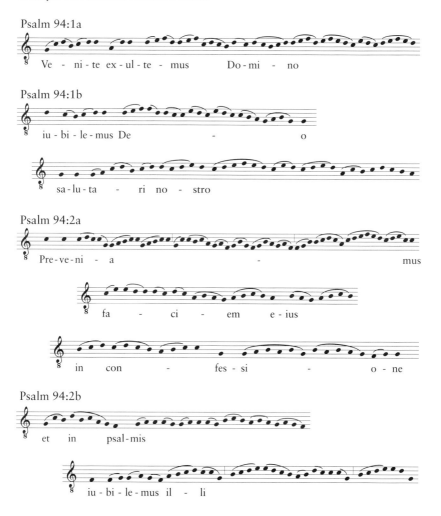

Psalm 94:1a

Ve - ni - te ex - ul - te - mus   Do - mi - no

Psalm 94:1b

iu - bi - le - mus De   -   o

sa - lu - ta   -   ri no - stro

Psalm 94:2a

Pre - ve - ni - a   -   mus

fa   -   ci   -   em e - ius

in con   -   fes - si   -   o - ne

Psalm 94:2b

et   in   psal - mis

iu - bi - le - mus il   -   li

while there are indications that the usage exists in the tenth century. Example 9.5 shows verses 1 and 3 of Psalm 94 as the alleluia for the Sunday after Easter in the G-authentic Constantinopolitan version.[11]

A further perspective on the Byzantine practice is had from a south Ital-

[11] Vat. gr. 345, fol. 26v; M. Arranz, *Le Typicon du monastère du Saint-Sauveur à Messine . . . A. D. 1131* vol. 185 of *Orientalia Christiana Analecta.* (Rome 1969), 257; J. Mateos, *Le Typicon de la grande église* Vol. 165–66 of *Orientalia Christiana Analecta.* (Rome, 1962–63).

Example 9.4. Old Roman Alleluia verses

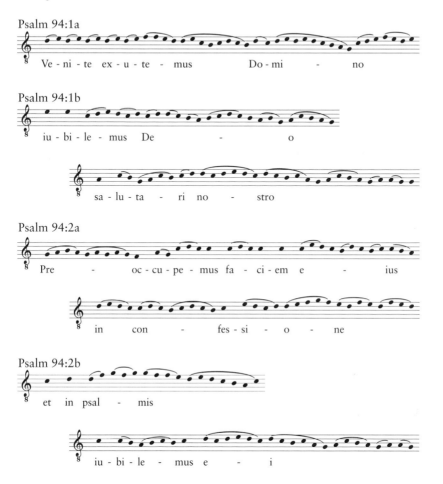

Psalm 94:1a

Ve - ni - te ex - u - te - mus   Do - mi   -   no

Psalm 94:1b

iu - bi - le - mus   De   -   o

sa - lu - ta   -   ri   no   -   stro

Psalm 94:2a

Pre   -   oc - cu - pe - mus fa - ci - em   e   -   ius

in   con   -   fes - si   -   o   -   ne

Psalm 94:2b

et   in   psal   -   mis

iu - bi - le   -   mus   e   -   i

ian Psaltikon recension of the thirteenth-fourteenth centuries. Its musical substances in Example 9.6[12] are related to those of Constantinople, but at times are more florid.

This sampling of same, yet different, realizations of Psalm 94 as G-authentic mass alleluia may support the view that psalm matrices continued to be dealt with improvisationally so long as the transmission remained aural, and that the introduction of neuming saw some of the later stage

[12] *Contacarium Ashburnhamense*, ed. Carsten Höeg, *Monumenta* Vol. 4: *Reproduction intégrale du Cod. Laur. Ashb, 64* (Copenhagen, 1956), fol. 222v–23.

Example 9.5. Byzantine Alleluia verses (Constantinopolitan)

improvised deliveries more or less faithfully recorded. Yet there are grounds for caution. Some of the psalmic chants, just like their idiomelic-automelic peers, may have settled into well-remembered fixity while still aurally transmitted. Then there are symptoms of written-editorial intervention in the Byzantine alleluias. A masterful analysis of the Psaltikon alleluia cycle by Christian Thodberg shows how fixed patterns and formulas are applied throughout the repertory, including the verses seen in

Example 9.6. Byzantine Alleluia verses (South Italian)

example 9.5.[13] On the Gregorian side, there are similar symptoms of writ-ten-editorial activity. The alleluia verses *Venite* and *Preoccupemus* (Ps. 94)

[13] Christian Thodberg, *Der byzantinische Alleluiarionzyklus,* vol. 8 of *Monumenta Mu-sicae Byzantinae* (*Monumenta Musicae Byzantinae, Subsidia* 8; (Copenhagen: 1956), 78f, 108, 147, 183, 196, 207, 229.

in example 9.2 share much of their style and conditions of transmission with the alleluia verse *Te decet hymnus* (Ps. 64); this too is in the G-mode, and may be said to have the same improvisatory ring; and it also has a place in the Pentecost dominical series. Yet the musical fabric of *Te decet* plays host to a significant patch of music that turns up elsewhere in the repertory, and not even in an alleluia. The offertory *Super flumina Babylonis* is one of a class of nonpsalmic offertories with possible Gallo-Hispanic roots, which may have attained idiomelic fixity by ca. 700 (see Ch. 3). In a characteristic trait of centonate process (see below), both the offertory *Super flumina* and the alleluia *Te decet* end with the same lengthy melisma on the word "Jerusalem," attached to what are otherwise different melodies (ex. 9.7).[14] What lies behind this is not clear. There may have been a common fund of such memorable entities upon which the shapers of the alleluia and offertory both drew; or the shared material may have acquired its melodic fixity in one chant and then been borrowed for the other. In that case, what can be surmised about the relative ages of offertories and alleluias suggests that the offertory melos came first. Whichever way it went, a musical fabric that might perhaps be seen as improvisational turns out to contain fixed melodic matter. All the same, the psalm matrix elaborations, as a class, may offer the likeliest windows on improvised preneumatic states.

4. *"Centonate"-formulaic compounds.* My fourth class contains Gregorian chants, like the alleluia *Te decet* and offertory *Super flumina,* in whose fabrics there are bits of melos that also appear in other chants, within other musical contexts, and generally attached to different words. The key question is, how much of what the notational versions show was there in the prior aural deliveries? There is much that suggests the more sophisticated features in the neumed states were the outcome of deliberate editorial or compositional actions taken with notational support.

Interest in centonate-formulaic process goes back to the 1890s and the analyses and tables offered by Dom Mocquereau and Dom Delpech in volume three of the *Paléographie musicale.*[15] This was intensified in the manuals of Wagner, Ferretti, Johner, and Apel;[16] it persists in undertakings today, such as Kainzbaur's "centologische Analyse" of the G-mode Tracts.[17] In earlier discussions, it went without saying that centonate-formulaic features were the result of "compositional" processes where no-

---

[14] *Graduale Triplex,* 306; Ott, *Offertoriale,* 122.

[15] pp. 25–77

[16] Peter Wagner, *Einführung in die gregorianischen Melodien,* vol. 3 of *Gregorianische Formenlehre* (Leipzig, 1921), 369–96; Paolo Ferretti, *Esthétique grégorienne* (Tournai, 1938), 1. 109–24; Johner, *Wort und Ton,* 311ff; Apel, *Gregorian Chant,* 344–50.

[17] Xaver Kainzbauer, *Der Tractus Tetrardus. Eine centologische Untersuchung,* vol. 11 of *Beiträge zur Gregorianik* (Regensburg, 1991).

Example 9.7. Alleluia *Te decet* and Offertory *Super flumina*

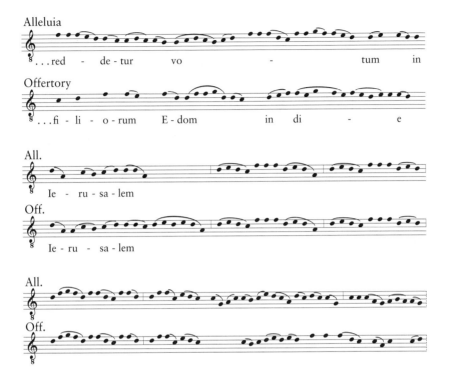

tation was involved. Since the acknowledgement of aural antecedents in 1950, the tendency has been to see centonate manifestations as carryovers from aural to notational states. Yet how much of the written was there before?

Gregorian chants have considerable range of centonate-formulaic densities. In 1950 Dom Hesbert addressed the question, "[s']il est possible de lire directement un manuscrit noté en neumes . . . ?"[18] He focused on a seven-pitch melisma, *re-mi-fa-mi-re-do-re* (the second pitch is a quilisma), that is used in eleven Gregorian mass chants (twice in two of them), which are spread throughout the liturgical year: five introits, three offertories, two communions, and a gradual. See example 9.8.[19] In the neumings of Saint Gall, that melisma was always noted the same; and when those neumes were translated into staff notations during the eleventh-twelfth centuries, the melodic substance itself also turns out the same, even

[18] "Groupes neumatiques à signification mélodique," *Atti del Primo congresso internazionale di musica sacra: Roma 1950* (1952), 229, cf. 230–35.

[19] Ibid., 231.

Example 9.8. Dom Hesbert's thirteen instances (1950)

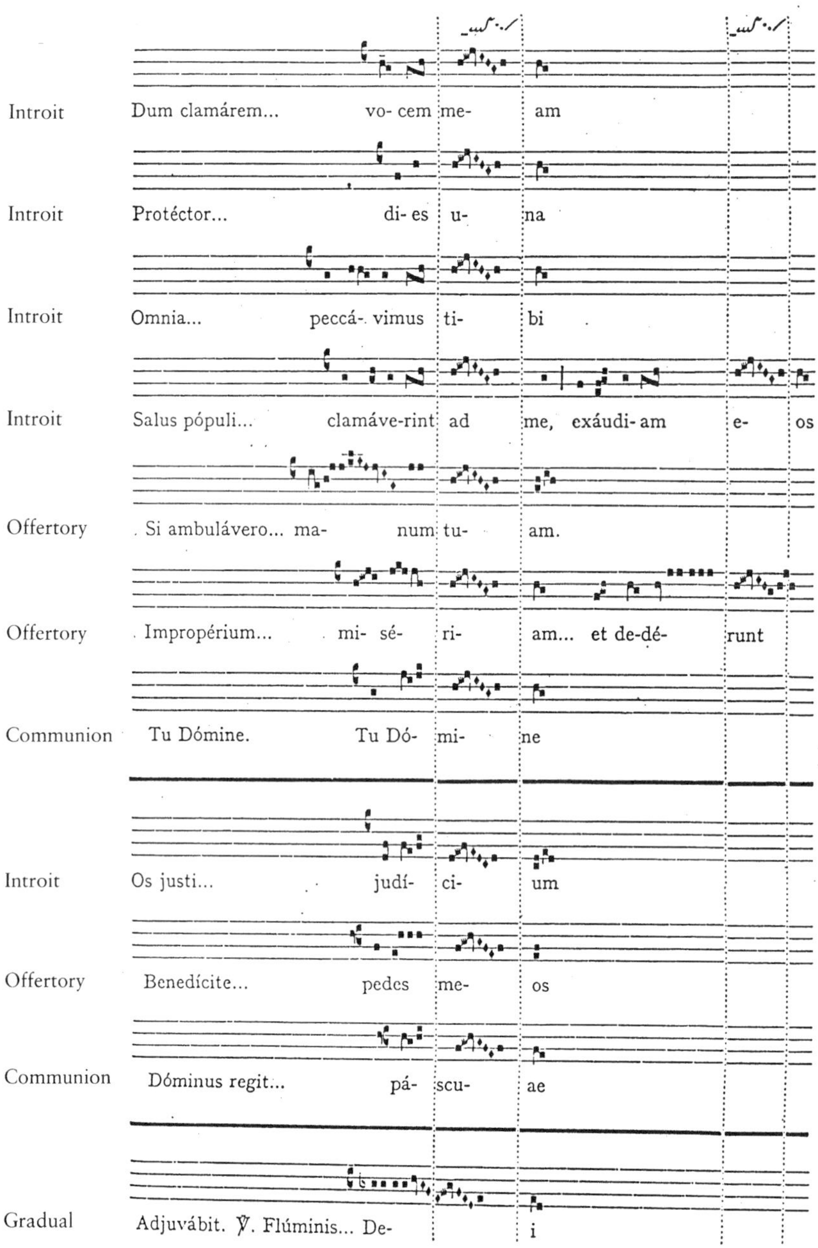

though its profile comes in three hexachordal positions: in nine instances with the *fa* on C, in three with it on F, and once on B-flat. Six of the eight Gregorian modes are represented: modes 2 and 6 with the C-hexachord; modes 3, 4, and 8 with the G-hexachord; and mode 5 with the F-hexachord. For Hesbert's question it sufficed to show that all the staffed realizations of this relatively rare neumatic entity turned out alike; hence singers over a span of centuries were able, using just staffless neumes, to remember the music quite accurately.

This can also be turned to the question at hand. Can such exact neumatic-melodic correspondences as these be the outcome of operations that were solely aural? Were performers in the heat of improvisational deliveries capable of plucking such particular formulaic units out of the reservoir of similar modal-melodic formulas; or does some written editorial intervention have to be supposed? Judging from the extent of this network, it seems less likely to be an outcome of actions taken in an aural-mnemonic environment than of editorial decisions made deliberately, with notation playing a role. Moreover, although two of these instances are in soloist's passages where an auralist's spontaneity might be displayed, the remainder are in choral passages where some prior agreement was necessary.

In yet another study Dom Hesbert dealt with an even more isolated relationship, where a centonate-formulaic bit appears just twice in the noted Gregorian mass book. The paschal offertory *Angelus Domini,* at the words "de celo," has the same music and neumatic details as the Pentecost offertory *Factus est repente* at the word "repente."[20] *Angelus* is an offertory of the standard Gregorian corpus, which for Hesbert meant Roman musical origin, and he took that to indicate as well the Roman origin of the rare and soon to be obsolete offertory *Factus est repente.* I have shown instead that offertories of the nonpsalmic type to which both *Angelus* and *Factus est repente* belong, likely had Gallo-Hispanic rather than Roman roots.[21] My present concern, however, is not with regional origins but with the conditions that produced this isolated melodic correspondence. As with example 9.8, there is the chance that it arose in an aural improvisatory sally, singled out from a roster of G-plagal modal-melodic bits resident in professional musicians' memories. However, with a connection that is literally as far-fetched as this, what is suggested instead is a decision contemplated at leisure in a notational medium, where the nicety might be identified as something that would be relished by others who encountered it in fixed, notational form.[22]

[20] See Chapter 4, figure 4.4.

[21] See Chapter 3.

[22] There may be a word-music play here involving the Gospel pericopes for Easter and Pentecost. The word "repente" of the Pentecost Gospel "Factus est repente de celo . . . . "

There are also situations of greater centonate density where considerable portions of a given chant are made up of melodic bits that lead other lives in other contexts. Example 9.9a shows the disposition of centonate-formulaic material in the gradual *Benedictus Dominus Deus Israhel;* example 9.9b shows their other contexts.[23] The range of correspondences, and the needs of choral as well as solo performers, again suggest that there were editorial/compositional decisions taken in a notational state.

The Gregorian repertory's most densely centonate chants are found among the tracts in G-plagal and the gradual verses in F-authentic. Their scope and complexity are suggested by tabulations of Ferretti, Apel, and others; whatever the tabulation's shortcomings, they show how intricate centonate manipulations could become.[24] For the formulaic relationships among the noted chants, in all likelihood there were aural antecedents of some sort. However, the levels of calculation and refinement shown by the notations are unlikely to have been attained without a written basis.

The indications of notation-based genesis reach beyond any narrowly defined centonate-formulaic class to embrace similar traits wherever they are found—among psalmic chants (as in the Byzantine Alleluia cycle) or among idiomelic chants (as in the offertories *Angelus Domini* and *Factus est repente*). A notational basis is also implied with the melodic adjustments that are made in class 2 (automelic chants) when fresh texts are accommodated to favorite models. Comparisons by Ferretti and Suñol have pointed up the subtleties in reconciling text and music in contrafact alleluias of the *Dies sanctificatus* type,[25] and in graduals of the *Justus ut palma* type.[26] Dom Cardine offered a pithy illustration of the latter complex; it is reproduced as example 9.10.[27]

(Acts 2), has the same music as "de celo" of the Paschal Gospel "Angelus Domini descendit de celo . . . " (Matthew: 28). In effect, the Paschal "de celo" anticipates the appearance of the Holy Spirit, "repente [de celo]," in the Pentecostal offertory. This refinement seems unlikely to have arisen in an oralist's summoning up of pertinent detail in the course of an improvised delivery; likelier it is a considered choice profiting from a written medium.

[23] Pointed out by Wagner, *Gregorianische Formenlehre,* 392ff and Johner, *Wort und Ton im Choral,* 313. Figure 9.9a: *Graduale Sacrosanctae Romanae Ecclesiae* (Tournai, 1952), 64. Figure 9.9b. A: Tract, Cantemus Domino (Mode 8; Easter Vigil), *Graduale,* 229; B: Tract, De profundis (Mode 8; Septuagesima?), *Graduale,* 76; C-1: Gradual, Audi filia (Mode 7, St. Cecilia, etc.), *Graduale,* 583; C-2: Gradual, Custodi me (Mode 1; Pentecost Sundays), *Graduale,* 345; C-3: Gradual, Salvum fac (Mode 7, Lenten), *Graduale,* 119; D: Gradual, Clamaverunt (Mode 7, St. Nereus, etc.), *Graduale,* [29]; E: Gradual, Liberasti (Mode 7, Pentecost Sundays), *Graduale,* 388.

[24] See Note 16.

[25] Ferretti, *Esthétique grégorienne,* 185–91.

[26] Grégoire Suñol, *Introduction à la paléographie musicale grégorienne* (Tournai, 1935), Planche F.

[27] *Semiologia gregoriana, Note raccolte dalle lezioni tenute da Dom Eugene Crdine* (Rome, 1958), p 120.

Example 9.9a. Gradual *Benedictus Dominus:* elements A through E

A single pattern is set to five different situations of text accent and syllable count, with adjustments made so that the accent falls on the same musical element, and other details are appropriately nuanced. For such fine-tuned accommodations as these, as for the more intricate cento-

Example 9.9b. Elements A through E: other contexts

Example 9.10. Accommodations, Gradual Type *Justus ut palma* (after Cardine)

nate networkings, there doubtless were aural antecedents. But the kinds of quick-think exploits that would be needed to produce some of the noted versions would seem to be beyond most auralists' abilities: imaginable, perhaps, in a select few, it is hard to imagine them in every one of the hundreds of choirmasters who were responsible for the musical liturgy throughout the Empire. The received, notational states are more readily seen as elaborations in writing of less developed aural states.[28]

Such speculations come down to matters of memory. There are accounts of prodigious mnemonic feats with verbal texts—the Bible, Homer, Vergil, Dante, etc.[29]—during antiquity and the middle ages. Yet all these depend ultimately on formulations that were visible; even for Homer, there was the Pisistratan text by the sixth century B.C. What brought them notice anyway was that they went beyond the ordinary memorist scope. In theory, there might be two sorts of memory at work in aural transmissions: one perhaps called continuity or narrative memory, the other perhaps referential or associative memory. Continuity memory would serve for music that came out in a progressive discourse, in a succession of melodic events, where one memorable quantum led to another, triggering recall. Such memory would be the custodian of most Gregorian music in its aural states: the remembered melodies in the idiomelic-automelic-prosomoiac classes, and any psalm matrix elaborations that reached melodic fixity before there was neuming. A window on continuity memory is had from the behavior of close multiples (like those for *Elegerunt apostoli*), which suggests that Merovingian musical memories controlled dozens of hours' worth of distinctively profiled, well-remembered, idiomelic melos without resorting to notation. Yet the music came out a bit differently at different places and occasions; continuity memory without the support of neumes fell short of verbatim recall.

Then the other sort of aural memory would be referential memory. This would serve for the melodic cross-referencings among centonate-formulaic chants, and for the adjustments made when contrafact texts were adapted to model melodies, or when hymnic music was intercalated with psalmody. With the centonate cross-referencings, that meant very random access to great quantities of intricately turned melos. That seems doubtful in itself. Add to it that close multiples for idiomelic chants show aural continuity memory falling short of accurate, verbatim recall, while precisely such recall is required by an ostensible referential memory's pinpoint search, quick connect operations. With some chants, such as the *Elegerunts*, the same melodic entities where continuity memory falls short

[28] The comparable situation with formulaic poetry was described by A. B. Lord: "At times the complexity of structural interconnections between verses in oral style is so great that it seems that man could have attained it only with the aid of writing. Such a conclusion has an almost ironic flavor; for the truth probably is that these intricate architectonics of expression were developed first in oral verse, thus establishing from very archaic times the techniques which many with writing inherited and then believed himself to have 'invented' with the stylus, the quill, and the pen"; "Oral Poetry," *Princeton Encyclopedia of Poetry and Poetics*, ed. A. Preminger (Princeton, 1965), 592.

[29] Mary J. Carruthers, *The Book of Memory: A Study of Memory in Medieval Culture*. (Cambridge, 1990), 18f, 74ff, 88.

are hosts to centonate and accommodative details that require such exactitude. But the two memory capabilities—one merely approximate, the other altogether precise—can scarcely be functioning as complements to one another within the same delivery. As clearly as anything can, this says that the notion of an aural referential memory, capable of managing the centonate and accommodative niceties found in the neumed versions, has to be abandoned. The centonate, etc., doubtless had a defining role in aural deliveries, but at lower levels of calculation and refinement than those in the noted states. What there is in neumes would, to a considerable extent, be the result of editorial or compositional decisions that were deliberately taken in the written medium.

The attempt has been made here to look back toward the Gregorian melos before it came to be neumed. Different kinds of behavior in notational states have been taken as indications of different behavior in aural states. The bulk of the aural repertory may have consisted of idiomelic chants whose melodic substances were by nature memorable, and which were likely to be firmed up in professional memories before neuming began. That firming, however, was less than absolute, and the music was not reproduced as exactly in aural deliveries as it was later on when the deliveries acquired the support of neumes. With chants based on the psalmic matrix, improvisational deliveries may have persisted for as long as the transmission remained neumeless, and that continuing improvisational stance may have induced Carolingian neumators to make faithful neumatic records of late stage aural, psalmic deliveries. With chants involving centonate-formulaic relationships, as with chants incorporating refined prosomoiac accommodations, the see through from notational back to aural would be much less. Aural states would have their centonate-formulaic characteristics, but the neumed states we have would owe much of their definitive shape to editorial-compositional input in the written medium. Centonate chants promise glimpses of earlier usage, yet of all the Gregorian chants they may reflect least well what their aural forbears were like.

CHAPTER 10

A Carolingian Visual Model

THE ECCLESIASTICAL REFORMS of Pippin and Charlemagne gave high priority to liturgical music. Local plainchant dialects that had flourished under a policy sanctioned by Gregory the Great were suppressed and a deliberately edited "Gregorian" compilation, nominally representative of Roman musical practice, was spread through Carolingian domains. The impulse for change came with the visit of Pope Stephen II to Francia in 753–54. When Stephen's successor Paul I sent liturgical books to the Frankish court in about 760, the list was headed by an *antiphonale* and *responsale*.[1] At Metz in the 750s and 760s, Bishop Chrodegang oversaw instruction in Roman ritual singing.[2] There was similar activity at Rouen under Bishop Remigius, who was Pippin's half brother.[3] In Charlemagne's time, an *Instructio pastoralis* of Archbishop Arno of Salzburg, ca. 798, directed his bishops to maintain schools where chant according to the

---

[1] "Direximus itaque excellentissime praecellentiae vestrae et libros, quantos reperire potuimus: id est antiphonale et responsale, insimul artem gramaticum Aristotelis, Dionisii Ariopagitis geometriam, orthografiam, grammaticam, omnes Greco eloquio scriptas, nec non et horologium nocturnum." *MGH, Epistolae mer. et kar. aevi* 1 *Tomus Epistolarum* 3, ed. Wilhelm Gundlach (1892), 529.

[2] "Cumque esset in omnibus locuples [Chrodegang], a Pippino rege omnique Francorum caetu singulariter electus, Romam directus est Stephanumque venerabilem papam, ut cunctorum vota anhelabant, ad Gallis evocavit . . . . Ipsumque clerum abundanter lege divina romanaque imbutum cantilena morem atque ordinem Romanae ecclesiae servare praecepit, quod usque ad id tempus in Mettensi ecclesia factum minime fuit"; Paul the Deacon (c. 783), *MGH, Gesta episcoporum Mettensium, Tomus Scriptorum,* 2. 268.

[3] In 760, Remigius (Remedius) brought Simeon, the *secundus* of the papal *schola cantorum,* from Rome to Rouen: "In [litteris vestris] siquidem conperimus exaratum quod praesentes Deo amabilis Remedii germani vestri monachos Symeoni scole cantorum priori contradere deberemus ad instruendum eos in psalmodii modulationem quam ab eo apprehendere tempore, quo illic in vestris regiminibus exstitit nequiverant; pro quo valde ipsum vestrum asseritis germanum tristem in eo quod non eius perfecte instruisset monachos. Et quidem, benignissime rex, satisfacimus Christianitatem tuam, quod nisi Georgius qui eidem scolae praefuit, de hac migrasset luce, nequaquam eumdem Simeonem a vestri germani servitio abstolere niteremur . . . . Propter quod et praefatos vestri germani monachos saepe dicto cantradidimus Simeoni eosque obtine collocantes sollerti industria eandem psalmodii modulationem instrui praecipimus et crebro in eadem, donec perfectae eruditi efficiantur . . . ecclesiasticae doctrinae cantilena disposuimus efficaci cura permanendum." *MGH, Epistolae mer. et kar. aevi,* 1, 553–54 (Paul I to Pepin III).

Roman rite was taught.[4] In 813–14, Archbishop Leidrad of Lyon reported to the aging emperor about similar activities in his own jurisdiction, including the establishment of a schola cantorum, with the assistance of a musically competent cleric from Metz.[5]

How much of this came about under which monarch is not clear. Charlemagne attributes most of it to his father,[6] and it may be that music's prominence in ceremonial was reason enough for it to be in the vanguard of change. Yet with Charlemagne's clerics still occupied in revising such major texts as the Sacramentary, Homiliary, Bible, and Lectionaries, it seems doubtful that decisive action with the music came sooner.[7] By ca. 800, in any event, a full, authoritative Gregorian repertory was established. Its verbal texts are mirrored roughly in the mass antiphoners, *Bland* and *Rheinau*, which were written at about that time.[8] Its music is harder to control. The first surviving manuscripts with neumes date only from ca. 900. Most specialists in these matters have supposed that the Gregorian chants reached their definitive melodic shapes at the same time their verbal texts were settled (in the later eighth century), but neumes were not yet invented at that time and the melodies were consigned to choirmasters' memories. My own supposition is that the very considerable tasks of editing the Gregorian melodic substances and accurately memorizing them required the support of neumes, and these were already in regular use during the late eighth century.

[4] "Episcopus autem unusquisque in civitate sua scolam constituat et sapientem doctorem, qui secundum traditionem Romanorum possit instruere et lectionibus vacare et inde debitum discere, ut per canonicas horas cursus in aecclesia debeat canere unicuique secundum congruum tempus vel dispositas festivitates, qualiter ille cantus adornet aecclesiam Dei et audientes aedificentur." *MGH, Legum sectio III. Concilia, Tomus II, Concilia aevi Karolini,* part 1 (Hanover, 1906), p. 199.

[5] "Et ideo officio quidem vestrae pietatis placuit, ut ad petitionem meam mihi concederetis unum de Metensi ecclesia clericum, per quem Deo iuvante et mercede vestra annuente ita in Lugdunensi ecclesia restauratus est orde psallendi, ut iuxta vires notras secundum ritum sacri palatii nunc ex parte agi videatur quicquid ad divinum persolvendum officium ordo deposcit. Nam habeo scola cantorum, ex quibus plerique ita sunt eruditi, ut etiam alios erudire possint." *MGH, Epistolarum Tomus IV. Karolini aevi, II,* ed. Ernst Duemmler, (Berlin, 1895) 542–43.

[6] In the *Admonitio generalis* of March 789: Ut cantum Romanum pleniter discant, et ordinabiliter per nocturnale vel gradale officium peragatur, secundum quod beatae memoriae genitor noster Pippinus rex decertavit ut fieret quando Gallicanum tulit ob unanimitatem apostolicae sedis et sanctae Dei aeclesiae pacificam concordiam. *MGH, Legum sectio II: Capitularia,* 1, ed. Alfred Boretius, (Hanover, 1883) 61; also the remarks in the *Libri carolini,* cited in Chapter 1, note 8.

[7] Rosamond McKitterick, "Royal Patronage of Culture in the Frankish Kingdoms under the Carolingians: Motives and Consequences" *Settimane di Studio del Centro Italiano di Studi sull'alto medioevo, XXXIX: Committenti e produzione artistico-letteraria nell'alto medioevo occidentale: 4–10 aprile 1991* (Spoleto, 1991): 93–135.

[8] *AMS,* xii–xviii; *CLLA,* nos. 1320, 1325.

The origins of neuming remain obscure. An isolated early Christian hymn survives from the late third century, fitted with notations for its pitch and rhythms, but those are alphabetic notations carried forward from Hellenistic practice, rather than neumes.[9] Isidore of Seville can probably be taken at his word, ca. 600, in the introductory paragraph on music in his encyclopedia, that "unless sounds are retained by memory they vanish, as they cannot be written down."[10] Antiphoners are mentioned in middle eighth century England but nothing really indicates they were noted.[11] The origin of neumes has, during most of the present century,

[9] Papyrus, Oxyrhynchus 1786; Egert Pöhlmann, *Denkmäler altgriechischer Musik,* vol. 31 of *Erlanger Beiträge zur Sprach- und Kunstwissenschaft* (Nürnberg, 1970), 106–9; Martin L. West, *Ancient Greek Music* (Oxford, 1992), 283, 324–26.

[10] *Isidori hispalensis episcopi etymologiarum sive originum, libri XX,* ed. W. M. Lindsay (Oxford, 1911), vol. 1: 3. 15. 2: "Nisi enim ab homine memoria teneantur soni, pereunt, quia scribi non possunt." A window is left open: there were still letter notations at the time, and Isidore may mean that notators using letters, or even staffless neumes, could not aspire to full accuracy.

[11] Egbert of York (d. 766), teacher of Alcuin: "Nos autem in Ecclesia Anglorum idem primi mensis jejunium (ut noster didascalus beatus Gregorius, in suo antiphonario et missali libro, per paedagogum nostrum beatum Augustinum transmisit ordinatum et rescriptum, indifferenter de prima hebdomada quadragesimae servamus .... Hoc autem jejunium [quarti mensis, secundo sabbato] idem beatus Gregorius per praefatum legatum, in antiphonario suo et missali, in plena hebdomada post Pentecosten, Anglorum Ecclesiae celebrandum destinavit. Quod non solum nostra testantur antiphonaria; set et ipsa quae cum missalibus suis conspeximus apud apostolorum Petri et Pauli limina." (*De institutione catholica dialogus:* Migne, PL 89, 441). At the Council of Cloveshoe in 747: *Capitulum 12:* "Duodecimo adjunxerunt edicto, ut presbyteri saecularium poetarum modo in ecclesia non garriant, ne tragico sono sacrorum verborum compositionem ac distinctionem corrumpant vel confundant, sed simplicem sanctamque melodiam secundum morem ecclesiae sectentur; qui vero id non est idoneus assequi, pronunciantis modo simpliciter legendo, dicat atque recitet quidquid instantis temporis ratio poscit; et qui/quae episcopi sunt, non presumant. Interea quoque presbyteri, de his quae propria sunt episcoporum in quibusdam ecclesiasticis officiis, nihil omnino tentent & praesumant agere. *Capitulum 13.* Tertiodecimo definitur decreto, ut uno eodemque modo dominicae dispensationis in carne sacrosanctae festivitates, in omnibus ad eas rite competentibus rebus, id est in baptismi officio, in missarum celebratione, in cantilenae modo celebrentur, juxta exemplar videlicet quod scriptum de Romana habemus ecclesia. Itemque ut per gyrum totius anni natalitia sanctorum uno eodem die, juxta martyrologium ejusdem Romanae ecclesiae, cum sua sibi convenienti psalmodia seu cantilena venerentur .... *Capitulum 15.* Quintodecimo definierunt capitulo, ut septem canonicae orationum diei & noctis horae diligenti cura cum psalmodia & cantilena sibimet convenienti observentur, & ut eamdam monasterialis psalmodiae parilitatem ubique sectentur, nihilque quod communis usus non admittit, praesumant cantare aut legere, sed tantum quod ex sacratum scripturarum auctoritate descenderit, & quod Romanae ecclesiae consuetudo permittit, cantent vel legant, quatenus unanimes uno ore laudent Deum." Joannes Dominicus Mansi, *Sacrorum conciliorum nova et amplissima collectio,* vol. 12 (Florence, 1761). Concilium Cloveshoviae, anno 747. cols. 399–400.

Chapter 12: "...that priests do not chatter in church like secular poets, or corrupt or confound with theatrical music (tragico sono) the substance and order (compositionem ac distinctionem) of the holy words. But let them conform to the simple holy melodies that are been assigned to the later years of the ninth century, and only recently has that edged backward, as the neuming of the prosula *Psalle modulamina* (found in Munich clm. 9543) is seen as datable to the second quarter of the ninth century.[12] Even so, the first systematic neumings of the Gregorian repertory are supposed to take place no sooner than the end of the ninth century, which is half a century later than some of the other, newer musical genres—such as the prosulae, tropes, and sequences—were routinely being neumed. This late start of Gregorian neuming has, essentially, just a single support: that traces of about a dozen Gregorian antiphoners survive from between the late eighth through late ninth centuries, and none of them is neumed; none has even the telltale spaces left for neumed melismas that make Albi 44, from the southern Aquitaine in the late ninth century, perhaps the earliest witness of Gregorian neuming.[13]

A likelier start for Gregorian neumings, as I see it, is in the later eighth century, when the neumes were needed by editors assembling the authoritative Carolingian melodic recension. This incorporates melodic refinements that would seem difficult to attain without the materials under visual-notational control. The neumes remained essential in the next stage, beginning near the eighth century's end, when those same melodies were sent to the realm's far-flung choirmasters with a mandate for their accurate memorization and reproduction.

---

the custom of the church. Whoever is not suited to this should speak and write in a simple speaking manner whatever the situation calls for . . . *Chapter 13:* . . . that in one and the same manner, on Sundays and on feasts of the Lord, and in all matters regularly pertaining to these, that is, in the office of baptism and at mass, that they celebrate according to the manner of chanting (modo cantilenae) that we have in the written exemplar from the church at Rome . . . *Chapter 15:* . . . that the seven canonical prayers of the day and night hours be observed with proper care and with the psalmody and chants (cantilena) appropriate to them. And that the same regularity of monastic psalmody be observed everywhere, and nothing is sung or read that is not of regular use, allowing only what comes from the authority of the holy scriptures. So that all together may as one praise God."

[12] Hartmut Möller, "Die Prosula 'Psalle modulamina' (Mü 9543) und ihre musikhistorische Bedeutung," in *La tradizione dei tropi liturgici. Atti dei convegni sui tropi liturgici (1985, 1987) organizzati dal Corpus Troporum sotto l'egida dell'European Science Foundation,* a cura di Claudio Leonardi ed Enrico Menesto. (Spoleto, n. d. [c. 1989]); facsimile, *MGG* 9, 1625.

[13] Albi, Bibl. municipale, Rochegude 44; forthcoming edition by John Emerson. Further possibilities are listed in *CLLA*, no. 1304a Vienna Nationalbibliothek. Cod. Vind. Ser. n. 3645, with a neumed office for Gregory the Great, was dated by Bernhard Bischoff to the middle or late ninth century; facsimile in Bruno Stäblein, *Schriftbild der einstimmigen Musik. Musikgeschichte in Bildern* vol. 3 of *Musik des Mittelalters und der Renaissance* 4 (Leipzig, 1975). Abb. 58; Michel Huglo has pointed out that the office was not composed before the tenth century: "Bilan de 50 années de recherches (1939–89) sur les notations musicales de 850 à 1300," *AcM* 62 (1990): 238. *CLLA*, no. 1304b (from Oxford, Bodl. Library, Cod. Auct. F 4, 26, flyleaf) is also dated on paleographic grounds by Bischoff to the second quarter of the ninth century; facsimile in E. Jammers, *Tafeln zur Neumenschrift* (Tutzing, 1965), Table 40.

In the prevailing theories of neume origins, the tendency is to group all the early manifestations of neuming together in what amounts to a single developmental stage. In my theory, two successive stages are distinguished. At the outset, during the later eighth century, a relatively short original stage 1, during which the repertory was assembled and edited. Following that, a much lengthier stage 2, beginning by ca. 800, with the repertory given its Empire-wide circulation; this stage then continued until the neumes themselves turned obsolete in the twelfth and thirteenth centuries, and in a sense it continued to modern times. In each of the two stages the primary achievement was a fully neumed edition of the Gregorian melodies. The earlier stage reached its peak with the promulgation of the first edition, which used Paleofrank neumes, and was limited in circulation to northern parts of France and Germany. Then the lengthier next stage would begin with a second, revised edition, substituting for the first. The melodies remained just as they were, but the neumings adopted a different calligraphic style and obeyed a fundamentally different operating rationale. This revised edition, with its fresh rationale, was the source for all of Gregorian chant's future melodic and notational developments.

Each of the two stages had a different practical purpose, and those purposes are reflected in the two different rationales of neuming. Stage 1's purpose was to establish the musical substance. One can imagine a gathering of specialists who set down the melodic raw materials and edited them to definitive form, all with the support of neumes. For much of the music, the likely source was Rome; but some of it was favorite Gallican music that the compilers-editors, themselves mainly northerners, were reluctant to lose; and some of it may have originated in fresh compositional initiatives that capitalized on the instrument of neumes. This stage would reach its end not long after the corpus of edited melodies was complete, with its full melodic substances stored in professional memories, and the profiles of those substances recorded in neumatic notation.

The neumes employed in stage 1 operations were of the type generally identified as Paleofrank; I would also describe them as "type 1." These neumes were well suited to the tasks of collecting and editing. Some decades ago, Handschin and Jammers drew attention to the archaic Paleofrank notations,[14] and Hourlier and Huglo quickly followed with amplifications and a comprehensive inventory.[15] Such neumings are among the oldest to survive. They date from the middle ninth through tenth cen-

---

[14] Jacques Handschin, "Eine alte Neumenschrift," *AcM* 22 (1950): 69–97; *AcM* 25 (1953): 87–8; E. Jammers, *Die Essener Neumenhandschriften der Landes-und Stadtbibliothek Düsseldorf* (Ratingen, 1952).

[15] Jacques Hourlier and Michel Huglo, "La Notation paléofranque," *EG* 2 (1957), 212–19.

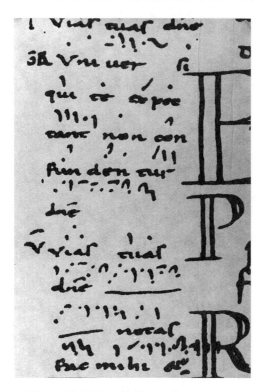

Figure 10.1. Type 1, Germanic neuming

turies (some perhaps from the early eleventh), and they represent northern regions, not far from the bases of Carolingian power. Figure 10.1 shows the gradual *Universi qui te expectant* in a north German representative of type 1; the music is entered in the margin of a sacramentary.[16] Figures 10.2a and 10.2b show the introit *Sacerdotes tui,* the gradual *Ecce sacerdos,* and the offertory *Inveni david,* in neumations added by a later hand to a full Missal which is the chief type 1 source from a region apparently in northeastern France.[17] The more orderly neuming of the sacramentary (Fig. 10.1) benefits from spaces left for melismas. The cramped, less elegant neuming of the missal (Fig. 10.2) lacks these, so that the neumator felt obliged to enter vertical strokes (not to be confused with neumes) to clarify the alignment of text and music.

[16] After Jammers, *Essener,* Table 5 (Düsseldorf D.1). A facsimile of the preceding introit appears in Chapter 5, Figure 7.

[17] After *La Notation musicale des chants liturgiques latins* (Solesmes, 1960), no. 1 (Paris, lat. 17305, fol. 15v).

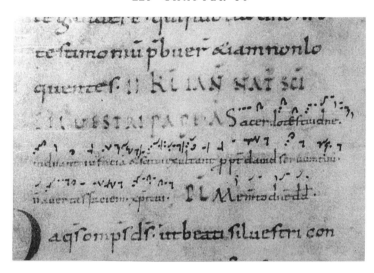

Figure 10.2a. Type 1, northeast France (?): Introit

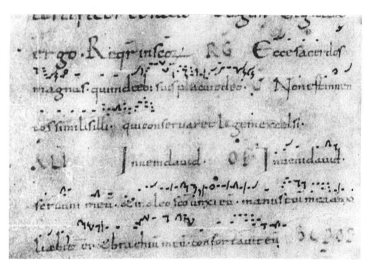

Figure 10.2b. Type 1, northeast France (?): Gradual and Offertory

Example 10.1 Gradual *Universi:* Type 1 Germanic neumes and Vatican Edition melody (=Saint Gall)

Grad. I.
U - ni-vér-   si * qui te exspéctant,

non confundéntur,   Dómi- ne.   ℣. Vi- as

tu- as Dó-mi-ne,

no-tas fac   mi-   hi :   et sé-

Carolingian music theory says little or nothing about type 1, Paleofrank neuming.[18] What is ventured here is based on its behavior and historical circumstances. Example 10.1 compares the beginning of the gradual *Universi qui te expectant* in the type 1 Germanic neuming and the Vatican Edition, the latter representing, by and large, the notational states and melodic implications of tenth-eleventh century St. Gall.[19] Type 1 neumes

---

[18] Aurelian of Réôme describes melodic motions in terms that suggest type 1 notations; Jacques Handschin, "Eine alte Neumenschrift," *AcM* 27 (1940): 69–73; E. L. Waeltner, "Die 'Musica disciplina' des Aurelianus Reomensis," *Berichte … VIIen Intern. Musikwissenschaftlichen Kongress (Köln, 1958)*, 293–95. Lawrence Gushee, *The Musica disciplina of Aurelian of Réôme*, Ph.D. Diss., Yale University, 1963), 215, 244–59; and such notations appear in the ninth century copy of the treatise in Valenciennes, Bibl. munic., 148.

[19] Düsseldorf, D.1, 126v; *Graduale Sacrosanctae Romanae Ecclesiae* (Tournai, 1952), 2.

can be seen as relatively straightforward descriptions of melodic events.[20] Their basic nature is to represent individual pitches as individual dots. Two or more pitches can also be connected in a straight or curved line, with the individual pitches maintaining implied positions as points in the line. Thus two pitches can take the form of an ascending or a nearly vertically descending diagonal, and linkages of three pitches, in a high-low-high, or low-high-low, relationship may, as one option, be represented by a half circle, facing up or down. Type 1 neumings also use wriggly dots and small curvatures of line to show liquescent and other ornamental deliveries; these describe the same melodic phenomena as the *oriscus, quilisma, strophici,* etc., but they would not yet bear those names. Longer durations are shown by lengthenings of individual dots into short horizontal strokes, and perhaps also by some anglings of linkage-ligature forms.

These neumings amount to graphs of relative highs and lows, with some pitch/performance nuances thrown in. Their rationale might be described as positional or graphic. That would suit the larger purposes of the stage 1 neumators: first to make records of aural versions and second to edit the raw written substances to finished melodic states. It was a practical way of launching the notational transmission, and the positional-graphic rationale identifiable here can be seen as a plausible basis for the origin of neuming.

Many other theories have circulated, most of them carrying much weightier conceptual baggage than the one just proposed. Alexandrian prosodic accents, Byzantine ekphonetic notations, Byzantine melodic notations, Latin punctuations, and the chironomics of choirmasters, both individually and in combination, have all been proposed as factors in neumatic origins.[21] Yet none may have had a role, as the kernel of origins

---

[20] Handschin ("Eine alte Neumenschrift") described most of their simple working basis; there are further valuable observations in Wulf Arlt, "Anschaulichkeit und analytischer Charakter: Kriterien der Beschreibung und Analyse früher Neumenschriften," *Musicologie médievale. Notations et Séquences. Actes de la Table Ronde du C.N.R.S., 6–7 Sept. 1982.* Études rassemblées par Michel Huglo (Paris, 1987), 29–55.

[21] See Chapter 5; also Arlt, *Anschaulichkeit.* The case for Alexandrian accents has been revived by Charles Atkinson, who draws perspectives from late ancient grammatical usage (Donatus, Martianus Capella, Isidore), from the verbiage of Aurelian of Réôme, and from the statement of the tenth?-century Vatican anonymous cited in his title: "De Accentibus Toni Oritur Nota Quae Dicitur Neuma; Prosodic Accents, the Accent Theory, and the Paleofrankish Script," in *Essays on Medieval Music in Honor of David G. Hughes,* ed. G. M. Boone. *Isham Library Papers* 4 (Harvard University, Department of Music, 1955), 17–42. Atkinson connects *accentus* with neuming. Aurelian, for one, seems to be using the word more casually to mean "melodic ups and downs," without neume technical signification. That is also the case in a poem by Alcuin used to preface single volume Carolingian Bibles: "Continet iste uno sancto sub corpore codex/Hic simul hos totos, munera magna Dei; . . . Quisque legat huius sacrato in corpore libri/Lector in ecclesia verba superna Dei/Distinguens sensus, titulos, cola, commata voce/Dicat, ut accentus ore sonare sciat" (*MGH, Poetae la-*

would lie in the adoption of the *positional-graphic* rationale whose work-ings are discernable in all the Type 1, Paleofrank neumings.

That original stage/type 1 would last only for a short time during the later eighth century. Near the century's end it would be replaced by stage/type 2, whose beginnings are marked by a fresh, authoritative neuming of the whole repertory in type 2 neumes. Example 10.1 shows the melos of the Gradual *Universi* in type 1 agreeing with the melos in the Vatican edition, itself representing a type 2 Saint Gall neuming. The massive tasks of edit-ing and memorizing were therefore complete in stage/type 1. When the neu-mators set about recasting the same melodies in a different, stage/type 2 no-tational dress, they had a fresh purpose, which was to assist in the accurate memorizing and reproduction of the melodies in the many places to which they were sent. That produced a different neumatic rationale. Under it, many of type 1's positional pitch dots were turned into type 2's more ex-pansive diagonal strokes. The essence of the change was that type 1 neumes were analogues of individual pitches, while type 2 neumes were analogues of melodic motions: thus the type 1 positional rationale was replaced by a type 2 rationale that can be described as directional.

Example 10.2 compares the treatment of individual pitches and of com-mon ligatures. Some pitches which in type 1 are rendered as individual dots are given greater substance in type 2, where they appear as direc-tional strokes, aimed more or less diagonally up or down. Then too, in-stead of type 1's straight and curved lines, where each pitch dot has at least an implied position on the line, there are type 2's ligatures, which are joinings-together of directional strokes.

I have described the type 2 neumatic rationale as directional. I would also describe type 2 as *gestural and chironomic*. Gestural suggests that the

---

tini aevi Carolini, ed., 183–86). Ernst Duemmler, (Berlin, 1881), 1. 287. The last four lines in David Ganz's version: "Whosoever as a reader in church reads in the sacred body of this book the high words of God, distinguishing the meanings, titles, cola and commata with his voice, let him say with his mouth as he knows the accent sounds"; Ganz, "Mass production of early medieval manuscripts: the Carolingian Bibles from Tours," in *The Early Medieval Bible: Its Production, Decoration and Use,* ed. Richard Gameson Cambridge Studies in Pa-leography and Codicology, ed. Albinia de la Mare and Rosamond McKitterick (Cambridge, 1994), 56. Alcuin is concerned here with full bibles, complete in one or at most two vol-umes; these would have punctuations, but there is only a slight chance of their having space for neumatic notations. *Accentus* again carries the implication of melodic ups and downs rather than written neumes. The same would apply, half a century later, to the descriptions of melodic motion by Aurelian; thus "Entgegen der allgemeinen Annahme sind diese Ter-mini [arsis, thesis, accentus acutus, accentus gravis, circumflexus, inflexio, ebenso Termini wie vox trumula, vox vinola, plenus sonus, percussio vocis] nicht als Namen für Neumen anzusehen. Die von Aurelian verwendeten Termini beschreiben vielmehr unmittelbar die Be-wegung der Stimme im Gesang. Darauf weise zahlreiche Verben, die in den Beschreibungen immer wieder auftreten, z. B. scandetur, sonabuntur, pronuntiabuntur, canitur," Waeltner, 294.

Example 10.2. Types 1 and 2: basic neume forms

Square-note shape	▪	⌐	⌐	⌐	♪	⌐	Ν	⌐
Type 1 / graphic	•	(none)	/	\	/	∩	∪	\
Type 2 / gestural	• (punctum)	/ (virga)	✓	∕	∕	∪	∿	/

neumings mirror the thrust of intervallic motions; and chironomic, an analogue of gestural, suggests that the hand motions of choir directors may have had a part in the conception. Chironomy has often been proposed as an agent in Latin neume origins, and perhaps as often it has been rejected.[22] The rejection seems justified to me, insofar as ultimate origins are concerned; there the graphic explanation would suffice. Yet, moving beyond neume origins, the rationale in all stage/type 2 neumings can be identified as directional, gestural, or chironomic.[23]

Reasons for the change in rationale, again, would lie in the different purposes to which the neumatic types were put. Type 1's graphic, positional, pitch-equals-dot rationale was suited to the operations of dictating and editing. Type 2's gestural-chironomic-directional rationale, particularly in species where ligatures were abundant, produced a different kind of visual image. With a general guideline that seems to be, "ligate what you can," the resulting neumatic forms are more plastic (individual strokes instead of dots, and extra strokes within ligatures). That increased shapeliness made the melodic transmission easier to manage. The more expansive strokes and the ampler presence of ligation in those gestural silhouettes gave the choirmasters' memories more substantial images to fix upon than the sometimes jumbled arrays of dots that appear in type 1 neu-

[22] Michel Huglo, "La Chironomie médiévale," *Revue de musicologie* 49 (1963): 155–71. Helmut Hucke, "Die Cheironomie und die Entstehung der Neumenschrift," *Mf* 32 (1979): 1–6.

[23] This is not an occasion to review the tangled history of the Latin term *neuma* and its musical correlatives. For more on this topic see Anne-Marie Bautier-Regnier, "A propos du sens de *neuma* et de *nota* en latin médiéval," *Revue belge de musicologie* 18 (1964): 1–9; Bruno Stäblein, *Schriftbild der einstimmigen Music* (Leipzig, 1975), 7–9, 61; Solange Corbin on "Neumatic Notations," in *NGD* 13, 128–29; David Hiley, *Western Plainchant*, 345. Such a review might take as a departure point the two different Greek terms behind the diverse Latin usages: *pneuma*—signifying airy, inspirational, having the breath of life—for the melodic, melismatic neumae of model antiphons, responsories, and sequences (Hiley in *NGD* 13, 123–25); and *neuma*—signifying nod, sign, control, expression of command (*Acts* 24:10: "and Paul answered, the governor having motioned him (*neusantos*) to speak")—for the type 2 neumings with their gestural rationale.

mations (see Fig. 10.2). Type 2's counterparts of directional intervallic motions may also have supplied paradigms for conductorial gesturings.

These observations about type 2 neumings have focused on situations where melismas tend to be disposed in ligatures. I would describe the ductus as conjunct. In a significant minority of type 2 neumations, however, the pitches tend to be represented as separate points rather than linked together. That can be described as disjunct, and at times it produces styles similar type 1/Paleofrank neumings. The essential difference is that this is done under the type 2 directional rationale, not the type 1 positional rationale. The most prominent type 2 disjunct species represent the regions of Brittany, the Aquitaine, and Lorraine. They have long posed problems for historians of neuming, being seen as too different in behavior and style from one another, and from the type 2 conjunct species, for them all to have a common departure point. This has supported the view that Gregorian neumings got an independent start at different places. My own view is that the type 2 neume species had nothing to do with neumatic origins, which are reflected only in type 1/Paleofrank species, and that type 2 had a common start in a neumation that was promulgated during Charlemagne's middle years as an authoritative model for the Gregorian repertory. The neumatic shapes in that model came from applying the directional-gestural-chironomic rationale to the melodies that choirmasters had already memorized with type 1 neumes. While the notation of the type 2 model's shapes was essentially conjunct, the disjunct neume species would descend from that same conjunct model, with their differences generated by reimplementing the model's directional-gestural rationale.

As already remarked, the calendar provisions and verbal texts of the type 2 model can be approached by way of the neumeless antiphoners, Rheinau and Bland, written ca. 800. Bland's own calendar agreements with the Gellone sacramentary, written at about the same time, speaks for the liturgical authority of both the sacramentary and the antiphoner.[24] However, the plainchant model's neumatic and melodic provisions can be approached only by way of much later descendents. One looks first to tenth and eleventh century neumings, representing nearly all of Germany, most of Italy, and much of France, all of which share an essentially conjunct neumatic ductus as well as significant amounts of notational and melodic detail. The agreements were showcased a century ago in the landmark collection of facsimiles published as volumes 2 and 3 of the *Paléographie musicale*, which concentrated on graduals of the *Justus ut palma* type. They have been confirmed over and again in the neumatic comparisons published by Gregorian semiologists in recent decades. Example

[24] Hesbert, *AMS* 115, compares the sanctorales of Bland and Gellone; *Liber sacramentorum Gellonensis*, ed. A. Dumas (Brepols, 1981).

Example 10.3. Semiologist's table (after Johannes B. Göschl)

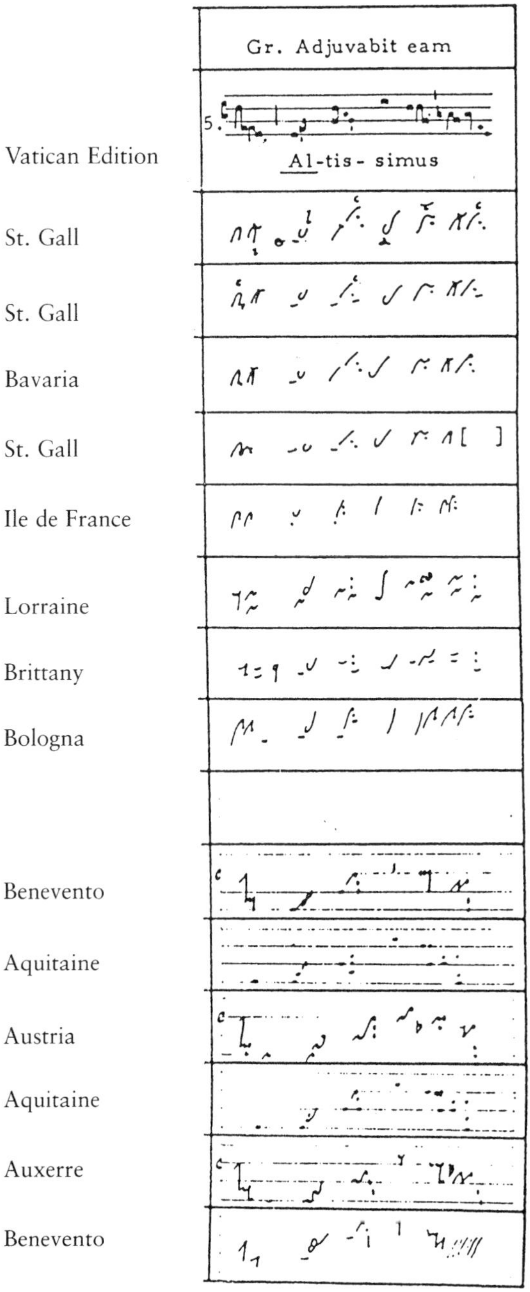

10.3 reproduces one such comparison from Göschl's admirable *Semiologische Untersuchung*.[25] Most of these neumations are conjunct, and they agree so well about particulars of ligature disposition and nuance that it is hard to see them as the outcome of independent notational initiatives.[26]

Example 10.4 carries this a step further with the ten-pitch melisma on "florebit" the fourth word of the Gradual *Justus ut palma*.[27] In its most common disposition, shown in example 10.4, the ductus is conjunct; with the climacus comprising pitches 4–6, all ten pitches are in effect ligated (3li 3li 2li 2li): porrectus, climacus, clivis, podatus). Fig. 10.3 shows this in ten neumations of the tenth through twelfth centuries, spread through Germany, Italy (Milan, Monza, Bologna, and Benevento), France (Burgundy and Touraine), and Poland.[28] This is the reading of the great majority of sources, representing nearly all regions. It is likely to reflect a common model with a similarly conjunct neumatic disposition.

In a significant number of conjunct neumings, however, the last four pitches do not divide 2li 2li, as in figure 10.3 but 3li si. Figure 10.4 shows this at Stavelot, Saint Gall, and Nonantola in north central Italy.[29] The 3 + 1 disposition represents the technique of neumatic disjunction or

---

[25] Johannes B. Göschl, *Semiologische Untersuchungen zum Phänomen der Gregorianischen Liqueszenz. Der isolierte dreistufige Epiphonus praepunctis, ein Sonderproblem der Liqueszenzforschung = Forschung zur älteren Musikgeschichte* 3/I–II. (Vienna, 1980) 2. 14, no. 24.

[26] Göschl himself puts this (1. 387): "Bestimmte im Verlauf unserer Untersuchungen gesichtete Fakten bekräftigen die Annahme, dass die gesamte handschriftliche Überlieferung letzlich auf eine einzige Urquelle zurückgeht und diese durch Abschrift weitertradiert wurde." However this position has been much criticized, as by Hartmut Möller, "Research on the antiphoner—problems and perspectives." 10 (1987): 1–14: "now the received idea of the chant as Gregory's work was fused with the aims and concepts of literary text criticism into an attitude of mind which has held sway in chant research right down to the recent work of some of the semiologists. According to the notion formulated by Mocquereau, the same constraints of transmission underpin 'Gregorian' chant as for a literary work such as the sermons of Pope Gregory. Treating the transmission of literary and liturgical musical texts as parallel is problematic" (p. 9).

[27] *GR* 38.

[28] The facsimiles, except for 10.3j, reproduce those of *PalMus* 2–3 (1891–93). *Fig. 10.3a*: Trier, Cathedral, 118; *PalMus* 3: pl. 111B (Bamberg). *Fig. 10.3b*: Zürich, Bibl. Canton. 71; *PalMus* 3: pl. 111A (Rheinau). *Fig. 10.3c*: Milan, Bibl. Trivulziana, *PalMus* 1: pl. 20 (Lombardy). *Fig. 10.3d*: Monza, Bibl. capit., C.12.75; *PalMus* 2: pl. 4B (Monza). *Fig. 10.3e*: Rome, Bibl. Angelica 123; *PalMus* 2: pl. 10 (Bologna); *Fig. 10.3f*: Monte Cassino 540; *PalMus* 2: pl. 21A (Beneventan). *Fig. 10.3g*: Montpellier, Fac. Médecine H.159, added leaf; *PalMus* 7: 2 (Burgundian?). *Fig. 10.3h*: Paris lat. 1087; *PalMus* 1: pl. 19 (Cluny). *Fig. 10.3i*: Tours, Petit Séminaire; *PalMus* 3: pl. 188A (Tours). *Fig. 10.3j*: Gniezno, bibl. capit. MS 149; *Antiquitates musicae in polonia*, ed. Hieronym Feicht: Vols. 11–12, ed. Krzyysztof Bieganski and Jerzy Woronoczak, (Graz, 1970) 12.34.

[29] *Fig. 10.4a*: Saint Gall 339; *PalMus* 1: pl. 14; *Fig. 10.4b*: Brussels 2031; *PalMus* 3: pl. 159; *Fig. 10.4c*: *PalMus* 2: pl. 15.

Example 10.4. Melisma on "*florebit*"

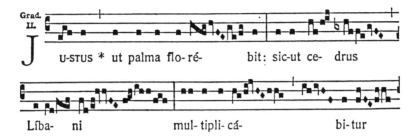

coupure, which was so brilliantly explained by Dom Cardine.[30] Here the *coupure* marks a lengthening emphasis on the penultimate pitch. Such use of ligature division to describe rhythmic nuance is common at Saint Gall, but it is found well beyond there and may have originated elsewhere, perhaps even among the type 1 Paleofrank neumations.

In addition, there are more elaborate neumings, as in Saint Gall 359 and Einsiedeln 121, which are again conjunct but also are rich in clarifications of melodic, rhythmic, and other performance details, with the use of episemata, "Romanus" letters, dots lengthened to horizontal strokes, undulants (oriscus, quilisma, pressus, strophici, etc.), and neumatic disjunctions. Figure 10.5 shows such a reading of "florebit" in SG–359, written ca. 900.[31] There are *episemata* attached to pitches 3 and 9, marking length emphasis; the *c[eleriter]* on pitch 4 signifies brevity; the final four pitches are disposed 3li si, effecting the *coupure.* With this abundance of clarifications, the reading might be described as nuance rich, distinguishing it from the majority of neume species which might be described as nuance poor. The spelling out of details in the nuance rich neumings is an indication of how precisely fixed and sharply etched on professional memories the melodic substances actually were. Of course, the notationally clarified details provided welcome support for the memories of Carolingian and Ottonian choirmasters.

Figure 10.6 compares nuance poor and nuance rich states of the Offertory *Elegerunt,* in the " Vulgate" melodic version that was analyzed in Chapter 6.[32] These two neumings, both conjunct, are nearly the same as to ligature disposition; almost certainly, they had a common neumatic departure point. Yet where Echternach (Fig. 10.6a) offers only a bare melodic profile, the neumator of Einsiedeln (Fig. 10.6b) has an enriched

---

[30] Eugène Cardine, "Sémiologie grégorienne," *EG* 11 (1970): 1–158.

[31] *PalMus* Series 2, vol. 2: 21–41.

[32] *Fig. 10.6a:* Paris, lat. 10510, 77 (Echternach): *Fig. 10.6b:* Einsiedeln 121; *PalMus* 4: p. 39 (Saint Gall).

Figure 10.3. "Florebit" melisma: conjunct, nuance poor, 2 + 2 division

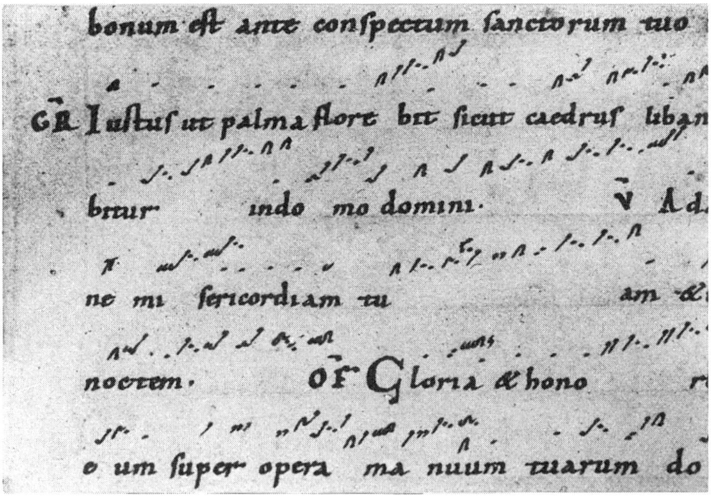

Figure 10.3a. Bamberg

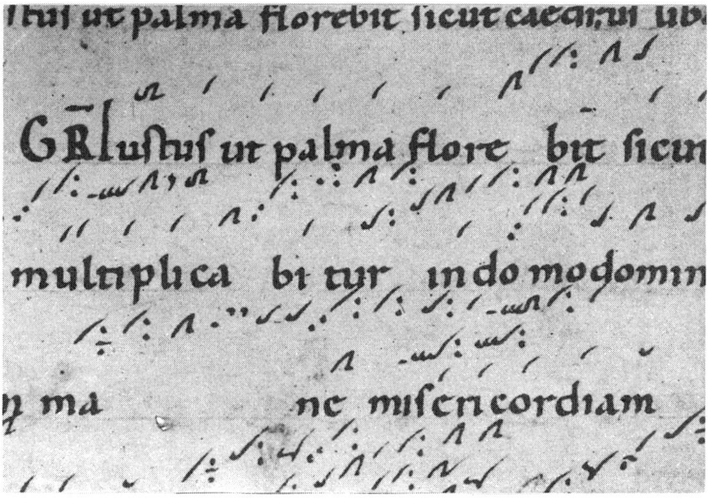

Figure 10.3b. Rheinau

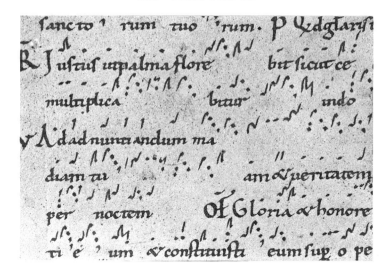

Figure 10.3c. Lombardy

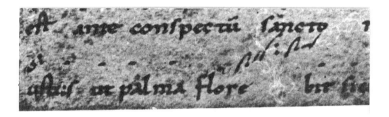

Figure 10.3d. Monza

profile with clarifications of pitch and duration. Which state was primitive? Most specialists, who have assigned a relatively late start, ca. 900, to Gregorian neuming, have also envisaged neumatic states that, at the outset, were relatively nuance rich, found in such sources as Saint Gall 359 and Laon 239. The nuance richness would continue for a century and longer in the hands of ambitious scribes (like that of Einsiedeln, ca. 1000); however, the majority of scribes were less ambitious, and they let the earlier nuance richness erode, so that by the eleventh century, neumings are generally reduced to nuance poor states.

In place of that, I set the start of Gregorian neuming farther back, and trace the variety of neume species which surface ca. 900 to a common type 2 neumed model of ca. 800. That reverses the developmental sequence, with

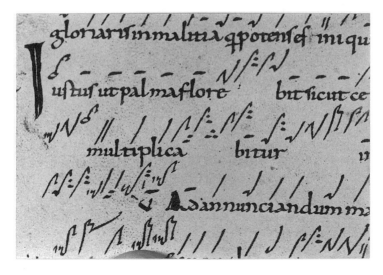

Figure 10.3e. Bologna

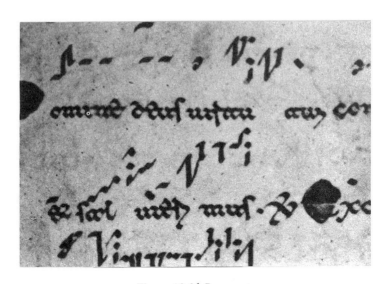

Figure 10.3f. Benevento

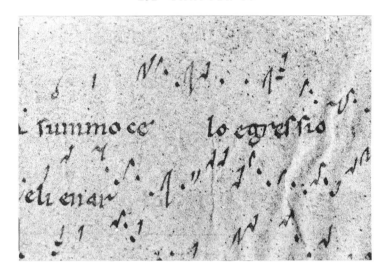

Figure 10.3g. Burgundy (?)

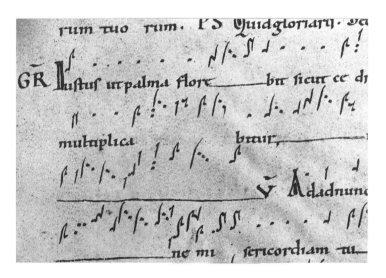

Figure 10.3h. Cluny

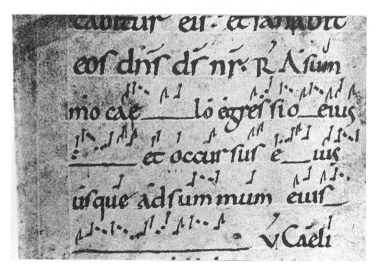

Figure 10.3i. Tours

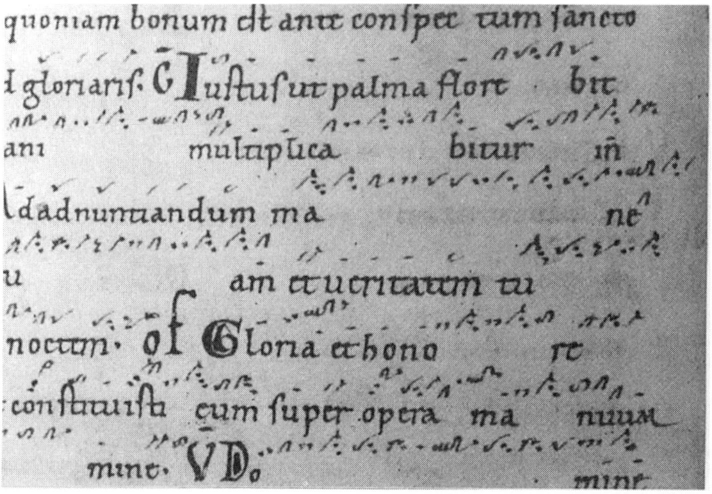

quoniam bonum est ante conspec tum sancto

I gloriaris G Iustus ut palma flore   bit

ani   multiplica   bitur   in

I dadnuntiandum ma   ne

u   am et ueritatem tu

noctem· of G loria et bono   re

constituisti cum super opera ma   nuum

mine· VD₀   mine

Figure 10.3j. Poland

Figure 10.4. "Florebit" melisma: conjunct, nuance poor, 3 + 1 division

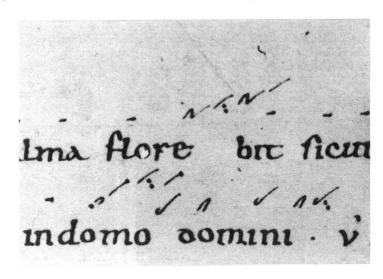

Figure 10.4a. Saint Gall

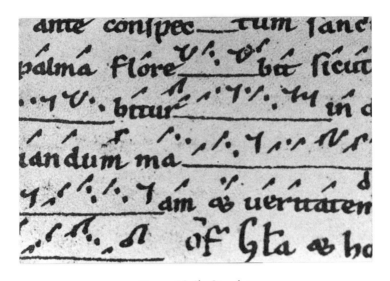

Figure 10.4b. Stavelot

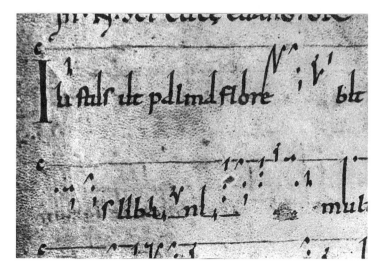

Figure 10.4c. Nonantola

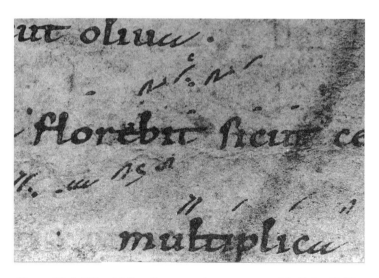

Figure 10.5. "Florebit" melisma: conjunct, nuance rich (Saint Gall)

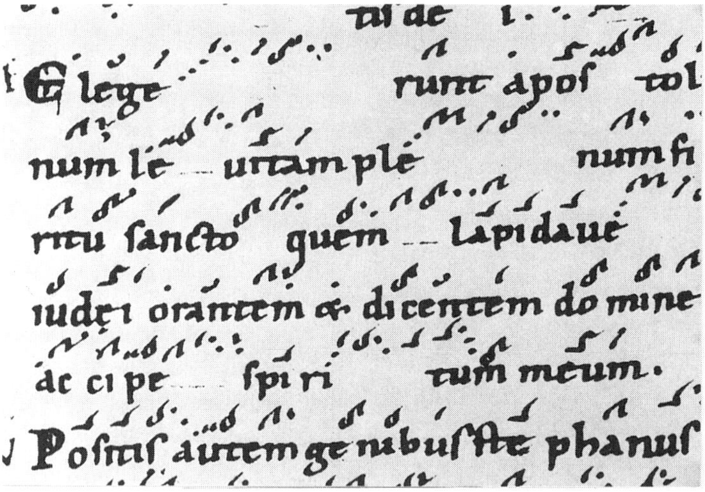

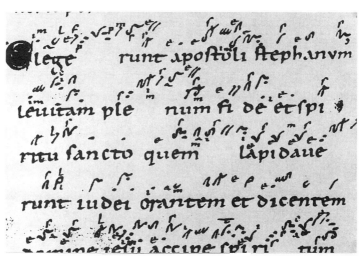

Figure 10.6a. "Elegerunt": nuance poor (Echternach)

Figure 10.6b. "Elegerunt": nuance rich (Saint Gall)

the early neumed model seen as nuance poor rather than nuance rich. Then the different local styles of neuming and the different techniques of nuance enrichment would develop during the ninth century, and be manifest in the variety of neumings that surface ca. 900. That the nuance enrichments vary from place to place, while the basic conjunct neumation and the melodic substance it represents are practically the same everywhere, indicates that the nuance rich readings were additions to the common nuance poor base.

Then there is the question of the disjunct neumings. In most theories of neume origins, a distinction is made between conjunct species, which make greater use of ligatures, and disjunct species, which favor individual signs for individual pitches.[33] The conjunct species are often seen as representing accent neumes, with some basis in the old Alexandrian accents;[34] the disjunct species represent point-neumes, with a tendancy to be more accurate in the approximation of pitch heightings; and Paleofrank neumes are thrown in with the point neumes. In this widely endorsed view, accent neumes and point neumes represent diverse and essentially irreconcilable notational principles which must have independent origins. Instead of that, my proposal has the Paleofrank neumes, with their graphic-positional rationale, situated apart from all others in an earlier stage 1; and then the other neume species, both conjunct and disjunct, are together in stage 2 as outgrowths of an archetypal type 2 model, all of whose neumatic shapes were governed by a directional-gestural rationale.

Figure 10.7 shows the neuming of the ten-pitch "florebit" melisma in the most prominent disjunct species: Lorraine, Breton, and Aquitainian.[35] The Lorraine species has long been identified with Metz, where the lore of authoritative Carolingian musical practice goes back to the later eighth century.[36] Among the early witnesses of Lorraine are the fragments of nuance rich antiphoners preserved in Laon 239 and Laon 266, both from the decades near 900.[37] Nevertheless, the neuming of Laon 239 seen here (Fig. 10.7a shows the melisma on "virtutem" of the gradual *Domine Deus virtutem*) hardly differs from the conjunct neumings of the same music in Figures 10.3 and 10.4. Laon distributes its last four pitches as 3li si, again a likely marker of rhythmic emphasis on the penultimate pitch.

In Breton neumings, the tendency is to dispose of melismas in disjunct dots rather than ligatures. Yet the Breton "florebit" in Figure 10.7b has the common conjunct disposition, with the concluding 3li si.

---

[33] See Chapter 5.

[34] See Note 21 above.

[35] *Fig. 10.7a:* Laon 239; *PalMus* 10: 15 (Lorraine). Fig. 10.7b: Angers 83 (Brittany); *PalMus* 1: 22a. *Fig. 10.7c* Paris lat. 776; *PalMus* 2: pl. 84 (Aquitaine).

[36] Claire Maître, *La Réforme cistercienne du plain-chant. Étude d'un traité théorique.* Cîteaux: Studi et Documenta, Vol. 6 (Brecht, 1995), 42–45.

[37] Peter Jeffery. "An Early Cantatorium Fragment Related to MS Laon 239," *Scriptorium* 36 (1982): 245–52.

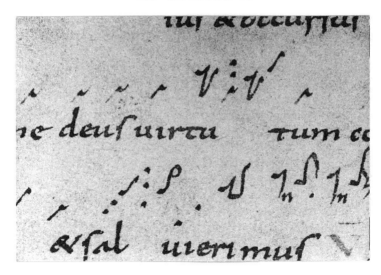

Figure 10.7a. "Florebit": Lorraine

Figure 10.7b. "Florebit": Breton

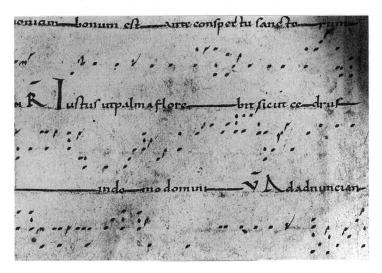

Figure 10.7c. "Florebit": Aquitaine

Of the three prominent disjunct species, only the Aquitaine departs considerably from the conjunct majority. However, the eleventh century Aquitainian neuming in Figure 10.7c was executed a century after the neumings of Lorraine and Brittany, and at two centuries' remove from a possible common source ca. 800. The rare survivals of archaic Aquitaine neumings have indications of a more conjunct ductus in earlier times.[38]

This sampling of the major disjunct species has shown no more than modest departures from the majority conjunct usage. It suggests that the disjunct species, like the conjunct, went back to the same model, with a common logic underlying them all. Their diversities in neumatic style and detail would be generated by the directional-gestural rationale whose license and constraint produced the model neuming and were exercised again by subsequent scribes whenever neumings were made. German scribes were often content to produce near replicas of the model; some continued using nuance poor, staffless styles into the fourteenth century, as in a Gradual of Schaffhausen(?).[39] Many scribes, however, became more deeply involved in the process of making their musical records. They

---

[38] Josiane Mas, "La Tradition musicale en septimanie," *Cahiers de Fanjeaux* 17 (1982): 280ff, with a facsimile of "préaquitaine" notation in Montpelier Bibl. Municipale, MS 4, facing p. 289; said to be ninth century.

[39] *PalMus* 3: pl. 130.

supplemented and altered the received neumatic shapes to produce more accurate, and more readily remembered, visual counterparts of the memorized melodic substances. Any and all scribal alterations and reshapings, however, remained regesturings of the universally familiar melodies. Whatever the notational changes, they all had the type 2 visual model as their ultimate point of departure.

In sum, there would be three main reasons for the notational diversities among the type 2 neume species. One was the impulse to assure melodic stability by clarifying the neumatic descriptions. When the type 2 model first circulated, the melodic substances must have seemed secure enough in professional memories, even though supported by no more than the nuance poor neumatic silhouettes. Then the need for better written support was felt and ninth century scribes went about improving on the model neumation. It led to the assorted states, some of them nuance rich, seen in the early tenth century; the continuation of such efforts, focused increasingly on pitch precision, led to the eleventh century's staff lines.

Another reason for the notational diversity would be esthetic. The neumators of type 1 scarcely seem concerned with visual elegance; what they would care about in their positional graphings is describing the music with tolerable accuracy.[40] Among type 2 neumators, calligraphic pretentions are greater and some of them give considerable play to local or personal tastes. This came about at the same time that literary scribes were engaged in developing the new Carolingian minuscule book hands. Musicians, entering their neumes between the lines of fashionably turned out texts, were surely tempted to stylize their own scripts.

A third reason for notational change would be that melodic substance was changed. That did not often happen. The music was meant to remain as it was when edited and committed to memory and neume by the Carolingians. Chapter 11 will trace something of the melodies' remarkable resistance to change over five centuries and more. Still, there were variabilities of memory that fostered melodic difference and occasioned neumatic change; and there were local variants, persisting from earlier times, that were judged worth recording. Italy was a natural place for such survivals; the Beneventan close multiple for *Deprecamur te Domine* (Chapter 2) may be one of them. France had its holdovers from Gallican usage, as with the close multiples for *Elegerunt apostoli,* seen in Chapter 6. Germany had the minor stylistic idiosyncracies of the German choral dialect; these might have entered the music without affecting the neumations, only to surface presently in the staffed versions, see Chapter 11.

For these reasons and perhaps others, stage/type 2 neumators would go beyond the received neumatic forms. However the notational changes

---

[40] See *Figs. 10.2a* and *10.2b* (Paris lat. 17305).

were generated under the same directional-gestural rationale that produced the model neuming.

A likely start for stage/type 1 neuming would be during the third quarter of the eighth century when the Carolingians launched their systematic efforts at Romanizing ecclesiastical music. Then a likely onset of type 1's obsolescence would come a generation or so later, signaled by the publication of the stage/type 2 neumed model. These dates would put the musical developments in line with the revisions of the homiliary, lectionary, sacramentary, and ordines that were the music's partners in the Carolingian liturgical reforms. The early date for the emergence of type 2 also leaves time for the nuance rich species of Saint Gall, Lorraine, etc., to reach the developed states in which they are first found ca. 900. However, the actual conversion from type 1 to type 2 neuming would not itself require much time. No major changes were made to the melodic substances; they were fixed and memorized in stage/type 1. The neume shapes needed to be altered. Types 1 and 2 are basically alike in translating pitch height into relative neume height, but their differences are such that type 1 does not easily convert into type 2; since it would take considerable erasure, it helps explain why no instances of conversion from type 1 to type 2 are known. Yet even with fresh antiphoners needing to be prepared, the change from type 1 positional to type 2 directional could be accomplished in little more than the time it took to write the new neumatic version out. It was not a huge task; in some tenth-eleventh century antiphoners, the full repertory of neumed mass propers fit within roughly four dozen folios.[41] Enough copies were needed to serve houses throughout Europe, but the mandate for reform was reason enough for this to be accomplished promptly.

The notion of an archetypal, directional-gestural, type 2 Gregorian neuming ca. 800 represents a considerable departure from the established view of the neumes as unavailable for any purpose before the second quarter of the ninth century, and then not applied to the Gregorian propers before ca. 900. Now that traditional view itself needs to be reviewed. It depends, at bottom, on just two arguments. One amounts to the difficulty of explaining how the neume species with disjunct ductus—point neumes—can have the same notational departure point as the rather different looking neume species with conjunct ductus—accent neumes. That is explained by the directional-gestural rationale as the active factor in shaping all type 2 neumings, both conjunct and disjunct.

[41] *Missale Basileense saec. XI: Spicilegium friburgense*, 35B, ed. Anton Hänggi and Pascal Ladner, *Faksimileband:* Max Lütolf, "Die Gesänge im Codex Gressly" (Freiburg, Switzerland, 1994).

The other argument is the total absence of Gregorian neumings before ca. 900. That cannot be lightly dismissed. Yet the fact is that antiphoners of any sort—with or without neumes—are a great rarity before ca. 1000. Traces of barely a dozen survive from before the early tenth century; and of those only two or three were written before the middle ninth century. None of them has neumes. Still, that near dozen unneumed antiphoners, half of them fragments, may be too meager, too accidental a sample to represent what there once was. There were hundreds of monasteries and churches under Carolingian control in the early ninth century, with each establishment of any size needing at least an unneumed antiphoner of its own. Library inventories tell of houses with more than one antiphoner,[42] and some high station clerics may have had their own. Of those hundreds of copies, only the handful of unneumed witnesses remains from between the late eighth and late ninth centuries, chiefly from the later end of the time span, and often they are mere fragments. Even the sacramentaries and lectionaries, to which the antiphoners are complements, have come down in not much greater numbers; their generally greater elegance should have increased the likelihood of survival.[43] Plainchants had a humbler ecclesiastical role than the prayers and biblical lections, and their manuscripts tended to be more humbly decorated. What elegance a music manuscript had tended to be lessened by the presence of scrawl-like neumes. Advances in the technology of neuming also made earlier neume states obsolete; the improvements in diastematy eventually did away with the neumes themselves. All that made a neumed antiphoner a ready candidate for disposal. In these circumstances, neither the limited survival of early antiphoners that lack neumes, nor the failure to survive of early antiphoners that bear neumes, may reflect anything more than accidents of preservation.

---

[42] Thus the six volumes of "Antiphonarii" in a Saint Riquier inventory of 831, cited by Stäblein, *MMMA* Vol. 2 (Kassel, 1979) 78*, n. 381.

[43] Carolingian Sacramentaries were more numerous than chant books, but even they have largely disappeared. The *Instructio pastoralis* of Arno of Salzburg, ca. 798, speaks of "presbyteros" " . . . Sacramentarium unusquisque habeat, quod episcopus debet considerare quomodo scriptum sit secundum ordinem, ut lex Domini per neglectum non pereat, sed cum summa reverentia sacerdos admoneat, qualiter per castitatem puram ad aecclesiam Dei veniant . . . . " *MGH, Legum sectio 3. Concilia. Tom. 2. Pars 1. Concilia aevi Karolini 1. Paris 1 (Hanover, Leipzig, 1906), 198.* Alcuin's *Epist.* 226 to the priest Symeon in 801 also suggests that abundance: "De ordinatione et dispositione missalis libelli nescio cur demandasti. Numquid non habes Romano more ordinatos libellos sacratorios abundanter? Habes quoque et veteris consuetudinis sufficienter sacramentari maiora. Quid opus est nova condere, dum vetera sufficiunt?" He goes on about Roman authority, doubtlessly meaning Carolingian-Roman: "Aliquid voluissem tuam incepisse auctoritatem Romani ordinis in clero tuo; ut exempla a te sumantur, et ecclesiastic officia venerabiliter at laudabiliter vobiscum agantur." *MGH, Epistolarum 4, Epistolae karolini acvi, tomus 2,* ed. Ernest Duemmler (Berlin, 1895), 370. The survivals of Carolingian Bibles are assessed in *The Early Medieval Bible,* ed. R. Gameson (Cambridge, 1994).

Then there are positive indications of an archetypal neuming present in the transmission during the ninth century, and perhaps already the later eighth century. Most significant are the close agreements, already remarked, among a wide spread of conjunct, nuance poor neumings, seen in Example 10.3 and Figures 10.3 and 10.4. It is hard to see these as the outcome of independent initiatives. A common neumed model ca. 800 would leave time for the notational differences ca. 900 to develop. The relatively moderate pace of notational change during the tenth century suggests that the neumatic differences ca. 900 have a remote, earlier departure point.

An early start for Gregorian neuming is also suggested by historical conditions. The division of Charlemagne's empire among the sons of Louis the Pious during the 840s (and particularly the Treaty of Verdun in 843) confirmed an already basic cultural division into eastern and western zones.[44] At the famous meeting between Charles the Bald and Louis the German at Strasbourg in February 842, oaths were taken in the vernacular *lingua romana* (this the earliest record of west Frankish dialect) and *lingua teudisca* by the two *populi*, who otherwise could not understand one another except in Latin. The widespread neumatic and melodic agreements among tenth and eleventh century antiphoners therefore suggest a common departure point before the middle ninth century.

There is the issue of memory, raised in the last chapter. Were Carolingian choirmasters, relying on memory without notational support, capable of maintaining the Gregorian melodic substances with near complete stability between an aural fixing ca. 800 and neumings that begin only a century later? Charlemagne's demand for accurate texts, in the *Admonitio generalis* of 789, extended to music for the service:

> Psalmos, notas, cantus, compotum, grammaticam per singula monasteria vel episcopia et libros catholicos bene emendate; quia saepe, dum bene aliqui Deum rogare cupiunt, sed per inemendatos libros male rogant. Et pueros vestros non sinite eos vel legendo vel scribendo corrumpere; et si opus est evangelium, psalterium et missale scribere, perfectae aetatis homines scribant cum omni diligentia.[45]

This is echoed a generation later in Abbot Helisachar's concerns with inaccuracies in the Gregorian antiphoner. Then ca. 850 (?) Aurelian is preoccupied with minute details of Gregorian melodies, which on inspection turn out to be exactly the same as those found later on in neumed antiphoners. For the whole of the extensive, and at times intricately worked,

[44] Rosamond McKitterick, *The Frankish Kingdoms Under the Carolingians (775–987)*, (London, 1983), 172; Janet L. Nelson, *Charles the Bald* (London, 1992), 120–23.

[45] *MGH, Leges: Capitularia*, 1 ed., A. Boretius (Hanover, 1883), 60.

Gregorian melodic corpus to be sustained by memory alone through nearly the whole of the ninth century supposes very ample capacities of verbatim recall in all of the realm's choirmasters. Many hours' worth of melos had to be strictly memorized.[46] Accomplishments of that order might be supposed for a select few of them, but it is harder to imagine they could all manage it without notational support, and all would have to do just that. A perspective comes from Guido of Arezzo's remark that his eleventh century contemporaries, who had the support of neumes, still needed ten years to master the repertory. That makes the undertaking without neumes seem impossible. In the last chapter, I considered the possibility of two different kinds of memory operating with unnoted plainchant: one, continuity (or narrative) memory, would oversee the melodic substances of idiomelic, automelic, and psalmic chants; the other, referential memory, would oversee the melodic substances with sophisticated centonate relationships and subtle accommodations. The close multiples examined in Chapter 6 tell us that continuity memory did not produce more than approximate recall; yet referential memory, in order to control the refinements in the eventual written states, would have required verbatim recall. The choirmasters' memories that were not up to verbatim recall in handling the narrative melos of close multiples were scarcely competent to control the centonate and accommodative fine tunings. That argues for noted support.

There are also some positive indications that Gregorian antiphoners carried neumes during the early ninth and even the later eighth centuries. Abbot Helisachar, as discussed in Chapter 7, implies as much about antiphoners ca. 820. A generation later, Aurelian has some neumes in his treatise, and though his many citations of Gregorian chants do without them, that suggests his readers had neumed antiphoners regularly available for consultation, see Chapter 8.

There is reason to suppose a Carolingian-Gregorian model antiphoner with type 2 gestural neuming reached south Italy by the early ninth century. Dom Hesbert believed one was there by c. 808, though he drew this conclusion before it was generally recognized that aural developments lay behind the received neumations, and as a matter of course he took the Beneventan transmission to be neumed.[47] Hesbert's dating also depended on the date of translation of St. Bartholomew's relics to the Lipari Islands, which has to be shifted from "before ca. 808" to "before

[46] Including such as the centonate cross referencings among fifth-mode graduals: P. Ferretti, *Esthétique grégorienne*, vol. 1 (Tournai, 1938), 117–24; the accommodative refinements among second-mode graduals: Grégoire Suñol, *Introduction à la paléographie musicale grégorienne* (Tournai, 1935), Planche F; or the accommodative refinements among alleluia verses of the type *Dies sanctifacatus*: Ferretti, *EG 1*, 185–91.

[47] *PalMus* 14: 450f.

ca. 838.[48] Nevertheless, the thrust of his argument stands, and it is further supported, by the musical and neumatic relationships between the offertories *Angelus domini,* and *Factus est repente,* discussed in Chapters 4 and 9. These suggest that a fully neumed Carolingian-Gregorian melodic corpus reached the Italian south by ca. 800, replete with the melodic-neumatic details it would have in its first surviving witnesses, ca. 1000.[49]

Against this background of early Gregorian neuming, what would be the earliest such indication stands out in fresh relief. This is the passage of Charlemagne's *Admonitio generalis* of 789, already cited, with the call for schools where boys will learn to read: "et ut scolae legentium puerorum fiant." Next comes the call for accuracy in major factors connected with worship: "Psalmos, notas, cantus, compotum, grammaticam per singula monasteria vel episcopia et libros catholicos bene emendate . . . . "[50] The frame of reference is liturgical—psalms, Gospels, calendar computations—and *notas,* fitting-in here between *psalms* and *chants,* seems more like a reference to neumatic notation than to Tironian notes[51] or legal jottings. The musical literacy such *notas* imply differed from the verbal literacies associated with Tironian shorthandings (where hundreds of signs must be controlled) or with legal documents; it imposed no large-scale obligation on learners. Verbal literacy—which Charlemagne himself may have had only up to a point—called for mastering an alphabet and a sizable vocabulary. The musical literacy of neuming meant no more than an ability to distinguish relatively higher pitches from lower ones. The nature of the neumatic notation was to represent sounds in relative positions on the page, and that was so, whether the reference in 789 would be to *notas* with a type 1 positional-graphic rationale, or to the successor *notas* with a type 2 directional-gestural rationale. The underlying principle was the same, and to grasp it was enough to make a noted melos accessible to memory recall—to make even a Carolingian schoolboy musically literate.

There remains the question of where an early archetypal Gregorian neumation would have been compiled. It was probably not done at Rome, although musical conditions there are too obscure before the later eleventh century for an adequate guess to be made. The origins of neuming, and the authoritative formulation of the Gregorian melodic and neumatic transmissions, in any case, seem likelier outcomes of organizational ener-

---

[48] "The Italian Neophytes' Chants," *JAMS* 23 (1970): 221, n. 100.

[49] *Angelus* is a standard Gregorian offertory; *Factus* is a Gallican aprocryphon found only in a small number of archaic south Italian and Frankish sources.

[50] *MGH. Leges: Capitularia,* 1, 60.

[51] The case for these is made by David Ganz, "On the History of Tironian Notes," in *Tironische Noten,* ed. Peter Ganz, *Wolfenbütteler Mittelalter Studien* vol. 1 (Wiesbaden, 1990,) 35–51.

gies in the Carolingian north. Saint Gall was long a favorite of specialists, but Dom Cardine surely improved on that, proposing the region "between the Seine and Rhine" as the source for Gregorian neumings whose beginnings he dated to the later ninth century.[52] Now in line with my own rearward shift of the starting date to the later eighth century, I would further narrow the geographical field and look to a type 2 neumatic visual model formulated in the region of the Meuse and Moselle-Rhine, particularly to the diocese of Trier,[53] which has Charlemagne's capital of Aachen to its north, and Metz to its south. It may well have been Metz, where legends of authoritative musical-liturgical activity reach back to the eighth-century era of Chrodegang, and then persist for some further centuries.[54] Substantial neumed relics at Metz begin only in the tenth century, at which time is found a disjunct Lorraine ductus that I would see as derived from, rather than directly reflective of, a conjunct neumed model. Close to Trier there are neumings of the abbeys of Prüm and Epternach, from the early eleventh century, with conjunct, relatively nuance poor provisions that fit with the notion of a conjunct neumed archetype of some two centuries earlier.

At Prüm, a monastery was founded by Charlemagne's great-grandmother in 720, and was revitalized in 752 by Pippin, for whom it remained a favorite spot. A richly decorated gradual-troper of the monastery of St. Salvator at Prüm was written between 990 and 1003, and was provided with neumes for the mass propers, ordinary, and tropes of major feasts.[55] Its archaic content includes the sole northern European neuming of the offertory *Factus est repente,* of which a facsimile is seen

---

[52] "Vue d'ensemble sur le chant Grégorien," *EG* 16 (1977): 174: "Ces notations sont attestées par les documents seulement dans la seconde moitié du IXe siècle, d'abord dans les pays compris entre le Rhin et la Seine."

[53] "Gregorian Chant and Oral Transmission," in *Essays on Medieval Music in Honor of David G. Hughes,* ed. by G. M. Boone. *Isham Library Papers* 4 (Harvard University, Department of Music, 1995), 285–86. There is a similar proposal concerning tropes by P.-M. Gy, "L'Hypothèse lotharingienne et la diffusion des tropes," in *Recherches nouvelles sur les tropes liturgiques, Recueil d'études réunies par Wulf Arlt et Gunilla Björkvall. Corpus Troporum. Acta universitatis stockholmiensis. Studia Latina Stockholmiensia* 36 (Stockholm, 1993), 231–37.

[54] Claire Maître, *La Réforme cistercienne,* 42ff; Hartmut Möller, "Die Feier des Metzer Osterofficiums im 9. Jahrhundert," in *Feste und Feiern im Mittelalter. Paderborner Symposion des Mediävistenverbandes.* eds. Detlef Altenburg, Jörg Jarnut, and Hans-Hugo Steinhoff (Sigmaringen, 1991), 309–22.

[55] Margaretha Rossholm Lagerlöf, *A Book of Songs Placed upon the Altar of the Saviour Giving Praise to the Virgin Mary and Homage to The Emperor, Research on Tropes. Proceedings of a symposium . . . Corpus Troporum, Stockholm, June 10–13, 1981,* ed. Gunilla Iversen, 125–78. *Konferenser 8 Kungl. Vitterhets Historie och Antikvitets Akademien;* (Stockholm, 1983), 125–78; p. 128; see also W. von den Steinen, *Notker der Dichter.* Editionsband, 154.

in Chapter 4, Figure 4.2. Prüm's nuance poor notation ignores *episemata* and some other characteristics of nuance rich neume species. It has some significative letters, but they are less common in the mainline Gregorian corpus than in the later and less familiar repertories of alleluias, offertory verses, tropes, and sequences, where such additional detail would have been particularly welcome.[56]

Echternach is represented by a full Sacramentary-Gradual, written shortly after 1028;[57] and again by a Gradual-Troper written later in that century. These are close to Prüm in generalities of neumatic style, being conjunct and relatively nuance poor, with rather thick forms; they distinguish punctum from tractulus and show undulants (oriscus, quilisma, etc.), but avoid episemata and significative letters. Figure 10.8 shows the two Echternach neumings for the introit *Letare Iherusalem*.[58]

Such neumations are common in Germanic regions during the tenth through twelfth centuries.[59] Their nuance poverty has usually been explained as a degradation from nuance rich states in such as Saint Gall 359 and Einsiedeln 121 (see Fig. 10.6 above), but recently their status has improved with a recognition of their old-German credentials.[60] I would see in them a conservative, conjunct, nuance poor usage that was particularly at home in the Carolingian heartland where the neumatic transmission

[56] Episemata are more variable than some of the more basic neumes in sequence tradition; Susan Rankin, "The Earliest Sources of Notker's Sequences," *EMH* 10 (1991): 231.

[57] Darmstadt, Hessische Landes- und Hochschulbibliothek, 1946. Facs. ed., *Codices selecti*, vol. 74 (Graz, 1982): *Echternacher Sakramentar und Antiphonar*. Introd. Vol., with commentary by Paul Ulveling: "l'écriture neumatique . . . appartient à l'école allemande répandue essentiellement dans une région englobant Echternach, Trèves, Bamberg, Strasbourg, Augsbourg, Würzbourg, Freising, Ratisbonne et jusqu' à l'Autriche"; "il serait faux pourtant de considérer l'écriture allemande comme une forme décadente de celle de St. Gall" (p. 128); he remarks also its "état d'esprit plus conservateur." The commentary is reprinted with other matter in Ulveling's *Essai historique et musicologique comparé sur le vocabulaire musical, son écriture mélodique et rhythmique jusqu'à l'époque du plain-chant, suivi d'un commentaire introductif au Sacramentaire et Antiphonaire d'Echternach.* (Graz, 1982), 514. See also Möller, "Deutsche Neumenschriften ausserhalb St. Gallens" in *De musica et cantu. Studien zur Geschichte der Kirchenmusik und der Oper, Helmut Hucke zum 60. Geburtstag,* ed. Peter Cahn and Anne-Katrin Heimer. (Hildesheim 1993), 225–42; (p. 227).

[58] *Fig. 10.8a:* Darmstadt, 1946; *Fig. 10.8b:* Paris BN lat. 10510.

[59] For instance, the main hands of the eleventh century Codex Gressly; Max Lütolf in *Spicilegium Friburgense,* 35B (1994).

[60] Thus the assessment of Darmstadt 1946 by Ulveling; also M.-E. Heisler, "Die Problematik des 'germanischen' oder 'deutschen' Choraldialekts." *Studia musicologica Academiae Scientiarum Hungaricae* 27 (1985): 67–82; Hartmut Möller, "Deutsche Neumen—St. Galler Neumen: Zur Einordnung der Echternacher Neumenschrift," *Studia Musicologica* 30 (1988): 415–30; Möller, "Deutsche Neumenschriften ausserhalb St. Gallens"; Möller, "Deutsche Neumenschriften ausserhalb St. Gallens"; Möller, *Das Quedlinburger Antiphonar* Berlin, Staatsbibliothek Preussicher Kulturbesitz Mus. ms. 40047, 2 vols (Tutzing, 1990); Fabian C. Lochner, "La 'Notation d'Echternach' Reconsidérée," *Revue Belge de Musicologie* 44 (1990): 41–55. In many respects, Saint Gall 339 belongs in this company.

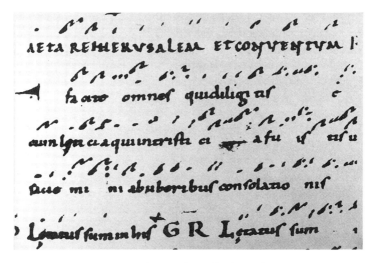

Figure 10.8a. Echternach, early eleventh century

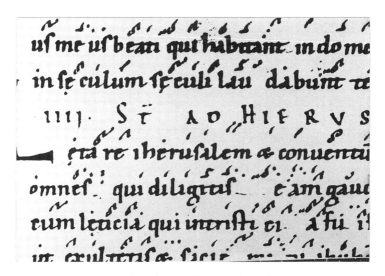

Figure 10.8b. Echternach, later eleventh century

began. Perhaps more faithfully than any others, they would reflect an archetypal neumation of ca. 800 that was the departure point for all the eventual stage/type 2 neumings.

The zone around Trier during the tenth-eleventh centuries also produced examples of the Lorraine species, with its tendancy to disjunction, and use of characteristic swallow-tail shapes for single pitches. As mentioned, these are found at Metz and they are also at Stavelot, to the north of Trier.[61] Gregorianists have reasonably emphasized the differences between the nuance rich, disjunct neumings of Lorraine, in such as Laon 239, and the nuance rich, conjunct neumings of Saint Gall, in such as Saint Gall 359 or Einsiedeln 121; those differences are manifest on almost any page of the Graduale Triplex. Yet the neumatic differences between the relatively nuance poor Germanic types at Echternach, Prüm, Stavelot, Bamberg (and even Saint Gall), and the relatively nuance poor Lorraine types at Metz and Stavelot, come to very little. Figure 10.9 shows three neumings.[62] The nuance poor Lorraine neuming of Stavelot (Fig. 10.9a) tends to separate pitches and swallow-tail shapes, but in other respects it is similar enough to the more Germanic species at Stavelot (Fig. 10.9b) and at Saint Gall (Fig. 10.9c) for all to derive from a common eighth-ninth century model.[63]

The main points have been these. Gregorian neuming got started in the latter half of the eighth century, using type 1, Paleofrank-style neumes that had a graphic or positional rationale. By ca. 800 a fresh type 2 neuming replaced type 1, based on a gestural, chironomic, or directional rationale. This was given official status in an archetypal formulation, a visual model, that likely was assembled by ca. 800 in the region of Aachen, Trier, and Metz. Copies were quickly spread through Carolingian dependencies. The model's own notation was conjunct, nuance poor and old-Germanic in style. It would be the source for all the later neume species. The differences that soon appeared among those species would be the result of reapplying, in the later neumings, the same directional-gestural (type 2) rationale that produced the model neuming.

Questions remain. One concerns the chronology of the stage/type 1 graphic neumings. Their earliest exemplars are slightly younger (the mid-

[61] J. Hourlier, "Le Domaine de la notation messine," *Révue grégorienne* 30 (1951): 96–113, 150–58.

[62] *Fig. 10.9a*: Brussels, BR, 2031; *PalMus* 3, pl. 159 (Stavelot-Lorraine). *Fig. 10.9b*: Brussels, BR, 2034; *PalMus* 3, pl. 121 (Stavelot-Germanic). *Fig. 10.9c*: Saint Gall 339 *PalMus* 1, pl. 14 (Saint Gall-Germanic).

[63] The Leipzig copy of the Tonary of Regino of Prüm (Leipzig, Universitätsbibliothek, Rep. 1.8.93 [olim 169]) is a product of the region, perhaps from Prüm itself, dating ca. 930. As a Tonary, its transmission differs from that of a mass antiphoner, however its conjunct neuming has most characteristics of the region's later antiphoners: paucity of letters and episemata, as well as lengthenings indicated by tractuli; some facsimiles: *PalMus* 13, 113, fig. 17; *MGG* 1, 879; *MGG* 8, 571; E. Jammers, *Tafeln zur Neumenschrift* (Tutzing, 1965), table 25, page 111. On the other hand, the tenth century Brussels copy of the Tonary (Brussels, Bibl. royale, 2750–65 [2751]), has neumes of the Lorraine type: diplomatic copy in *CS* 2. 1–72.

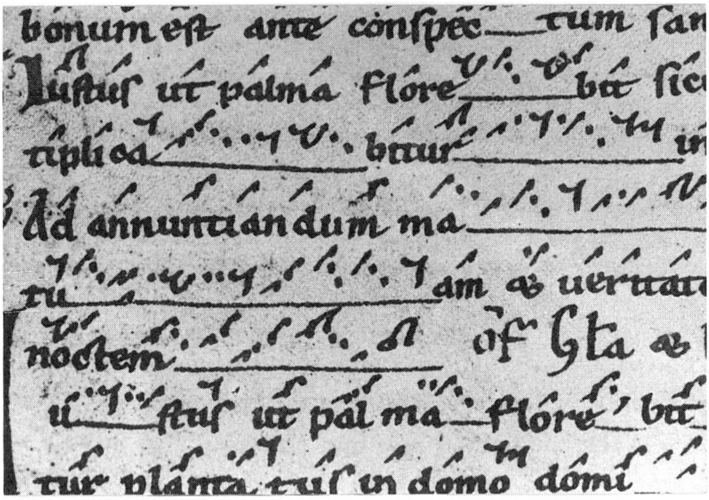

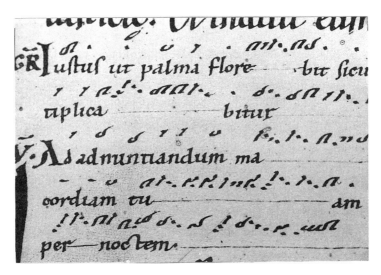

Figure 10.9a. Stavelot, "Lorraine" type

Figure 10.9b. Stavelot, "German" type

dle ninth century) than the earliest of type 2 gestural neuming (which include *Psalle modulamina*, datable to the second quarter of the century).
Now if type 1 was already made obsolescent by the publication of an authoritative type 2 visual model ca. 800, then such ninth century dates lack

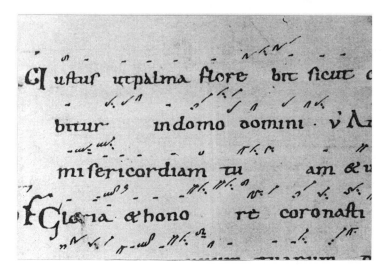

Figure 10.9c. Saint Gall, "German" type

significance. In any case, type 1 seems a straggler during the ninth and tenth centuries, while type 2, supplanting it on its home ground, generated a growth cycle that would continue for centuries. Still, there are isolated appearances of type 1 two centuries or more after its alleged decline set in. Some scribes may have preferred it for its positional rationale, with the straightforward picturing of melodic events; a similar preference may have led the neumators of Breton and Aquitainian type 2 species to turn from a conjunct to a more accurately heighted disjunct ductus. Some other scribes may have clung to type 1 because notational preferences die hard.[64]

Another question is raised by the appearance within type 1 linkages (or ligatures) of traits that reflect the type 2 rationale. A type 1 linkage may contain a directional stroke rather than a dot as representative of a single pitch—thus a gestural impulse within the type 1 positional-graphic rationale. Yet the ambiguity is slight, and the scribe may have settled for a cursive form that came readily to hand; that is the more likely since all surviving type 1 documents were executed at times when type 2 was already universal.

A final question concerns ligatures again, here the reasons governing the two types' distributions of the melos between ligiatures and single

[64] Elements of Lorraine-style neuming survive in Valenciennes 128, written in 1512; Hourlier, "Domaine de la notation messine," 105.

Example 10.5. Six Paleofrank neumings for low-high-low: Paris lat. 2291

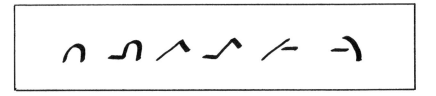

pitches. In the conjunct neumings of type 2, scribes have a roster of standard two- and three-pitch figures (the eventually named clivis, podatus, climacus, etc.), to which leader and/or follower dots are attached; the apparent principle is to ligate what one can, using the standard figures; the apparent aim is to produce neumatic images whose shapeliness lets them be readily registered by the eye and consigned to memory. In the type 1 neumings a different principle of linkage may be operating. It is suggested by such as the Saint Amand Sacramentary, Paris lat. 2291 (end of ninth century), where, within the space of twelve noted lines the Paleofrank neumator describes the melodic pattern low-high-low in half a dozen different ways. (See Ex. 10.5.)[65] These differences may have conveyed some of the same information about duration and emphasis that are shown in the nuance rich type 2 species by lengthenings, angularities, episemata, and coupures. Some of the Paleofrank forms may also be showing articulations, with separate points for detachés and ligations for legatos. That would fit the progression which has, at the outset, a graphic stage/type 1, focused on relatively accurate picturings of melodic details; and following that a successor, gestural, nuance poor stage/type 2, starting with lessened accuracy but compensating with an increased plasticity of neumatic profile that makes the melodic substances more memorable. The relationships between type 1 linkages and type 2 ligatures need to be pursued further, but that may have to wait until a more adequate documentation of type 1 neuming becomes available.[66]

[65] That observation by Handschin, "Eine alte Neumenschrift," 77, is taken up by Susan Rankin, "Carolingian Music," in *Carolingian Culture: Emulation and Innovation,* ed. Rosamond McKitterick (Cambridge, 1994), 302.

[66] This will be helped by Wulf Arlt's forthcoming publication of the Paleofrank leaves which he and Fritz Reckow have uncovered in Wolfenbuttl 510; there are two leaves of a full gradual of the tenth(?) century (Kloster Lamspringe?), designed to bear notation, and supplied with type 1 Paleofrank neumes that are entered by a main hand throughout; see Arlt, "Anschaulichkeit und analytischer Charakter" in *Musicologie médievale. Notations et Séquences,* ed., Michel Huglo (Paris, 1987), 29–55. I am grateful to Professor Arlt for information about these leaves.

CHAPTER 11

Memory, Neumes, and Square Notations

IN EARLIER CHAPTERS, the focus was on Gregorian chant's path from aural to notational transmission. Musical developments there are obscure. For much that went on no record was kept, and even after neuming began, for a long time little or nothing may have been preserved. This final chapter turns to developments during later centuries, when notational records are ample, and what happened has had much careful study.[1]

The term " written" takes on a special meaning with medieval chant, implying both more and less than it does with medieval transmissions that involve words alone. Gregorian music begins its written, or better its "notational," transmission in a partnership between memory and neumes. There memory, an unwritten or aural factor, still plays a dominant role, much as it did before neuming was introduced; even with the neumes, the full record of melodic substance rested only in memory, while the notational signs were merely memory aids. Then the technique of music writing evolved, and by the middle eleventh century the staffless neumes were accurately heighted on staff lines. With that, the basic relationship between memory and writing changed so that the notational factor became primary and memory was reduced to an auxiliary role. Yet long after the precisely pitched notations were universal, memory maintained something of its grip, helping keep the music close to its Carolingian antecedents.

My proposal has been that the Gregorian musical repertory received not only its definitive melodic fixing in the times of Pippin and Charlemagne, but also its decisive neumatic recording. These belonged to the same operation. By ca. 800, there was an authoritative neuming for the full melodic repertory circulating throughout Carolingian domains. The melodic substances were stable, down to fine details. These were memorized tunes that choirmasters reproduced exactly and were meant always and everywhere to sound the same.[2] This music was accurately profiled in the staffless

---

[1] Thomas Kohlhase und Günther Michael Paucker, *Bibliographie Gregorianischer Choral*, vol. 9–10 of *Beiträge zur Gregorianik* (1990); *Addenda 1*, vol. 15/16 (1993).

[2] This early archetype view of the start of Gregorian neuming departs considerably from the widely accepted late independent view, which sees the repertory fixed as to melody ca. 800, with melody transmission done aurally and Gregorian neumings starting up roughly a century later, ca. 900, and generated independently at different places; see Chapter 1. It departs even farther from the re-improvisation view, which sees the Gregorian melos as not yet stabilized during the ninth and even some later centuries, and with melodic shapes, even in the epoch of neume writing, still potentially variable.

neumes which, while they were imprecise about pitch, were so precise about other melodic aspects—duration and certain nuances—that the full music could be accurately recalled. As for pitch, the neumes had a simple principle, which was to show higher pitch at a relatively higher position on the page, and lower pitch at a relatively lower position.

In the early stages of this partnership between memory and neumes, the notation's inaccuracy with regard to pitch was not an obstacle to the integrity of the transmission. Yet its consequence was that neither partner could function without the other. The neumes were not exact enough for the full melodic substances to be read from them alone; they were useless unless there was someone around who already had the tunes in memory. Without the reminders given by the staffless neumes, it seems doubtful that choirmasters everywhere could have managed routinely the accurate recall of the full repertory's melodic substances. Close multiples, like those dealt with in Chapters 2, 3, and 6, tell us that before there was neuming, a memorized melody came out somewhat differently at different places; but then the memories, which without notational support managed only approximate recall, were raised to the level of verbatim recall by the presence of neumes.

At the beginning of notational transmission, the alliance between verbatim memory and staffless neumes would have seemed an adequate guarantor of melodic stability. But shortcomings were soon apparent, and through much of the ninth century efforts were made to improve neumatic accuracy, with different sorts of clarification tried at different places. These led to the diversities in style and technique that are seen ca. 900 in the first surviving Gregorian neumings. Any and all modifications or supplements to the neumatic shapes of 800, however, were made with the understanding that those original shapes were generated by a directional-gestural-chironomic rationale, and that the same rationale continued as the generator of all subsequent neumings. Most later neumators left the model shapes pretty much as they were received. At Saint Gall, there were clarifications in the form of letters, episemata, etc., added to what otherwise remained near replicas of the model. For more enterprising neumators, as in the Aquitaine, Lorraine, and Brittany, the received shapes were even more susceptible to change. Scribes there journeyed farther from the originals and produced quite varied neumatic stylizations. Yet whatever the technical or calligraphic changes might be, all the neumations were still meant to describe the same melodic substances that were authoritatively fixed in Pepin's and Charlemagne's times; and all continued to be governed by the same directional-gestural rationale.

These workings of the memory-plus-neumes syndrome and the gestural rationale can be observed in the *Graduale Triplex,* where the Vatican-Solesmes square note Gregorian edition is paralleled with staffless neum-

Example 11.1. Offertory, *Ad te Domine* (Graduale triplex)

ings of Laon and Saint Gall. Example 11.1 shows the opening of the Offertory *Ad te Domine levavi* in this arrangement.[3] Each of the tenth century neumings has something of its own notational means and style. However, the melodic substances they describe are almost the same and the considerable melodic agreements give strong indication that they are musically close to the melodic state that was fixed by the late eighth century Carolingian editors. Furthermore, the Vatican-Solesmes melodic version, thanks to the considerable reliance of its own editors on excellent, tenth century Saint Gall neumings, offers respectable restorations of the presumed Carolingian melodic substances. There is need for proper scientific restorations of the melodic and neumatic formulations of the eighth-ninth centuries, yet for many purposes, including those of the following discussion, the Vatican's melodic readings can be taken provisionally as representative of the early melodic details.[4]

Something of the fate of those details during the tenth through eighteenth centuries can be judged from Example 11.2, where the opening in-

[3] *GT,* 17.

[4] A consensus of tenth and eleventh century neumations suggests that in its ligature oriented, conjunct ductus, the Saint Gall neumation of ca. 1000 (Einsiedeln 121), used in the *Graduale Triplex,* was close to that of the model, ca. 800. Some of the nuance rich features in Saint Gall would, however, be less representative of the model; that same consensus suggests it was better represented by such as the nuance poor neumings from the region of Trier (Stavelot, Echternach, Prüm, etc.); see Chapter 10.

cises of the Offertory *Ad te Domine* are shown in a spread of regional readings.[5] The Vatican reading (ex. 11.2a) here stands for the authoritative Carolingian melody, and the other readings allow something of the scope and mechanism of melodic change to be gauged. Example 11.2b represents the Empire's western zone at eleventh century Dijon. This manuscript's double notations (alphabetic and neumatic) provide the earliest pitch specific readings of the full Gregorian melodic repertory. Its version of the Offertory *Ad te Domine* is close to that of the Carolingian (Vatican) edition (ex. 11.2a).

From the eastern zone, there is the twelfth century version of Klosterneuburg near Vienna (ex. 11.2c), which again scarcely departs from the Carolingian (Vatican) reading. Two centuries or more after the memory-plus-neumes transmission began, the melodic substances and notational shapes are almost exactly what they were in the earlier traditions at Saint Gall, Laon, and Dijon. Nevertheless, one notices a preference for higher pitches and wider skips in Klosterneuburg's rise to F (rather than E) on "a-ni-MAM" and "ME-am." These are symptoms of the German choral dialect,[6] which would reflect regional style preferences and/or slackenings of memory. These may have become encrusted in the transmission long before the twelfth century, though remaining undetected behind the facade of staffless neumes. They represent a significant stylistic impulse, yet when measured against the overall scope of melodic agreements throughout Europe, these Germanic divergences are of minor consequence.

The thirteenth century Chartres version (ex. 11.2d) is again close to the Carolingian (Vatican) melos. For its upper pitch on "a-ni-MAM" and "ME-am," it has the Carolingian E rather than the Germanic F.

The easternmost version is represented by Esztergom (Gran), where the Hungarian kings were crowned (ex. 11.2e). Dating from before 1341, this is in the Germanic line. It generally maintains the neumatic model's conjunct, nuance poor provisions (Chs. 5 and 10), while agreeing with Klosterneuburg-Vienna (ex. 11.2c) as to pitch details: again the high, Ger-

---

[5] Example 11.2a (Carolingian model=Vatican edition): *GT,* 17. Example 11.2b (Dijon): *PalMus* 7, 205. Example 11.2c (Vienna/Klosterneuburg): *PalMus* 19, fol. 2. Example 2d (Chartres): *Missale Carnotense (Chartres Codex 520),* Facsimile, ed. David Hiley, *MMMA,* vol. 4 (Kassel, 1992) 1, fol. 10. Example 11.2e (Gran): *Missale notatum strigoniense ante 1341 in Posonio,* ed. Janka Szendrei and Richard Rybaric; *Musicalia Danubiana* 1; (Budapest, 1982), fol. 1v. Example 11.2f (Passau): *Graduale Pataviense (Wien 1511),* Facsimile, ed. Christian Väterlein *Das Erbe Deutsche Musik,* Abteilung Mittelalter, vol. 24; (Kassel, 1982), fol. 1v. Example 11.2g (Edit. Medicaea): *Graduale de Tempore iuxta ritum Sacrosanctae Romanae Ecclesiae, cum cantu, Pauli V. Pont. Max iussu reformato . . .* Typographia Medicaea, anno 1614, fol. 2v. Example 11.2h (Grenoble): *Graduale Romanum . . .* (Gratianapoli, 1730), 4.

[6] Maria-Elisabeth Heisler, "Die Problematik des 'germanischen' oder 'deutschen' Choral-dialekts." *Studia musicologica* 27 (1985): 67–82.

Example 11.2. Offertory, *Ad te Domine,* incises 1–4

a. Vatican Edition

Ad   te   Do - mi   -   ne   le   -   va   -   vi

b. Dijon sec. 11 (transposed)

c. Vienna sec. 12

d. Chartres sec. 13

e. Gran sec. 14

f. Passau 1511

g. Medicaea 1614

h. Grenoble 1730

manic F on "a-ni-MAM" and "ME-am"; also an F on "Do-mi-NE." There is a touch of melodic slackening in the stepwise filling-in of the melisma on "con-FI-do."

The Passau Gradual published in 1511 (ex. 11.2f), again an eastern version, still remains close to the Carolingian (Vatican) reading. It has the Germanic high Fs.

These widely scattered readings, spanning six centuries, reveal just minimal departures from the posited Carolingian melodic formulation. That persistence of the melos would confirm the faith placed in the partnership between memory and neumes by the formulators of the notational transmission.

A century later, with the *Editio Medicaea* of 1614 (the Gradual of Paul V, ex. 11.2g), the differences are more considerable. They are attributable

Example 11.2. (Continued)

a. Vatican

  a — ni - mam me - am

b. Dijon

c. Vienna

d. Chartres

e. Gran

f. Passau

g. Medicaea

h. Grenoble

in part to the reform nature of that compilation. Its Offertory *Ad te Domine* has marks of the tamperings for which the *Medicaea* is known: the word "Domine" has been excised; melismas are shortened or suppressed; melismas are added rarely, as on "le-VA-vi," perhaps to compensate for the absent "Domine," or perhaps, in the spirit of the time, as a madrigalesque ornament. There also are modal tailorings, as on "e-ru-bes-CAM," where the cadence on the low D adds weight to the ostensible tonic.

A later reading of *Ad te Domine levavi* is that of the *Graduale* published by Pierre Favre at Grenoble in 1730 (ex. 11.2h). Distant by eight or nine centuries from its Carolingian source, the music is still much as it was.

The melodic stability that is manifest throughout Example 11.2 can be attributed in part to the continuing action of memory. Even after staff no-

Example 11.2. (Continued)

a. Vatican

De - us me - us in te con - fi - do,

b. Dijon

c. Vienna

d. Chartres

e. Gran

f. Passau

g. Medicaea

h. Grenoble

tations emerged, the venerable tunes lived on in musicians' ears, and that helped in resisting change.

Something more of this can be seen in Example 11.3, which has the opening of the offertory *Elegerunt apostoli,* for St. Stephen, in five of the seven sources that supplied Example 11.2.[7] This music is a bit less stable than *Ad te Domine.* Its more melismatic style and its narrower liturgical application (there were other options for a Stephen offertory), doubtless left it more vulnerable to change. Again, the Vatican version can stand for

[7] Example 11.3a (Carolingian model=Vatican edition): *GT* 634; C. Ott, *Offertoriale* (Tournai, 1935), 161; *PalMus* 7, 267. Example 11.3b (Vienna/Klosterneuburg): *PalMus* 19, fol. 16. Example 11.3c (Gran): *Missale notatum strigoniense ante 1341,* fol. 14. Example 11.3d (Passau): *Graduale Pataviense (Wien 1511),* Facsimile, fol. 14v. Example 11.3e (*Medicaea*): *Graduale . . . Pauli V. Pont. . . . Typographia Medicaea, anno 1614,* fol. 24.

Example 11.2. (Continued)

a. Vatican

non   e - ru - be - scam

b. Dijon

c. Vienna

d. Chartres

e. Gran

f. Passau

g. Medicaea

h. Grenoble

an authoritative Carolingian melodic state; it was actually based on the eleventh-century Dijon reading (ex. 11.3a). Much the same melos appears in both the eastern and western zones. At twelfth-century Klosterneuburg (ex. 11.3b), there are again the earmarks of the Germanic dialect: a high F rather than an E on "LE-vi-tam"; and a C rather than a B-flat on "PLE-num." At fourteenth century Gran, (ex. 11.3c), the melisma on "E-le-GE-runt" is compressed. Passau in 1511 (ex. 11.3d) stays close to the Carolingian (Vatican,) yet its *Elegerunt* is a bit freer than its *Ad te Domine*. The *Medicaea* of 1614 (ex. 11.3e) has again for its own reasons come a greater distance.

With *Elegerunt* there is something more. Its regional witnesses reveal an exceptional range of melodic variants that likely reflect its origin as a Gallican offertory. Some versions are far enough removed from the Vati-

Example 11.3. Offertory, *Elegerunt,* "Vulgate" melody

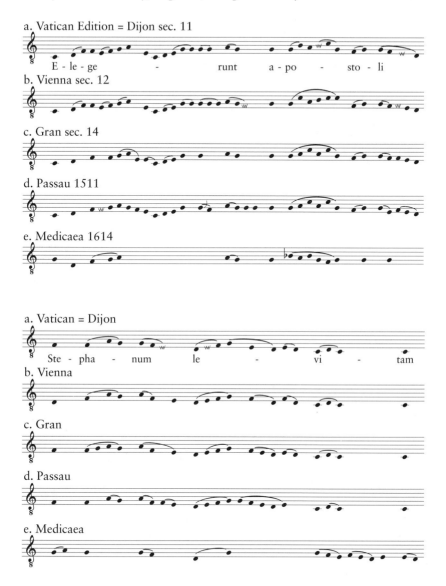

a. Vatican Edition = Dijon sec. 11

E - le - ge - runt a - po - sto - li

b. Vienna sec. 12

c. Gran sec. 14

d. Passau 1511

e. Medicaea 1614

a. Vatican = Dijon

Ste - pha - num le - vi - tam

b. Vienna

c. Gran

d. Passau

e. Medicaea

can "Vulgate" reading in Example 11.3a to be reckoned as close multiples—descendents of Gallican neumings which began as independent local dictations, rather than outgrowths of the Carolingian formulation. A number of these have been examined in Chapter 6. Two others have become available since then, representing Chartres and Grenoble.

Example 11.3. (Continued)

a. Vatican = Dijon

ple - num fi - de

b. Vienna

c. Gran

d. Passau

e. Medicaea

The thirteenth century Chartres Elegerunt (ex. 11.4)[8] might be taken for a descendent of the Carolingian "Vulgate" version (Vatican recension) in example 11.3a, except that the melodic differences between the Vatican and Chartres versions of *Ad te Domine levavi* (Exx. 11.2a and 11.2d) are so much less than those between their *Elegerunts* (comparing ex. 11.3a with ex. 11.4). The Chartres *Elegerunt* represents a region where an old Gallican melodic tradition might survive, and this melody strays far enough from the Vulgate to be counted as a multiple. Its closest musical and geographical ties are with the *Elegerunt* of Auxerre (Ch. 6, Ex. 6.3). Both may descend from a common source, or Chartres may descend from an independent dictation that is not otherwise documented.

Similar possibilities exist with the *Elegerunt* published at Grenoble in 1730 (ex. 11.5).[9] Here again is a region where traces of an Old Gallican version might flourish, though by this time one may also be dealing with neoGallican liturgical-musical initiatives of the seventeenth and eighteenth centuries. In any case, where Grenoble's *Ad te Domine* descends from the Carolingian (Vatican) version, its *Elegerunt* is far enough removed from the "Vulgate" version to suggest that it too is a close multiple. Yet it is so far from *Elegerunt's* other multiples that it is hard to say which, if any of them, it reflects.

[8] *Missale Carnotense*, ed. David Hiley (1992), fol. 37.
[9] *Graduale Romanum* . . . (Grenoble, 1730), 23.

Example 11.4. Offertory, *Elegerunt*, "Chartres" melody

These comparisons, although limited to parts of just two offertories, allow some general conclusions about the condition of Gregorian melos between the tenth and eighteenth centuries. The musical substances remain remarkably stable during all that time. The stability is greatest at the outset, before the notations become precisely pitched; thus the first pitched versions to emerge, in the eleventh and twelfth centuries, show the melos still almost the same everywhere. Much of that would be the result of the notation's own insufficiency with respect to pitch, for it obliged the mem-

Example 11.5. Offertory, *Elegerunt,* "Grenoble." 1730 melody

ories to be accurate. After the staffed pitch notation entered, the melodies might have lost any further susceptibility to change. Yet it worked the other way, with the transmission becoming less stable. The lessened reliance on memory eroded memory's efficacy and the availability of staff notation let self-confident professionals perpetuate what were at times mistaken memories, as well as indulge in editorial compositional forays of their own. The overall picture, however, is one where departures are remarkably slight. By and large, sixteenth-century readings are still close to those of the ninth and tenth centuries.

Gregorian semiologists have been very active in recent decades, describing, localizing, and interrelating the many neume species and melodic differences that are found in tenth through thirteenth century sources. The present papers propose changes in the historical and conceptual assumptions on which some of those studies are based. Until now, the general view has been that while Gregorian chants reached melodic fixity and the ideal of verbatim reproduction during the later eighth century, this was accomplished by means of memory alone, and the first systematic neumings of the repertory began only a century later. My alternative proposal is that an authoritative neumation was promulgated at the same time (by ca. 800) that the authoritative melodic formulation was made, and this model neuming was the reference point for all subsequent neumings. Along with this, I would identify a directional or gestural rationale as the generating principle for notational behavior in the model neuming and all its descendents. These proposals fall short of proof, but I believe there is much that recommends them. By their means, a way is opened to simple solutions for some of the more puzzling aspects of musical and notational relationships in the tenth and eleventh centuries. In the end, they emphasize the good sense of the eighth century Gregorian editors, who by seating the musical transmission in a mutual dependency between verbatim memory and gestural neumes, managed so well to assure the melodies' long-term resistance to change.

Index

Page references in italics indicate that an example or figure is included.

About the Author

KENNETH LEVY is Scheide Professor of Music History Emeritus
at Princeton University. He is well known for his work
in medieval music, particularly Byzantine and Latin plainchant.
He is the author of *Music: A Listener's Introduction.*

DATE DUE

			Printed in USA

HIGHSMITH #45230